SMALL-SCALE ENTERPRISES IN DEVELOPING AND TRANSITIONAL ECONOMIES

Small-Scale Enterprises in Developing and Transitional Economies

Edited by

Homi Katrak

and

Roger Strange

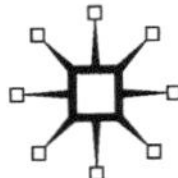

First published 2002 by
PALGRAVE
Houndmills, Basingstoke, Hampshire RG21 6XS and
175 Fifth Avenue, New York, N. Y. 10010
Companies and representatives throughout the world

PALGRAVE is the new global academic imprint of St. Martin's Press LLC Scholarly and Reference Division and Palgrave Publishers Ltd (formerly Macmillan Press Ltd).

ISBN 0–333–96864–6

This book is printed on paper suitable for recycling and made from fully managed and sustained forest sources.

A catalogue record for this book is available from the British Library.

Library of Congress Cataloging-in-Publication Data

Small-scale enterprises in developing and transitional economies / edited by Homi Katrak and Roger Strange.
p. cm.
Includes bibliographical references and index.
ISBN 0–333–96864–6
1. Small business—Developing countries—Case studies. 2. Small business—Europe, Eastern—Case studies. I. Katrak, H. (Homi) II. Strange, Roger.

HD2346.5 .S63 2002
338.6′42′091724—dc21

2001036988

10 9 8 7 6 5 4 3 2 1
11 10 09 08 07 06 05 04 03 02

Printed and bound in Great Britain by
Antony Rowe Ltd, Chippenham, Wiltshire

Contents

List of Tables vii

List of Figures ix

Notes on the Contributors x

List of Abbreviations xiv

1 Introduction and Overview 1
Homi Katrak and Roger Strange

Part I Small Is Beautiful? A Reappraisal

2 The Efficiency of Small Enterprises in Developing Countries: An Empirical Analysis 11
John Weeks

3 Small Enterprises and Immiserizing Growth: A Cautionary Tale from the Chinese Silk Industry 31
Roger Strange and Jim Newton

4 Small is Not Always Beautiful: Environmental Enforcement and Small Industries in India 50
Nandini Dasgupta

Part II Small-Scale Enterprises and Market Competition

5 Entry, Exit, and the Role of the Small Firm in China's Industrial Transformation 77
Qing Gong Yang and Paul Temple

6 Economic Liberalization and Growth of Small-Scale Enterprises: The Indian Experience 99
Homi Katrak

7 Venezuelan Manufacturing, SME Decline, and Failed Transition 115
Alan Mulhern

8 European Integration and the Survival of Polish Small Enterprises 137
Subrata Ghatak, George Manolas, Costas Rontos and Ioannis Vavouras

9 The Impact of Adjustment-led Transformation on Small-Scale Manufacturing in Bulgaria 157
Berhanu Kassayie

Part III Clusters: One Fit for All Situations?

10 A Cure for Loneliness? Networks, Trust and Shared Services in Bangalore 185
Mark Holmström

11 Promoting Small-Scale Industries in Indonesia: A Review of Recent Policies and Programmes 214
Henry Sandee

12 The Determinants of Competitiveness in SME Clusters: Evidence and Policies for Latin America 229
Manuel Albaladejo

Part IV New Developments: Technology Upgrading

13 Firm Size, Technological Capabilities and Market-orientated Policies in Mauritius 255
Ganeshan Wignaraja

14 Information, ICTs and Small Enterprise: Findings from Botswana 285
Richard Duncombe and Richard Heeks

Index 305

List of Tables

2.1	Employment by size of manufacturing establishment in six developing countries (various years)	13
2.2	Employment by size of manufacturing establishment in three developed countries (various years)	14
2.3	Value-added per worker and average wages in manufacturing establishments in four developing countries	17
2.4	The size–productivity relationship and technical efficiency in small enterprises in three developing countries	20
2.5	Returns to scale in the industrial sectors of six developing countries	26
3.1	World production of raw silk, 1938–98	36
3.2	Raw silk production and export in China, 1983–98	37
5.1	The hazard model covariates	92
5.2	Estimated hazard functions for enterprises in Liaoning Province, 1987–96	94
5A.1	The size composition of the sample of firms	96
6.1	Estimated regression equations explaining the growth of small-scale enterprises in Indian industries	109
6.2	Estimated regression equations incorporating interdependent effects on the growth of small-scale enterprises in India	110
7.1	Per capita GDP for selected countries, 1970 and 1988	116
7.2	Venezuela's economic performance, 1995–9	120
7.3	Estimated regression equation explaining the change of the SME share in Venezuelan manufacturing value-added	129
8.1	Explanatory variables in the logit model	140
8.2	Empirical results from estimation of the logit model	147
8.3	Frequencies of each category in the sample of Polish enterprises	148
8.4	Detailed empirical results from estimation of the logit model	149
8.5	Expected impact of accession to the European Union on the sample of Polish SMEs, by branch of economic activity	150

8.6 Profitability of the sample of Polish SMEs, 1998, by branch of economic activity 151
9.1 Origins of private manufacturing firms in selected Central and East European countries 159
9.2 Survey sample of Bulgarian firms, analyzed by size and year of entry into operation 163
9.3 Survey sample of Bulgarian firms, analyzed by size and legal form of organization 165
9.4 Survey sample of Bulgarian firms, analyzed by sector 166
9.5 Regional distribution of private manufacturing firms in selected Central and East European Countries 168
9.6 Legal organization of private manufacturing firms in selected Central and East European countries 169
9.7 Size distribution of private manufacturing firms in selected Central and East European countries 171
9.8 Survey sample of Bulgarian firms, analyzed by value, and type and size of firm 173
9.9 Survey sample of Bulgarian firms, analyzed by source of technology, and type and size of firm 174
9.10 Size distribution of the Bulgarian sample of firms, 1990–5 175
9.11 Average annual growth rates of firms in the Bulgarian sample, 1991–5 176
9.12 Effects of size on the average annual growth rates of the firms in the Bulgarian sample, 1991–5 178
11.1 Size distribution of Indonesian manufacturing establishments, 1986 and 1996 218
13.1 Technology index of the sample of Mauritian firms 267
13.2 Average technology index for large firms and SMEs in the Mauritian sample 268
13.3 Estimated regression equations explaining the technological capabilities of garment firms in Mauritius 272
13.4 Mean values of the variables for large firms and SMEs in the Mauritian sample 273
13.5 Estimated regression equations explaining the export performance of garment firms in Mauritius 275
13A.1 The technological capability scoring scale 277
13A.2 Correlation matrix 279
14.1 Respondent profile from the questionnaire survey in Botswana 288

List of Figures

2.1	Efficient and inefficient production techniques	18
2.2	Optimal firm size in the standard neo-classical case	23
2.3	The long-run average product of labour and returns to scale: logical possibilities	24
2.4	Coefficients of variation for the optimal establishment size in twenty industrial sectors	27
3.1	Technical progress at constant terms of trade	33
3.2	Technical progress and immiserizing growth	35
5.1	Contributions to output growth of Chinese firms, 1987–96	84
5.2	Contributions of entry, exit and survival to the output growth of Chinese firms, 1987–96	85
5.3	Contributions of entry, exit and survival to the productivity growth of Chinese firms, 1987–96	86
6.1	The effects of trade liberalization on the outputs of small-scale enterprises and large enterprises	102
6.2	The effects of trade liberalization on the relative outputs of small-scale enterprises and large enterprises	105
7.1	Real per capita GDP in Venezuela, 1961–93	117
7.2	Real manufacturing value-added and labour productivity in Venezuela, 1961–95	124
7.3	Employment and numbers of firms in manufacturing in Venezuela, 1961–95	125
7.4	The SME shares of employment, total firm numbers, and manufacturing value-added in Venezuela, 1961–95	126
7.5	Manufacturing value-added in SMEs in Venezuela, 1961–95	130
9.1	New entrants in Bulgarian private manufacturing, 1989–95	161
9.2	The establishment and operational start-up of the sample of Bulgarian firms, 1989–95	162
9.3	A comparison of the sectoral distribution of the Bulgarian sample with the national distribution, 1995	166
12.1	The determinants of competitiveness in SME clusters	231
14.1	A systemic view of information and communication technologies	286
14.2	The enterprise information systems model	289
14.3	A systemic view of enterprise	296

Notes on the Contributors

Manuel Albaladejo is an Industrial Economist working as an research associate at the International Development Centre of the University of Oxford. His areas of interest are competitiveness and technological capabilities in SMEs and clusters, industrial and technology policy, and business development services. Some of his most recent work includes UNECA's strategic framework to enhance the competitiveness of SMEs in Africa, and UNIDO's SME policy framework to help the AfDB design lines of credit to promote SMEs.

Nandini Dasgupta is a Reader in Development and Environment at the University of Greenwich and has spent over 25 years as a lecturer and consultant in the field of development. Her recent research includes work on the greening of small-scale industries and on environmental policy in developing countries; on the links between energy efficiency and poverty alleviation; and on small enterprises and sustainable livelihood.

Richard Duncombe is a lecturer/researcher in the Institute of Development Policy and Management at the University of Manchester. His research interests include information and communication technologies (ICTs), information systems, ICTs and enterprise development, ICTs in developing countries, and technology and development. He has worked extensively in Sub-Saharan Africa, undertaking consultancy and other research projects concerning ICTs and development. He is currently completing a PhD degree at the University of Manchester.

Subrata Ghatak is Research Professor and Director of Graduate Research Studies in Economics at Kingston University. Before that, he was a Reader in Economics at Leicester University. He has been a visiting Professor at the University of Florida at Gainesville and at Guelph University in Canada, and has acted as a consultant to many international organizations, including UNCTAD and the World Bank. He has authored or co-authored several books, and has contributed numerous articles to national and international journals.

Richard Heeks is a Senior Lecturer at the University of Manchester in the Institute for Development Policy and Management, a postgraduate centre for managers from developing and transitional economies. He has a PhD on industrial development which led to the publication of *India's Software Industry* (Sage, 1996). He has provided consultancy inputs to public and private–sector organisations worldwide, and currently directs a Masters programme on 'Management and Information Systems.' His homepage is located at <http://www.man.ac.uk/idpm>.

Mark Holmström is a social anthropologist specialising in studies of industrial societties. Most of his fieldwork has been in Indian cities, where he has studied industrial workers' careers; formal and informal sector labour; small firms, flexible specialization, industrial districts and clusters. He has also written about workers' co-operatives and other forms of industrial democracy in Italy and Spain. Since retiring from the University of East Anglia in 1999, he has worked on SMEs and clusters in Spain (especially in the toy industry), and is planning further research in India. His main publications are *South Indian Factory Workers: their Life and their World* (Cambridge University Press, 1976), *Industry and Inequality: The Social Anthropology of Indian Labour* (Cambridge University Press, 1986), *Industrial Democracy in Italy: Workers Co-ops and the Self-Management Debate* (Gower 1989), *Work for Wages in South Asia* (Manohar, 1990), *Spain's New Social Economy: Workers' Self-Management in Catalonia* (Berg, 1993), and *Decentralized Production in India: Industrial Districts, Flexible Specialization, and Employment* (Sage and French Institute of Pondicherry 1998, edited with Philippe Cadēne).

Berhanu Kassayie is a Lecturer in the Political Economy of Transition at South Bank University and a Lecturer in Development Studies at Birkbeck College, University of London. He has a PhD in SME Studies.

Homi Katrak is a Visiting Professor in Economics at the University of Surrey. He has also been a part-time consultant at the National Institute of Economic and Social Research, London. His research areas are development economics and industrial economics and his studies on Indian industries have been published in leading academic journals in the UK and USA.

George Manolas is a Senior Economist at the Greek Ministry of National Economy. His major research interest is applied economic policy, and he has contributed to many books and journals such as *Regional Studies*, *Rivista Internationale*, *Statistics in Transition*, *Greek Economic Review*, and the *Journal of Asia Pacific Economy*.

Alan Mulhern is Senior Lecturer at Kingston University. His teaching specialisms include the theory of the firm and the business environment. His research specialism is the small firm in Latin America, and his publications in this area include 'Venezuelan Small Businesses and the Economic Crisis: Reflections from Europe', in *International Journal of Entrepreneurial Behaviour and Research*, and 'Long and Short Run Determinants of Small and Medium Size Enterprise Share: The Case of Venezuelan Manufacturing', in *Economics of Planning*.

Jim Newton teaches International Business at the University of Hong Kong's School of Business and was previously Director of the University's MBA Programme. His research interests concern issues in international trade in both goods and services, especially in Asia and between Asia and the West. The focus of current studies is on the international political economy of specific sectors of importance to Hong Kong, China and Asia. He is also a contributor to the School's Centre for Asian Business Cases which is producing a library of case studies for use in both local and international management and business programmes.

Costas Rontos is a Senior Economist at the National Statistical Service of Greece, and also lectures at the University of Aegean. His major research interest is applied statistics, and he is the author of several articles in scientific journals.

Henry Sandee is a Senior Research Fellow in the Department of Development Economics at Vrije Universiteit Amsterdam. He was previously attached to Satya Wacana Christian University in Indonesia. He is the author of *Innovation Adoption in Rural Industry: Technological Change in Roof Tile Clusters in Central Java, Indonesia*. He has published several articles on small-scale industry development in Indonesia, Vietnam, and Sri Lanka. His current research concerns small industry exports and business development services in Southeast Asia.

Roger Strange is Senior Lecturer in Economics, and formerly Head of the Management Centre, at King's College London. He has published widely on Europe–Asia economic relations. His most recent books are *Japanese Manufacturing Investment in Europe: Its Impact on the UK*

Economy (Routledge, 1993), *Business Relationships with East Asia* (Routledge, 1997, edited with Jim Slater), *Management in China: The Experience of Foreign Businesses* (Frank Cass, 1998, editor), *Trade and Investment in China* (Routledge 1998, edited with Jim Slater and Limin Wang), and *The European Union and ASEAN: Trade and Investment Issues* (Macmillan, 2000, edited with Jim Slater and Corrado Molteni).

Paul Temple is currently Lecturer in Economics at the University of Surrey. Previously he has worked as an Economic Adviser at the National Economic Development Office in London and as a Research Fellow in the Centre for Business Strategy at the London Business School. He has published widely in the area of economic performance, with recent papers in both *Economic Journal* and *Oxford Economic Papers*. He is also a joint editor of *Britain's Economic Performance* (Routledge, 1998, 2nd edn) and *Investment, Employment and Growth: Perspectives for Policy* (Routledge, 1999).

Ioannies Vavouras is Professor of Economic Policy at Panteion University, Athens. He was previous head of the department of public administration, and has been Rector of the University since April 2000. He is the author of a large number of books and articles, mainly in the fields of macroeconomic theory and policy, economic planning, public sector economics, economic development, economic and monetary union, and the shadow economy.

John Weeks is Head of Economics at the School of Oriental and African Studies at the University of London, and Director of the Centre for Development Policy and Research. In the 1970s, he was one of the first researchers to investigate the so-called 'informal sector'.

Ganeshan Wignaraja is Chief Programme Officer in the Export and Industrial Development Division of the Commonwealth Secretariat. He is responsible for the Secretariat's advisory work on industrial competitiveness strategies and SME development policies, and has published widely on these issues.

Qing Gong Yang has worked as a statistician in Liao Ning Statistics Bureau, China, and as a Visiting Scholar in the Department of Economics at Newcastle University. He is currently reading for a PhD in the Department of Economics at the University of Surrey researching into enterprise performance in China.

List of Abbreviations

2-D	two-dimensional
APEMEFAC	National Footwear Makers' Association (Peru)
APIC	Association of Small-Scale Garment Manufacturers (Peru)
ASEAN	Association of Southeast Asian Nations
BDS	business development services
bn	billion
BOCCIM	Botswana Confederation of Commerce, Industry and Manpower
CAD	computer-aided design
CEDT	Centre for Electronic Development and Technology, Indian Institute of Science
CEE	Central and East European (countries)
CETPs	central effluent treatment plants
c.i.f.	cost in freight
CIS	Commonwealth of Independent States
Clik	Consortium of Electronic Industries of Karnataka (India)
CMTI	Central Machine Tools Institute (India)
CNCs	computer numerically controlled (machine tools)
CNSIEC	China National Silk Import and Export Corporation
COEs	collectively-owned enterprises
crore	10 million (100 lakhs)
DCSSI	Development Commissioner – Small-Scale Industries (India)
DF	dominant firm (model)
DFID	Department for International Development (India)
DGTD	Directorate General of Technical Development (India)
ECLA	Economic Commission for Latin America
EPZ	export processing zone
EU	European Union
FAO	Food and Agriculture Organization of the United Nations
FDI	foreign direct investment
FTCs	foreign trade corporations
GATT	General Agreement on Tariffs and Trade

GDP	gross domestic product
GML	*La Gazeta Mercantil Latinoamericana*
ha	hectare
ICTs	information and communication technologies
IIED	International Institute for Environment and Development (UNIDO)
ILO	International Labour Office
IMF	International Monetary Fund
ISO	International Organization for Standardization
ISI	import-substitution industrialization
IT	information technology
ITC	International Trade Centre
ITI	Indian Telephone Industries
ITU	International Telecommunications Union
JETRO	Japan External Trade Organization
KASSIA	Karnataka Small Scale Industries Association (India)
lakh	100,000
LDCs	less developed countries
LEs	large enterprises
m	million
MEDIA	Mauritius Export Development and Investment Authority
MNC	Multinational Company
MOFERT	Ministry of Foreign Economic Relations and Trade (China)
MVA	manufacturing value-added
NBER	National Bureau of Economic Research
NIEs	Newly Industrializing Economies
NPC	National Productivity Council (India)
NSSG	National Statistical Service of Greece
NTTF	Nettur Technical Training Foundation, India
OCEI	Organizacíon Central de Estadística y Información (Venezuela)
OECD	Organisation for Economic Co-operation and Development
OLS	ordinary least squares
PCBs	printed circuit boards
PPF	production possibility frontier
PRC	People's Republic of China
PYME	*Pequeña y Mediana Empresa*
PYMI	*Pequeña y Mediana Industria*

R&D	research and development
RAPA	Regional Office for Asia and the Pacific (FAO)
SAAT	South Asian Multidisciplinary Advice Team (New Delhi)
SIC	Standard Industrial Classification
SIDO	Small Industries Development Organization
SISI	Small Industries Service Institute (India)
SMEs	small and medium-sized enterprises
SMMEs	small, medium and micro-enterprises
SOEs	state-owned enterprises
SPSS	Statistical Package for the Social Sciences
SSEs	small-scale enterprises
SSI	small-scale industries
TFP	total factor productivity
TI	technology index
UMP	Urban Management Programme (UNCHS)
UNCHS	United Nations Centre for Human Settlements
UNCTAD	United Nations Conference on Trade and Development
UNDP	United Nations Development Programme
UNIDO	United Nations Industrial Development Organization
US	United States of America
USAID	United States Agency for International Development
WEP	World Employment Programme (ILO)
WTO	World Trade Organization

1 Introduction and Overview

Homi Katrak and Roger Strange

Since around the 1960s, the governments of many of the developing countries have been concerned to promote their small-scale enterprises (SSEs). The rationale for helping those enterprises could be summed up neatly in the often-heard saying 'small is beautiful'. This view arises for a number of diverse reasons, which have tended to differ from one country to another. However, the more well-known reasons have included the following:

- SSEs offer greater opportunities for employment;
- they are the 'seed bed' out of which larger enterprises grow;
- they are independent and can help the dispersion of industry away from the urban areas; and
- they can help to restrict the market domination of the larger enterprises.

The policy instruments used to help the SSEs have also been quite diverse. These have included credit facilities (to meet set-up expenses and some operating costs); subsidies for the purchase of some inputs; advice on technological upgrading, production and marketing; reservation of certain items for exclusive production by the SSEs; and exemption from certain regulations and taxes.

Now, while the arguments for helping the SSEs have considerable appeal, they also raise a number of important questions. Some questions are mainly of a practical nature, while others are concerned with the overall rationale of SSE policies.

Any policy to support SSEs needs to consider an initial practical question: What criteria should be used to distinguish SSEs from other (medium and large) enterprises?[1] This question is important in particular for the government agencies that administer support policies. There is a choice of input-based or output-based criteria (for example, number of employees, value of physical assets, and value of sales). However, all these criteria require a cut-off point in order to distinguish SSEs from other enterprises. But this creates a problem. If different enterprises use different types of technologies, and/or produce different quality/price products, the grouping of 'small' enterprises may alter between the various criteria. In the event, in the absence of any a priori guidelines, decisions about cut-off points have sometimes been influenced by the lobbying power of pressure groups. An alternative criterion rests on certain characteristics of the enterprises. For example, SSEs would be those enterprises that have family ownership and employ only family members. This criterion would avoid the problem of the cut-off points. But there may instead be a problem of defining 'the family'. The obvious inference from this brief discussion is that no one criterion is unquestionably better than the others. This may well explain why different countries (and even different agencies within a country) have tended to use different criteria.

A second important question concerns the overall objective of SSE support policies. Should those policies be designed to help mainly the SSEs? Or should they have a broader perspective, namely to help SSEs enhance the country's overall economic welfare? The former objective would emphasize mainly the benefits and needs of the SSEs, while the latter would also be concerned with those enterprises' competing and/or complementary relationships with medium and large enterprises.

In past years, when many developing countries had implemented regulatory and protectionist policies, considerations of efficiency and competition were not always of major importance. Instead, the objectives of national self-reliance and of promoting particular industries and types of enterprise were of greater interest. Policies towards SSEs and medium and large enterprises were often influenced by the lobbying efforts of their respective pressure groups. The relationships between the different types of enterprise were usually not taken into account.

This economic background gave rise to three types of problem for SSEs. First, some of the claims made for these enterprises were based on empirically untested grounds. Second, some other claims were seen to be conflicting with each other. And third, government support for SSEs was offset by some policies to help other enterprises. Each of these problems is well known, and is thus only given a brief mention here.

One of the major claims for the SSEs concerned their employment potential. This claim was based initially on the belief that these enterprises have higher labour requirements (per unit of output) than do other enterprises. However, empirical research has shown that SSEs do not always have higher unit labour requirements. Moreover, even where they do have higher unit labour inputs, the underlying reason could be that they are less efficient in the use of both labour and capital, and/or because they are exempt from labour union pressures that face the larger enterprises. The important implication is that higher labour intensities *per se* are not an argument for supporting SSEs. A further point is that SSEs' employment potential depends also on their level and growth of output, and these aspects may compare unfavourably with the medium and larger enterprises.

The second of the problems is that some of the claims for the SSEs could be conflicting with each other. Consider the argument that SSEs are independent, and so can be located in geographically dispersed areas, far from large urban centres. If those SSEs were to sell their output mainly in their small local markets, they would have limited sales, and hence limited employment potential. On the other hand, if they aimed to sell in the large urban markets, they would have a location disadvantage *vis-à-vis* some of their larger competitors and consequently would not be able to check the market domination of the latter.

The third problem was that government support for SSEs was sometimes neutralized by other policies that were aimed at helping the larger enterprises. Tariffs and other barriers to competing imports may have helped larger enterprises in particular, because their products are closer substitutes for imports (than are the products of SSEs). Consequently, import restrictions may have caused some shift of resources away from SSEs and towards the larger enterprises.

Recognition of all these problems has led to research into new roles and policies for the SSEs. There is now greater interest in those enterprises' contribution to overall economic welfare, both via improvements in their own efficiency, as well as through their competing–complementary relationships with medium and large enterprises. These issues have acquired considerable relevance recently, as many countries have introduced wide-ranging economic reforms, shifting away from the earlier inward-looking and regulatory policies to a more outward-looking and market-orientated approach.

The chapters in this volume address a number of the issues raised above. Some of those issues have been relevant during the years of the inward-looking regimes, and continue to be so, while others have emerged with recent economic reforms. Part I is made up of three chapters examining major concerns about SSEs' contribution to overall economic welfare, namely efficiency, immiserizing growth, and pollution. Part II contains five chapters, which look at some more recent concerns as SSEs face increased competition. These concerns are about growth and survival, as well as the need to mobilize government support. Parts III and IV discuss the important roles of industrial clusters, and technological upgrading. These are two of the strategies that may help SSEs compete with foreign enterprises, as well as against their larger domestic rivals.

The chapters in Part I provide a critical perspective on the idea that 'small is beautiful'. In Chapter 2, John Weeks investigates the relationship between the size of production units and efficiency. He finds little empirical support for the view that small enterprises in manufacturing are relatively employment-generating, or that small enterprises represent a more efficient response to market conditions than do medium and large ones. Rather, he notes that wages in small enterprises typically are lower than in medium and large ones, and concludes that there would be no change in employment even if wages in the latter fell to the level of the former. Thus he questions the wisdom of small enterprise development, unless it can be shown (and here he draws attention to the paucity of the required data) that small enterprises possess dynamic advantages.

In Chapter 3, Roger Strange and Jim Newton also sound a cautionary note about the merits of small-enterprise development. They draw on the experience of the silk industry in China to show how reform and liberalization during the 1980s gave rise to a massive increase in the numbers of small reeling plants and silk processing factories. This expansion in capacity led to a collapse of the world silk market, and to the subsequent immiserization of the Chinese industry. The role of the state in the demise of the industry is critically examined, and lessons are drawn for countries wishing to promote the development of SSEs in export-orientated industries.

Nandini Dasgupta, in Chapter 4, focuses on the environmental impact of the growth of small-scale enterprises. She notes that there is now recognition not only that pollution by small-scale industries is a problem, but also that the poor typically suffer more than the better-off because of the proximity of low-income housing to clusters of small, polluting industries in many cities in developing countries. She argues that a fundamental difficulty in providing a solution lies in the conceptualization of the environmental problem, and that the ability to deal with the problem varies with the size of the enterprise. Thus she concludes that a technocratic approach is inadequate, but that an interactive and participatory approach may prove to be a more fruitful means of implementing cleaner production strategies.

The chapters in Part II address the effects of market competition on SSEs. In Chapter 5, Qing Gong Yang and Paul Temple examine the role of entry and exit processes in the context of China's gradualist industrial reforms, particularly during the latest phase of transition to a socialist market economy. They conclude that competitive selection processes operate, for small firms and collectively owned enterprises (COEs), in a manner consistent with a private market economy, and that the probability of exit for these firms has increased with the reforms. In contrast, they find that no such processes appear to operate for state-owned enterprises (SOEs), nor has this situation changed in the most recent phase of reforms. They conclude that competitive selection in China is not infact providing a sufficiently important substitute for corporate governance mechanisms based on ownership.

Homi Katrak, in Chapter 6, considers whether India's economic liberalization policies, introduced in 1991, have had a beneficial, or a detrimental effect on the growth of SSEs. He suggests that some aspects of liberalization might have favoured the SSEs, while others were more likely to help the competing larger enterprises. His analysis focuses on those products that compete with the output of the larger enterprises, rather than those where the relationship is complementary (for example, under subcontracting relationships). He concludes that the SSEs' growth was significantly lower in the product groups where they initially had a lower output share, and was also lower when the growth of the competing larger enterprises was higher. But the effect of competition from the larger enterprises was dampened somewhat by liberalization, to the benefit of the SSEs.

In Chapter 7, Alan Mulhern addresses the causes of the relative decline in the importance of small and medium size enterprises (SMEs) in the manufacturing sector in Venezuela since 1960, and their absolute decline since the late 1970s. Venezuela's economic system has been characterized by two attempts at 'transition' to a modern economy: the first in 1958 at the start of its democratic system; and the second in 1989, when it attempted to bring into being an open free-market economy. Mulhern highlights structural barriers in manufacturing, and a lack of efficiency and innovation efforts by the SMEs, as the key economic determinants of the decline, which he attributes to the deeply exclusionary nature of the economic structure. Furthermore, he suggests that the decline of the SMEs highlights not only an economic problem in Venezuela, but also the wider political problem that a genuine transitional economy requires a participative economic democracy with access for everybody to the productive resources of the economy.

In Chapter 8, Subrata Ghatak, George Manolas, Costas Rontos and Iohanies Vavouras consider the possible effects on Polish SMEs of accession to the European Union (EU). They note that Poland underwent one period of rapid economic transformation during the 1990s, and that a second period will be required as the country faces up to the challenges ahead. The chapter contains the results of a questionnaire survey of Polish SME owners/managers about the perceived impact of EU accession on their enterprises. This reveals that the majority of Polish managers were optimistic, but that there was considerable variation in the degrees of optimism between firms from different locations, in different industries, and with different characteristics. These results provide the basis for the authors to put forward a number of policy initiatives which they maintain should help Polish SMEs not only to survive, but also to prosper in the environment of increased competition in the Single European Market.

Berhanu Kassayie looks at another European country, Bulgaria, in Chapter 9, and considers the impact of reform and liberalization on the establishment and expansion of manufacturing SMEs. He finds that the emerging small manufacturing sector was founded primarily on spin-off start-ups from large SOEs during, and in the period immediately following, the initiation of system reform in 1990. The rate of new firm entry appeared to slow down in the aftermath of the introduction of the 'shock therapy' of reform institutionalization in 1992, compounded by inconsistencies in reform implementation. Furthermore, he detects a tendency towards larger new manufacturing start-ups in Bulgaria, concurrent with the beginnings of institutional transformation, and suggests that this has been effected through favoured access for the larger 'small' enterprises to equipment and external finance. He also concludes that reform has had a positive impact on the expansion of existing firms, and that this impact has been stronger for the larger 'small' firms.

The chapters in Part III consider the role of clusters in the development of SSEs. In Chapter 10, Mark Holmström investigates the extent and limits of co-operative networking between SSEs in the electrical and electronic industries in Bangalore, the 'real' services (for example, advice, training, testing) provided by public-sector bodies, and the use that firms make of them. He takes a very positive view of industrial clusters and the associated 'flexible specialization' that allows the firms to achieve 'collective efficiency', and to overcome the disadvantages of small size. He then considers the lessons that may be learned from Bangalore's experience of the promotion of industrial districts, not just in India but also in other developing countries, and emphasizes the need to build trust if such initiatives are to succeed.

Henry Sandee explores the performance of Indonesia's small-scale industries, before and after the Asian financial crisis, in Chapter 11. He points out that government policies in Indonesia were biased towards larger firms in various ways during the period 1986–96, and that initiatives to foster SSEs had been both limited and not very successful. But this changed in the aftermath of the crisis, which the small-scale industries weathered rather better than their larger counterparts. At a governmental conference in December 1999, the need was identified for a more conducive environment for SSEs, for the rationalization of assistance to small firms, the strengthening of support services, the privatization of programmes, and for institutional capacity building.

In Chapter 12, Manuel Albaladejo considers the determinants of competitiveness in SME clusters, citing evidence from five clusters in Latin America. He laments the varied growth experience of these clusters, which he ascribes to the increasingly dynamic nature of competitiveness in global markets. Few clusters in developing countries have been able to compete with innovative and high-quality products. Albaladejo identifies not only the 'cluster-level' determinants of competitiveness associated with the 'collective efficiency' approach, but also the 'firm-level' and 'country-level' factors that are also required. He concludes that clustering on its own does not guarantee economic success, but that policies designed to strengthen inter-firm co-operation should be combined with government interventions at the national level, and with specific schemes to build up the technological capabilities of SMEs.

Finally, Part IV contains two chapters on the issue of technological upgrading. In Chapter 13, Ganeshan Wignaraja explores the relationship between firm size and the acquisition of technological capabilities, using data from a sample of firms in the garment industry in Mauritius. He constructs a 'technology index' for the firms, and identifies not only firm size but also technical manpower, employee training, and external technical assistance as important determinants. He further demonstrates that export performance is related to size and to technological capabilities. The large firms appear to have acquired the requisite competitive capabilities to produce to the high standards of price, quality, delivery and so on demanded by foreign buyers, but the SMEs have not reached the same levels of achievement. He suggests that supplier linkage programmes and the provision of business development services might be useful ways of incorporating SMEs into effective clusters around the large enterprises, so improving their capabilities.

And, in Chapter 14, Richard Duncombe and Richard Heeks assess the potential contribution of information and communication technologies (ICTs) to small enterprise development. They report the findings from a questionnaire survey of current information practices and needs in formal sector enterprises in Botswana. The survey first mapped current enterprise information systems, finding that there was a strong reliance on informal systems. It also mapped current information needs. They conclude that information gaps are certainly an issue for small entrepreneurs, but may be less important than (but intertwined with) the needs for other resources such as finance, skills and new markets. Where information services merit improvement, changes to informal, non-electronic systems must be considered alongside changes to formal ICT-based systems. Interventions, whether by entrepreneurs or support agencies, must also be differentiated.

Note

1. For some purposes, SSEs and medium-sized enterprises may be aggregated as small and medium-sized enterprises (SMEs). For other purposes, a finer categorization may be appropriate. In Chapter 9 of this volume, for example, the distinction is made between 'micro' enterprises, 'medium–small' enterprises, and 'small' enterprises.

Part I

Is Small Beautiful? A Reappraisal

2 The Efficiency of Small Enterprises in Developing Countries: An Empirical Analysis

John Weeks

INTRODUCTION

While there exists a wealth of literature on the process of industrialization in developing countries, and on policies to foster industrialization, one finds relatively little analysis, theoretical or empirical, of the relationship between the size of production unit and key variables such as choice of technique, wage behaviour, and employment growth. This relative absence is in contrast to the voluminous number of articles and books on the size distribution of production units in agriculture. This chapter investigates these issues, with particular attention to the efficiency of enterprises by size.

As Cortes *et al.* (1987) have pointed out, attempts to measure efficiency by size of establishment are fraught with difficulty, both for conceptual reasons and because of data problems. Here, published data on size distributions are used and, to compensate for potential problems with the data, various measures of efficiency are employed. The general conclusion from the statistical exercises is that, in general, small manufacturing enterprises, defined as those having fewer than fifty workers, do not appear to be efficient, either technically or economically.

First, I shall review the common arguments in favour of promoting small enterprises, and test for whether the alleged characteristics on which these arguments are based are supported empirically. The statistics indicate that, overall, small enterprises have characteristics consistent with them being 'labour intensive' in the narrow sense of lower output per worker. The second section presents the theoretical tools to be used in assessing 'efficiency'. The subsequent section applies these to the empirical information for several developing countries.

SMALL ENTERPRISES IN DEVELOPED AND DEVELOPING COUNTRIES

Perhaps one of the most universal characteristics of capitalist production is the variation in the size and efficiency of production units within the same product line. This variation was pointed out by the so-called 'classical' economists, especially David Ricardo and Karl Marx, and these early theorists considered it sufficiently important to require both a coherent explanation and to be incorporated into their modelling. Neo-classical economists, on the other hand, tended to have a literal reading of Marshall's famous 'representative firm', treating this concept as an approximation of reality rather than as an abstraction from the complexity of reality.[1] Except in extremely concentrated sectors of production, the norm in both developed and developing countries is a striking variation in scale of production, and the persistence of that variation indefinitely. That this persistence of differences in scale could reflect a static equilibrium outcome challenges credibility, though not the ingenuity of the neo-classical school (Lucas, 1978).

Tables 2.1 and 2.2 provide an indication of the extent to which establishments are differentiated by size in different countries. The developing countries listed in Table 2.1 are those that will be treated empirically in this chapter. For comparison, statistics are given for three developed countries in Table 2.2. It is beyond the scope of this chapter to consider trends over time in countries (Weeks, 2000). Here, the discussion is restricted to an inspection of the importance of small enterprises in selected countries. In both tables, establishments are divided into three size ranges: small (10–49 employees), medium (50–499 employees), and large (500 or more employees). For every country, statistics are available for a minimum of twenty years. The country (albeit a city state) in which small establishments account for the largest share of employment is Hong Kong, with an average of 28 per cent over almost half a century. In three of the six developing countries (that is, Brazil, Colombia and Korea) the employment share of small enterprises is between 20 and 24 per cent of total employment. For Pakistan and South Africa, the share is significantly lower, at 12 per cent and 13 per cent, respectively. The variation among the three developed countries is considerably more: one-third for Japan; about 13 per cent for the USA, and slightly higher than the latter in France.

While the tables contain data on only a few countries, these are sufficient to demonstrate that there are no simple stories about what determines the importance of small enterprises. For example, among

Table 2.1 Employment by size of manufacturing establishment in six developing countries (various years)

Country	Year	Employment as percentage of total		
		Small	Medium	Large
Brazil	1960	20.6	47.7	31.7
	1965	16.4	47.2	36.3
	1970	24.9	52.3	22.8
	1975	25.9	52.6	21.5
	1980	24.1	54.9	21.1
Colombia	1956	31.0	n/a	n/a
	1960	28.3	n/a	n/a
	1965	25.1	n/a	n/a
	1970	19.6	n/a	n/a
	1975	19.7	n/a	n/a
	1980	19.5	51.8	28.7
	1985	21.1	51.0	27.8
	1990	20.5	n/a	n/a
Hong Kong	1951	22.8	49.4	27.9
	1955	24.2	48.1	27.6
	1961	25.1	50.5	24.4
	1965	20.3	52.7	27.0
	1971	24.8	48.2	27.0
	1975	27.5	48.8	24.0
	1980	29.4	51.3	19.3
	1985	32.0	51.3	16.6
	1990	35.4	48.9	15.7
	1996	34.3	47.4	18.3
Korea	1958	43.2	n/a	n/a
	1962	33.8	n/a	n/a
	1966	25.9	40.1	30.0
	1970	22.6	38.5	38.8
	1975	13.6	40.8	45.6
	1980	15.6	41.4	43.0
	1985	20.3	41.9	37.8
	1990	21.7	38.7	31.6
Pakistan	1954	18.4	20.8	60.8
	1960	17.1	28.9	54.1
	1966	13.7	28.8	57.5
	1970	12.3	27.2	60.5
	1975	7.9	25.3	66.8
	1980	10.3	28.5	61.2
	1985	10.1	30.1	59.8
	1988	10.6	32.9	56.5

Table 2.1 (contd.)

Country	Year	Employment as percentage of total		
		Small	Medium	Large
South Africa	1950	18.2	52.4	29.4
	1960	15.2	52.3	32.5
	1970	11.0	47.5	41.5
	1979	11.1	47.1	41.8
	1988	12.1	48.2	39.6

Notes: Small establishments are defined as those with 10–49 employees; medium as those with 50–499 employees; and large as those with 500 or more employees.
Source: See Appendix.

the three developed countries, it does not appear that a relatively low degree of regulation in itself fosters small enterprises; indeed, it was the most regulated and protectionist country, Japan, in which small enterprises accounted for more than twice the share of employment than in the relatively *laissez faire* USA. The same point applies to the six developing countries. While the share of small enterprise employment

Table 2.2 Employment by size of manufacturing establishment in three developed countries (various years)

Country	Year	Employment as percentage of total		
		Small	Medium	Large
France	1962	14.8	33.3	51.9
	1977	12.4	32.3	55.3
	1990	19.1	36.1	44.7
Japan	1967	30.5	39.8	29.7
	1975	31.5	39.9	28.6
	1990	32.9	42.8	24.3
USA	1967	11.7	41.5	46.7
	1977	12.8	45.0	42.2
	1987	15.3	47.4	37.4

Notes: Small establishments are defined as those with 10–49 employees; medium as those with 50–499 employees; and large as those with 500 or more employees.
Source: OECD (1992).

is greatest in the most open economy, Hong Kong, the percentages are much the same for Brazil and Korea, though the former country was considerably less open to trade in the 1960s and 1970s than the latter.

The statistics from a limited number of countries suggests that the prosperity or otherwise of small enterprises is a complex phenomenon. The argument of this chapter is that, while policies matter, the performance of small enterprises is determined ultimately by their efficiency relative to larger enterprises. It is to this issue that we turn in the following sections.

THE ARGUMENTS FOR SMALL ENTERPRISES

The empirical point of departure of this chapter is that, within sectors of manufacturing, even narrowly defined, production units vary in scale, and this variation occurs within a dynamic setting of expansion and decline. Indeed, that portion of the rather small literature on the size distribution of establishments that focuses on developing countries takes an implicitly or explicitly dynamic approach. The focus of this literature, the obsession one might say, is over the relative benefits of fostering small and medium-sized enterprises on the one hand, and large enterprises on the other. At one extreme is the 'economies of scale' position, which argues that large enterprises are inherently more efficient, for a range of reasons: narrowly-defined cost economies that are associated with scale, greater technological dynamism, and higher rates of profit and investment from internal funds. At the other extreme is the 'small enterprise' position, which argues that the alleged scale economies are illusory. For the former, large enterprises exist as a consequence of objective economic and technological laws, and small enterprises are either failed large ones or inefficient producers subsidised by the low wages paid to socially and politically vulnerable workers. For the latter, small enterprises are the efficient adapters to market conditions, while large producers exist only in consequence of market distortions that are designed specifically to foster their survival.

It is beyond the scope of this chapter to review the analytical and empirical debates between the two positions, which has been done with clarity by Cortes *et al.* (1987) and Little *et al.* (1987). For present purposes it is sufficient to note the crucial empirical dimension of the small enterprise position. In the context of developing countries, the essence of the small enterprise argument is that establishment size is a close, if not exact, proxy for labour intensity. In this view, labour intensity is correlated negatively with scale, and small enterprises, because they pay lower wages, choose more labour-intensive techniques. The lower wages in small enterprises are alleged to reflect more closely the social opportunity cost of labour than do the higher wages enjoyed by workers in large establishments. The higher wages in the latter are attributed to 'market distortions', either trade-union power or government regulation of wage levels. The large enterprises exist, despite paying higher wages, because of a range of government-sponsored benefits (for example, trade protection, subsidized credit, and self-serving health and safety regulations). Whatever the validity of the small enterprise position, it rises or falls on key empirical tests: that output per worker and wage levels are correlated positively with scale of production. If output per worker is not lower in small establishments, then they do not create more employment per unit of output, and the employment justification for fostering them is lost.

Prior to an analytical treatment of the issue, the scale of production and labour intensity hypothesis is tested for four countries in Table 2.3. The statistical procedure was as follows:

- for each country, establishments were divided into three size ranges, as in Tables 2.1 and 2.2: small (10–49), medium (50–499), and large (500-plus employees) at the three-digit level of the International Standard Industrial Classification;
- both value-added per worker and average wages were normalized in each year such that the index for large establishments was 100; and
- a regression was estimated, with dummy variables for each three-digit sector (with the miscellaneous sector 390 omitted), and for small and medium establishments (with the category for large establishments omitted).

The procedure, which accounts for differences by sector, provides support for the labour-intensity and scale hypothesis. For all four countries, output per worker is significantly below that for large establishments, for both small and medium enterprises, and in all cases the differential is greater for small enterprises than for medium ones. The variation in wages across size categories is considerably smaller in all countries. For Hong Kong, the wage differential for small establishments is slightly less than 10 per cent, and non-significant for medium-sized units. That the fall in output per worker as size declines is greater than the fall in wages implies that labour's share in value-added falls with size. This is consistent with the labour intensity hypothesis.

Table 2.3 Value-added per worker and average wages in manufacturing establishments in four developing countries

Country	Value-added per worker[2]		Average wage[3]	
	Ratio	T-statistic	Ratio	T-statistic
Brazil (1960–80)[1]				
Small	55.9	12.1*	64.4	17.7*
Medium	76.2	6.5*	79.8	10.1*
Colombia (1970–89)[1]				
Small	46.0	16.8*	50.3	19.0*
Medium	70.4	9.2*	71.4	10.9*
Hong Kong (1977–90)[1]				
Small	65.6	6.1*	90.5	2.9*
Medium	88.5	2.0*	100.0	0.8
Korea (1970–91)[1]				
Small	40.9	14.1*	68.9	17.4*
Medium	74.4	6.1*	80.8	10.8*

Notes: 1. Data were available for Brazil for 1960, 1966, 1970, 1975 and 1980; for Colombia for 1970, 1975, 1980, 1985 and 1989; for Hong Kong for 1977, 1980, 1983, 1985 and 1990; and for Korea for 1970, 1975, 1980, 1985 and 1991.
2. Output per worker is measured in terms of value-added, and normalized in each year such that the figure for large establishments was 100.
3. Average wages were normalized in each year such that the figure for large establishments was 100.
Small establishments are defined as those with 10–49 employees; medium as those with 50–499 employees; and large as those with 500 or more employees.
A significant ($p < 0.05$) T-statistic is shown by *.
The numbers of observations for each country were as follows: Brazil, 270; Colombia, 360; Hong Kong, 195; and Korea, 360.
Source: See Appendix.

However, the statistics in Table 2.3 do not confirm the hypothesis. They indicate that overall, for the four countries, output per worker increases with the size of establishment. Whether this is because labour intensity is related negatively to size, or because small or medium-sized establishments are technically inefficient (using more labour and more capital) is not clear from the table. The generalization that output per worker is related positively to size is only the first step in considering the possible benefits of small enterprises. The issue of efficiency is pursued in the next section.

ARE SMALL ENTERPRISES TECHNICALLY EFFICIENT?

Under purely competitive conditions, with efficient factor markets and perfect foresight, no enterprise would operate with a technique that employed more of all factors per unit of output than were employed by other enterprises in the sector. However, one or all of these conditions may not hold in developing countries, creating the possibility of inferior techniques. It is this possibility that we consider in this section.

Figure 2.1 shows graphically the analytical point, using the familiar factor price frontier, and taking the special case in which the frontiers are linear.[2] The diagram shows three profit–wage trade-offs for the same product. Techniques A and C are efficient *alternatives*, in the sense that each is more profitable than the other over some range of wage levels. Specifically, technique A is the more profitable for wages

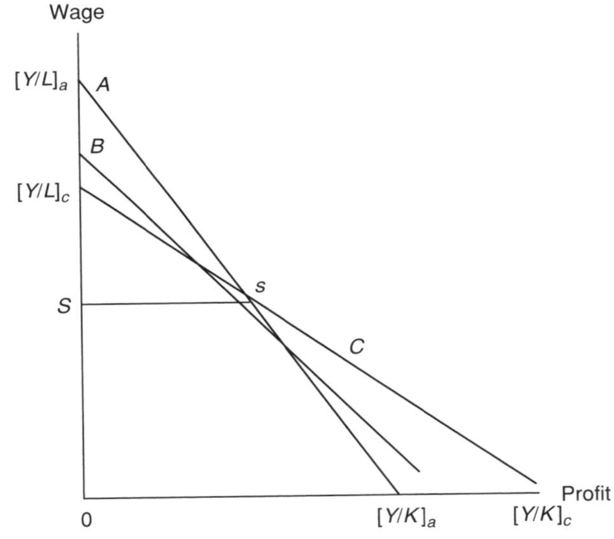

Figure 2.1 Efficient and inefficient production techniques

Note: Techniques A and C are both efficient; technique B is inferior.

above point *S* on the vertical axis, and technique C is the more profitable for wages below that level (with *s* the 'switch point'). The vertical intercepts measure the average product of labour, and the horizontal intercepts the average product of capital. It is deduced directly that technique A is the more capital-intensive. Technique B is inefficient (inferior): that is, there is no combination of the wage level and profit rate that would induce a rational capitalist to employ it under competitive conditions with perfect foresight. While at some wage levels it is more profitable than technique A, and at others more profitable than technique C, at no positive wage is it more profitable than both.

There are a number of reasons why, in practice, technique B might be used. First, and most generally, unanticipated technical change may render existing techniques inferior, reducing the value of existing capital to near zero. A rational response by an 'inferior' producer would be to continue to produce with the inefficient technique for a time period that balanced the loss of current profit against the deadweight loss of the unrealized capital stock. Less generally, new techniques may require a substantially larger scale of production. Small producers, rendered inefficient by technical change, may not have access to the financial institutions that would allow them to move up to the larger scale of production.

To investigate empirically whether techniques are alternatives or inferior, one requires data on the value of the capital stock. The formal conditions are as follows:

- technique A is an alternative to technique C if $[Y/L]_c > [Y/L]_a$, but $[Y/K]_c < [Y/K]_a$; and
- technique A is inferior to technique C if $[Y/L]_c > [Y/L]_a$, and $[Y/K]_c > [Y/K]_a$.

The necessary data are available for three developing countries (namely, Korea, Colombia and Pakistan) and the results are presented in Table 2.4. The table reports the outcome of testing two hypotheses. The first hypothesis is that value-added per worker is lower in small establishments than in medium or large ones. This might be called the 'weak labour-intensity hypothesis'. If small enterprises are more employment-generating, the necessary condition is that output per worker is lower than for larger enterprises. Second, the 'strong labour-intensity hypothesis' is tested; namely, that the formal conditions for technical efficiency given above are satisfied. In order that small enterprises may be more employment-generating, both hypotheses must be sustained. The 'weak' hypothesis was tested as follows:

- for each sector and size category, mean output per worker and the standard deviation of that mean were calculated;[3]
- a simple difference of means test was applied for each size category with respect to all others; and
- size categories were judged to have different means if the test was significant at the 10 per cent probability level.

The 'strong' hypothesis was tested by calculating labour per unit of output and capital per unit of output, and averaging these across years. For each year, these ratios were normalized with respect to the sector average.

Table 2.4 The size-productivity relationship and technical efficiency in small enterprises in three developing countries

Sector	Colombia	Korea	Pakistan
311/312: Food	NLI Not efficient	LI Not efficient	NLI Inefficient
313: Beverages	LI Not efficient	LI Not efficient	LI Inefficient
321: Textiles	NLI Not efficient	NLI Not efficient	NLI Inefficient
322: Apparel	LI Not efficient	NLI Not efficient	NLI Inefficient
323: Leather products	NLI Not efficient	LI Not efficient	NLI Efficient
324: Footwear	NLI Not efficient	NLI Not efficient	LI Efficient
331: Wood products	LI Not efficient	LI Not efficient	LI Efficient
332: Furniture	LI Not efficient	LI Efficient	Not available
341: Paper products	LI Not efficient	LI Efficient	LI Efficient
342: Printing	LI Not efficient	LI Inefficient	LI Inefficient
351: Industrial chemicals	LI Efficient	LI Inefficient	LI Inefficient
352: Other chemicals	LI Not efficient	Not available	LI Inefficient

Table 2.4 (*contd.*)

Sector	Colombia	Korea	Pakistan
355: Rubber	NLI Not efficient	LI Efficient	LI Inefficient
356: Plastics	NLI Not efficient	LI Inefficient	NLI Efficient
361: Pottery, china	NLI Not efficient	LI Inefficient	NLI Inefficient
362: Glass	LI Efficient	LI Inefficient	Not available
369: Non-metallic minerals	LI Not efficient	LI Inefficient	Not available
371: Iron and steel	LI Not efficient	NLI Efficient	LI Efficient
372: Non-ferrous metals	NLI Efficient	LI Efficient	Not available
381: Metal products	LI Not efficient	LI Inefficient	LI Inefficient
382: Non-electric machinery	NLI Not efficient	LI Inefficient	LI Inefficient
383: Electric machinery	LI Not efficient	NLI Inefficient	LI Inefficient
384: Transport equipment	NLI Not efficient	LI Inefficient	LI Inefficient
385: Professional equipment	NLI Not efficient	NLI Inefficient	Not available
Summary: Labour intensive and efficient	1/24	4/23	4/19

Notes: The data for Colombia were from 1971, 1975, 1980, 1985 and 1989; for Korea from 1962, 1966, 1970, 1975, 1980, 1985 and 1991; and for Pakistan from 1965, 1970, 1975, 1980, 1985 and 1987.
Labour-intensive (LI) and not labour intensive (NLI) refer to the output per worker criterion. Efficient and not efficient refer to labour–output and capital–output ratios. See text for further details.
Source: See Appendix.

Table 2.4 shows that, while small enterprises use more labour per unit of output than medium or large enterprises in a majority of cases, there are many exceptions. Small enterprises are not labour-intensive by the weak definition in six out of twenty-three cases for Korea, eleven out of twenty-four cases for Colombia, and six out of nineteen cases for Pakistan. Thus, for 35 per cent of the three-digit sectors, small enterprises do not appear to generate more employment per unit of output, even by the weak definition. Further, about half of these cases (eleven out of twenty-three) occur in so-called light industries (food and clothing), sectors that are usually assumed to be more labour-intensive than manufacturing as a whole. The test for technical efficiency (inferior techniques, the strong definition) produces a result even more unfavourable to the hypothesis that small enterprises might be a source of employment generation. For Colombia, small enterprises seemed to be technically efficient in only three sectors; for Korea, in five sectors; and for Pakistan, in six sectors – that is, less than 25 per cent of sectors for the three countries. In only nine of these fourteen cases of technical efficiency were the small enterprises efficient *and* labour-intensive. Thus the three countries provide little support for the view that, in manufacturing, small enterprises are relatively employment-generating.

One cannot draw strong conclusions from the tables, for several reasons. First, a general judgement cannot be made on the basis of only three countries. Second, it may be that the capital stock data are unreliable. While neither of these problems can be resolved, the possible bias arising from both can be reduced by employing an alternative test of efficiency that does not require capital stock data. This will both eliminate the use of possibly unreliable data, and increase the number of countries that can be investigated. This is done in the next section.

TESTING FOR THE OPTIMAL SIZE OF ESTABLISHMENT

The neo-classical theory of the firm provides a vehicle for an alternative measure of efficiency, albeit on restrictive assumptions. In this section, we make the necessary assumptions to generate an estimate by three-digit sector of the establishment size (measured by number employed) that is associated with the highest output per worker. Under those assumptions, that establishment size would be the most economically efficient were all establishments to face the same input prices (whatever those prices might be).

The basic theoretical tools are demonstrated in Figure 2.2. The north-east quadrant of the diagram is the capital (K) and labour (N) space, and it is assumed that for each product there is only one activity vector, the line K/N. Along this line there are four logical possibilities: output increases more than proportionately to the inputs (increasing returns to

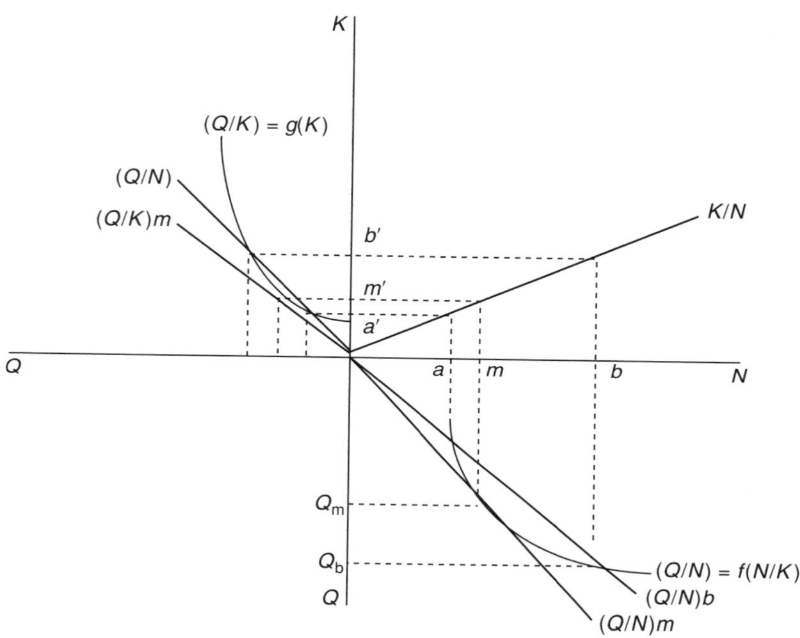

Figure 2.2 Optimal firm size in the standard neo-classical case

scale); proportionately (constant returns); less than proportionately (decreasing returns); or passes successively through each of these. The latter yields the so-called U-shaped total cost curve if all establishments face the same input prices. If input prices vary across establishments, but the output prices are the same, output per worker by employment size remains unique to the given technology, in the form of an inverted 'U'. The inverted 'U' outcome is shown in the south-east quadrant, which traces the function $Q/N = f(N/K)$ in output–labour space. Three levels of input use are indicated on the labour axis. In the range *a* to *m* there are increasing returns to scale, and from *m* to *b* (and beyond) there are decreasing returns to scale. The point defined by (m, Q_m) is the maximum for output per worker (and output per unit of capital, shown in the north-west quadrant).

The function $Q/N = f(N/K)$ can be approximated by a simple algorithm:

$$(Q/N)_i = \alpha_0 + \alpha_1 N_i + \alpha_2 N_i^2.$$

The turning point of this function is found by setting the first derivative to zero. Thus the 'optimal' establishment size, if there is one, measured by employment is:

$$N^* = -(\alpha_1/2\alpha_2).$$

The parameters α_1 and α_2 determine the returns to scale outcome:

if $\alpha_1 > 0$ and $\alpha_2 > 0$, or $\alpha_1 > 0$ and $\alpha_1 = 0$, increasing returns to scale;
if $\alpha_1 = 0$ and $\alpha_2 = 0$, constant returns to scale; and
if $\alpha_1 < 0$ and $\alpha_2 = 0$, or $\alpha_1 < 0$ and $\alpha_1 < 0$, decreasing returns to scale.

These logical outcomes are summarized in Figure 2.3, which shows output per worker as a function of the level of employment. This procedure tests for *economic* efficiency, because it assumes that all enterprises are *technically* efficient. Further, there is by definition a trade-off between economic efficiency and employment generation, since the former is defined by output per worker. If, for example, small establishments lie below the most efficient size of unit, they

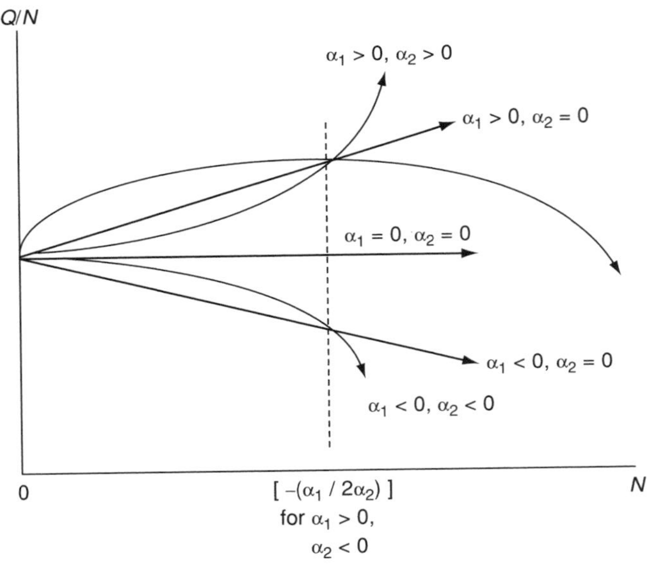

Figure 2.3 The long-run average product of labour and returns to scale: logical possibilities

would be more employment-generating per unit of output. A policy fostering them would involve a political judgement, and not an economic one.

It could be argued that this statistical exercise assumes what it wants to prove: having previously established that there is in general a positive correlation between value-added per worker and establishment size, it follows that any regression exercise linking the two will yield a result showing that larger establishments are more economically efficient. However, the statistical results are not trivial, for two reasons. First, Table 2.1, which showed the positive correlation, presents data at the aggregate level, rather than sector by sector, as is done here. Second, in Table 2.1, establishments were divided into three broad categories: small, medium, and large. Here, all size ranges available from the country sources are used (see notes at the bottom of each part of Table 2.4).

The quadratic approximation could be estimated at the three-digit level for six countries,[4] and the results are shown in Table 2.5. The number of sectors included varies from a low of fifteen for South Africa, to a high of twenty-four for Colombia. First, it should be noted that no sector showed decreasing returns, which imparts some credibility to the results. Of the 117 sectors across six countries, the values of the two parameters implied that 69 per cent showed had an inverted 'U' shape (the neo-classical case), 22 per cent were consistent with constant returns, and 9 per cent implied increasing returns. If we take 500 employees as the lower bound of the 'large' category, and treat increasing returns as implying that large establishments are most efficient, then for over 60 per cent of sectors, 'large' was the most economically efficient. For another 14 per cent, 'medium' units were the most efficient (nine in Colombia, six in Hong Kong, and one in South Africa). In no sector did the most efficient size fall into the 'small' category, though the finding that 22 per cent of sectors showed constant returns is consistent with small establishments not being inefficient.

The estimates of the most efficient establishment size appear credible for several reasons. As noted above, no sector shows continuous decreasing returns. Such a result would be non-credible, because it would imply that in the long-run there should be no production. Second, while there are no *a priori* grounds for a predicted result, none of the estimated sizes is outrageously large (that is, in excess of actual plant sizes in the countries in question, as indicated by the published data). Third, and perhaps most interesting, for several

Table 2.5 Returns to scale in the industrial sectors of six developing countries

Returns to scale[1]	**Brazil**	**Colombia**	**Hong Kong**	**Korea**	**Pakistan**	**South Africa**	**All Sectors**	
							(No.)	**(%)**
Unique optimal size	17	13	15	21	9	6	81	69.2
of which employment								
< 100 employees	0	0	0	0	0	0	0	0.0
100–499 employees	0	9	6	0	1	2	18	15.4
500–999 employees	6	3	5	14	6	3	37	31.6
> 1000 employees	11	1	4	7	2	1	26	22.2
Constant returns	0	5	3	2	7	9	26	22.2
Increasing returns	1	6	2	1	0	0	10	8.5
Total sectors	18	24	20	24	16	15	117	100.0

Notes: 1. See the text for the definitions of optimal size, constant returns, and increasing returns to scale. Data were available for Brazil for 1960, 1966, 1970, 1975 and 1980; for Colombia for 1965, 1970, 1975, 1980, 1985 and 1990; for Hong Kong for 1977, 1980, 1985 and 1990; for Korea for 1966, 1970, 1975, 1980, 1985 and 1991; for Pakistan for 1965, 1970, 1980, 1985 and 1987; and for South Africa for 1977, 1980, 1985 and 1990.
Source: See Appendix.

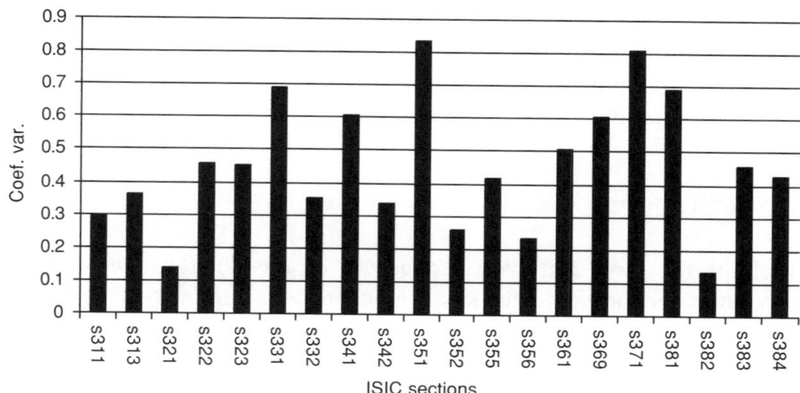

Figure 2.4 Coefficients of variation for the optimal establishment size in twenty industrial sectors

Note: The coefficients of variation are calculated for each sector across at least four of the six developing countries (Brazil, Colombia, Hong Kong, Korea, Pakistan and South Africa).
Source: See Appendix.

sectors the variation in estimated establishment size across countries is rather low, as shown in Figure 2.4. For those sectors that could be estimated for at least four countries, the average and standard deviation of most efficient establishment size were calculated, to produce the coefficient of variation, which is presented in the graph. For no sector is the statistic greater than unity, and for just over half it is below 0.5. If one thinks that foreign direct investment and other mechanisms of technology transfer tend to establish a common international technology, Table 2.5 provides some support for this view.

While this statistical exercise in itself is not conclusive, given the limitations of the data and the restrictive assumptions on which they are based, they are consistent with the evidence of the previous section. They offer sufficient reason to doubt the generalizations made frequently about the benefits of policies to foster small enterprises. In particular, they suggest that small enterprises do not necessarily represent a more efficient response to market conditions than large ones. The evidence indicates that wages in small enterprises typically are lower than in medium and large ones. However, if small enterprises are not economically efficient, even more if they are not technically efficient, the lower level of wages takes on negative implications. First, it implies that were wages in medium and large enterprises to fall to the level of those in small enterprises, there would be no shift in employment from the latter to the former. Second, it follows that in some, if not many, circumstances lower wages serve as a worker subsidy to capital, to maintain small enterprises in existence.

CONCLUSIONS

Perhaps the most impoverished aspect of the debate over whether governments should foster small enterprises is the lack of empirical evidence to assess contending views on the issue. To an extent, this is understandable, since the data on which informed judgements could be made are quite limited. As a result, positions tend to be based on case studies that frequently do not include information on costs, *a priori* arguments incorporating restrictive assumptions sometimes not made explicit, and causal empiricism.

The lack of appropriate data is especially frustrating, because it is collected regularly by governments of middle-income countries, and even of some low-income countries, as the basis for their manufacturing surveys. In the past it could be argued that the resources required to collate establishment data by size were excessive, given the utility of doing so. Whether or not that was true in the past, it is now no longer the case, given that most countries enter such data in electronic format, requiring only simple programming to sort it by establishment size. The shining example of how such data should be collected and presented is Korea, whose industrial surveys since the 1970s have been published with all major production and employment indicators by establishment size, disaggregated to the five-digit level. The frustration is only increased by the fact that, coincident with greater ease of collecting size distribution data, the number of countries that publish them on a regular basis has declined. In the 1970s and 1980s, over a dozen countries did so, half of which have since discontinued publication (and perhaps collection). Of the six countries included in the tables in this paper, only three provided data into the 1990s (Hong Kong, Korea and South Africa).

Fostering collection, sorting and publication of data by size would seem to be an obvious task for UNIDO, and the policy uses should also be obvious. Many, if not most, governments of developing countries give at least rhetorical support to small enterprise development. However, policies and policy discussions are rarely based on a systematic analysis of the viability of small enterprises, either at the sectoral or at the macro level. It may well be that systematic analysis would reveal the vibrancy and dynamism of small enterprises, but this cannot be taken as given.

Appendix

The database for the study is described in detail in Weeks and Letteri (1994), and more briefly in Weeks (2000). It is available from the author. All data are taken from country publications. In the case of Brazil, data were reported only in the five years shown in Table 2.1 (except for 1981, whose data were non-comparable). The Colombia data were reported for almost every year (1955–91) and then discontinued. For Hong Kong, reporting was intermittent for 1975–91, then on an annual basis. Korean statistics were reported every year from 1970, and continue. After an almost continuous annual series (1954–88), Pakistan appears to have discontinued reporting. South African data have appeared irregularly, usually every three years. The 1992 manufacturing survey had not been published when this chapter was written.

Listing the original sources for these six countries would be space-consuming, because the publications have changed names, or because the data have appeared in different publications over the years. The details, and the worksheets on which the analytical statistics were generated, are available from the author.

Notes

1. In the context of his writings as a whole, Marshall's representative firm would seem to be equivalent to Marx's concept of 'socially necessary labour time' or 'average conditions of production'. The Marxian concept refers to the establishment, through competition, of a norm of efficiency in a sector, and not to the actual convergence of producers to common technology and management standards.
2. For a simple presentation of the conditions under which factor price frontiers are linear, see Weeks (1989).
3. Output per worker by size category was normalized to the sector mean for each year.
4. For a few sectors, the estimation is at the two-digit level, because of the non-availability of data at the three-digit level.

References

Cortes, M., Berry, A. and Ishaq, A. (1987) *Success in Small and Medium-Scale Enterprises: The Evidence from Colombia*, New York: Oxford University Press.

Little, I. M. D., Mazumdar, D. and Page, J. M. Jr (1987) *Small Manufacturing Enterprises: A Comparative Study of India and other Economies*, New York: Oxford University Press.

Lucas, R. E. (1978) 'On the Size Distribution of Business Firms', *Bell Journal of Economics*, vol. 9, pp. 508–23.

Organization for Economic Co-operation and Development. (1992) *Manufacturing Data for Selected OECD Countries*, Paris: OECD.

Weeks, J. (1989) *A Critique of Neoclassical Macroeconomics*. London: Macmillan.

Weeks, J. (2000) 'The Role of Small Enterprises in Developing Countries in the Long Run: An Empirical Analysis', Working Paper, SOAS Centre for Development Policy and Research, London: CDPR. Accessible on website www.soas.ac.uk

Weeks, J. and Letteri, C. (1994) 'Employment, Wages and Establishment Size in Selected Developing Countries: An Empirical Analysis', Working Paper, SOAS Centre for Development Policy and Research, London: CDPR. Accessible on website www.soas.ac.uk

3 Small Enterprises and Immiserizing Growth: A Cautionary Tale from the Chinese Silk Industry

Roger Strange and Jim Newton

INTRODUCTION

The promotion of small-scale enterprises (SSEs) is viewed widely as a key component of the development strategies of many developing and transitional economies, and is often supported actively by governments and/or international agencies. This chapter sounds a cautionary note by drawing on the experience of the silk industry in China, where a massive increase in the numbers of small reeling plants and silk processing factories has been accompanied by the collapse of the world silk market. Furthermore, we demonstrate that this was not just an unhappy coincidence, but that the expansion in capacity and the collapse of the market were related. We are thus able to identify theoretical circumstances under which technological innovation may in fact harm the growing economy: this is analogous to the phenomenon of 'immiserizing growth' first identified by Jagdish Bhagwati (1958).

The silk industry in China has a long history, and is a major source of both employment and foreign exchange (Newton and Strange, 2001). For many years, silk had an expensive image, and was used almost exclusively for the manufacture of *haute couture* garments. Garment manufacture was carried out largely in Western Europe, Japan and the United States, and required high-quality raw silk as the essential raw material, which came predominantly from China. However, this international division of labour was disturbed by two linked technological innovations. The first was the development and adoption in China during the 1980s of a US process known as 'sand-washing', which permitted the manufacture of garments using much-lower-quality silk. This resulted in a substantial expansion of the

Chinese silk-processing industry, a boom in Chinese exports of silk products, and substantial economic benefits to the Chinese economy. Unfortunately, not just for the Chinese but also for all involved in the world silk industry, the popularity of 'sandwashed' silks was short-lived, as the flooding of Western markets, together with consumer dissatisfaction over the poor quality of the products eventually gave rise to a 'trivialization' of the image of silk. This dissatisfaction catalyzed the second innovation, namely the development during the 1990s of a range of silk-like fabrics such as cuprammonium and lyocell which imitated many of the desirable characteristics of silk while being more amenable to production in large quantities at consistently high levels of quality. The market for silk collapsed.

The structure of this chapter is as follows. The theory of immiserizing growth is outlined in the first section. The second section provides a brief description of the silk-manufacturing process, and contains a review of the structure of the world silk industry and its development since the mid-1980s. This establishes the importance of China both as the dominant supplier of raw silk in international trade, and as the country that was at the vanguard of the production of sandwashed silk garments in the late 1980s and early 1990s. The third section will review the process of reform and liberalization in China from the 1980s onwards, and the repercussions of this for the indigenous silk industry. It will focus in particular on how the liberalization process gave rise to chaos in the industry, and how the state subsequently tried (and largely failed) to re-establish a measure of central control. The fourth section will highlight the effects of the two technological innovations on the Chinese silk industry, and demonstrate how immiserization has arisen for rather different reasons than in the standard Bhagwati case. The role of the state will be examined critically in the concluding section, and lessons drawn for countries wishing to promote the development of SSEs in export-oriented industries. Can technological innovation lead to perverse outcomes for SSEs?

TECHNOLOGICAL INNOVATION AND IMMISERIZING GROWTH

Technological innovation pushes out the production possibility frontier (PPF) of the economy, but the resultant growth is biased towards the sector experiencing the technical progress. If there is no effect on relative prices, then the output of this sector rises while that of other sectors falls, and there is a concomitant reallocation of the factors of production. In Figure 3.1, technical progress in the textile industry shifts the PPF out horizontally by a constant percentage amount from PPF_1 to PPF_2. Production shifts from a point such as P_1 on the original PPF_1 to P_2 on the new PPF_2, if relative prices (given by the slope of the line R_1) are unchanged. The output of the textile industry expands, while that of the other industries contracts. National income is increased (the 'wealth' effect) and this enables the economy to increase consumption of both textiles and the other goods[1] (from C_1 to C_2) and attain a higher indifference curve (Ω_2 rather than Ω_1).

If the technological innovation takes place within an exporting industry (as in Figure 3.1), then the country's volume of trade expands

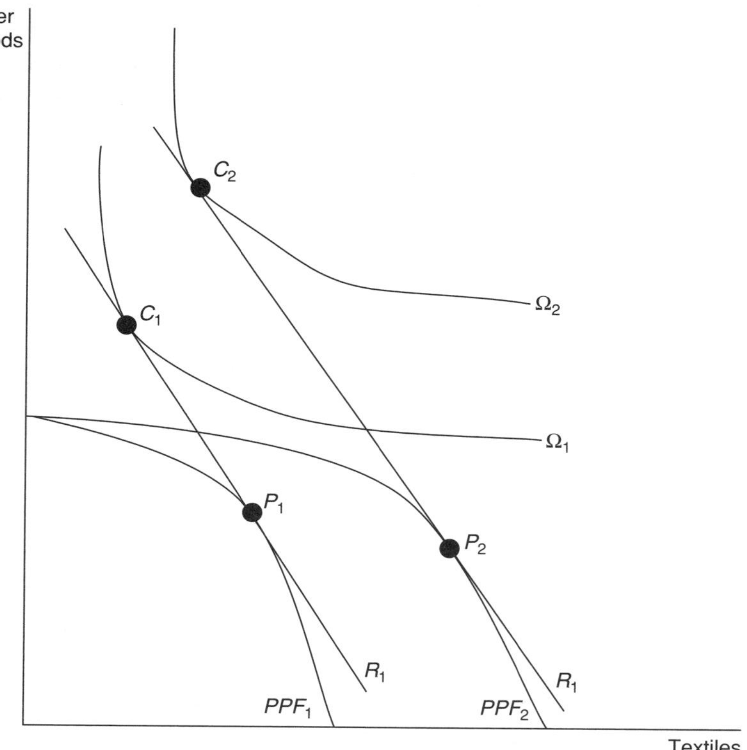

Figure 3.1 Technical progress at constant terms of trade

at the original terms of trade. If the country is 'small', then this expansion in the volume of trade will have a negligible effect on the world prices of the exportable (for example, textiles) and importable goods. But if the country is 'large', then the additional world supply of exportables will give rise to a fall in the world price, and the terms-of-trade will worsen for the growing economy – though the effect will be beneficial for the importing countries as they are now able to buy these goods at lower prices. If world demand is very price inelastic, then the terms-of-trade effect may be so severe as to outweigh the positive wealth effect – see Figure 3.2. Here production shifts from P_1 to P_3, but the additional output of textiles has caused relative prices to change from R_1 to R_3. Consumption of both textiles and the other goods falls (from C_1 to C_3), and the economy can only attain an indifference curve such as Ω_3 which is inferior to Ω_1. The technical progress has in fact reduced the value of national income and potential consumption: this is the phenomenon first identified by Bhagwati (1958) known as immiserizing growth.

If the technological change takes place within an import-competing industry, then the country's volume of trade contracts at the original terms of trade. If the country is 'large', then the reduced world demand of importables will give rise to a fall in the world price, and the terms of trade will improve for the importing economy – though the effect will be harmful for the exporting countries as they will then only be able to sell their goods at lower prices.

In summary, immiserizing growth of the Bhagwati type[2] requires four conditions:

- the growth must be export-orientated, so that a negative terms-of-trade effect is a possibility;
- the growing economy must be 'large', so that the additional supply has a significant effect upon the world market;
- world demand for the product must be price inelastic, so that the additional supply gives rise to a substantial fall in price; and
- the exported product(s) must account for a substantial proportion of the economy's output, so that the negative terms-of-trade effect outweighs the positive wealth effect.

Subsequent theoretical work has identified other circumstances where immiserizing growth may take place in a 'small' economy: when there is capital growth or technical progress in a tariff-protected importing sector (Johnson, 1967), or where there is foreign investment in a tariff-protected importing sector (Brecher and Diaz Alejandro, 1977).

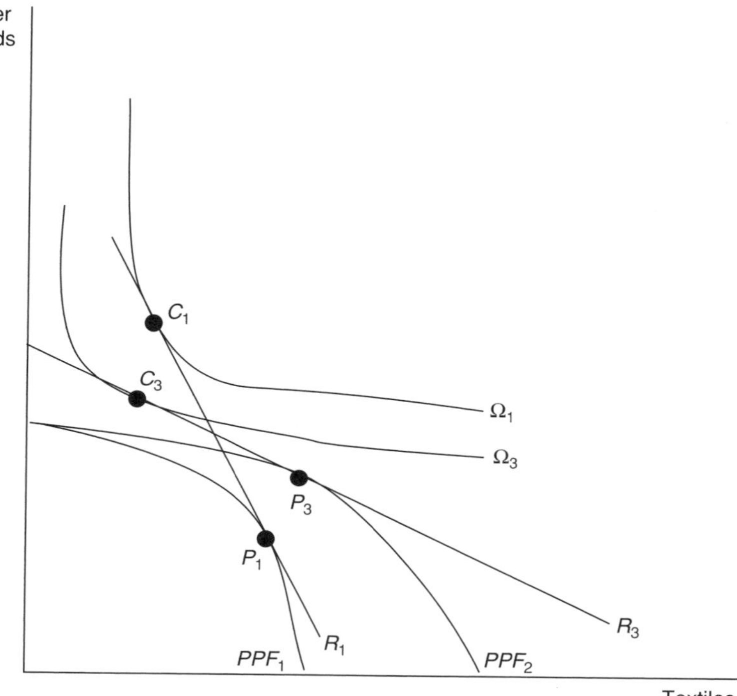

Figure 3.2 Technical progress and immiserizing growth

SILK MANUFACTURE AND THE WORLD SILK INDUSTRY

The process of mulberry silk manufacture comprises a number of stages (Watkins, 1997; pp. 21–2). The first involves the cultivation by farmers of mulberry trees. The second is the raising of silkworms, fed on the mulberry leaves, from eggs to cocoons. The selling of the cocoons marks the boundary of sericulture (which is an agricultural activity) and textile production. The buying and selling of cocoons typically takes place within cocoon exchanges, and nearly all cocoons are further processed where they are produced (Watkins, 1997; p. 25). The third stage is silk reeling, and involves the unravelling of the cocoons into a continuous filament called raw silk. The silk filaments are then combined and twisted during the fourth stage of throwing to form a variety of silk yarns. Any waste silk from the above manufacturing processes is spun to form spun-silk yarns. The filament or spun-silk yarn is woven or knitted in the fifth stage to produce greige fabric, which is dyed and finished during the sixth stage. And the seventh and final stage is the manufacture of silk garments and other made-up goods from the fabric. There is a substantial international trade in many of these silk products (that is, raw silk, silk yarn, silk fabric, and silk garments and made-up goods), but only a limited trade in cocoons.

China is at the time of writing, and has been since the late 1970s when it surpassed Japan, the dominant world producer of raw silk (see Table 3.1), with India, Brazil and Japan being other significant producers. China is also the predominant supplier of raw silk to the international market, and provides more than 80 per cent of world imports of raw silk and yarn (International Trade Centre, 1997, p. 15). It should be noted, however, that the share of China's raw silk output being exported has declined significantly over the years (see Table 3.2), as has the share of raw silk in China's overall silk trade, as China has

Table 3.1 World production of raw silk, 1938–98

Year	Total	China	India	Japan	CIS	Brazil	Others
1938	56 500	4 855	690	43 150	1 900	35	5 870
1978	49 360	19 000	3 475	15 960	3 240	1 250	6 435
1983	56 576	28 140	5 681	12 456	3 899	1 362	5 038
1984	56 129	28 140	6 895	10 800	3 999	1 456	4 839
1985	58 887	32 000	7 029	9 592	4 000	1 553	4 713
1986	62 460	35 700	8 280	8 220	4 000	1 680	4 744
1987	64 440	37 620	8 400	7 860	4 000	1 680	4 839
1988	61 260	34 380	9 300	6 840	4 000	1 740	6 322
1989	66 900	40 800	10 020	6 060	4 010	1 680	5 206
1990	70 983	43 800	10 200	5 700	4 009	1 680	4 699
1991	76 732	48 480	10 800	5 520	4 000	2 100	4 940
1992	82 419	54 480	12 600	5 100	4 000	2 280	3 783
1993	97 337	69 300	13 200	4 200	4 000	2 340	3 750
1994	100 388	72 000	13 200	3 900	3 000	2 520	5 800
1995	105 138	77 900	12 884	3 240	n/a	2 468	n/a
1996	85 192	59 000	12 927	2 580	n/a	2 270	n/a
1997	79 590	55 117	14 048	1 920	n/a	2 120	n/a
1998	71 727	49 430	14 000	1 080	n/a	1 821	n/a

Notes: All figures are in tonnes; CIS = Commonwealth of Independent States.
Sources: 1938–85 International Silk Association.
1986–98 Desco von Schulthess AG.

Table 3.2 Raw silk production and export in China, 1983–98

Year	Production	Exports	Exports as percentage of production
1983	28 140	9 473	33.7
1984	28 140	8 557	30.4
1985	32 000	10 893	34.0
1986	35 700	9 394	26.3
1987	37 620	9 292	24.7
1988	34 380	9 404	27.4
1989	40 800	11 361	27.8
1990	43 800	8 594	19.6
1991	48 480	9 016	18.6
1992	54 480	8 899	16.3
1993	69 300	8 664	12.5
1994	72 000	13 049	18.1
1995	77 900	12 710	16.3
1996	59 000	12 101	20.5
1997	55 117	11 089	20.1
1998	49 430	9 169	18.5

Sources: 1983–85 International Silk Association.
1986–98 Desco von Schulthess AG.

moved into the manufacture of downstream products. Whereas, in 1981, China's exports of ready-made garments and made-up silk articles accounted for only 12.5 per cent of the country's total silk export earnings, this proportion had risen to 20 per cent by 1989, and to 70 per cent by 1993 (Watkins, 1997, p. 129).

The main silk processing (converting) areas are Europe (France, Germany, Italy, Switzerland, and the United Kingdom), and Japan, and these countries, together with the United States and Japan, are major importers of made-up silk goods. The European countries rely entirely on imports of their raw materials, which come mainly from China. Most of India's raw silk production is consumed in the domestic market, while Brazil's output is exported mainly to Japan, where it supplements domestic production.

In short, China is very much the key to the international silk trade. As the International Trade Centre (1997, p. 15) notes, 'Announcements by Chinese authorities of new plans and export strategies are studied carefully by the world's silk converters and importers.' Furthermore, the silk industry in China is a very significant source of both employment and foreign exchange.

ECONOMIC REFORM AND LIBERALIZATION IN THE CHINESE SILK INDUSTRY

For about thirty years after the creation of the People's Republic of China (PRC), the production of silkworm cocoons, raw silk, and silk fabrics was governed by the national economic plans. Annual production targets were set by the State Planning Committee, and allocated to provinces, and from there to cities and counties (FAO/RAPA, 1989, pp. 12–15). The system was managed by specialist departments in various Ministries: cocoon production by agricultural departments; the procurement of cocoons by the National Federation of Supply and Marketing Co-operatives; domestic silk sales by the Ministry of Commerce; and silk imports and exports by the China National Textiles Import and Export Corporation. In February 1982[3], these specialist organizations were brought together with the establishment of the China Silk Corporation to provide unified management of the purchasing of cocoons, and the production, supply and sale of raw silk and silk textiles. These institutional arrangements were, however, dismantled in October 1986, when the China Silk Corporation was dissolved; silk production was put under the control of the Ministry of Textile Industry; domestic silk sales under the Ministry of Commerce; cocoon purchase and the import/export of silk under the China National Silk Import and Export Corporation (CNSIEC)[4].

Largely as a result of this system of central control, market conditions were stable and predictable up to the mid-1980s. Foreign textile producers purchased raw silk at the biannual Guangdong trade fair by paying the officially announced prices, and both delivery and quality were very reliable (Watkins, 1997, p. 134). Notwithstanding fluctuations in world demand, the price of Chinese raw silk thus rose gradually from about US$20 in 1975 to about US$30 at the end of 1987, and there was a concomitant increase in silk consumption in most importing countries. The 'orderly market' was, however, disrupted in the mid-1980s by a combination of circumstances: reforms in the agricultural sector; foreign trade reform; and increased processing by the domestic silk industry.

First, as regards the agricultural sector, the major reform was the introduction by the Chinese Government of the 'production responsibility' system in the late 1970s[5]. Under this system, each farm household was assigned a piece of land and was held responsible for delivering a given quantity of a certain product to satisfy the procurement requirement, but any surplus could either be retained by the farm household or sold in the market at market prices (Chow, 1994, p. 10). Essentially, therefore, each farm household had control over the land it used and could choose what to produce and how to market its products. The FAO (FAO/RAPA, 1989; p. 124) notes that mulberry planting and silkworm rearing had been anchored strongly in China's earlier collective village structure. But new mulberry planting under the previous 'four-around' policy (the policy of planting systematically on all open spaces around houses, villages, fields, roads, canals, railroad lines, river embankments and so on in order to maximize protective and productive vegetation) carried out by the community had ceased with the abolition of the collective village structure. Indeed, there was much uncontrolled felling of mulberry trees, as producers of mulberry leaves switched their land and labour to more lucrative food products. Mulberry acreage was reported to have shrunk in 1987 by some 10 000 ha, for the first time in over forty years. Moreover, many village-run silkworm hatcheries have been abandoned, with the result that, mainly in the proximity of the coastal areas of Jiangsu, Zhejiang, Anhui and Fujian, where the 'rural modernization' drive has been most intensive, many farming families gave up sericulture. Furthermore, central control over the purchase of silk cocoons was abolished, with the result that a two-tier pricing system came into operation: cocoons sold by CNSIEC were offered at one price while those sold by non-state enterprises were generally offered at higher prices. Individual businessmen began speculating in the major cocoon-producing provinces, and the resultant confusion, which was particularly acute during the so-called 'cocoon wars' of 1987–8, led to spiralling prices (Glasse, 1995, p. 94).

Second, as regards foreign trade reform, the central government took a series of measures designed to stimulate the growth of exports.[6] One of the first steps was to decentralize the authority to engage in foreign trade transactions. In 1979, all foreign trade transactions were handled by a dozen national foreign trade corporations (FTCs). By the mid-1980s, MOFERT had approved the creation of 800 separate FTCs,[7] each of which was authorized to engage in foreign trade within specified product ranges. These FTCs were of several types: some had been created by national production ministries; hundreds were established by provincial governments to handle trade in their regions; and a few were set up by large enterprises. A second development was the series of initiatives designed to encourage foreign investment, with particular help being given to firms that were export-oriented or that introduced advanced technology (Wu and Strange, 1997). Other measures included, *inter alia*, the use of export licences to forestall or alleviate potential domestic market shortages; the introduction of a system of tax rebates on export goods; the relaxation of exchange control; the opening of 'foreign exchange adjustment centres' which provided a *de facto* devaluation of the yuan; and several other export promotion measures.

Third, the 1980s also witnessed a significant increase in processing by the domestic silk industry. As is evident from the data presented in the previous section, China's 'traditional' role had been as a supplier of raw silk for export to processors in Western Europe, the United States and Japan, and made-up silk products only accounted for 12.5 per cent of China's total silk exports by volume in 1981 (Watkins, 1997, p. 129). But the commercialization of 'sandwashed' silks[8] during the decade, and the lure of quick profits, fuelled by a buoyant world market not only for silk but for textiles in general (Watkins, 1997, p. 1), encouraged numerous small-scale plants to move into the production of made-up silk goods for export. This move into downstream processing was facilitated by liberalization and further encouraged by the Chinese government through a variety of measures, notably the dual exchange rate system and the use of export taxes. Watkins (1997, p. 138) also notes that the Chinese government announced in 1987 that it intended to halt exports of raw silk to encourage domestic downstream processing, but that this statement was later amended to the 'slowly phasing out' of raw silk exports.

The situation in China at the end of 1987 thus combined a falling supply (and rising prices) of cocoons, buoyant world demand for silk products, fast-increasing domestic demand for raw silk to meet the requirements of domestic processors, and the possibility of government action to reduce or even to halt raw silk exports. The inevitable result was an increase in the price of raw silk – the official Chinese price (quality 3A, denier 20/22) rose from less than US$30 at the end of 1987 to US$51 per kg in January 1989 (ITC, 1990, p. viii) – together with supply shortages. The situation was exacerbated by the practice of 'parallel trade', whereby various provinces, empowered by trade liberalization, started exporting raw silk directly to foreign markets (especially Hong Kong) rather than selling through CNSIEC.[9] The situation became so serious[10] that there were considerable delays, and even cancellations, during the first half of 1989 in CNSIEC executing the orders of its foreign buyers (ITC, 1990, pp. 15, 42).

The disarray in the channelling of raw materials caused the Chinese government to step back from its liberalization policy and try to re-establish some central control, much to the relief of foreign buyers. In 1990, new measures were instigated to bring supplies of mulberry leaves and cocoons back under state control. Incentives in the form of scarce chemical fertilizers were offered to farmers who traded with CNSIEC. Manufacturers were required to secure production and quality licences from CNSIEC in order to have their products approved for export, and tariffs of 80–100 per cent were levied on goods that bypassed the CNSIEC (Watkins, 1997, p. 134).

Meanwhile, the high price for cocoons and raw silk encouraged farmers to expand the land they devoted to mulberry cultivation. Raw silk production in China continued to rise through the late 1980s and early 1990s – see Table 3.1. Much of this increased production was destined for domestic processing, and Chinese production of made-up silk goods continued to increase. By 1991, the proportion of made-up goods in China's silk exports had risen to 40 per cent, and this figure increased to almost 70 per cent in 1993 (Watkins, 1997, p. 43). This remarkable transformation in export composition was generated partly by the new consumer market for 'sandwashed silks', and exacerbated by the economic recession of the early 1990s, which led to falling demand for raw silk by the Western processors. The official price of Chinese raw silk fell from US$51 in late 1990, to $24 by the end of 1993. These adjustments were undertaken not only in response to the supply and demand situation in the world raw silk market, but also as a partial attempt to reconcile the discrepancy between the export prices of raw silk and Chinese-made silk products (Hyvarinen, 1993, p. 16). Foreign importers of Chinese raw silk had to pay for their purchases at the official exchange rate, while domestic processors were able to export their goods and receive payment at the swap rate. In essence, China's effective monopoly of the raw silk trade, combined with its dual exchange rate system, allowed its domestic silk manufacturers the luxury of subsidized competition.

The boom in the export of Chinese silk products was further associated with a proliferation of SSEs producing silk fabrics and garments. Many of these were joint ventures, either with firms from Hong Kong or with Western department stores. The share of total silk sector exports provided by rural enterprises rose from 21.4 per cent in 1988 to 54 per cent in 1992 (Yan, 1995). New factory capacity was coming onstream at a faster rate than the increase in output of raw materials, and gave rise to overcapacity (Watkins, 1997, p. 7). By 1994, reeling capacity in China had reached 4.5m reeling ends, which required a cocoon supply considerably in excess of the normal annual yield. This overcapacity dragged cocoon prices upwards, in turn providing incentives for farmers to take an interest in sericulture, which flourished unchecked in many places, regardless of conditions. The quality of cocoons went down, as did the quality of raw silk. The immediate consequences were twofold. On the one hand, the many small reeling mills, using outdated technology and unable to take advantage of economies of scale, could only turn out poor-quality products, and thus wasted valuable raw materials and energy. On the other hand, the larger and better-equipped reeling mills suffered from raw material shortages and rising production costs, and were accordingly obliged to reduce or even stop production (ISA, 1996, pp. 1–2).

The year 1994 proved to be something of a turning point, both for the Chinese industry and for the silk industry world-wide. There were a number of institutional developments. First, the dual exchange rate system was abolished with effect from 1 January, and replaced by a single floating rate for holders of contracts and licences. The effective subsidy to domestic processors was thus removed, though export sales were still subject to export taxes (Watkins, 1997, p. 71). Second, the China Cocoon and Silk Exchange was established in late 1993[11] to facilitate silk futures trading and provide some control over fluctuating prices. Third, the State Council issued a directive on 14 March to provincial governments on new regulations designed to control the purchases of silk cocoons and protect the interests of farmers.[12] The directive stipulated, *inter alia*:

- that silk cocoon purchases were to be handled by CNSIEC and its branch offices in the provinces, and that no unauthorized individuals or organizations would be permitted to buy cocoons from the market;
- that the purchase prices of cocoons would be fixed by CNSIEC, and provincial governments were not permitted to alter these prices;
- that provincial governments should monitor the quantity and quality of silk cocoons to be harvested, and should take steps to discourage the establishment of small-scale silk mills; and
- that surplus cocoons should be consigned to the National Silk Textile Trading Market.

Fourth, both the United States and the European Union (EU) introduced quotas on the import of Chinese made-up silk goods.[13] The EU quotas were punitive and, in a sharp departure from previous practice, imposed unilaterally in March 1994. While similar goods made from other materials, especially cotton and synthetics, had faced trade restraints for several years, the applicable quotas had been negotiated bilaterally within the framework of the GATT Multi-Fibre Agreement. The new EU trade policy was unusual in being formulated without consultation with the Chinese authorities, and it was also the first time that silk had been subject to trade restraints across the European Union. The quotas were greeted with dismay both by the Chinese exporters and by the European retail trade, particularly the large multiple store groups (Watkins and Phillips, 1994, p. 105). US quotas were also imposed in 1994, but were rather less severe and the changes were negotiated bilaterally in consultation with the Chinese authorities. Interestingly, the pressure for the quotas came primarily from the US cotton and manufactured fibre textile and apparel industry, who alleged that the imports of cheap Chinese silk garments was encroaching on their market (Watkins, 1997, p. 107).

These developments, however, were overshadowed by the collapse in Western demand for imported garments from China, caused by the deterioration in silk's image as a result of the marketing of low-quality goods after the commercialization of sandwashed silk. In his 1997 report to the International Silk Association,[14] the French delegate, Olivier Fournier, observed that 'silk's trivialisation and the destruction of its prestige in Europe, led of course to its desertion by designers as an absolute reference for quality, in favour of more modern yarns. As the silk clothes that they were being proposed [*sic*] were no longer flattering for them, women started to bring up the question of the constraints due to the particular measures that have to be taken for its care, and they started to compare it to other materials, when it should remain beyond compare.'

The depression in the export trade of Chinese made-up goods had knock-on effects for the production of mulberry and silkworm cocoons. The cocoon shortages of the early 1990s gave way to overstocking in 1995, and there were reports of mulberry trees being uprooted in some areas.[15] The government adjusted the export tax rebate on silk products three times between 1996 (9 per cent) and July 1999 (15 per cent), but exports continued to fall. By 1998, it was estimated that 65 per cent of the trading and exporting enterprises dealing in silk textile goods were making losses, in no small part as a result of suicidal price competition.[16] The companies were quoting different export prices for the same products, to secure more orders, while foreign buyers were able to request quotations from several different enterprises and to force them to cut prices by showing them lower quotations from their competitors.

IMMISERIZING GROWTH AND THE CHINESE SILK INDUSTRY

What insights can this experience provide for the theory of immiserizing growth? To answer this question, it is useful to summarize the recent history of China's silk industry in four periods[17]. Up to the mid-1980s, the industry consisted primarily of sericulture and the reeling of raw silk in numerous state-owned silk mills. The central authorities set production targets and prices for both cocoons and raw silk, monitored quality, and arranged delivery to foreign purchasers. In short, market conditions were 'orderly'. There was very limited domestic processing of the raw silk, and China's role within the world silk industry was as the pre-eminent supplier of the essential raw materials to processors in the developed markets of Western Europe, the USA and Japan. Notwithstanding its monopoly position in the provision of raw silk, in which it accounted for 90 per cent of international trade, China did not abuse its market power in any systematic way, and the Western processors were able to secure sufficient quantities of raw silk at reasonable prices.[18] It was a period marked by an international division of labour that appeared to benefit all parties. The Western processors had their guaranteed supplies of raw silk from which to manufacture *haute couture* garments and other expensive silk products; and the Chinese government had a steady and profitable source of foreign exchange.

This cosy coexistence was shattered in the late 1980s by the combination of technological innovation and economic liberalization. The innovation was the development of the sandwashing process, and its widespread deployment was facilitated by the adoption of the 'production responsibility' system and the liberalization of foreign investment and trade. Even without government support, this potent combination would no doubt have generated an export boom as Chinese entrepreneurs, aided and abetted by Western retailing interests, scrambled to take advantage of the valuable pickings in the new market for sandwashed silk garments. That the Chinese government favoured an increase in the share of made-up goods in China's total silk exports and was prepared to provide appropriate incentives was an added bonus.

The untrammelled flowering of free enterprise soon came into conflict with China's traditional role as a supplier of raw silk to the Western processors, and the early 1990s witnessed a variety of muted Chinese initiatives to re-establish some degree of central control over the indigenous silk industry. This was undoubtedly a bad period for the European processors (though not for the European retail interests), who were caught between high prices for their essential raw material and the massive inflow of cheap silk goods from China. For China, on the other hand, the situation was more ambivalent. Although there was official embarrassment about the cancelled deliveries in 1989 and consternation about the extent of parallel trading (and the concomitant loss of central government revenues), and the fall in the export sales of raw silk was more than offset by the additional revenues generated by the buoyant sales of sandwashed silk garments.

However, Chinese equanimity disappeared with the collapse of the market for sandwashed silks in the late 1990s. The causes were twofold. On the one hand, there was consumer dissatisfaction with the poor quality of many of the silk garments that were emanating from China, which gave rise in turn to doubts about the continued worth of silk goods in general. On the other hand, there were the technological innovations that gave rise to fibres such as cuprammonium and lyocell, which replicate many of the desirable characteristics of sandwashed silk while allowing greater quantities of garments to be manufactured to a consistent quality standard (Watkins, 1997, p. 15). In short, silk had been reduced to the status of a mere commodity, whereas once it had been the 'Queen of Fibres'. This demotion in status was bad news for all involved in the world silk industry, but especially for China, given the scale of its involvement. Not only was China hit by falling export sales and the prices of raw silk, but it also suffered from declining export sales of made-up silk goods. And the Chinese authorities were powerless to do anything about the situation, except to stem the financial losses of the industry by reducing capacity.

The innovation of sandwashing did not initially lead to the oversupply of silk garments, but rather created an entirely new market which was at first complementary to the traditional market for *haute couture* goods. Thus, from the Chinese viewpoint, the innovation did not give rise to a worsening of the terms of trade, but instead created additional demand (and hence higher prices) for raw silk. This highlights the importance of careful definition of products and industries. It is misleading to conceive of a market for 'silk garments' *per se*, because there were two separate markets: one for '*haute couture* silk garments' and one for 'cheap, easy-care, textile garments'. The *direct* impact of sandwashed silks was on the latter, as evidenced by the reasons put forward for the imposition of US import quotas in 1994 (Strange and Newton, 1999). The development of sandwashed silks did, however, have an *indirect* impact on the *haute couture* market through the negative impact it had on silk's luxury image, and through the stimulus it provided for the development of the imitative, 'silk-like' products. This innovation from the Western importing countries reduced demand for sandwashed silk products and worsened China's terms of trade. Taking its history since the 1980s as a whole, therefore, and treating the two innovations as linked, the Chinese silk industry has experienced immiserizing growth.

But the conditions that have generated this immiserizing growth are rather different from the Bhagwati case. Certainly, the growth has been export-orientated and the growing economy has been 'large', so developments in the Chinese industry have had a significant effect on the world market. But prices have not fallen because of an expansion of export volume (indeed, Chinese exports of raw silk in 1998 were lower than in 1988), but because silk has lost its image and become a 'commodity'. The growth did not lead to a movement along the demand curve, as in the Bhagwati case, but stimulated an inward shift in the demand curve.[19] This is the distinctive feature of the immiserizing growth in the Chinese silk industry.

CONCLUSIONS

What can one say about the role of the Chinese authorities in permitting a situation to develop where the indigenous silk industry, which had prospered for thousands of years, and over which China enjoyed an effective monopoly in the production of raw silk, to be brought to its knees? To what extent was the situation a result of governmental myopia, or was it simply an unfortunate consequence of economic liberalization? It would be a harsh judgement to blame the Chinese authorities for encouraging the boom in sandwashed silks, and for failing to foresee the eventual collapse both in that market and in the market for *haute couture* silk garments[20]. The more important lesson concerns the fact that the authorities were unable to re-establish any real control over the indigenous silk industry even when it became obvious that problems were emerging. This was a direct result of liberalization, and of the replacement of a state monopoly with hundreds of SSEs employing out-of-date equipment to produce goods of poor quality. The problem was exacerbated by the fact that silk manufacture is a commodity chain, but there was little integration between those involved in sericulture, those involved in the various silk processing activities, and those involved in foreign trade. So when problems did emerge, no form of concerted response was possible, and fierce competition between the SSEs simply made matters worse.

This study of the Chinese silk industry has not only provided a new theoretical variant for the immiserizing growth literature, but it has also raised a number of policy issues regarding the promotion of SSEs in developing and transitional economies. First, there are dangers in liberalizing an industry which is very export-orientated, and where the state had formerly held an effective export monopoly: the inevitable lower prices benefit foreign consumers at the expense of domestic producers. Second, there is a need to maintain quality, particularly when a large proportion of the output is exported to developed country markets. Third, there is also a need to ensure that the SSEs are aware of trends in their export markets, particularly when there are several stages in the production process, and each stage is under separate control.

Notes

1. Assuming consumer tastes are homothetic.
2. The standard textbook example is of the expansion of the coffee sector in Brazil in the 1930s.
3. The State Council issued a notice on the establishment of the China Silk Corporation in December 1981, having initiated a feasibility study in early 1978. The Corporation was founded officially on 27 February 1982; it also undertook the management of the silk research institutions and silk engineering institutes. It was under the direct control of the State Council.
4. CNSIEC officially went into business in January 1987, and was under the control of the Ministry of Foreign Economic Relations and Trade (MOFERT).
5. The system was adopted formally by the Fourth Plenum of the Eleventh Central Committee of the Communist Party in September 1979. See Chow (1994), pp. 9–11.
6. This paragraph draws heavily on Lardy (1992) ch. 3, and World Bank (1994). There were also a series of measures related to imports.
7. And there were more than 5000 a few years later (Lardy, 1992, p. 39).
8. See Newton and Strange (2001) for further detail on the development of sandwashed silks.

9. The incentive for parallel trade was provided by the dual exchange rate system: CNSIEC paid for raw silk at the official exchange rate, whereas the raw silk producers could obtain the (higher) swap rate if they exported directly.
10. Watkins (1997, p. 134) estimates that only 44 per cent of the raw silk trade in 1988 was taking place through authorized channels, with the remaining 56 per cent occurring illicitly.
11. The Exchange (located in Jiaxing, Zhejiang province) started trial operation on 28 July 1993, and trading began in October 1993 (Watkins, 1997, p. 141).
12. See the report in *Textile Asia* (June 1994) pp. 75–6.
13. See Strange and Newton (1999), and Newton and Strange (2001) for detailed analyses of the quotas and of the circumstances of their imposition.
14. See the report in the *International Silk Association Monthly Newsletter*, No. 201 (November 1998) p. 4.
15. See the *International Silk Association Monthly Newsletter*, No. 181 (February 1996) p. 3.
16. *Textile Asia* (December 1999) pp. 63–4.
17. See International Silk Association (1993, p. 56) for an account of the development of the silk industry in the period between 1949 and the mid-1980s.
18. Indeed, the 1980 Agreement on bilateral trade in textile products between China and the European Community included an undertaking by China (Article 11) to supply minimum guaranteed quantities of certain textile products (including raw silk) to the EC industry at the normal trade price (Strange, 1998, p. 68).
19. The graphical representation in terms of PPFs and indifference curves would be exactly the same as in Figure 3.2.
20. Though any wise Marketing Director would always be wary of selling a cheap imitation of its main product.

Bibliography

Anon (1994) 'Regulated Buying', *Textile Asia* (June), pp. 74–6.

Anon (1999) 'Silk in Excess', *Textile Asia* (December), pp. 63–4.

Bhagwati, J. (1958) 'Immiserizing Growth: A Geometrical Note', *Review of Economic Studies*, vol. 25, no. 68 (June), pp. 201–5.

Brecher, R. A. and Diaz Alejandro, C. F. (1977) 'Tariffs, Foreign Capital and Immiserizing Growth,' *Journal of International Economics*, vol. 7, no. 4 (November), pp. 317–22.

Chow, G. C. (1994) *Understanding China's Economy*, Singapore: World Scientific Publishing.

FAO/RAPA (Food and Agriculture Organization of the United Nations/Regional Office for Asia and the Pacific). (1989) *Sericulture Development in Asia*, RAPA Publication No. 1989/5, Bangkok: FAO/RAPA.

Glasse, J. (1995) *Textiles and Clothing in China: Competitive Threat or Investment Opportunity?* Special Report No. 2638, Wilmslow: Textiles Intelligence Limited.

Hyvarinen, A. (1993) 'Trends in the World Silk Market', *Textile Outlook International*, No. 47 (May), pp. 9–59.

ISA (International Silk Association). (1993) Report on the XIXth Congress – Nanjing/Suzhou: 31 October–6 November, Unpublished.

ISA (International silk Association) (1996a) 'Extricating China's Silk Industry from its Present Predicament', Speech by Chen Youzhe, Newsletter No. 181 (February), pp. 1–4.

ISA (International Silk Association) (1996b) 'International News', *Monthly Newsletter*, no. 181 (February), pp. 1–3.

ISA (International Silk Association) (1998) 'France: Annual Report', *Monthly Newsletter*, no. 201 (November), pp. 3–4.

ITC (International Trade Centre, UNCTAD/GATT) (1988) *Silk*, ITC/072/B3/88–IX, Geneva: UNCTAD/GATT.

ITC (International Trade Centre, UNCTAD/GATT) (1990) *Silk Review 1990*, ITC/128/B3/90–X, Geneva: UNCTAD/GATT.

ITC (International Trade Centre, UNCTAD/WTO) (1997) *Silk Review 1997: A Survey of International Trends in Production and Trade*. 5th edn, Geneva: ITC.

Johnson, H. G. (1967) 'The Possibility of Income Losses from Increased Efficiency or Factor Accumulation in the Presence of Tariffs', *Economic Journal*, vol. 77, no. 305 (March), pp. 151–4.

Lardy, N. R. (1992) *Foreign Trade and Economic Reform in China, 1978–1990*, Cambridge University Press.

Newton, J. and Strange, R. (2001) 'Here We Go Round the Mulberry Bush: EU–China Trade in Silk', in M. D. Hughes and J. H. Taggart (eds), *International Trade: European Dimensions*, Basingstoke: Palgrave, pp. 248–62.

Strange, R. (1998) 'EU Trade Policy Towards China', in R. Strange, J. Slater and L. Wang (eds), *Trade and Investment in China: The European Experience*, London: Routledge, pp. 59–80.

Strange, R. and Newton, J. (1999) 'Conflicting Interests in the Formation of EU Trade Policy: The Case of Silk Imports from China', Paper presented at the Academy of International Business, Northeast Regional Meeting, Philadelphia, USA, June.

Watkins, P. (1997) *World Markets for Silk: Forecasts to 2000*. Special report No. 2641, London: Economist Intelligence Unit.

Watkins, P. and Phillips, P. (1994) 'Global Changes in the Market for Silk and Silk Products', *Textile Outlook International*, vol. 55 (September) pp. 93–127.

World Bank (1994) *China: Foreign Trade Reform*, Washington DC: The World Bank.

Wu, X. and Strange, R. (1997) 'FDI Policy and Inward Direct Investment in China', in J. Slater and R. Strange (eds), *Business Relationships with East Asia: The European Experience*, London: Routledge, pp. 199–217.

Yan S. (1995) 'Export-oriented Rural Enterprises', *JETRO China Newsletter*, No. 118 (September–October), pp. 8–16,22.

4 Small Is Not Always Beautiful: Environmental Enforcement and Small Industries in India

Nandini Dasgupta

INTRODUCTION

Most developing and industrializing nations have for decades actively promoted the growth of small-scale industries because of their employment-generation capacity, but there was scant attention to possible environmental impacts. It was only during the 1990s that there was recognition that pollution from small-scale industries is a problem. Hamza (1991) noted that in some instances small enterprises pollute more per unit than large industries. Satterthwaite and Hardoy (1992) and Dasgupta (1998) have shown that there are considerable social costs of pollution associated with this sector: the proximity of low-income housing to clusters of small, polluting industries in cities of developing economies means that the poor suffer more than the better-off from environmental pollution. There is now a greater understanding of the nature of the environmental problem, and of the need to identify and develop sector-specific and size-specific policy options that will address these issues.

National governments can chose from a range of options. Environmental policy has several instruments (market-based and command-based), and there are different approaches to enforcement (sanction-based and compliance-based). The choice and combination of policy instruments and enforcement strategy are crucial to addressing the environmental problems in this sector.

Based on a review of the literature and case studies, this chapter argues that the solutions to these problems in the small-scale sector lie in a combination of sanction-based and compliance-based strategies. Compliance-based strategies should be adopted to allow interactive and participatory approaches to problem-solving, and sanctions and penalties to deal with persistent deviant behaviour: that is, a 'carrot and stick' policy. Some policy shifts are already occurring in countries such as Thailand (Kritiporn *et al.*, 1990); Indonesia (World Bank, 2000) and Hong Kong (Lei and Yang, 1993). In contrast, countries such as India, Vietnam (Mol *et al.*, 1997) and Kenya (Frijns *et al.*, 1999) still pursue enforcement policies of sanctions and penalties, often with little or no environmental impact.

In these countries, the fundamental difficulty lies in the conceptualization of the environmental problem. Sanction-based strategies are underpinned by a technocentric attitude, which assumes that pollution is a 'technical problem', and hence can be tackled by the application of modern technology. In India, this is still the dominant perception of industrial pollution. Additionally, it comes with the assumption that all polluting units, irrespective of size, are able and willing to adopt and change to meet national environmental standards (Dasgupta, 2000c; p. 15).

Evidence from small industries in developing countries shows that such a conceptual approach is inappropriate and inadequate. The environmental problem in this sector is multidimensional in nature. Dasgupta (2000b, p. 946) has shown that 'relations between capital, labour and technology in small-scale units in a developing country are more influenced by the socio-economic context than by the efficiency needs of the production process'. Under conditions of structural poverty and limited livelihood opportunities for many social categories, small industries are often the only opportunity for income generation for those with limited capital, skills and knowledge.[1] This conditions the relationships between the three inputs and determines the structure of the firm, its labour composition and its reactive, absorptive and adaptive capabilities, particularly to technological change (Dasgupta, 2000b, p. 946). This implies that attitudinal and capability problems need to be addressed first, to facilitate technological change and the implementation of cleaner production strategies.

Admittedly, the overall financial, technical and attitudinal problems of environmental management may cut across size groups, but the argument here is that the ability to deal with the problem varies with size. The large-scale industrial sector has reasonably well-developed factor and product markets, capital stock, professional management and an ability to change. Such units have the means to acquire the technology and expertise necessary to improve environmental management. However, in common with the small units, the will is often missing, as they try to externalize the cost of pollution for as long as possible (Dasgupta, 2000c).

Designing appropriate enforcement strategies thus requires an understanding of this 'environmental problem'. The objectives in this chapter are twofold. First, there is a need to demonstrate why a technocratic approach is inadequate to address these problems. Case studies from India are used to analyze the environmental problems and to show why the scale of operation makes a difference. It will make evident that the issues are complex and require policy instruments that are size and sub-sector specific. Second, based on the experience of more successful cases, it will be argued that participatory and interactive approaches to implementing cleaner production strategies could be the way forward.

The structure of the chapter[2] is as follows. The next section gives a brief background to this study, and then shows that technocratic conceptualization is inadequate because it fails to encapsulate the multidimensional nature of environmental problems associated with small[3] industrial units. The third section uses three case studies to illustrate the constraints to change and the perceptions of owners in this sector to environmental issues. The penultimate section discusses the use of a 'carrot and stick' policy, based on the understanding that there is a problem but the sector lacks the initiative, willingness and ability to resolve it. The final section summarizes the conclusions.

ENVIRONMENTAL ENFORCEMENT AND THE POVERTY CONTEXT

This section[4] will first define sanction and compliance-based strategies, and describe India's environmental enforcement strategy briefly. This is followed by a discussion of conceptual issues defining the environmental problems in India's small-scale industries.

Environmental policies consist of several instruments. Dasgupta (2000b) notes that most of these instruments fall broadly into two categories: 'economic' or 'market based' instruments, and 'command and control' instruments. The former are based on the 'rational polluter pays' hypothesis; that is, the industry weighs the costs and benefits of environmental compliance, and decides to act only when benefits dominate. The instruments of 'command and control' (for example, banning of CFCs after the expiry of the phase-out period) are used when economic instruments may be impractical. Doeleman

(1992) notes that this group of instruments tends to impose uniform technical solutions.

For convenience, the approaches to enforcement of environmental policy are often divided into (i) sanction-based approaches; and (ii) compliance-based approaches. It is pertinent to note that this division is artificial, as most enforcement approaches may contain elements of both. Sanction-based approaches aim to enforce regulation by compulsion and coercion, with a penal approach[5] to dealing with deviant activity, given that regulations are in place. An example would be the use of judicial orders to close down polluting industries. Compliance-based approaches begin by recognizing that the detection of deviant activity is the first step towards prevention, rather that than prosecuting deviance (Lane *et al.*, 1999). The environmental agencies would have to be more proactive, and determine the best way of achieving the environmental standards. The stress is on shared responsibility, where the environmental agencies work with the polluters to reduce pollution with the least social and economic cost. The emphasis is local and emancipatory. However, there is always the concern that 'co-operation may become collusion', and fail to reduce pollution (Lane *et al.*, 1999).

Enforcement Strategies in India

Following the Stockholm Conference on Human Environment in 1972, India and several other developing countries sought to develop their own environmental control systems. The only available model at that time was the sanction-based one, as used in the developed countries. Not surprisingly, the process of environmental policy development in the West, though piecemeal (Turner and Opschoor, 1994), concurrently had produced a large body of environmental laws.

It is pertinent to note here that since then there have been considerable shifts in environmental policy in developed economies. There is now an emphasis on market-based instruments and complementary approaches for environmental improvements in large and medium-scale industries, with a move away from sole reliance on command and control strategies. Furthermore, it has been recognized in the United Kingdom that policies developed for large and medium-scale industries may not be appropriate for small industries. Spence (1998), following an extensive review of small industries in the United Kingdom, concluded that this sector has specific constraints that need to be acknowledged in any initiative.

In contrast, India has legislated extensively to strengthen its command and control system.[6] Its first law was enacted in 1974. The Water Act provided for the prevention and control of water pollution, and for the maintainance or restoration of the quality of water. It also put in place the infrastructure for monitoring and control. Under the Act, a Central Pollution Control Board and State Pollution Control Boards were set up. Their tasks are essentially inspection, monitoring and regulation. The Law also set out the penalties for non-compliance, and procedures for enforcement. Legislation in 1981, 1982 and 1983 provided for prevention, control and abatement of air pollution. The Environmental Protection Act of 1986 gives individual citizens the right to bring polluters to court (Dasgupta, 2000c).

Generally, the environmental agencies pursue three different methods for environmental improvement in small industries. The first is to require industries to install end-of-pipe abatement measures. The second is the threat of closure or relocation if environmental standards are not achieved. And the third is to recommend to clusters of units the construction of central effluent treatment plants (CETPs) to clean up effluents. As might be expected, the level of non-compliance is high, as industry is unable and unwilling to change, and the agencies do not have enough resources for effective monitoring (Dasgupta, 2000c).

Consequently, there was a considerable rise in the number of judicial actions against industry in the 1990s. This may be attributed to three sources: (i) cases brought against a unit or a cluster of units by a Pollution Control Board; (ii) cases brought against a unit or a cluster of units by environmental activists; and (iii) when activists have taken the state Pollution Control Board to court for not enforcing the environmental standards, as seen in the case of Delhi.[7] The Delhi Pollution Control Committee[8] in turn passed court orders affecting nearly 90 000 units. Though it has made little difference to large industries, who have the means to engage in protracted litigation, or who have used it as a pretext to shut down unprofitable factories,[9] small-scale units have faced closure and relocation.

Dasgupta (1998, 2000b) demonstrates that not only are these measures not working, they are detrimental to long-term environmental governance. Installing abatement equipment without a shift to cleaner technology means that the owner sees no economic benefit from pollution reduction. Thus, the industry does not make the link between economic gains and environmental benefits. This has generated a very negative perception of environmental investment. In 1995, Harlankar

(1995) noted that 15 000 small units had been closed in India by court orders. Closures and relocations led to job losses. In 1998, the closure of 163 units (of which three were large) in Delhi led to estimated losses of 125 000 jobs. Furthermore, court orders do not require relocating units to use cleaner technology (Dasgupta, 2000b), implying that it merely shifts pollution out of the urban bubble. Recommending the construction of CETPs in instances which are inappropriate (Dasgupta, 2000b), and the failure to execute these projects quickly and effectively[10] when it is appropriate, means that factories continue to pollute.

Developing Countries: Pollution in the Poverty Context

Environmental problems in small industries are complex in scope and magnitude. This can be attributed to the social and economic role this sector plays, and the consequent articulation of capital, labour and technology under conditions very different from those in large-scale manufacturing. It is important to distinguish the three dimensions: economic, social and technical.

As regards the economic dimension, the post-independence strategy for modernization and growth in most developing economies has been based on developing a capital-intensive, large-scale industrial sector. This generates employment for those with financial and human resources. The small-scale sector with its low barriers to entry is expected to generate livelihood for those with limited human and financial resources. In many countries (for example, Bangladesh, India, Indonesia or Colombia),[11] this sector has been encouraged with subsidies, credit facilities and product protection. Little *et al.* (1989) have argued against encouraging the small-scale sector, as it does not make efficient use of either labour or capital, and Sandesara (1991) has suggested that the arguments for protecting this sector in India are social, and not economic. However, more recently, both the ILO/UNDP (1997) and Ronnas *et al.* (1998) note that small and medium-sized industries are fundamental to the efficient translation of economic growth into enhanced employment opportunities and income.

There are three economic characteristics of the small-scale sector that are relevant to this analysis: (i) the short-term perspective of firms; (ii) intra-sectoral diversity; and (iii) the insecure position of the workers. According to Sandesara (1991), the objective of many small firms tends to be profit maximization in the short-term, even though it means lower income in the long-run. This often leads to a lower investable surplus. Furthermore, it makes it difficult to sell the 'business' argument that waste reduction and better material recovery leads to improved profits in the long run (Dasgupta, 2000b). There is considerable intra-sectoral diversity in size and product. The size variation makes the issue of affordability paramount, while product diversity means that multiple waste streams have to be tackled. The majority of workers are drawn from low-income households with few skills. This, combined with high labour turnover, makes the overall level of human development low. Additionally, the wage market in this sector is poorly developed, and the owner arbitrarily determines the wage rate. The absence of any form of contract further means that there are no safeguards against dismissal and accidents.

The social dimension becomes important because of the generally lower levels of human resources among owners, and low levels of literacy among workers, particularly in the very small firms. This has implications for (i) the available knowledge and information base; and (ii) available skills. 'The level of knowledge and information is fundamental to the way change is managed' (Dasgupta 1997, p. 297). The ability to handle and absorb new information is generally limited by low exposure to information in general. The study of lead smelting units showed that the owners failed to understand either the environmental regulations or the standards they were expected to meet. When owners have a limited information base, as in this case, decision-making tends to become family-based and/or intuitive. For example, Sethuraman (1992) notes that the choice of product when starting a unit is influenced partly by the family's social contacts and partly by familiarity with the product. Reaction to, and interpretation of, new information is then greatly conditioned by the socioeconomic background of the owner, with implications for environmental information dissemination.

One important aspect of small industry is that it enables people to start their own businesses, and to provide employment to members of their family who may be unemployable or less gainfully employed elsewhere (Sandesara, 1991). This is indicative of the possibilities that the managerial and technical ability among owners and managers may generally be low. Regarding the quality of entrepreneurship, Sethuraman (1987) notes that entrepreneurs may possess some capital or access to credit, but have limited managerial ability, as they rarely have formal training. This means that very often the entrepreneur lacks adequate education and skills. Patel (1987) argues that 'not all persons can become entrepreneurs'. Some may possess traits that may be honed through training and/or experience, but training in entrepreneurship is not so common.

The impact of these factors is that the organizational structure in small firms is dominated by the entrepreneur, who takes all the decisions at the work-place and spends most of his/her time managing the day-to-day business. There is little delegation of responsibilities. The short-term economic perspective combined with social characteristics largely condition the adaptive and reactive capacities of this sector.

As regards the technical dimension, the choice of technology and process in a small industry is not a technical decision but is, according to Sethuraman (1992), adapted to the availability of capital, space, raw materials and skills – locally and in the family. This contrasts with the behaviour of large enterprises, which choose optimal combinations of resources depending on the technology used. The technology used in small industries is the cheapest. In some countries, formal and/or informal start-up credit can easily be made available,[12] but with little attention to long-term technical and financial viability. This, combined with little subsequent investment, means that the technology is soon outdated, inefficient and inefficacious.

Pollution results from inefficient energy use, process inefficiencies, poor work practices, and poor housekeeping and absence of waste management (UNIDO, 1995). There is little maintenance or upgrading of technology, and no attempt to control pollution. Externalizing the cost of pollution is taken as given, and cheap skilled and unskilled labour is often a disincentive to technological change (Dasgupta, 1997). The impact of this pollution is borne primarily by the workers, and by the poor neighbourhoods (Satterthwaite and Hardoy, 1992). Additionally, those most vulnerable to technological change are the workers in this sector, who in any case have low levels of entitlements.[13] As seen in the case of Delhi (Dasgupta, 1998), the loss of employment by the male head of households leads to considerable distress, and to shifts in household survival strategies.[14]

The 'Environmental Problem'

At the conceptual level, environmental problems have been classified into two groups. According to Karshenas (1992; p. 16), the problems in the first group are 'related to the application of modern technology; to economic growth, to advances in technology and to high income and consumption levels'. Sethuraman (1992) refers to this as the 'income effect'. The problems in the second group are related to economic backwardness, poverty, unemployment, stagnant technology, and slow growth in general. Sethuraman describes this as 'substitution effect', since the poor draw on natural resources in the absence of purchasing power. Karshenas calls it 'forced degradation'. These conceptual categories are important explanatory tools, and they together encapsulate the processes, dynamics and effects of pollution in small industries.

In developing economies, small industries embody the risks and consequences (positive and negative) of technological change and growth on one hand, and the effects associated with poverty, unemployment, stagnant technology and low levels of human resources development on the other. As noted above, technological progress increases the productivity of labour and incomes, generates higher investible surpluses, and improves competitiveness. This raises the capability of coping with environmental problems and making the necessary adjustments. This would also be generally true for large-scale modern industry in developing economies. Apart from the new, high-technology industries (information technology, manufacture of automobile components and electronics goods, some export-orientated and niche-market sub-sectors) the bulk of small industries is at the margin of technological change. It draws on technology that is easily available and relatively cheap. The negative outcome of the application of technology is that small industries bring with them all the environmental problems of air and water pollution, and soil contamination. The positive outcome is that they do provide a livelihood to millions who would otherwise have difficulty in obtaining gainful employment.

However, the flip side is that they embody generally low levels of human resource development and low levels of investment. This reverses the decision-making process at the firm level, where the availability of skills and knowledge determine the product, the choice of technology, and the production process. Thus, introducing cleaner technology and waste management techniques, and changing work practices, are not merely questions of the availability of technology and resources. Major barriers to improving environmental management are the low ability to cope with, and low willingness to accept, change. Studies in Nairobi (Frijns *et al.*, 1997) and Calcutta (Dasgupta, 1997) both concluded that technological change is constrained by attitudinal, organizational and economic barriers. Additionally, the short-term profit perspective and little investible surplus limits their financial ability to cope with change and with the problems it generates. Together, these constraints would make environmental management of small units notionally and operationally different from environmental management of large and medium firms.

In summary, this section has shown that there is a time lag between the existing environmental policies of some developing countries and those of the developed economies. While the West has moved from relying solely on command and control strategies to a mix of market-based instruments and command and control strategies, India has seen little change to its environmental policy since the 1970s. It is still reliant on a command and control policy backed by a penal approach to enforcement. The underlying assumption to this approach is that industry has the resources (financial, technical, skills, information) and hence the ability to achieve the national environmental standards and regulations. The evidence suggests that such an assumption is unrealistic.

Overall, the financial, technical and attitudinal problems to change may cut across industry groups of all sizes. However, the manifestation of the problem varies with size. Several constraints are specific to the small-scale sector:

- Low reactive, absorptive and adaptive capabilities to change. This may be attributed largely to low levels of education among owners and workers; to reliance on informal and dated knowledge bases for decision-making; and to a short-term economic perspective and limited investible surplus.
- Resistance to change and a reluctance to deal with technical issues, largely attributable to limited exposure to environmental information and to low levels of technical education.
- Organizational constraints as small firms tend to be dominated by the owner with little delegation of responsibility. This means that the owner has little or no time for dealing with environmental issues.
- Attitudinal constraints lie in low environmental awareness and low cognisance of laws and regulations.
- The short-term perspective makes it difficult to sell the business argument that environmental improvements make long-term gains.

The policy to address environmental problems in small industries must therefore acknowledge both substitution and income effects. It must note that the barriers to technological change are rooted in the relations between capital, labour and technology, which in small industries are conditioned by the socioeconomic context of limited livelihood opportunities for many social categories.

CASE STUDIES FROM INDIA

The case studies[15] presented in this section highlight the complex nature of the environmental problems, and the difficulties of resolving them with a technocratic approach. The three sub-sectors examined are: acid-processing firms in north-east Calcutta; lead-smelting units in Picnic Gardens, Calcutta; and the glass industry in Ferozabad.

Acid-Processing Firms in North-east Calcutta

The case study of these factories shows how they operate, the constraints they face, the environmental problems which arise from the use of primitive technology, and the totally inadequate response of the environmental agency to the problem.

There are about 172 acid-processing firms in a cluster of 200 chemical processing and/or converting plants located in the Bagmari area. The cluster occupies nearly forty-two acres. The first acid-processing factories were set up in the 1940s, when Calcutta was a thriving manufacturing and trading centre. The entrepreneurs saw a market in distilling and concentrating commercial grade sulphuric, hydrochloric and nitric acids – by-products of large industries – into AR (analytical reagent) and GP (general purpose) grades.

In 1972, the vacant land to the north of these firms was occupied and housing erected. A pond, which was an important source of water for these factories, was filled in. No infrastructure support had been provided to these firms. At the time of the survey in 1997 there was no piped water supply, no drains, no sewage system and no paved roads, only narrow, muddy, densely built-up lanes, covered with ash from these factories. The piped water supply stops outside the cluster and water has to be collected regularly by users.

About fifty-five of the 172 acid-processing firms are tiny, one-person firms where the owner undertakes all the functions of purchase, processing and delivery. A majority of these owners have little or no education. At the other end of the spectrum are ten firms, each employing 12–14 workers (including clerical staff), with an average annual turnover of around Rs30 lakhs (£4286). In the middle, and dominating the sector, are 107 firms, each employing 8–9 workers (including clerical staff), with an annual turnover of Rs15–20 lakhs (£2143–£2857). Sixty metric tonnes of commercial grade acid is delivered daily to this cluster by 5–6 tankers. This is distributed among the firms according to their requirements.

The aim is to concentrate the commercial grade acids to the purer AR and GP grades using the glass-flask condenser method. This involves heating the dilute acid and capturing the concentrate by condensation in another glass flask. The efficiency of the process depends on the amount of water available for cooling and proper insulation of the equipment to prevent leakage of acid vapour.

A row of open clay *chullas* (stoves) fuelled by smokeless coal briquettes is used to heat flasks of acid, each of which sits on a cast iron *karai* (two-handled pan). There is an opening in the front of each *chullah* to stoke the fire. At the back is another row of flasks connected by the condenser to receive the concentrated acid. The cooling water is reused until it is too contaminated for further use. The water and the air are contaminated by fumes that escape because of mismatched and ill-fitting stoppers, connector pipes and inadequate insulation. The air in the factories, in the cluster and in the adjoining residential area is polluted with the smell of acid. The Preliminary Report, submitted by a government task force set up in 1978, identified inefficiencies which result in pollution. It noted that 34 kg (20 per cent) of acids were lost per day during handling, by spillage, evaporation during storage and other process losses. Another 34 per cent was unaccounted for.

It is clear that considerable air and water contamination is associated with these acid-processing factories. It is also clear that the lack of a water supply, process inefficiencies, lack of knowledge and understanding of health, safety and environmental issues, and poverty are at the root of this pollution. Ironically, it also means that low-cost measures, such as better insulation and matching pipe sizes, can reduce acid loss and pollution considerably. Since the development of low-income housing around this cluster, residents have complained about the high incidence of respiratory diseases among both young and old residents. Local community groups have developed a case for people versus industry. This approach has increased social tensions, as jobs are threatened, and has exacerbated an already difficult situation.

The response of the Pollution Control Board was to recommend the construction of a central effluent treatmen. plant! The response was inadequate and inappropriate for three main reasons. First, it did not address the main source of the pollution – that is, the inefficiencies in process flows, in work practices, and the poor knowledge of health and safety issues. These inefficiencies could have been addressed cheaply and provided increased returns to industry. Second, trying to force the industry to adopt measures that were inappropriate and unaffordable by the majority of owners was unhelpful to long-term environmental governance. Third, the stance of the Pollution Control Board reflected a technocratic attitude and showed a limited understanding of the problem. Needless to say, the status quo continues, and these firms continued to pollute as late as the year 2000.

Lead-Smelting Firms in Picnic Gardens, Calcutta

This case study[16] indicates the problems faced in the lead-smelting sector, and the role that the environmental agency played in trying to resolve them. Lead smelting is a highly polluting activity. The main pollution results from the emission of lead dust from furnace inefficiencies and from the lack of abatement measures. In August 1994, twenty-four factories in Picnic Gardens were threatened with closure if they did not comply with the regulations within one year (that is by August 1995). This was after years of campaiging by members of the surrounding middle-income residential communities. Most firms installed some form of pollution abatement equipment supplied by the private sector, often at great cost, but there was no reduction in ambient or workplace pollution. Furnace inefficiencies had not been addressed. The owners were bitter that they were being asked to undertake further investment.

Unlike in the case of acid-processing factories, some engineers from the State Pollution Control Board were involved directly in trying to identify the inefficiencies in process flows and work practices, after the initial round of investment failed to have an impact. They noted that furnace efficiency could be increased by 75 per cent with low-cost measures. This in turn would reduce abatement costs. However, the available inspectors and engineers were over-stretched and they admitted that there were no ready solutions to outdated technology. Iterative change needs time and exchange of information over a lengthy period. The Department of the Environment was neither structured nor resourced to participate in such programmes.

Furthermore, most owners, though prosperous, were illiterate, and did not understand the technical specifications and implications of the pollution standards they were expected to meet. Consequently, the owners were unable to ask the 'right questions' in their dealings with firms selling abatement equipment. They also failed to appreciate the limitations and the maintenance requirements of the equipment they installed. In most cases, the equipment malfunctioned.

This experience shows that technical change for greening businesses is a complex, multi-faceted problem. Important issues such as knowledge and understanding of processes employed, organizational issues and work practices, and attitudes to change have to be addressed to initiate technological change for pollution abatement. This case also indicates the nature of official assistance that could be provided.

The Glass Industry in Ferozabad

This case study[17] provides an analysis of an initiative by the Development Commissioner – Small Scale Industries (DCSSI) of the Government of India, to aid the cluster of glass industries in Ferozabad as it was threatened with closure, being in the Taj Trapezium.[18] The sector is a high-energy user with high levels of air pollution. As in the case of the lead-smelting industry, information and pressure to change were also buffeting the owners here. The study shows that, despite considerable efforts by the DCSSI to demonstrate the benefits of improved furnace efficiencies, the uptake of new technology was negligible. The reasons for failure offer lessons for the future.

The programme undertaken by DCSSI concentrated on improving furnace efficiency.[19] The melting process typically consumes 70–80 per cent of total energy requirements, and large-scale savings were possible. Three types of furnace are used in the glass industry: tank furnaces, pot furnaces, and muffle furnaces. Heat is also used for screen printing on glass, for grinding, and for cutting bangles. There were 1200 units in the cluster. Twenty large firms had continuous tank furnaces, using regenerative heat recovery systems. Some were oil-fired, with a majority of them fired indirectly by coal through a separate gasification system. There were 75 firms using pot furnaces, with 2–3 tonnes melt capacity per day, using coal as fuel. The design is inherently inefficient and very little effort has been made to improve the basic design. Typical pot furnaces operating in the United Kingdom and the Czech Republic are equipped with recuperative systems. None of the pot furnaces in Ferozabad employ heat recovery systems, and all of them use a central fixed bed of coal to effect melting. Muffle furnaces are used for making bangles. The programme was aimed at improving the tank and pot furnace technologies.

Since the number of tank furnace users was comparatively small, they were targeted individually to improve the gasification plant. For the pot furnace, the methodology used was to go in with the improved technology and set up a demonstration centre. DCSSI then undertook training and information dissemination. The officer interviewed noted that, even after several years of information dissemination, the rate of uptake remained very low. He saw major shortcomings in the approach to the problem and in project design, as it failed to address the constraints to technological change. He noted that several lessons from this experience could be used to inform future strategy:

- There was a need to counter the basic reluctance towards new development. Before owners are asked to make major investment in items such as a furnace, the benefits of change have to be demonstrated at the firm level. This implies addressing issues of housekeeping, work practices and process improvements first, before major investment in technology change. For example, educating the owners about the benefits of improving instrumentation and better insulation, and demonstrating that the melting efficiency of furnaces also depends on raw-material quality, batch preparation and mixing.
- However, to be able to achieve these improvements in process efficiency it would be necessary first to undertake firm-level studies, to assess the needs and constraints as perceived by the owners.
- Fundamental to these would be evaluation at the firm level to establish furnace design changes. This would help to demonstrate that efficiency gains were possible even with existing technology through adaptation and change. Interacting with Research and Development (R&D) institutions dealing in the glass industry would be crucial. Indigenous technology should first be investigated before importing technology that is difficult to adapt to conditions in small firms. In this case, technology was imported from the Czech Republic.
- An initiative should establish the scope for continuous absorption of technology. Its long-term success will be assured only if the initiative for change comes from the owners: that is, following attitudinal change.
- The programmes have to distance themselves from the environmental agencies.

To summarize, it is clear that change for improved environmental management cannot be an overnight process. To prepare the ground for technological change it is essential first to address issues of attitude to change, of inadequate knowledge and information base, and of poor work practices and housekeeping. This implies that the process of technological upgrading is as much about improved management input as about technology itself. To undertake such a task, requires a flexible, participatory approach with in-depth knowledge of the targeted sub-sector. Furthermore, the question of affordability by tiny firms in this sector has to be recognized, and alternative strategies developed. The environmental argument that small firms will eventually be forced out cannot be applied where survival economics dominate (Lardinois and van de Kluder, 1995; Dasgupta, 2000b).

Additionally, the owners of small enterprises need to accept that higher environmental standards have altered the parameters under which they operate. The technology mix employed may be appropriate to the scale of operations, but the higher environmental performance now required renders the technology outdated and expensive.

The discussions with owners and workers in all three sub-sectors made it clear that the present sanction-based approach of trying to impose end-of-pipe measures has been detrimental to long-term governance, for two reasons: (i) industry fails to make the link between pollution control and prevention, and economic gains; and (ii) this in turn is generating a negative perception of environmental investment. Furthermore, as seen in the case of lead smelting units, the private sector selling abatement equipment can act rather unscrupulously, generating even greater scepticism.

TOWARDS CLEANER PRODUCTION STRATEGIES IN SMALL-SCALE INDUSTRIES

The present environmental strategies in India are not working. The complexity, the sub-sectoral diversity, and low levels of environmental awareness and education among owners and workers indicate the need to develop interactive, participatory approaches to environmental problem-solving: 'To make such approaches operational, policy must ensure that industry co-operates with the appropriate programme. This could be done through a carefully designed package of incentives and penalties informed by the micro-realities of the sector. The "carrot and stick" policy could provide a framework for the multiple participatory programmes that would be necessary to deal with the varied problems of diversity, size, products and of processes employed' (Dasgupta, 2000b, p. 959).

The 'Carrot and Stick' Policy

The starting point in this policy approach is to recognize that there is a problem that needs to be resolved, but the initiative to resolve it is not forthcoming from the sector involved. An understanding of the constraints, or the micro-realities, to improved environmental management should therefore be the next step. These realities would inform the design of the package of incentives, whose aim would be to address and/or counter the shortcomings and reluctance that inhibit compliance. The balance between incentives and penalties will be guided by the fundamental principle that cleaning up makes better sense than continuing to pollute. However, it is not only important to address the problems and constraints in a sector but also to ensure compliance. Hence the need to combine sanction and compliance strategies. Compliance-based strategy is needed for problem-solving and to indicate a way forward, and sanctions to ensure compliance and to deal with persisting deviant behaviour (Dasgupta, 2000b, p. 959).

In reality, the carrot and stick policy has taken various forms. Hong Kong has used this policy to improve waste management in small and micro units. As Lei and YANG (1993) report, tiny units that generate chemical waste are required to store the waste safely for collection, and there is a heavy penalty for non-participation. Eight thousand units are registered on the programme. Indonesia's policy initiatives under the programme called 'PROPER' combine a package of information dissemination, incentives, and a 'name and shame' policy for non-compliance. The head of pollution control, Nabiel Makarim, notes that Indonesia realized by 1978 that its weak institutions would not be able to support command and control strategies, and opted for alternative methods. The following ten years of the environmental programme were devoted to institution-building and awareness-raising. The PROPER programme was started in 1995. Incentives to industry are provided through cheap credit and soft loans for the purchase of pollution-control equipment. Permits are awarded depending on the level of compliance, starting with green (most compliant) and moving through blue and red to black (non-compliant). Those in the red and black categories are named and shamed. According to Makarim, social castigation becomes an alternative, because law enforcement does not work. The programme appears to have had some success. The improvements in the 187 factories targeted by PROPER are discussed in detail in World Bank (2000).

The Participatory Approach

'The participatory approach can be defined as a systematic, but semi-structured activity carried out in cluster-based small industrial units (to maximise demonstration effect) by a team of technical officers and facilitators to help owners identify sources of inefficiencies, waste and poor work practices and to provide technical and environmental information for raising awareness and for problem solving' (Dasgupta, 2000b, p. 960).

Examples of the participatory approach to problem-solving are more difficult to find than examples of the 'carrot and stick' policy. The National Productivity Council (NPC) of India has adopted an *ad hoc* participatory approach based on an understanding and acknowledgement of the three dimensions – economic, social and technical – discussed earlier. The Waste Management Circles Programme,[20] developed by NPC and funded by the World Bank, targeted clusters of small-scale units that were major polluters. The programme has had some success in reducing waste in six of the ten clusters targeted in Phase 1. To implement the participatory approach, engineers were trained as facilitators. Though their goal was environmental improvement, their marketing strategy was 'how to help small industries increase their profitability'. Their objective was first to build confidence, and then to go slowly through the processes employed to assess the procedures used; undertake input–output analyses, involving owners at every stage; brainstorming and allowing the solutions to come from the owners, so that they have a sense of ownership. Along the way they addressed issues of work practices, instrumentation, and the need for monitoring inputs and outputs. However, they failed in four of the ten clusters and did not target the tiny units (with fewer than six workers), as these would not have been able to afford the changes necessary. The reasons for failure were that the sub-sector in Panipat producing furnishings for the export market was very successful and not interested; and the lock industry in Kanpur, though flourishing, lacked the foresight to undertake change.

Based on the evidence provided in this chapter and the experience of the NPC, enabling activities would include the following:

- Help firms to analyze and understand the process flows used, and to identify inefficiencies. For example, in the acid-processing units, the workers and owners should be helped to appreciate that most of the pollution is associated with the use of ill-fitting stoppers and mismatched connector pipes. This should be related to the increased efficiency of acid recovery via the flask and condenser method.
- In the case of lead-smelting units and in the glass industry, guide owners and workers to appreciate that the melting efficiency of the

furnace depends on the timing of the load, and on the quality of the batch mix.

- Help industry to appreciate the benefits of instrumentation, of better work practices, and of monitoring the quality and quantity of inputs. Improve work practices, for example, washing lead plates before smelting so that battery acid does not enter the smelting process.
- Help firms to understand the links between improved resource recovery and lower waste generation, and its impact on pollution abatement costs. For example, enable owners in the lead-smelting units to appreciate that incremental change to furnace design can increase resource recovery considerably. This would also reduce ash and lead oxide particle in the smoke, and thus lower abatement cost. In the acid-processing industry, improving insulation would increase acid recovery and reduce pollution.
- Demonstrate the benefits through low-cost measures at firm level, and initiate an attitudinal change.
- For longer-term environmental management, help businesses to understand and establish environmental goals, set priorities, and assess the costs and benefits of the technological changes required.
- With regard to tiny firms, the agencies involved would need to help units develop alternative, and affordable, survival strategies.

This package of measures can only be delivered through a proactive, flexible approach, backed by an understanding of the inherent constraints of the sector, and combined with an appreciation of sub-sector specific obstacles. It requires resources in terms of engineers who can also act as facilitators of the process, and whom the industry could trust, and sometimes expert technical inputs from already established institutions for R&D, as underscored by the case of the glass industry. The emphasis is on enabling industry to appreciate, understand and improve environmental management. The initiative to change must ultimately come from the owners. Financial assistance is not recommended, as this would only strengthen the culture of dependency in this sector.

This change, which requires attitudinal shifts, cannot occur overnight. The present command and control strategies do not have the scope to deliver the necessary information and advice in the format appropriate to small units. While the NPC demonstrates a useful way forward, the initiatives remain *ad hoc* and project-specific. If environmental improvements are to be achieved at the sectoral level, there also have to be shifts at the policy level.

CONCLUSIONS

There is growing evidence that pollution from clusters of small industrial units has to be addressed, as it has considerable local impact. However, the development of an appropriate policy mix is hindered by a narrow conceptualization of the problem. A technocratic approach is unable to address the problems of implementing cleaner production strategies in this sector. This is because the social and economic role played by this sector impinges on the articulation of capital, labour and technology at the firm level. It reverses the decision-making process where knowledge and skill determine the choice of product, technology and production process. The consequence is that small-scale firms create problems of environmental pollution without the ability to tackle them.

An understanding of the constraints to resolving, and the perception of, environmental problems is crucial. The case studies all revealed technical, organizational, knowledge and attitudinal barriers, in varying degrees. The attitudinal constraints have to be addressed first, to prepare the ground for technological change, and this can be achieved only if it can be demonstrated to owners that they will benefit from undertaking the recommended changes (Dasgupta, 2000c). All the case studies showed that much of the problem can be reduced through low-cost changes, such as better materials recovery, improvements in work practices, and the adoption of a more scientific approach to materials use (for example, the use of instrumentation). The achievment of such improvements can help to demonstrate some of the benefits to owners.

To address these issues requires a flexible, interactive approach at sub-sectoral level. However, this has to be backed by sanctions that would ensure participation in programmes, and compliance in the case of persistent deviant behaviour. The package of incentives and penalties needs to be tied to timeframes and environmental targets, with procedures to ensure uptake and participation built into policy design. To develop and implement such strategies requires the strengthening of institutional capacity, and new management tools and systems. Donor agencies can play an important part in encouraging institutional development for improved environmental management.

Acknowledgement

I am grateful to *World Development* (Elsevier) for permission to reproduce this chapter.

Notes

1. This chapter does not consider the small, capital- and technology-intensive sub-sectors such as information technology, modern units making spare parts for cars, and some niche-market export enterprises.
2. The chapter is based on three previous publications (Dasgupta, 2000a, 2000b and 2000c), and includes extracts from these papers.
3. The term 'small' refers to the size of the production unit. A variety of methods and criteria may be used to define it, but an in-depth discussion is not within the scope of this chapter. As this chapter has an India focus, the official Indian definition is given: 'Small-scale sector in India is defined in terms of investment ceilings on the original value of the installed plant and machinery. Under the Notification No. 857 dated 10.12.97, a small-scale undertaking is one where the fixed assets in plant and machinery does not exceed Rs.300 lakhs (Rs.30 million; £430,000 approx.)' (DCSSI, 1998). 'Tiny' or 'micro-enterprises' are those with investment up to Rs25 lakhs (£36 000 approx.). In addition to these there are a large number of unregistered units. This study focuses on registered small, including tiny, units.
4. The discussion in this section is reproduced from Dasgupta (2000b).
5. For a more detailed discussion see Lane *et al.* (1999).
6. Central Pollution Control Board (1997) reproduces all the environmental legislation, rules and regulations issued in India.
7. For a detailed discussion, see Dasgupta (1998).
8. The Delhi Capital Region is designated a Union Territory. However, it functions like a state in administrative matters. The Delhi Pollution Control Committee is regarded as, and has all the powers held by, a State Pollution Control Board.
9. India's exit policy and strong unions in the large-scale industries make it very difficult to close down a factory.
10. In the late 1980s it was recommended that a CETP be constructed to treat the effluents generated in the Industrial Estate at Wazirpur. At the time of the author's survey in 1998, the land for the construction of the CETP had yet to be identified.
11. See Little *et al.* (1989) on Colombia and Pardo (1991); Little *et al.* (1989) on India and Thomas (1991); Mannan (1993) on Bangladesh; and Mehmet (1995) on Indonesia.
12. In some countries where the small sector enjoys market and product protection, cheap credit is also made available. See Sandesara (1991) on India, and Mannan (1993) on Bangladesh. For social categories that are hesitant to take up the offer of formal credit, informal credit networks and family savings are commonly used (Dasgupta, 1997).
13. 'Entitlement' refers to the complex ways in which individuals or households command resources. Though the concept was originally developed for the rural sector, it is useful in explaining how poverty affects different people. See Sen (1981) for details.
14. In the context of the trade-off associated with environmental options, the ILO makes the point that the present environmental debate unfortunately does not discuss the consequences for employment. It emphasizes the need to address the environment–employment dilemma.

15. For in-depth analyses of these sectors, see Dasgupta (2000c), Dasgupta (1997) and DFID (1999), respectively.
16. This case study draws on Dasgupta (1997), and was undertaken in September 1995.
17. The analysis was undertaken by the author for a DFID study in 1998–9. For a detailed and in-depth discussion, see DFID (1999) and Dasgupta (2000a).
18. The Taj Trapezium was created to protect heritage monuments and cities, all located in close proximity to Agra, from industrial pollution. The Trapezium covers an area of $10\,400\,\text{km}^2$, and stretches from Aligarh in the north, to Mathura and Bharatpur in the west, and from Aligarh in the east to Etawah in the south-east. Ferozabad is in the middle of the zone. Industries in the Taj Trapezium have been threatened with relocation.
19. It is important to note that the most effective method of improving efficiency and reducing pollution could be the substitution of oil or gas for coal. However, this is not an option available to the Ferozabad glass producers. The natural gas pipeline has by-passed the cluster, contrary to expectations. Oil is a heavily taxed and expensive fuel, so continued use of indigenous coal is likely. Furthermore, the quality of coal required by the glass industry is 'steam grade B', but the industry receives inferior grade coal with high ash content. Hence, efforts have concentrated on improving the efficiency of coal-fired furnaces (Dasgupta, 2000a).
20. For a detailed discussion of the programme, see the newsletters of Waste Management Circles (1997–8) and DFID (1999).

References

Bhalla, A. S. (ed.) (1992) *Environment, Employment and Development. A World Employment Programme study*, Geneva: ILO.

Central Pollution Control Board (1997) *Pollution Control Acts, Rules and Notifications Issued Thereunder* New Delhi: Government of India, Ministry of Environment and Forests.

Centre for Science and Environment (1985) *The Citizen's Report*, New Delhi: Centre for Science and Environment.

Chandak, S. P. (1994) 'DESIRE: Demonstration in Small Industries For Reducing Waste', *Industry and Energy*, vol. 17, no. 4, pp. 41–5.

Chiu, H. and Tsang, K. L. (1990) 'Reduction of Treatment Costs by Using Communal Treatment Facilities', *Waste Management and Research*, vol. 8, no. 2, pp. 165–7.

Dasgupta, N. (1992) *Petty Trading in the Third World*, Aldershot: Avebury.

Dasgupta, N. (1997) 'Greening Small Recycling Firms: The Case of Lead Smelting Units in Calcutta', *Environment and Urbanisation*, vol. 9, no. 2 (October), pp. 289–305.

Dasgupta, N. (1998) 'Tall Blunders: Present Strategies Do More Harm than Good', *Down to Earth*, vol. 30 (September), pp. 22–5.

Dasgupta, N. (2000a) 'Energy Efficiency and Environmental Improvements in Small-scale Industries: Present Initiatives Are Not Working', *Energy Policy*, vol. 27, no. 14, pp. 789–800.

Dasgupta, N. (2000b) 'Environmental Enforcement and Small Industries: Reworking the Problem in the Poverty Context', *World Development*, vol. 28, no. 5, pp. 945–67.

Dasgupta, N. (2000c) 'Policy Implications for Environmental Improvements in India's SSI', *Small Enterprise Development*, vol. 11, no. 2, pp. 15–27.

DCSSI (Development Commissioner – Small Scale Industries) (1998) *Small-Scale Industries*, New Delhi: Government of India.

DFID (Department for International Development) (1999) *Energy Efficiency and Poverty Alleviation*, London: DFID.

Doeleman, J. A. (1992) 'Employment Concerns and Environmental Policy', in A. S. Bhalla (ed.), *Environment, Employment and Development*, A WEP study, Geneva: ILO, pp. 41–95.

Frijns, J. and van Vliet, B. (1999) 'Small-scale Industries and Cleaner Production Strategies', *World Development*, vol. 27, no. 6, pp. 967–83.

Frijns, J., Malombe, K. and van Vliet, B. (1997) 'Pollution Control of Small-scale Metal Industries in Nairobi', WAU, Wageningen, Department of Sociology.

Hamza, A. (1991) 'Impacts of Industrial and Small Scale Manufacturing Wastes on Urban Environments in Developing Countries', Paper prepared for the Urban Management Programme, United Nations Centre for Human Settlements, Nairobi: UMP/UNCHS (September).

Harlankar, S. (1995) *The Calm before the Storm*, New Delhi: Centre for Science and Environment.

Hillary, R. (1995) *Small Firms and Environment. A Groundwork Status Report*. Birmingham: Groundwork.

Humphries, J. and Rubery, J. (1995) *The Economics of Equal Opportunity*, Manchester: Equal Opportunities Commission.

IIED (International Institute for Environment and Development) (1997) *Market-based Instruments for Pollution Prevention: A Case Study of Indian Steel Industry* IIED/UNIDO. Available on website www/iied.org/creed/case_isi.htm

ILO (International Labour Organization) (1993) *India: Employment, Poverty and Economic Policies*. Report prepared under a project sponsored by the United Nations Development Programme (UNDP) Technical Support Services – 1, New Delhi: ILO.

ILO (International Labour Organization) (1996) *Economic Reforms and Labour Policies*. Report prepared by the ILO – South Asian Multidisciplinary Advice Team (SAAT) under United Nations Development Programme (UNDP) Technical Support Services – 1, New Delhi: ILO.

ILO (International Labour Organization)/(UNDP) (United Nations Development Programme) (1997) *Jobs for Africa: A Policy Framework for an Employment-Intensive Growth Strategy*, Geneva: ILO.

Karshenas, M. (1992) 'Environment Development and Employment: Some Conceptual Issues', in A. S. Bhalla (ed.), *Environment, Development and Employment, A World Employment Programme study*, Geneva: ILO, pp. 10–30.

Kent, L. (1991) *The Relationship between Small Enterprises and Environmental Degradation in the Developing World (with Emphasis on Asia)*. Review prepared for USAID, Washington DC: USAID.

Kritiporn, P., Pnanyotou, T. and K. Charnprateep (1990). *The Greening of Thai Industry: Producing More and Polluting Less*, Bangkok: Thailand Development Research Institute Foundation.

Lane, S. N., Richards, K. S. Sinha, S. and Wu, S. Y. (1999) 'Screw the Lid Even Tighter? Water Pollution and Enforcement of Environmental Regulations in Less Developed Countries', in S. T. Trudgill, D. E. Walling and B. Webb (eds), *Water Quality: Science and Policy*, New York: John Wiley.

Lardinois, I. and van de Kluder, A. (1995) *Plastic Waste: Options for Small-scale Resource Recovery*, Amsterdam: Tool Publications.

Lei, P. C. K. and Yang, D. S. C. (1993) 'The Implementation of Controls Over the Management of Chemical Waste in Hong Kong', Proceedings of the Pacific Basin Conference on Hazardous Waste, Honolulu, November.

Lin, C. M. (1994) 'Cleaner Production in Small and Medium-Sized Industries', *Industry and Environment*, vol. 17, no. 4, pp. 68–70.

Little, I. M. D., Mazumdar, D. and Page, J. M. Jr (1989) *Small Manufacturing Enterprises*, Washington DC: World Bank.

Makarim, N. (1998) 'Summary of Proceedings of Theme IV', 27 October. Available on website pollmgt@jazz.worldbank.org

Mannan, M. A. (1993) *Growth and Development of Small Enterprises: The Case of Bangladesh*, Aldershot: Avebury.

Mehmet, O. (1995) 'Employment Creation and Green Development Strategy', *Ecological Economics*, vol. 15, pp. 11–19.

Mol, A. P. J. and Frijns, J. (1997) 'Ecological Restructuring in Industrial Vietnam: The HoChiMinh City Region', Paper prepared for the Euroviet III Biannual Conference, Amsterdam: IIAS/CASA.

Pardo, E. F. (1991) 'Urban Employment and the Role of the Small-scale Manufacturing Sector In Colombia', in H. Thomas, F. Echevarria and H. Romijin (eds), *Small Scale Production*, London: Intermediate Technology Publications, pp. 208–30.

Patel, S. V. (1987) 'Developing Indigenous Entrepreneurship: The Gujarat Model', in P. A. Neck and R. E. Nelson (eds), *Small Enterprise Development: Policies and Programmes*, Geneva: ILO, pp. 187–202.

Ronnas, P., Sjoberg, O. and Hemlin, M. (1998) *Institutional Adjustment for Economic Growth: Small-scale Industries and Economic Transition in Asia and Africa*, Aldershot: Ashgate.

Sandesara, J. C. (1991) 'Small-scale Industrialisation: The Indian Experience', in H. Thomas, F. Echevarria and H. Romijn (eds), *Small Scale Production*, London: Intermediate Technology Publications, pp. 131–51.

Satterthwaite, D. and Hardoy, J. (1992) *The Squatter Citizen*, London: Earthscan Publications.

Scott, A. (1989) 'The Environmental Impact of Small-scale Industries in the Third World', ESRC Global Environmental Change Program, Briefings No. 19, (May).

Sen, A. K. (1981) *Poverty and Famines: An Essay on Entitlements and Deprivation*, Oxford: Clarendon Press.

Sethuraman, S. V. (1987) 'Technology and Small Enterprise Development', in P. A. Neck and R. E. Nelson (eds), *Small Enterprise Development: Policies and Programmes*, Geneva: ILO, pp. 187–202.

Sethuraman, S. V. (1992) 'Introduction', in A. S. Bhalla (ed.), *Environment, Development and Employment, A World Employment Programme study*, Geneva: ILO, pp. 1–9.

Shin, E. (1992) *Economic Evaluation of Urban Environmental Problems: With Emphasis On Asia*, Washington DC: World Bank, Urban Development Division, Infrastructure and Urban Development Department.

Spence, L. J. (1998) *Small Businesses and Environmental Issues in the UK and the Netherlands: A Literature Review and Research Agenda*, Kingston, UK: Kingston University Business School.

Thomas, H. (1991) 'Labour and Work in Small Enterprises', in H. Thomas, F. Echevarria and H. Romijn (eds), *Small Scale Production*, London: Intermediate Technology Publications, pp. 60–85.

Tikkoo, V. (1992) 'Case Study on Hazardous Wastes from Small-scale Industries in Bombay, India', Paper prepared for the Urban Management Programme, United Nations Centre for Human Settlements, Nairobi: UMP/UNCHS (October).

Turner, R. K. and Opschoor, H. (1994) 'Environmental Economics and Policy Instruments', in R. K. Turner and H. Opschoor (eds), *Economic Incentives and Environmental Policies: Principles and Practice*, Dordrecht: Kluwer, pp. 1–24.

UNIDO (United Nations Industrial Development Organisation) (1995) *Study of Cleaner Production Techniques and Technologies Covering Clusters of Small-scale Industries in Selected Areas*, New Delhi: UNIDO.

Waste Management Circles (1997–8) *Newsletters*, India: National Productivity Council.

World Bank (2000) *Greening Industries*, Washington DC: World Bank.

Part II

Small-Scale Enterprises and Market Competition

5 Entry, Exit, and the Role of the Small Firm in China's Industrial Transformation

Qing Gong Yang and Paul Temple[1]

INTRODUCTION

Since the 1980s, while transforming itself from a centrally planned economy to an emerging market economy, China has achieved a 10 per cent average rate of growth in Gross Domestic Product (GDP), with GDP per head more than quadrupling. The contribution of small firms to this performance has been truly remarkable, with the numbers of small enterprises increasing rapidly from 344 000 in 1978 to nearly 8 million in 1995 (Wang and Yao, 1999). They have provided increasingly large shares of both output and employment; this process has been particularly important in the production of consumption goods and services.

China's recent economic performance is considerably more impressive than that of other transition economies in Eastern Europe and the countries of the former Soviet Union. However, a central paradox of this record is that it has been achieved in the absence of a number of factors commonly deemed to be essential in a successful transition economy. These include reasonably complete market liberalization, large-scale privatization, secure private property rights, and democracy. Resolution of the paradox is important when assessing the role of current and future reforms. It is argued here that small firms have had a vital role in creating a competitive market environment, and have acted as a partial substitute for a large-scale privatization process (and for forms of corporate governance based on private ownership). An investigation of this point is a key element in our understanding of the more recent phase of reforms, and of the 'competitive selection process' by which firms enter and leave industries. This process is shown to be especially important for small firms in the electrical engineering sector we investigate, and for which we model the impact of the latest phase of reforms on competitive selection.

The chapter is organized as follows. The second and third sections provide an overview of the reform process and its implications for the performance of manufacturing enterprise in China. The fourth section considers the dynamics of output, employment and productivity growth in an important sector of Chinese manufacturing – electrical engineering – in Liaoning province. A key objective of this section is to ascertain whether the latest phase of reforms has changed the pattern of growth substantially as it relates to the entry, exit and survival of firms. The fifth section considers in more detail the empirical analysis of exit. In the penultimate section, we employ a hazard rate model to explore the determinants of industrial exit. The final section concludes. We conclude *inter alia* that, notwithstanding the important contribution of small firms to growth, the competition that they provide for larger state-owned enterprises cannot as yet be regarded as an effective substitute for ownership-based corporate governance mechanisms.

THE TRANSITION PROCESS IN CHINA

The 'reform and opening up' policy proposed in the Third Plenum of The Eleventh Congress of the Communist Party on 18–22 December 1978 marked the beginning of China's reform era. At the beginning of the reform process, China's policy-makers had reasonably clear objectives relating to the increase of productivity and the improvement of living standards. But at that time, even in Western countries, let alone in socialist countries, deregulation and privatization remained controversial topics. Hence there was no obvious model to serve as a guide. The reforms consequently proceeded by using an experimental method, referred to as 'crossing the river by groping for stones'. Reforms were established in a few cities, before they were implemented at the national level.

A further landmark occurred when the Fourteenth Party Congress met in September 1992. For the first time, the 'socialist market economy' was endorsed as a description of the nature of China's reform goal. The meeting thus establishes a rather rough periodization of the reform process as a whole. The first stage lasted from 1978–92; it was characterized by the continued dominance of the planning mechanism while trying to establish a balance between the plan and the market. Official ideology vacillated between the idea of 'planning supplemented by market' and that of a 'planned commodity economy'. The second stage, from 1993, envisaged the explicit goal of establishing a 'socialist market economy' to replace the old planning system. This goal is discussed in more detail in the next section.

It is widely recognized that the Chinese transition process has a number of features that distinguish it from those elsewhere; primarily, this involves so-called 'gradualism', which entails not only a 'dual track' approach (Cao *et al.*, 1997) in production and pricing, but also in relation to ownership structure. A variety of reasons for China's choice of this gradualist strategy have been advanced. They include the following:

- China's economic and political reforms have not changed the political foundation, the leadership of the Communist Party, and the control of the state-owned economy, especially that of the strategically important sectors.
- Second, the Chinese reformers realized that economic and political reforms were likely to be very costly, since they involved not only transforming the formal institutions, but also those 'informal' institutions that have evolved over time and are still a feature of much economic organization.
- Third, reform is of necessity a process of reallocating socio-economic and political rights. So, to the extent that those currently holding rights will be affected, they will frequently be in a position to challenge the reform, or to negotiate exemptions from its implementation. Alternatively, they may be in a position simply to ignore the reform, and hold on to existing control rights backed by the old institutions. Gradualism recognizes that too rapid a pace of reform is likely to be frustrated.
- Fourth, the Chinese government realized from the outset of reform that there were no successful precedents for economic reform in socialist countries from which China could learn. Indeed, even if such a successful precedent existed, it would probably not be possible for China to transfer the necessary processes and institutions in any straightforward fashion.
- Fifth, and closely related to the fourth point, is that there is no unique capitalist pattern to follow. Private ownership patterns differ considerably even among the advanced capitalist economies. Indeed there are differences between the Anglo-Saxon economies, where ownership is highly dispersed and control tends to be exercised 'externally' via the capital market, and other countries, where ownership tends to

be more concentrated and cannot be liquidated easily, favouring 'internal' control and monitoring of management (Morris, 1996).

THE CURRENT PHASE OF REFORMS: THE SOCIALIST MARKET ECONOMY

By the end of 1992, China's economic system had reached a halfway point between a planned system and a market system. In September of that year, the Fourteenth Congress of the Chinese Communist Party endorsed for the first time the objective of building a 'socialist market economy' as the goal of the reforms. The explicit nature of the target should be contrasted with the old philosophy (see above) of 'groping for stones'. In November 1993, the Third Plenum of the Fourteenth Party Congress began to establish a rule-based system, with related market-supporting institutions. In 1997, the Fifteenth Party Congress made a breakthrough on ownership issues, with private ownership being upgraded to an 'important component of the economy' rather than being merely a 'supplementary component'. And more recently, in 1999, private ownership and the Rule of Law were incorporated into the Chinese Constitution, and private ownership was given equal standing with state-owned enterprises (SOEs).

The reforms in this stage recognized that the phase of dual-track development may have reached its conclusion. Before 1994, the liberalization of foreign exchange markets was carried out by means of a dual-track policy, with an official planned exchange rate and a market rate existing simultaneously. In 1994, the planned allocation of foreign exchange was abolished completely, and the dual-track exchange markets were merged into one. In 1996, China went one step further in announcing current account convertibility of its currency, while, however, retaining control of the capital account. This proved compatible with both a stable currency and an increased inflow of foreign direct investment.

Further important reforms were introduced to the fiscal, monetary and social security regimes. Far stricter controls are now imposed on both local and central governments with regard to borrowing and possible monetization of deficits. Local governments must now balance their budgets. From the perspective of this chapter, monetary reforms have been important, especially in the wake of the Asian financial crisis. There is now an increased resolve on the part of the central bank to discipline financial institutions. We may note here that, before 1994, 70 per cent of the Central Bank's loans to SOEs were made by the central bank's local branches, which were heavily influenced by local governments. In 1993, the Central Bank centralized its operations, and since then the local branches have been only supervised by the Bank's headquarters. In 1998, the Central Bank further replaced its thirty provincial branches with nine cross-province regional branches. These reforms have reduced the influence of local government on monetary policies and on credit allocation decisions substantially.

As regards the enterprise system, the post-1992 reforms introduced some significant changes, which established the foundations of a modern company system. At the outset of this stage, enterprises were merged to take advantage of scale economies as well as to help mobilize resources. Most of the merger decisions were made by the government rather than at the level of the enterprises themselves. Some enterprises were incorporated, and some accessory services were spun off. Intra-enterprise contracts of various kinds have also been introduced widely. Since 1995 there has been large-scale privatization of small and medium SOEs, and of collectively-owned enterprises (COEs), as well as the beginnings of layoffs of state workers on a large scale, with some insolvent enterprises being allowed to go bankrupt. Larger companies were also floated on the stock market, and at the time of writing, in China's Shanghai and Shenzhen stock markets, there are more than 1000 listed companies. Debt conversion to equity is now beginning to be implemented for larger companies, and the monopoly in telecommunications has been dismantled. In order to wipe out the debt incurred by the historical and policy burdens of the large and strategically important SOEs, and in order to strengthen the discipline of both SOEs and state banks, four asset management companies have been established by the four state commercial banks. Those asset management companies take up SOEs' debt as shares in SOEs.

Ostensibly, therefore, the reforms since 1992 may have been expected to have impacts on enterprise performance via both product market and capital market effects. Our concern in this chapter is largely with the former, and with some measurable dimensions of the competitive process. We assess the respective roles played by entry, exit and incumbent firm growth in one sector of manufacturing in one province. Accordingly, the next section performs some relatively straightforward decompositions of output and productivity growth. The ensuing sections develop a more formal econometric model to investigate the question of whether the new regime has in fact sharpened the competitive selection process and facilitated the transfer of resources from weaker to stronger enterprises by means of a measurable impact on the hazard of exit faced by enterprises.

COMPETITIVE DYNAMICS IN THE ELECTRICAL ENGINEERING SECTOR

There are a number of ways to judge the effectiveness of the reform process, and to evaluate the role played by small firms. The most popular approach has been to compare total factor productivity (TFP) over time and across different kinds of firm.[2] A possible problem with this technique is the difficulty of comparing like with like. Given the tendency of the small-firm sector to enter market niches, it seems likely that the comparison may not be robust to the output deflators employed. Further, the approach represents something of a black box from a micro-dynamic perspective. Is TFP growth indicative of what is happening to incumbent firms, or the impact of entry and exit? As we shall see, this question is particularly important given the high rates of 'churning' of the small enterprises observed. An alternative approach is to consider explicitly the underlying processes, and to gauge the extent to which they have improved as a result of the latest phase of the reforms. Below we attempt to gain a picture of the effectiveness of the competitive process by examining measurable characteristics of the processes of entry, exit and growth, and how they have changed with reform.

The creation, survival and growth of the newly-established firms and the downsizing and exit of the traditionally large, dominant, state-owned firms are vital to the success of both the transition process itself and also to the long-term health of those economies. But while the role of the entry of newly-established firms has been a focus of attention for both academics and policy-makers (for example, Jackson *et al.*, 1999; Qian, 1999), the role of the exit of old and inefficient firms has largely been ignored. Arguably, the entry and exit of firms deserve equal emphasis, since these are two sides of what Schumpeter termed 'creative destruction' (Stiglitz, 1999). Moreover, the process of exit is likely to become much more important as the movement of surplus labour from the countryside to the towns slows down.

The dataset we use in this investigation covers almost the complete population of Chinese firms in the electrical engineering industry in Liaoning, a Northern China province, over the ten-year period from 1987 to 1996. This province used to be the centre of China's manufacturing industry, and is an area where the central planning system had perhaps been most deeply rooted. Of its fourteen cities, five are coastal; one of the latter – Dalian – was one of the earliest cities to have been opened up to the outside world. Arguably, therefore, the enterprise reforms in this province, especially the reform of the state-owned enterprises (SOEs), is representative of the enterprise reforms in China's manufacturing sector more generally. The electrical engineering industry is, moreover, a sector where traditionally the SOEs have dominated, but where currently the new entry of non-SOEs is relatively easy, so that our selection of this sector should be regarded as being to some extent representative of the current reform situation. This sector accounts for around 5 per cent of the province's gross industry output. The dataset is an unbalanced panel of 3992 firms – the number of different entities appearing at any stage over the whole period examined from 1987–96; there were 1092 in 1987, and 1638 in 1996 (see Appendix). First we consider some simple decompositions of output change by firm type and in terms of survivorship (that is, the sub-set of firms that existed both at the beginning and at the end of the period in question).

Figure 5.1a depicts how the various size classes contributed to output growth over the period 1987–96. Two sub-periods are considered, corresponding to the periods before and after the most recent set of reforms. It should be noted that the contribution of small enterprises, while still being considerable, in fact falls somewhat between the two sub-periods. Figure 5.1b examines the pattern of growth by ownership type. The main point to note is that that there was a big fall in the contribution of the SOEs. This is accounted for mainly by the sharp rise in the contribution of foreign-related ownership (including investment from Hong Kong, Macao and Taiwan) in the most recent sub-period. Figure 5.1c concentrates on the small firms themselves. Small-firm activity is concentrated mainly among the COEs, although foreign-firm participation and other types have latterly become much more significant.

Figure 5.2 shows the contribution to the growth of output of entry, exit and survival for the whole period, and for the two sub-periods. Figure 5.2a suggests that there was a big increase in the importance of 'churning' of enterprises between the two sub-periods, with both the positive contribution of entry and the negative contribution of exit increasing substantially. Indeed, in the sub-period since the reforms, the net impact of entry and exit is clearly more important than the growth of surviving firms. Figure 5.2b concentrates on the small-firm sector. It shows that a similar phenomenon was also occurring here, with big increases in the roles of both entry and exit.

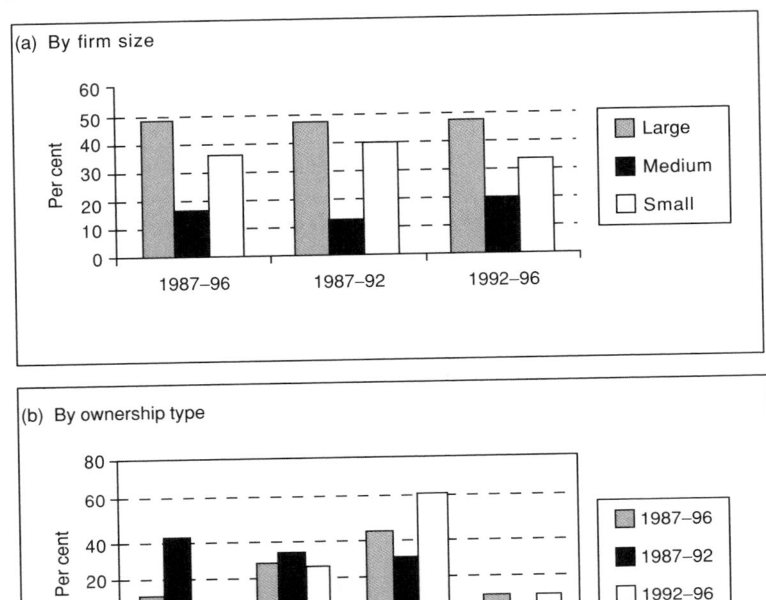

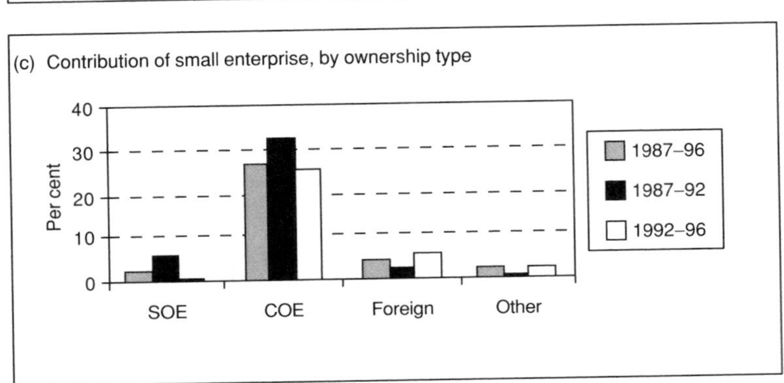

Figure 5.1 Contributions to output growth of Chinese firms, 1987–96

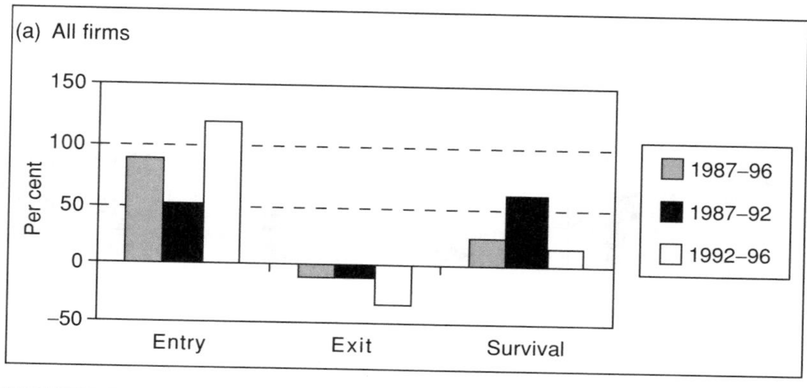

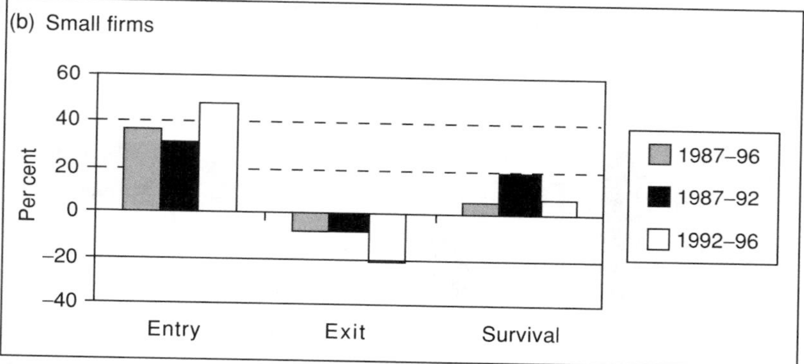

Figure 5.2 Contributions of entry, exit and survival to the output growth of Chinese firms, 1987–96

Superficially, the evidence from Figure 5.2 suggests a sharpening of the competitive process over the period under investigation. Establishing such a result, however, requires a more explicit assessment of both the hazard represented by exit and the competitiveness of new entrants. For this we need a performance measure. Here we focus on labour productivity. Ideally, we would want to examine total factor productivity. However, we expect that, within a specific sector, movements in labour productivity may provide a reasonable proxy for movements in total factor productivity. Figure 5.3a shows the contribution of entry, exit and survival to the sector's productivity growth. It suggests that all three (on average) made positive contributions to productivity growth over both sub-periods. However, the major impact is coming from the entrants, with only a limited part being played by survivors and exits.

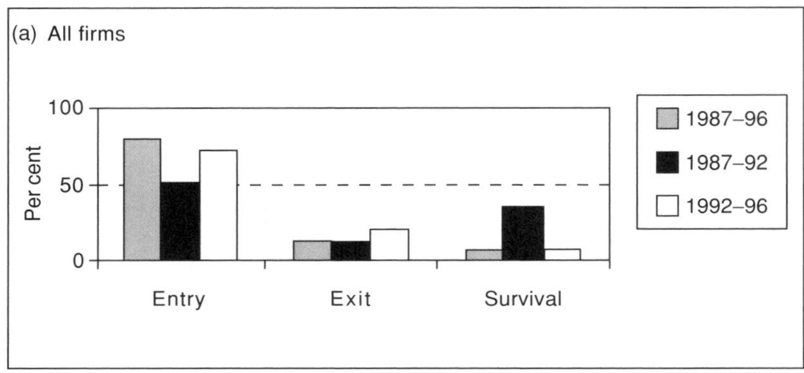

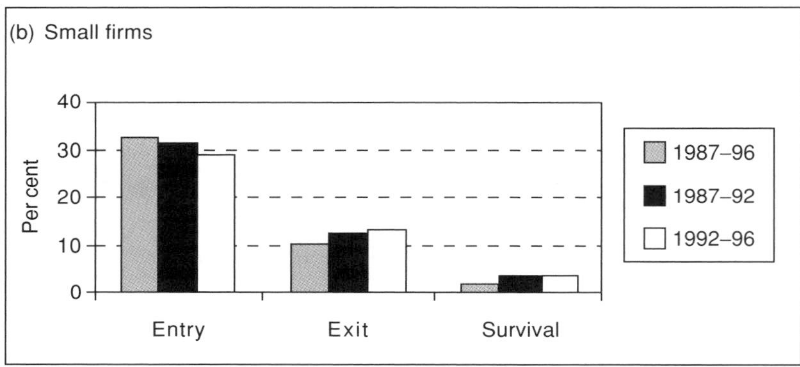

Figure 5.3 Contributions of entry, exit and survival to the productivity growth of Chinese firms, 1987–96

Exits do appear to have increased their role a little over the sub-periods, but there is clearly no large impact from the contributions of survivors. Looking solely at the contribution of small enterprises to overall productivity growth, Figure 5.3b suggests that survival is less important, while exit is considerably more important. We now turn explicitly to the determinants of exit behaviour.

THE EMPIRICAL ANALYSIS OF EXIT BEHAVIOUR

In this section we discuss and develop the empirical analysis of industrial exit. A number of studies – for example, Hart and Prais's (1956) pioneering work on the growth of British companies – have examined the dynamic aspects of firm behaviour in the context of advanced economies. We are, however, unaware of similar work for the transition economies, where the focus has tended to be on the role of new entries, or on the restructuring of large, state-owned enterprises.

In the context of economic growth at full employment, the exit of inefficient and value-destroying firms in transition economies may be an important element in reducing social waste and helping to mobilize resources more efficiently. In the Chinese context, this process may take on an added significance, with a gradual decline in the extent of under-employment in the countryside. In addition, of course, the exit process also provides a credible threat to the incumbent firms, which may then hasten their own restructuring. As the objectives of the transition are to eliminate the subsidies to the state sector and to reallocate the resources to their best use, the state-owned enterprises – which were built for the old central planning system and where inefficiency is allegedly pervasive – are less likely to survive the competition from newly-established firms. That the old state-owned enterprises are more likely to exit seems to be a logical assumption. However, we suspect that, in the Chinese case, the high economic and social costs associated with the closure of state-owned enterprises create strong barriers to exit. This prevents the more inefficient state-owned enterprises from closing down. We are particularly concerned with the question of whether barriers to exit have changed to any great extent as a result of the reforms taking place under the socialist market economy.

But exactly what kind of hazard is posed by exit? In China, there are many possible reasons for the disappearance of firms in our dataset. One is that the owner (either a government department in terms of the SOEs, the 'community' in terms of the COEs, or private individuals in the case of both foreign and domestic privately-owned enterprises) may decide to close down an under-performing enterprise. Another important cause is merger and acquisition. The bureaucratic overlord of the enterprises may decide to merge a poor performer with a successful one, with the aim of saving the former from bankruptcy. The merger may also happen voluntarily, without the interference of the government. A third reason is a change of ownership. This may take various forms: joint ventures where foreign capital dominates, firms being sold to the public, firms being sold to individuals, and firms being sold to employees and management. The final reason for exit is that a firm may change its main industry.

It is helpful at this stage to consider some existing work on economic models of industrial evolution, and the processes that generate entry, exit, productivity growth, and market share or factor use. In many of these models, each of the these dimensions of enterprise performance is depicted as the optimal behaviour of forward-looking entrepreneurs with rational expectations but limited information. For example, Hopenhayn (1992) considers a relatively straightforward model in which firms differ only in terms of their productivity levels, which evolve according to an exogenous Markov process. New firms enter when the distribution from which they draw their initial productivity level is sufficiently favourable for their expected future profit stream, net of annual fixed costs, to cover the sunk costs of entry. Firms exit when they experience a series of adverse productivity shocks, driving their expected future operating profits sufficiently low for exit to be their least costly option. This particular model shares a number of implications with other representations of industrial evolution developed by Jovanovic (1982) and Ericson and Pakes (1995). At any point in time, an entire distribution of firms with different sizes, ages and productivity levels coexist, and simultaneous entry and exit is the norm. Young firms have not yet survived a shakedown process, so they tend to be smaller and to exit more frequently. Large firms are the most efficient, on average, so their mark-ups are the largest. None the less, despite the heterogeneity, equilibrium in both the Jovanovic and Hopenhayn models maximizes the net discounted value of social surplus. Thus market interventions generally make matters worse and, in this sense, the competitive process is optimal.

Empirical studies of the processes of entry and exit for the developed economies tend to indicate that industry characteristics explain a large amount of the variation observed not only between industries, but also within industries over time. The variables associated with the observed differences across industries include sunk costs, absolute capital requirements, minimum efficient scale, and market concentration. Moreover, as Shapiro and Khemani (1987) showed in a study of 143 four-digit Canadian manufacturing industries over the period 1972–6, these variables tend to be associated with both barriers to entry and barriers to exit. A number of other studies have indeed confirmed the correlation between entries and exits.[3] The positive correlation between entry and exit flows, which appears to be especially marked among small firms, has been described as a revolving door at the bottom of the industry size distribution.

Other studies indicate that entry and exit rates tend to be influenced by both expected rates of return in the industry, and by its growth rate. Firm-specific effects have also been found to be important: for example, small firm size is generally thought to be important (Lieberman, 1990). Some of the important features of the firm pre-exit, and which have a significant effect on the closure decision, have not been considered in previous studies of firms' entry and exit. These factors include profitability, productivity, R&D activities, marketing strategies, financial leverage, the firm's governance structure and so on. Nickell (1995) suggests that firm heterogeneity arises from differences in prices and technology; the latter including both effort and organization as well as the use of innovation.

In addition to the effects generally found to be important in the advanced economies, it is clear that a number of additional factors need to be considered in the context of transitional economies in general, and the Chinese economy in particular. In our empirical work, we need to consider the following:

- *The ownership form.* The ownership form is likely to be an important determinant of exit in the Chinese context, though the relationship may be complex. While, for example, SOEs may be inefficient, the probability of their exit may be influenced by a consideration of the social costs and resistance associated with closure. Moreover, the differential fiscal and legal treatment of enterprises according to their ownership form (and for which we cannot adequately control) may also be important. Our data allows us to classify enterprises into six groups: SOEs, COEs, domestic privately-owned enterprises, shareholding companies, foreign-funded enterprises, and Taiwan, Hong Kong and Macao-funded enterprises. Because of the small numbers of domestic privately-owned enterprises and shareholding companies during the sample period, we in fact classified our sample into four groups: SOEs, COEs, foreign-funded enterprises (including the Taiwan, Hong Kong and Macao-funded enterprises), and other ownership forms. The SOEs were taken as the baseline ownership type, and dummy variables (COE, Foreign, Other) were used to identify the other three forms of ownership.
- *The age of the enterprise (Age).* Typically, those enterprises that have survived the longest have established themselves in the market, may be better able to survive an adverse shock of given size (for example, through 'goodwill' and established links to suppliers or to the capital market). However, in the context of transition economies, the effect may be strengthened, since established firms frequently are those where the traditional planning mechanisms and vested interests are rooted most deeply.

- *Enterprise size*. In this study, we use the logarithm of the physical size of an enterprise to capture the possible advantages of large firms over small firms with regard to scale economies, as well as advantages relating to capacity for investment in R&D and marketing. The inclusion of this variable will also control for differential effects of government policies with regard to enterprises of different sizes. We expect to see a negative effect on a firm's probability of exit. We include measures based on both capital stock (*lncap*) and employment (*lnemp*). It should be noted that size variables may also capture the characteristics of sunk costs of firms in an imperfect market environment, especially in transition economies where capital markets are underdeveloped. An additional control for sunk costs is a measure of capital intensity (*Capinte*). This may also be important for another reason. In the 1980s, electrical engineering was targeted by the government in ways that may well have encouraged entry by enterprises with less than optimal capital intensity.
- *Enterprise performance*. In a market economy, this is the key to the competitive selection process, with poor performance punished by exit. In the context of transition economies, however, the relationship may not be so straightforward, as efficient firms may be 'punished' by higher taxation, and inefficient firms may be 'encouraged' by state subsidies. As suggested by the literature, we include measures of both profitability and productivity. It is important to include productivity (*Prod*) as well as profitability (*Prof*), as the latter may have ambiguous effects – high profitability firms may also be prone to exit through acquisition.
- *The expected industrial profit rate*. As a measure of the level of the returns within a sector, we use the one-year lagged national profit to fixed capital ratio (*Exprofit*) as an indicator of the expected profit rate. A higher expected profit rate of an industry will tend to attract more firms to enter the industry, which will increase competition in the market, and may tend to increase the closure probability.
- *The extent to which a firm orients its behaviour towards the market*. We measure the extent an enterprise produces for the market by the ratio of the firm's market sales revenue to its gross output value (*Salerate*). If a firm adopts a more market-orientated strategy, this ratio should be higher. The more a firm adopts a market-orientated strategy, the more likely it is to survive in the market, therefore the lower the closure probability. Therefore, we expect a negative effect of market-orientated behaviour on the firm's closure probability.

- In order to allow for differences in the market environment, we also include indicators of *the degree of market competition* and *the extent of financial constraints*. We use the proportion of output produced by the four largest firms (*Conc*, *Conc2*) as an indicator of the degree of market competition, and use the ratio of interest to fixed capital for individual firms (*Inrate*) as an indicator of the degree of financial constraints faced by those firms. In a more concentrated market, the existence of monopoly power makes smaller firms more prone to failure. The hardening of the financial constraints eliminates or decreases the support to under-performing firms, therefore it will increase the closure probability of firms.
- *Other controls*. We also include some other variables to reflect possible regional or governmental influences. *CEPR* indicates an enterprise controlled by central or government influences; *CITY* and *County* indicate city or county government-controlled enterprises, respectively. In addition, we use *Ratio* (the share of electrical engineering in total manufacturing) and *Growth* to capture industry and market environment factors.
- Finally, we use a dummy variable (*P92*) to incorporate the impact of the post-1992 reforms.

Table 5.1 provides a full listing of the variables used in the empirical analysis.

A HAZARD RATE MODEL OF EXIT BEHAVIOUR

This section reports the results from experiments on the impact of reform on the exit hazard faced by the firm. The approach adopted in this chapter models exit as a hazard rate: that is, as the conditional probability that an enterprise exits in a small interval of time, given that it has not already exited at time t. The hazard rate, $\lambda(t)$, is related to the more familiar survival probability, $S(t)$, in the following manner:

$$S(t) = 1 - F(t) = \text{Prob}(T \geq t),$$

where $F(t)$ is the cumulative density function that an individual firm will have exited;
Prob $(T \geq t)$ = the probability that the survival of an individual firm is of length at least t; and

Table 5.1 The hazard model covariates

Variables	Definition
Firm-level factors	
COE	Collective-owned enterprises, dummy variable
Foreign	Foreign-funded enterprises (joint ventures and privately-owned)
Other	Firms other than *SOE*s, *COE*s and *Foreign*
CEPR	Central- or provincial-government-controlled enterprises
CITY	City-government-controlled enterprises
County	County-government-controlled enterprises
Age	Years since establishment
Prof	The ratio of profits to sales revenue
Prof 92	The interaction of *Prof* and *P92*
Prod	Productivity, defined as the ratio of output to employment
Lncap	Logarithm of firm's fixed capital
Lnemp	Logarithm of the number of employees
Prate	The ratio of productive fixed capital to total fixed capital
Inrate	The ratio of interest payment to fixed capital
Capinte	Capital intensity, defined as the ratio of capital to employment
Capint92	The interaction of capital intensity and *P92*
Salerate	The ratio of sales revenue to gross output value
Industry-level factors	
Exprofit	One year lagged industry profit rate
Ratio	Share of the electrical engineering industry to manufacturing industry
Conc	Regional concentration ratio, defined as the output ratio of the four largest enterprises in the region in electrical engineering
Conc2	The square of the concentration ratio
Market environment	
Growth	The growth rate of overall Chinese GDP
P92	Dummy variable (*P92* = 1 if year > 1992; *P92* = 0 if year ≤ 1992)

$$\lambda(t) = f(t)/S(t),$$

where $f(t)$ is the probability density function.

Estimation proceeds on the assumption of proportionality: that is, that the impact of the specific exogenous factors of interest (covariates) on the hazard rate acts as a constant multiple of the so-called 'baseline hazard' (Cox, 1972):

$$\lambda(t) = \lambda_0(t) \exp\{\mathbf{X}'\beta\},$$

where $\lambda_0(t)$ is the baseline hazard;
$\mathbf{X}$ is a vector of co-variates; and
β is the vector of coefficients to be estimated.

Given the above assumption, estimation may follow a variety of paths, depending on the degree to which a functional form is imposed. A common approach is to use semi-parametric estimation based on Cox (1972); this imposes no functional form for the hazard function, and the results of this estimation method are presented here. However, we experimented with a variety of functional forms, and differences were not found to be significant. This finding is in keeping with other econometric studies of hazard rates (for example, Karshenas and Stoneman, 1993).

Our approach to analyzing the specific impact of the latest batch of reforms on the competitive process was to consider the reform as a specific covariate. The dummy variable (P92 $= 1$ if $t > 1992$) thus represents the impact on the hazard rate facing all enterprises in the sample. However, our experiments also allowed for the reforms to impact differentially according to ownership type, firm size, measures of profitability, and capital intensity. Here we may note that pre-1992 policies may have encouraged excessive entry by enterprises with inefficiently low capital intensity. We estimated this possibility first by introducing interaction terms combining these variables with the reform dummy. Second, we allowed for entirely different hazard functions by estimating different equations by ownership type and for small firms. Separate estimations for larger firm sizes were precluded by the numbers of observations. The results are presented in Table 5.2.

Column (1) provides a benchmark, without any interaction terms. It can be seen that a number of the covariates have significant and correctly signed influences on the hazard rate. The SOE is the baseline ownership type. In comparison, collective and other forms of ownership demonstrate significant positive impacts on the hazard rate. By way of example, the hazard rate facing a COE was nearly 19 per cent above that for an SOE. We also find that the regional concentration ratios exert a positive influence. Negative impacts come from foreign ownership, the age of the enterprise, both its productivity and profitability levels, and employment as a measure of size. The proxies for liquidity and gearing do not appear to be significant. More importantly in the current context is that the coefficient on the impact of the reforms (variable P92), while correctly signed, is not particularly large

Table 5.2 Estimated hazard functions for enterprises in Liaoning Province, 1987–96

Covariate	All enterprises	All enterprises	SOEs	COEs	Small enterprises
	(1)	(2)	(3)	(4)	(5)
COE	0.17499*	0.19116**			0.2221*
Foreign	–0.26227	–0.25112			–0.1927
Other	0.27180	0.21820			0.2794
CEPR	–0.05078	–0.07960	–0.58733	–0.16163	–0.0916
CITY	0.07020	0.08348	–0.6041**	0.19113**	0.0926
County	0.00110	0.00758	–0.6249**	0.03259	0.0146
Age	–0.01691***	–0.01642***	0.00583	–0.02025***	–0.0161***
Prof	–0.00014**	–0.00043***	–0.0067	–0.00041***	–0.0004***
Prof 92		0.00033**	0.00584	0.00031**	0.0003**
Prod	–0.02799*	–0.03005**	–0.15484	–0.03006*	–0.0298*
lncap	–0.07036***	–0.07590***	–0.1467**	–0.06554***	–0.7767***
lnemp	–0.12968***	–0.12073***	–0.0677	–0.12987***	–0.1186***
Prate	–0.00023	–0.00014	–0.0014	–0.00014	–0.0001
Inrate	0.02581	0.02586	–0.0286	0.03306	0.0256
Capinte	0.00023	0.01020***	0.0111*	0.13767***	0.0106***
Capint92		–0.00987***	–0.00743	–0.01319***	–0.0103***
Salerate	–9.13 E-7	–2.51 E-6	–0.00106	–8.37 E-7	–2.46 E-6
Exprofit	–0.18007***	–0.09632***	–0.25915***	–0.09078***	–0.0967***
Ratio	–3.36824***	–2.25727***	–4.3055**	–2.30560***	–2.2868***
Conc	0.42781***	2.47304***	0.54813***	2.47756***	2.4848***
Conc2		–0.03801***		–0.03822***	–0.0382***
Growth	0.10107***	0.05283***	0.16507***	0.04927***	0.0530***
P92	0.03459	0.58769***	0.24662	0.59242***	0.5792***
Number of observations[1]	13304	13304	1529	11349	12688
Log-likelihood	–14552.5	–14489.4	–612.1	–12857.1	–14293.7

Notes: ***indicates significant at 1% level; **indicates significant at 5% level; *indicates significant at 10% level

1. This is an unbalanced panel, with the number of observations equal to the number of firms separately identified times the number of arrival observations available for each.

(effectively increasing the baseline hazard by only about 3 per cent), and is statistically insignificant.

Column (2) introduces the interaction terms indicated by Prof92. The additions are not only significant, but also sharpen the estimates significantly. The following points should be noted. Most importantly, the coefficient of P92 is now both positive and highly significant. While profitability now exerts a larger negative impact on the probability of exit, the interactive term is both significant and *positive*. We believe that this may reflect a higher propensity under the new regime for the more profitable firms to exit through acquisition. We also now observe that capital intensity effects exist only prior to 1992.

Column (3) examines the SOEs only. While there is a positive coefficient on the reform dummy (P92), this is statistically insignificant at conventional levels. Furthermore, it may be observed that neither productivity nor profitability appear to be significant, either pre- or post-reform. Performance therefore does not appear to matter.

Column (4) offers a contrast by considering only COEs. Here we obtain results that are much more consistent with a competitive selection process. Unlike the SOEs, productivity and profitability are important influences on exit rates, as is the new regime itself for all COEs, as indicated by the large positive and highly significant coefficient on P92. This pattern is largely replicated in column (5) for small firms; this is not surprising, since the samples are largely coextensive.

Our results therefore largely confirm the discussion and the evidence presented in the section on the competitive dynamics in the electrical engineering sector. The reforms have increased considerably rates of churning in this key sector of manufacturing, a process which affects small firms and COEs in particular. On the other hand, we find little evidence that the reforms have had an impact on the SOEs, and that in neither sub-period do conventional indicators of enterprise performance appear to have much influence on the probability of exit.

CONCLUSIONS

In this chapter, we have examined aspects of the competitive selection process in an important sector of Chinese manufacturing, looking in particular for changes resulting from the latest stage of reforms, namely the transition to the 'socialist market economy'. We have argued that these dynamic processes are likely to be increasingly important, for two main reasons. First, as the agricultural sector as a source of surplus labour begins to decline, the release of resources for the continuing growth of manufacturing may have to come increasingly from the exit of relatively inefficient enterprise. Second, the peculiarities of the reform process in China place additional emphasis on the role of competition (and probably from small firms in particular) as a substitute for more traditional forms of corporate governance.

Our analysis suggests that for small firms and COEs, the competitive selection process operates much as we would expect in a private market economy. The study also suggests that it is insufficient to analyze the competitive process from the point of view of new firm entry and incumbent firm growth alone. Indeed, the substantial rate of churning of enterprises that we observe in this sector means that a study of exit is just as important as that of entry. Moreover, this rate of churning appears to have increased substantially in the latest phase of reform. Our estimation of a hazard model for exit probabilities suggests that exits do contribute to efficiency within the small firm/COE sector, since performance indicators serve as useful predictors of rates of industrial exit. However, we do not find evidence that profits or productivity are any better predictors of exit as a result of the latest reforms.

On the other hand, our analysis suggests an entirely different role for SOEs. The conventional enterprise performance indicators are not good predictors of their demise, and we can find no evidence that things have changed since 1992. While their role in the economy is declining as other sectors have established faster growth rates, their continuing privileged status does not yet appear to have come under serious threat. Consequently, we do not as yet find convincing evidence that competitive selection is in fact providing a sufficiently important substitute for corporate governance mechanisms based on ownership. This may represent a considerable challenge for the future.

Appendix: The Size Composition of the Sample of Firms

Table 5A.1 The Size Composition of the Sample of Firms

	1987	**1992**	**1996**	
Large	17	24	32	The original value of productive fixed capital >40 million yuan RMB
Medium	23	41	51	The original value of productive fixed capital is between 10 million and 40 million yuan RMB
Small	1052	1353	1555	The original value of productive fixed capital is less than 10 million yuan RMB
Total	1092	1418	1638	

Notes

1. The authors are grateful for comments received from the participants at the conference on 'Small-scale Enterprises in Developing and Transitional Economies' held at King's College London, September 2000. We are also grateful to the editors for encouraging this study. All errors remain our own.
2. For a recent review in the case of small firms see Wang and Yao (1999).
3. See, for example, Dunne *et al.* (1988) for US manufacturing industries, Schwalbach (1991) on German manufacturing industries, Geroski (1991) on British firms, and Baldwin and Gorecki (1989) on Canadian industries.

References

Baldwin, J. R. and Gorecki, P. K. (1989) 'Firm Entry and Exit in the Canadian Manufacturing Sector', *Statistics Canada, Research Paper Series 23* (Fall).

Cao, Y. Z., Fan, G. and Woo, W. T. (1997) 'Chinese Economic Reforms: Past Successes and Future Challenges', in W. T. Woo and S. Parker (eds), *Economies in Transition: Comparing Asia and Europe*, Cambridge, Mass.: MIT Press, pp. 19–39.

Cox, D. (1972) 'Regression Models and Life Tables', *Journal of the Royal Statistical Society, Series B*, vol. 34, pp. 187–220.

Dunne, T., Roberts, M. J. and Samuelson, L. (1988) 'Patterns of Firm Entry and Exit in U.S. Manufacturing Industries', *Rand Journal of Economics*, vol. 19, no. 4, pp. 495–515.

Ericson, R. and Pakes, A. (1995) 'Markov Perfect Industry Dynamics: A Framework for Empirical Work', *Review of Economic Studies*, vol. 62, pp. 53–82.

Geroski, P. A. (1991) 'Domestic and Foreign Entry in the UK: 1983–84', in P. Geroski and J. Schwalbach (eds), *Entry and Market Contestability: An International Comparison*, Oxford: Basil Blackwell, pp. 63–88.

Hart, P. E. and Prais, S. J. (1956) 'The Analysis of Business Concentration: A Statistical Approach', *Journal of the Royal Statistical Society*, vol. 119, no. 2 pp. 150–91.

Hopenhayn, H. (1992) 'Entry, Exit and Firm Dynamics in Long-Run Equilibrium', *Econometrica*, vol. 60 pp. 1127–50.

Jackson, J., Klich, J. and Poznanska, K. (1999) 'Firm Creation and Economic Transitions', *Journal of Business Venturing*, vol. 14, no. 5 (September), pp. 427–50.

Jovanovic, B. (1982) 'Selection and Evolution of Industry', *Econometrica*, vol. 50, pp. 649–70.

Karshenas, M. and Stoneman, P. L. (1993) 'Rank, Stock, Order, and Epidemic Effects in the Diffusion of New Process Technologies: An Empirical Model', *Rand Journal of Economics*, vol. 24, no. 4 (Winter), pp. 503–28.

Lickerman, M. B. (1990) 'Exit from Declining Industries: "Share-out" or "Stake-out"?', *Rand Journal of Economics*, vol. 21, no. 4, pp. 538–54.

Morris, D. (1996) 'The Reform of State-owned Enterprises in China: The Art of the Possible', *Oxford Review of Economic Policy*, vol. 11, no. 4 pp. 54–69.

Nickell, S. (1995) *The Performance of Companies: The Relationship between the External Environment, Management Strategies and Corporate Performance*, Oxford and Cambridge, Mass.: Basil Blackwell.

Qian, Y. (1999) 'The Institutional Foundations of China's Market Transition', Paper presented at the Annual World Bank Conference on Development Economics, Washington DC.

Schwalbach, J. (1991) 'Entry, Concentration, and Market Contestability', in P. Geroski and J. Schwalbach (eds), *Entry and Market Contestability: An International Comparison*, Oxford: Basil Blackwell, pp. 121–42.

Shapiro, D. and Khemani, R. S. (1987) 'The Determinants of Entry and Exit Reconsidered', *International Journal of Industry Organisation*, vol. 5, no. 1, pp. 15–26.

Stiglitz, J. E. (1999) 'Whither Reform? Ten Years of the Transition', Paper presented at the Annual World Bank Conference on Development Economics, Washington DC.

Wang, Y. and Yao, Y. (1999) 'Technological Capacities and Development of China's Small Enterprises', Beijing University, China Center for Economic Research, Working Paper No. E1999 003, Beijing: Beijing University.

6 Economic Liberalization and Growth of Small-Scale Enterprises: The Indian Experience

Homi Katrak

INTRODUCTION

Many developing countries are interested in promoting their small-scale enterprises (SSEs). These enterprises are considered to be important as they may (i) be the 'seed bed' for economic growth; (ii) have great scope for generating employment; and (iii) help the geographic dispersion of industry.

The policy instruments used to support the SSEs have differed somewhat from one country to another. In many countries, however, the instruments include concessions on finance, subsidies for the purchase for certain inputs, advice on technological upgrading and marketing, and exemption from certain taxes. An important question that continues to be debated is whether these measures to help the SSEs have been complemented, or offset, by the countries' recent economic liberalization programmes. Under these programmes, earlier inward-looking and regulatory policies, including tariffs on (and other barriers to) competing imports, restrictions on the imports of technology and licensing of industrial capacity, are being replaced by more outward-looking and market-orientated policies. Had the earlier policies disadvantaged the SSEs, and have the economic reforms helped those enterprises?

Some writers, including UNDP (1998), Ahmad (1993), and Rodriguez and Tescon (1998) have argued that the earlier import barriers had mainly helped the large enterprises (LEs). Those enterprises, being better able to lobby for government favours, had obtained relatively higher protection for the product groups (and industries) in which they predominated[1] and, within particular product groups, had higher protection for the types of item that they made. Consequently, resources had been diverted towards the LEs. Trade liberalization may thus be expected to redress this bias against the SSEs.

Other writers, however, have taken a different perspective. Parker *et al.* (1995) found that, in five African countries, economic reforms have had both positive and negative effects on SSEs; liberalization brought easier access to material inputs but also greater competition from imports of final products. Sandesara (1991) has argued that a distinction should be made between the SSEs that have to compete with the larger enterprises and those that do not; if liberalization helps the LEs, the competing SSEs may be affected adversely, but the others may either benefit or not be affected[2].

Indian governments have, for over four decades, implemented wide-ranging policies to promote SSEs. In addition to the support measures adopted in various countries mentioned above, Indian SSEs are exempt from certain regulations concerning employment and layoff, and receive a price preference on government procurement. A further policy is the 'reservation' of some items for the SSEs only; the LEs may not make those items, unless they export 75 per cent of their output.

The effect of these policies on the SSEs' performance has, however, not been very impressive. Aggregate data, reported by the Confederation of Indian Industries (1998), show that between 1989–90 and 1996–7 the SSEs' share in total industrial production decreased from 57.4 to 51.5 per cent, though their share in exports increased from 27.6 to 34 per cent. These aggregate figures may perhaps be indicating that the SSEs are mainly concentrated in the industries that have had lower growth of domestic demand but higher growth of export demand.

More detailed analyses have shown up problems regarding the SSEs' use of inputs and their outputs. The main concerns about the inputs are as follows. Bhalla (1992) observed that the SSEs' size cannot allow a division of labour among employees. Seth (1995) noted that small enterprises sometimes employ low-cost casual labour that lacks experience, and Ramaswamy (1994) estimated that the SSEs' low-cost labour advantage is more than offset by their lower productivity. Bala Subrahmanya (1998) reported that SSEs have paid little attention to technological upgrading. As regards the SSEs' outputs, Little *et al.* (1987), Kashyap (1988) and Morris *et al.* (1997) have pointed out that the SSEs' products are of lower quality than those of the LEs, while Katrak (1999) found that the establishments making reserved items have relatively higher unused capacities.

This chapter focuses on Indian SSEs that compete with the LEs. The aim is to examine how the 1991 economic liberalization affected those

SSEs' growth and market shares. Our interest covers two topics. First, have the economic reforms helped the SSEs to increase their growth of output? Second, has the competing impact of the LEs on the SSEs' growth been dampened, or intensified, since the liberalization? The results of the analyses may be of interest for the government's reservation policy.

The structure of the chapter is as follows. The second section presents theoretical models which may be used to make predictions about the effects of liberalization on the small enterprises' growth of output. The third section contains a discussion of the empirical procedures to test those predictions. The data to be used in the tests are then described and, in the penultimate section, the results are reported. The final section summarizes the main findings and considers some implications.

SOME THEORETICAL ARGUMENTS

To begin with it will be helpful to use the Dominant Firm (DF) model, from the Industrial Economics literature,[3] to examine how India's economic liberalization policies may have affected the SSEs' production and market shares. The model can allow for some major aspects of the economic reforms: (i) the decrease in the barriers to competing imports, and (ii) the relaxation of the industrial licensing policy as well as of the restrictions on the imports of technology.

The DF model envisages competition between a large number of SSEs and one (or a few) LEs. For simplicity, let us assume that there are two large enterprises. Initially, we also make two further assumptions. First, the LEs have agreed, at least implicitly, to collaborate and maximize their joint profits. Second, all the enterprises make a homogeneous product. However, the product is differentiated vertically from the competing imports; the latter are relatively high quality/price items[4].

Figure 6.1 illustrates the effects of trade liberalization. The schedules are drawn linearly for convenience only. S^*S is the supply curve of the SSEs, and L^*L is the marginal cost curve of the large enterprises. D_1d_1 is the demand curve facing the domestic industry in the period before trade liberalization. The LEs then face the 'residual' average revenue curve $A_1T_1 = (D_1d_1 - S^*S)$; the corresponding marginal curve is M_1E_1, extended to A_1. The market equilibrium is as follows: the LEs' profit-maximizing output is J_1P_1 leading to price OP_1, and so the SSEs, being price takers, produce P_1Q_1; the aggregate output J_1Q_1 clears the market.

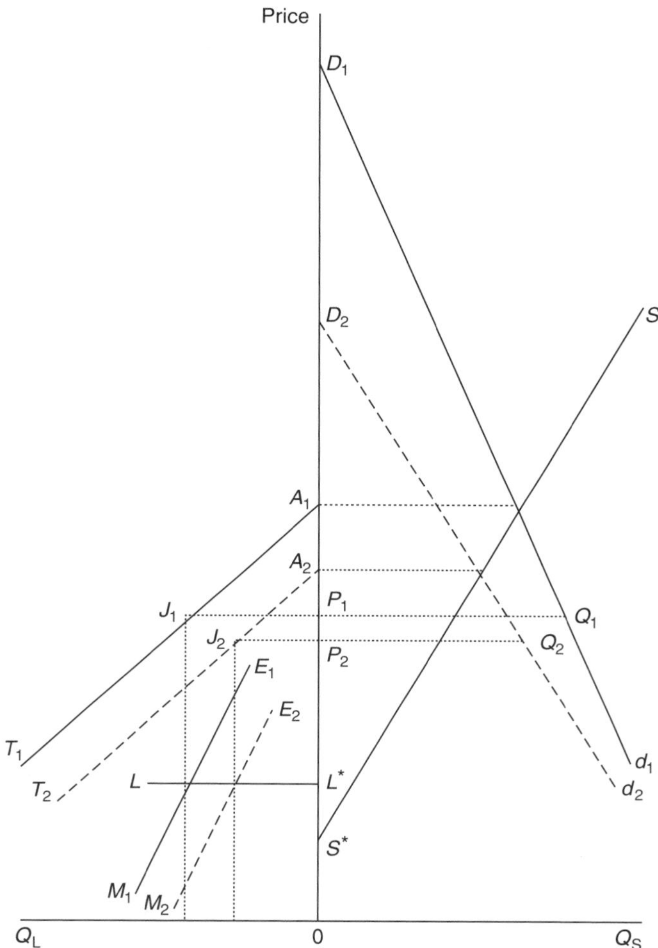

Figure 6.1 The effects of trade liberalization on the outputs of small-scale enterprises and large enterprises

Import liberalization will affect both the LEs and the SSEs adversely. The liberalization will shift the industry demand curve downwards, also the LEs' average revenue curve. Their new locations are D_2d_2 and A_2T_2 respectively. Consequently, the LEs' output will decline to J_2P_2, the price will fall to OP_2, and so the SSEs production will also be reduced, to P_2Q_2. The DF model thus suggests that import liberalization may not benefit the SSEs.

The LEs' and SSEs' products may not be identical and homogenous. In fact, as mentioned above, the former's products tend to have a higher quality/price. The LEs' products may thus be closer substitutes for the competing imports. Import liberalization may thus have a greater (negative) impact on the LEs. However, this need not benefit the SSEs. The overall effect on the SSEs may depend on the responses of the larger enterprises. One possibility is that the increase in import competition may cause the LEs to abandon their earlier agreement on joint profit maximization. Each of these enterprises may decide to increase their own output.[5] That, in turn, would cause a decrease in the price of the SSEs' product, and hence lead to a decrease in their level of output.

The likelihood that the LEs will increase their output is also suggested by two other elements of the policy reforms. Liberalization of the industrial licensing regime and of the imports of technology are both likely to favour the LEs. The earlier licensing regime had restricted in particular the LEs' capacities and production; in terms of Figure 6.1, the output of those enterprises' would have been kept below the profit-maximizing level, J_1P_1. Delicensing would allow the LEs to expand output. As regards the imports of technology, as Katrak (1997) has observed, the larger enterprises are better able to search for a suitable foreign technology and, moreover, the foreign suppliers prefer to deal with licensees that can generate a large volume of output. Liberalization of those imports is thus more likely to benefit the LEs.

Some other recent policy changes may also have helped the LEs. First, the export obligation required of the LEs that make reserved products has been reduced from 75 per cent to 50 per cent. Consequently, the number of LEs making these items will increase. Secondly, Rekhi (1995) has reported that the duties on imports of capital goods discriminate against low-value equipment; the duty on items whose c.i.f. value exceeds Rs 20 crore (£ 3 million) has been eliminated, but lower valued items still face a duty of 15 per cent. Third, Srinivasulu (1997) reports that changes in the excise duties on cigarettes have affected the small-scale producers of Beedis adversely; the decrease in the duty on mini-cigarettes (less than 60 mm in length) has led some LEs to start producing those items, thereby increasing competition for the Beedis.

A final point is that, since the liberalization, the LEs may have moved increasingly towards higher quality/price products. This may have been helped by the delicensing policy, and by the liberalization of the imports of technology and may, perhaps, have been given an impetus by competition from imported products. Consequently, the LEs may have been engaging increasingly in competition among themselves and/or with the imported products, rather than with the SSEs. That, in turn, will have dampened the (negative) impact of the LEs' competition on the SSEs; the former may have begun to have a less adverse effect on the latter. In this case, liberalization may, at least indirectly, have helped the SSEs.

In view of all the arguments discussed in this section, it seems that the net effect of economic liberalization on the SSEs' growth of output cannot readily be predicted on a priori grounds. It is therefore best to approach the empirical analysis in an agnostic manner.

THE PROCEDURES FOR THE EMPIRICAL TESTS

The empirical tests will focus on competing products made by the SSEs and the LEs. There are two main questions of interest. First, has the SSEs' output (or growth of output) increased since the 1991 liberalization? And second, has their output (or growth) been affected adversely by the LEs?

Figure 6.2 illustrates how the competing outputs of the SSEs and LEs may be affected by liberalization. The vertical axis measures the quantities produced by the SSEs. The schedule S_1A_1 shows that their production is affected negatively by competition from the LEs. The horizontal axis and the schedule L_1B_1 pertain to the LEs. The locations of the intercepts and the slopes of the schedules reflect the intensity of competition facing the two types of enterprise. Equilibrium will be at E_1, with the SSEs producing E_1J_1 and their output share shown by the slope of OE_1.

Liberalization may affect the SSEs' output in two ways. First, a 'direct' effect because of the policy changes that affect only the SSEs and cause a shift in their schedule. Second, there will be a 'rival' effect, due to policies that shift the LEs' schedule[6]. Suppose that the diverse aspects of liberalization lead to an outward shift of both the schedules. Let the new locations be S_2A_2 and L_2A_2 respectively. The direct effect on the SSEs' output is the increase from E_1 to E_2, while the rival effect causes the decrease from E_2 to E_3. The 'net' effect is thus the change from E_1 to E_3.

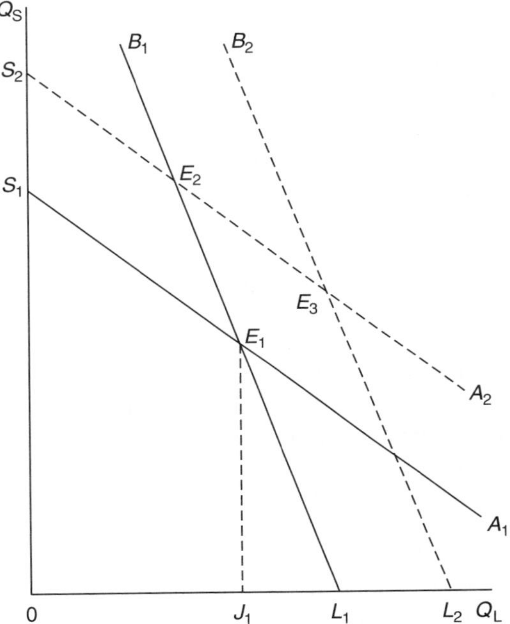

Figure 6.2 The effects of trade liberalization on the relative outputs of small-scale enterprises and large enterprises

In view of the competition between the SSEs and LEs, it is important to separate out the rival effect. One possibility would be to employ a simultaneous equation model. Unfortunately, the data on the additional variables that would be required for that approach are not available. The alternative procedure used here takes account of data availability. The data pertains to the output of fifteen products shown separately for the two types of enterprise. Details of the data are in the next section. The tests will pool the data for the years before and since liberalization to give thirty observations. We test whether the SSEs' growth rate of output during the years since the 1991 liberalization has been greater (or less) than in the years before the policy change.

The growth of output will be measured over the period 1987–8 to 1991–2 before liberalization, and 1992–3 to 1996–7 subsequent to the policy change.[7] The measure of the SSEs' growth, taken from Evans (1987), is:

$$G_S = [\log(Q_{SE}) - \log(Q_{SB})],$$

where Q_S is the quantity produced, and the subscripts E and B are for the end and beginning years of each 5-year period.
The LEs' growth, denoted by G_L, will be measured similarly.

We first examine the effect of liberalization on the SSEs' growth, without reference to the LEs. The regression equation will be:

$$G_S = a_1 + b_1 R_S + c_1 DVT + \varepsilon_1, \tag{6.1a}$$

where G_S is the SSEs' growth of output;
R_S is the 'relative output' at the beginning of each 5-year period, defined as (Q_{SB}/Q_{LB});
DVT is a time dummy variable with values of zero and unity, respectively, for the years before and since liberalization; and
ε_1 is a random disturbance term.

R_S is included to capture some changes that might have occurred even in the absence of liberalization. With the growth of incomes, some consumers may switch from the SSEs' products to the higher quality/price items of the LEs' (and/or to competing imports). The SSEs' growth will be lower than in the absence of the switch in demand. Now the greater the SSEs' relative output at the start of a 5-year period, the greater the scope for such a switch and hence the lower will be the SSEs' growth.[8] So we expect that the coefficient of R_S will have a negative sign.

Equation (6.1a) may be expanded to include the growth of the LEs:

$$G_S = a_2 + b_2 R_S + c_2 DVT + d_2 G_L + \varepsilon_2. \tag{6.1b}$$

We expect that if the LEs exert a rival effect, the coefficient of G_L will be negatively signed. And if the coefficient of DVT is not significant it will mean that, even when the LEs are taken into account, liberalization has had no impact on the SSEs' growth.

An alternative regression to isolate the presence of the LEs is:

$$UG_S = a_3 + b_3 R_S + c_3 DVT + \varepsilon_3, \tag{6.1c}$$

where UG_S is defined as that component of the SSEs' growth that is not related to the LEs. It is obtained as the unexplained residual of a regression in which the dependent and explanatory variables are the growth of the SSEs and the LEs respectively.[9]

In terms of Figure 6.2, UG_S corresponds to the movement from E_1 to E_2 only; this movement is unrelated to any shift of the LEs' schedule. The coefficient of DVT in the regression in Equation (6.1c) should thus reflect only the direct effect of liberalization.

It should be noted that, in the above equations, DVT is being employed to test for an intercept shift; that is, to examine whether liberalization has had some effect on the SSEs' growth independently of the other variables. Suppose now that these tests find that DVT is not significant; that is, there has been no intercept shift. We would then proceed to a second set of tests, and examine whether liberalization may have had an interdependent effect. In other words, could liberalization have had some impact on the SSEs' growth such that the effect has depended on one of the other explanatory variables?

There are two possible interdependencies. One possibility is that the impact of liberalization on the SSEs' growth may be dependent on their relative output. If the earlier policy regime had constrained the SSEs' relative output of certain products, we should find that liberalization would lead to comparatively higher growth in those products. This argument will be examined with the following regression:

$$G_S = a_{21} + b_{21}LR_S + c_{21}DLR_S + \varepsilon_4, \tag{6.2a}$$

where $DLR_S = (DVT^* LR_S)$.

The effect of liberalization will be indicated by the sign of c_{21}. For instance, if c_{21} turns out to be negatively signed, it would mean that the negative influence of R_S on the SSEs' growth has been intensified since liberalization, particularly in those products where initially there was a low rate of growth.[10] The second possibility is that the effect of liberalization on the SSEs depends on the growth of the competing LEs. This possibility will be examined by employing the product term $DG_L = (DVT^* G_L)$ in the following regression:

$$G_S = a_{22} + b_{22}LR_S + c_{22}G_L + d_{22}DG_L + \varepsilon_5. \tag{6.2b}$$

If the coefficient d_{22} turns out to be positively signed, it would indicate that the negative impact of the LEs has diminished since liberalization, particularly in the products where the SSEs initially had a low rate of growth.[11]

THE DATA

The major source of data on India's SSEs is the Census of Registered Small-Scale Industrial Units (or establishments). These are undertaken by the Development Commissioner – Small-Scale Industries (DCSSI), under the purview of the Small Industries Development Organization (SIDO). However, these data are not very helpful for our tests. The latest available data are for 1987–8, and are thus prior to the 1991 liberalization. Moreover the data are only provided for twenty broad-based manufacturing 'industries', and so are not sufficiently detailed for a study of competing SSEs and LEs.

An alternative dataset for the SSEs, also collected by the DCSSI, covers eighteen product groups, defined at the four-digit level of the Indian Standard Industrial Classification. The eighteen products are of importance for small-scale producers. These data were obtained from a sample of 4800 establishments located in geographic centres of importance for the particular products. Comparable data for the LEs were collected by the Directorate General of Technical Development (DGTD) upto 1995, and since then are from the Department of Industrial Policy and Promotion. Both datasets are shown in EPW Research Foundation (1998), for all years from 1987–8 to 1996–7. A more detailed discussion of the data is in Pradhan and Saluja (1998).

Three features of the data are worth mentioning. First, the output produced by the SSEs and LEs of the eighteen items accounts for 8.44 per cent of the weight assigned to the manufacturing sector in the Census of Industrial Production. Three of the eighteen items had to be omitted because their data were not reported suitably: the data are either in current year values or in physical units that differ between the SSEs and LEs. Thus we keep to fifteen products for which the data are in physical units common to both SSEs and LEs. Second, the enumerating unit in all cases is the production establishment, rather than the enterprise. This would seem appropriate whenever decisions about choice of technique, product quality and so on are made at the level of the establishment. The terms SSEs and LEs will henceforth be used to mean small and large (and medium) establishments. The third point is that the threshold size of establishment that distinguishes between the SSEs and the others has periodically been revised upwards. The threshold is based on the purchase value of capital equipment (that is, plant and machinery), and this value is revised upwards to allow for inflation in the price of the equipment. A problem may arise if the revisions result in hitherto medium-sized (and large) establishments being reclassified as SSEs. This reclassification would show up as an increase in the number of SSEs, and hence in the level of output attributed to them. The implications of this will be considered further when interpreting the results of the empirical tests.

THE EMPIRICAL RESULTS

Simple correlation tests showed no significant association between liberalization and the SSEs' growth. The correlation between the dummy variable *DVT* and G_S is only −0.08, and the correlation between the former and UG_S (that is, the SSEs' growth that is unrelated to the large enterprises) is only −0.15.

Table 6.1 reports the initial set of regression results. Equation (6.1a) includes only the relative output and the dummy variable. The coefficient of DVT is not significant. However, the coefficient of LR_S is negative and significant at the 1 per cent level: the SSEs' growth has been lower the higher was their initial relative output. Equation (6.1b) includes also the growth of the LEs. The coefficient of G_L is negative and significant, showing an adverse 'rival' effect on the SSEs. However *DVT* is still not significant. In Equation (6.1c) the dependent variable is UG_S, to test for the direct effect only. Here too *DVT* is not

Table 6.1 Estimated regression equations explaining the growth of small-scale enterprises in Indian industries

	Explanatory variables	**Equation**		
		(1a)	**(1b)**	**(1c)**
	Constant	0.35**	−0.34**	−0.02
		(2.93)	(3.08)	(0.16)
LR_S	Log (relative output of SSEs)	−0.15**	−0.15**	−0.14**
		(3.20)	(3.37)	(3.43)
DVT	Time dummy variable	0.04	0.09	0.09
		(0.27)	(0.56)	(0.62)
G_L	Growth rate of LEs		−0.64*	
			(2.60)	
Corrected R^2		0.23	0.36	0.25

Notes: The regressions are based on thirty pooled observations, each relating to one of fifteen (3-digit or 4-digit) product groups over two 5-year periods(1987/8–1991/2 and 1992/3–1996/7).

The dependent variables in Equations (1a) and (1b) is the growth of the SSE's output over the 5-year periods, and in Equation (1c) it is the growth of the SSE's output that is unrelated to the larger enterprises. See the text for definitions of the explanatory variables.

The *t*-statistics are shown in brackets. The coefficients marked by * are significant at the 5% level; those identified by ** are significant at the 1% level.

Table 6.2 Estimated regression equations incorporating interdependent effects on the growth of small-scale enterprises in India

	Explanatory variables	Equation	
		(2a)	(2b)
	Constant	0.33** (3.83)	0.31** (4.16)
LR_S	Log (relative output of SSEs)	−0.17* (2.62)	−0.12** (3.24)
DLR_S	$(DVT^{*}LR_S)$	0.04 (0.51)	
G_L	Growth rate of LE_s		−1.16** (3.81)
DG_L	$(DVT^{*}G_L)$		1.11* (2.55)
Corrected R^2		0.23	0.48

Notes: The regressions are based on thirty pooled observations, each relating to one of fifteen (3-digit or 4-digit) product groups over two 5-year periods (1987/8–1991/2 and 1992/3–1996/7).
The dependent variable in Equations (2a) and (2b) is the growth of the SSE's output over the 5-year periods. See the text for definitions of the explanatory variables.
The *t*-statistics are shown in brackets. The coefficients marked by * are significant at the 5% level; those identified by ** are significant at the 1% level.

significant. Clearly, then, there has been no intercept shift; liberalization has had no independent effect on the growth of SSEs.

Table 6.2 reports the regression results for the interdependent effects. In Equation (6.2a), the coefficient of LR_S is again negative and significant, but the product term DLR_S does not perform well. So liberalization does not have an interdependent effect with relative output. Equation (6.2b) has a more interesting result. The coefficient of the product term DG_L is positive, while that of G_L is negative, and both are significant. This suggests that the (negative) rival effect of the LEs has diminished since liberalization, particularly for those products where the SSEs initially had a low growth of output.

Considered together, the results show that liberalization has had no direct effect on the growth of SSEs. However, allowing for interdependence with the LEs' (negative) rival effect, we see that liberalization has, at least indirectly, helped the SSEs' growth. The remaining task is to explain this dampening of the LEs' rival effect. Could it be that these enterprises have themselves suffered lower growth since liberalization? We can analyse the LEs' growth with the following regression (*t*-statistics in brackets):

$$G_L = -\,0.03 + 0.01\ LR_S + 0.02\ DVT$$
$$(0.30)\ (1.08)\qquad (1.77)$$

The coefficient of *DVT* is positive and significant at the 10 per cent level. Clearly, liberalization has not reduced the LEs' growth. So this cannot explain the weakening of the LEs' effect on the SSEs. An alternative explanation is that liberalization has pressurised and/or enabled the LEs to engage increasingly in competition with each other (and also with imports) rather than with the SSEs. The LEs are moving to higher quality/price products, and so those products are becoming less close substitutes for those of the SSEs.

SUMMARY AND IMPLICATIONS

This chapter has examined whether India's economic liberalization policies, introduced in 1991, have had a beneficial, or adverse, effect upon the growth of the SSEs. The analysis has focused on SSEs' products that compete with those of the LEs. The case of complementary products (for example, those produced under subcontracting arrangements) and of handicrafts is left for another exercise.

Our interest in the competing products arises because of two considerations. First, the SSEs' products are differentiated from those of the LEs, and often have a relatively lower quality-price. Second, some of the diverse aspects of liberalization may have discriminated between the two types of enterprise: whereas the decrease in foreign trade barriers may have favoured the SSEs, the relaxation of restrictions on industrial capacity and on imports of technology are likely to have helped the LEs. Consequently, the overall effect of liberalization on either type of enterprise could not readily be predicted on a priori grounds.

The empirical tests examined the SSEs' growth over two 5-year periods, 1987–8 to 1991–2 and 1992–3 to 1996–7. It was found that, over both periods, the SSEs' growth was significantly lower in the product groups where they initially had a low output share and, moreover, was lower the higher was the rival growth of the LEs. The results for liberalization were as follows. An intercept dummy variable showed that the SSEs' growth rate did not differ significantly between the two 5-year periods. Another trial using a slope dummy showed that liberalization has dampened the LEs' (negative) rival effect on the SSEs. Thus, in either case, there was no evidence that liberalization has harmed the SSEs.

These results could well reflect some of the diverse and opposing influences of India's economic reforms. The effect of relaxing the restrictions on industrial capacity and on imports of technology, which are likely to have favoured the LEs, may have been offset by the (albeit limited) decrease in foreign trade barriers, which may have helped the SSEs.

Do the results imply a pessimistic, or optimistic, future scenario for India's SSEs? The answer depends on three considerations, which could be examined in further research. First, will the above results hold for a broader dataset than was used here? Second, it will be interesting to see whether the more recent decreases in foreign trade barriers help the SSEs. Third, will government (and other) agencies play an increasing role in helping the SSEs to upgrade their technologies?[12]

Notes

1. The empirical evidence in support of this argument is, however, rather mixed. Ahmad (1993) found that, in a sample of sixteen aggregate industries (two-digit ISIC), the average size of establishments was correlated positively with the capital intensities, and the latter were related positively to the effective rates of protection. However, these relationships did not hold for eighty-seven detailed (five-digit) industries. Moreover, it is not clear whether such inter-industry relationships would also apply to different-sized establishments within industries.
2. The products that are likely to benefit are those made under subcontracting arrangements for the LEs, while those that may not be affected by the LEs include handicrafts.
3. The Dominant Firm model is discussed in Clarke (1985).
4. The competing imports, in the Indian context, are likely to be mainly from the economically advanced countries, and consequently will be technologically more advanced and of a higher quality/price than the domestic products.
5. For example, as is well known in Industrial Economics literature, in the case of a linear demand schedule and constant marginal costs, the competing output of two identical enterprises in a Cournot model is one-third greater than their joint profit-maximizing level of output.

6. The policies that may bring about an outward shift of the SSEs' schedule might include government support for their technological upgrading, marketing, and so on, while the policies that will mainly shift the LEs' schedule will include relaxation of restrictions on industrial capacity and/or on imports of technology.
7. The reporting period for each year is the twelve months ending in March. The years chosen for the empirical test will thus correspond quite closely to the five-year periods just before and after the start of the end-1991 economic reforms.
8. Strictly speaking, the switch from the SSEs' products could be towards the higher quality/price imports, as well as to the products of the LEs. However, the former possibility will be ignored, since a switch to imports may not be very likely, particularly in view of trade barriers. Moreover, the data for imports and for production are not always comparable.
9. The resulting regression is: $G_S = 0.39\ (3.84) - 0.66G_L\ (2.44)$; the *t*-values are in brackets.
10. This argument may be visualized in terms of a diagram where G_S and R_S are plotted on the vertical and horizontal axes respectively, and the influence of R_S on G_S is shown by a negatively-sloped schedule. Liberalization may not affect the intercept of the schedule (on the G_S axis), but may make its negative slope steeper.
11. Following the lines of the preceding note, the influence of G_L on G_S would be shown by a negative-sloped schedule, and liberalization would make the schedule less steep.
12. Katrak (1998) has reported that, in recent years, some industrial research institutes have improved on their performance in developing and transferring technologies for user enterprises.

References

Ahmad, J. (1993) 'Trade and Industrial Policies and Small-Scale Industry: The Case of Indonesia, Pakistan and Sri Lanka', *Canadian Journal of Development Studies*, vol. 14, pp. 43–53.

Bala Subrahmanya, M. H. (1998) 'Shifts in India's Small Industry Policy', *Small Enterprise Development*, vol. 9, pp. 35–45.

Bhalla, A. S. (1992) 'Innovations and Small Producers in Developing Countries', in A. S. Bhalla (ed.), *Small and Medium Enterprises: Technology Policies and Options*, London: Intermediate Technology Publications, pp. 83–100.

Clarke, R. (1985) *Industrial Economics*, Oxford: Basil Blackwell.

Confederation of Indian Industries (1998) *Handbook of Statistics, 1997*, New Delhi: Confederation of Indian Industries.

EPW Research Foundation (1998) 'Industrial Production Statistics of India', *Economic and Political Weekly*, vol. 33, pp. 1271–84.

Evans, D. S. (1987) 'The Relationship between Firm Growth, Size and Age: Estimates for 100 Manufacturing Industries', *Journal of Industrial Economics*, vol. 35, pp. 567–81.

Kashyap, S. P. (1998) 'Growth of Small Enterprises in India: Its Nature and Content', *World Development*, vol. 16, pp. 667–81.

Katrak, H. (1997) 'Developing Countries' Imports of Technology, In-house Technological Capabilities and Efforts: an Analysis of the Indian Experience', *Journal of Development Economics*, vol. 53, pp. 67–83.

Katrak, H. (1998) 'Economic Analyses of Industrial Research Institutes in Developing Countries: the Indian Experience', *Research Policy*, vol. 27, pp. 337–47.

Katrak, H. (1999) 'Small-scale Enterprise Policy in Developing Countries: An Analysis of India's Reservation Policy', *Journal of International Development*, vol. 11, pp. 701–15.

Little, I. M. D., Mazumdar, D. and Page, J. M. Jr (1987) *Small Manufacturing Enterprises: A Comparative Study of India and Other Economies*, Oxford University Press.

Morris, S., Basant, R., Das, K., Ramachandran, K. and Kashy, A. (1997) *Overcoming Constraints to the Growth and Transformation of Small Firms*, (Ahmedabad: Indian Institute of Management.

Parker, R. L. et al. (1995) 'Small Enterprises Adjusting to Liberalization in Five African Countries', African Technical Department Series, World Bank Discussion Paper No. 271, Washington DC: World Bank.

Pradhan, B. K. and Saluja, M. R. (1998) 'Industrial Statistics in India: Sources, Limitations and Data Gaps', *Economic and Political Weekly*, vol. 33, pp. 1263–70.

Ramaswamy, K. V. (1994) 'Small-scale Manufacturing Industries: Some Aspects of Size, Growth and Structure', *Economic and Political Weekly*, vol. 29, pp. M13–M23.

Rekhi, S. (1995) 'Growth Trade-off: Changes Bank on Imports to Give a Boost to Exports', *India Today*, 30 April, p. 65.

Rodriguez, E. R. and Tescon, G. (1998) 'Liberalization and Small Industry: Have Manufacturing SMEs in the Philippines Benefited?', *Small Enterprise Development*, vol. 9, pp. 14–22.

Sandesara, J. C. (1991) 'New Small Enterprise Policy: Implications and Prospects', *Economic and Political weekly*, vol. 26, no. 42, pp. 2423–6.

Seth, A. (1995) 'Cost-Efficiency of Small Manufacturing Enterprises: Implications for Employment Policy', *Economic and Political Weekly*, vol. 30, pp. M130–M134.

Srinivasulu, K. (1997) 'Impact of Liberalization on Bedi Workers', *Economic and Political Weekly*, vol. 32, pp. 515–7.

UNDP (United Nations Development Programme) (1998) *Development of Rural Small-Scale Industrial Enterprises*, Vienna: UNDP.

7 Venezuelan Manufacturing, SME Decline, and Failed Transition

Alan Mulhern

INTRODUCTION

There has been a growing awareness of the importance of small firms and their revival within developed economies. Birch (1981) signalled this importance two decades ago when he pointed out that the majority of new jobs were being generated in the USA by small firms. Acs and Audretsch (1989) confirmed this by presenting evidence from 1976–86 showing that this increase in the employment share of smaller firms was occurring not only in the US economy as a whole but especially in manufacturing – thus confounding those who attributed this rise in the share of small and medium-sized enterprises (SMEs) to a structural shift to a service economy. Storey (1994) confirmed the existence in the United Kingdom of what came to be seen as a 'U-shaped' trend in SME manufacturing employment share. He located the change in trend in the late 1960s – a date often referred to in other studies of this phenomenon in developed economies. A famous study by Sengenberger *et al.* (1990) concluded that, from around the mid-1960s, there had been a general revival of small firms in many industrialized countries, measured as a recent increase in their share of total employment. Evidence from other authors (Nugent, 1996; Spilling, 1998; Trau, 1997) with respect to countries as far apart as Korea, Norway and Italy pointed to a similar reversal of trend, and has lent support for this claim. A subtext of this hypothesis is a belief that such a revival constitutes a transitional state to a post-industrial economy. The postulated revival of SMEs is seen as being vital to this reassertion of economic democracy.

The structure of the chapter is as follows. First, the economic background of Venezuela over recent decades will be outlined. Second, the evidence for the decline in manufacturing SMEs from 1962–95 will be presented. Third, the results of recent economic modelling of the Venezuelan manufacturing sector will be summarized in order to highlight the key economic explanatory variables of SME decline. Fourth, the institutional, political-economic factors that underlie the decline of the SMEs will be explained. In conclusion, I will point to the deep structural changes needed in the Venezuelan economy, and in government policy, if there is to be any future for this stratum.

THE ECONOMIC BACKGROUND

In 1970, Venezuela had a per capita Gross Domestic Product (GDP) higher than Spain, Hong Kong or Singapore. Only eighteen years later, and in spite of the oil boom that fuelled its economy, the GDP of these three countries was approximately 2.5 times greater than that of Venezuela. Table 7.1 shows the average annual growth rates of per capita GDP for various countries between 1970 and 1988, using Venezuela as the point of comparison, with an index figure of 100 in 1970. The impact of different growth rates between economies over this short period is striking. Table 7.1 shows the relatively poor rates of growth for five of the six Latin-American economies listed. Singapore in 1970 had an index figure of 76 compared to Venezuela's 100. By 1988, Singapore had risen to 262 while Venezuela's fell to 92.

Table 7.1 Per capita GDP for selected countries, 1970 and 1988

Country	**Per capita GDP (Venezuela 1970 = 100)**		**Average annual GDP growth rate (%)**
	1970	**1988**	
Ireland	106.50	224.90	4.9
Venezuela	100.00	92.98	− 0.4
Greece	94.35	143.41	2.4
Spain	90.08	237.05	5.5
Singapore	76.61	246.65	6.7
Hong Kong	72.58	262.89	7.4
Argentina	73.39	75.45	0.2
Brazil	36.29	67.03	3.5
Chile	68.55	47.37	− 0.2
Colombia	27.42	35.99	1.5
Mexico	57.26	57.49	0.0

Source: Enright *et al.* (1996).

Venezuela, during this period, experienced an absolute decline in per capita GDP. The 1980s have been called the decade of lost growth in Latin America. This especially applies to Venezuela, and was acknowledged explicitly in 1989 when new policies, embracing a different economic paradigm, were put in place. Figure 7.1 shows that there was a structural break in the growth of per capita GDP in Venezuela in the late 1970s. Prior to 1979, the long-term per capita growth rate averaged 1.7 per cent per annum. After 1979, this rate reversed to become an average negative figure of −1.9 per cent per annum.

The strong growth of the first period reflected Venezuela's immensely rich natural resources and the fact that the country was starting from a very low economic base. The population was very small and economic growth rapid. Given these factors, plus the world economic expansion during this period, such growth was not surprising. However, the development strategies guiding the economy were to lead the country into a blind alley. Venezuela, in common with many other Latin-American countries, adopted inward-looking policies of import-substitution industrialization (ISI), strong state control, and an extensive range of paternalistic and clientilistic practices. Most economic resources were controlled by the government. The country relied mainly on its oil exports, which accounted typically for over 80 per cent of total exports, and over 50 per cent of government revenue. This was its strategy to make the transition from a pre-modern to a modern economy.

Paradoxically, high oil prices have often been followed by poor economic performance. For example, the 1973–4 oil price rise produced

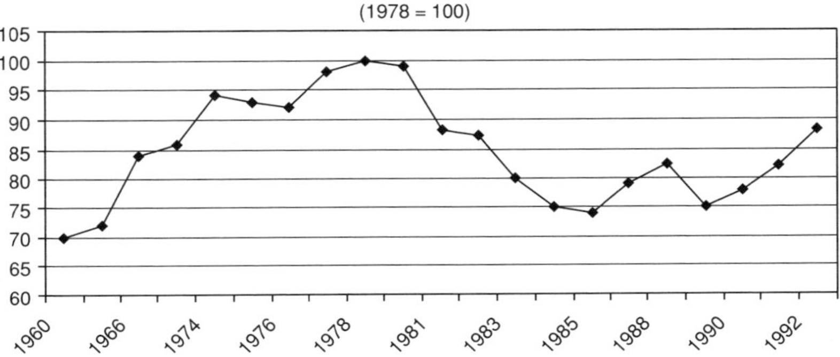

Figure 7.1 Real per capita GDP in Venezuela, 1961–93 (1978 = 100)

Source: Organización Central de Estadística y Información, Venezuela.

a short-term boom, led by rising demand within the economy. The result was two years of negative per capita GDP growth, while the 1979 price rise was followed by negative per capita growth each year up to 1985, by which time per capita GDP had been reduced to the level of the mid-1960s. Oil revenues, controlled and distributed by the government, became the main focus of state activity. There was growth from 1986–8, based on rising external debt, but the demand-led expansionary policies that fuelled this expansion led to shortages, inflation, and the depletion of external reserves. The government's response of placing controls on prices, credit and foreign exchange further damaged manufacturing and the private sector, while the economy remained even more dependent on the vicissitudes of oil prices and revenue. It became clear by the early 1980s that the crucial task of 'sowing the oil revenues' and achieving the transition to a modern participative economy had not being achieved. Large amounts of the vast oil revenues supported the government as it ran up budget deficits, employed an expanding bureaucracy, provided funds to support and bail out nationalized industries, provided finances for elephantine projects, and made deals with unions that gave concessions to workers that would otherwise have been impossible. Oil revenues therefore supported the status quo, and those who were privileged by virtue of political power to be 'insiders' to this system. Those who were 'outsiders' were excluded from the benefits. The growing informal sector, which came eventually to employ half the labour force, was the most noticeable of the outsiders.

Inflationary policies, sustained by rising international debt, produced only short-term growth in the late 1980s, and inevitably caused rising prices – despite price controls. The exchange rate deteriorated as external reserves diminished, while shortages of key goods arose. The government responded by tightening controls on credit, prices and foreign exchange, which further distorted the market structure, exasperating the competitive conditions of the non-oil economy. Serious productivity declines continued to characterize an economy dependent chronically on state-led industrialization and the vicissitudes of international oil prices.

The year 1989, when GDP fell by 8 per cent, and public and private investment by 53 per cent, marked a change in policy that was named '*el Gran Viraje*' – the great turning point – so-called because of the determination to turn away from the previous disastrous development strategies and embrace structural reforms. This involved the adoption of free-market reforms and attempts to dismantle parts of the government and bureaucratic apparatus. This was the second major attempt at 'transition' – in this case, to a free-market economy. The reforms included:

- moving from an exchange rate and interest rates system that had been fixed by the government, with highly discretionary rules determining who was to benefit, to a market-determined exchange-rate system;
- moving from high and variable tariffs on imports to low and more uniform tariffs;
- deregulating investment, opening the public sector to competition, and the privatization of some public enterprises;
- cutting generalized food subsidies; and
- restructuring Venezuela's external commercial debt.

The economy responded quickly and positively to these reforms, with strong GDP growth (7.4 per cent per annum) from 1990–2, while public and private investment leaped by 80 per cent in 1991, and a further 37 per cent in 1992. Other measures of economic growth such as private exports and fiscal deficit reduction also showed dramatic improvements. However, a notable feature of popular and democratic feeling in Venezuela was the resistance to the moves towards a free market. The structural reforms inevitably exasperated short-term inequalities. Riots, in which 300 people died, occurred when fuel prices rose and, in 1992, there were two unsuccessful military coups. They led to the paralysis of the reforms, and even the careful control of the fiscal deficit was abandoned: it grew to 6.3 per cent of GDP in 1992. The privatization programme and other such measures were stopped. Eventually, the president resigned. Venezuela abandoned the search for a liberalized economy, and chose a former president associated with the early days of its democracy – that is, it returned to the paternalistic style typifying the pre-1989 order. When faced with a crisis, Venezuela turned politically towards the past. A political stalemate ensued, with the authorities unwilling to enact unpopular measures. The economic situation deteriorated, and inflation rose from 32 per cent in 1992 to 46 per cent in 1993, while GDP growth fell from 6.1 per cent in 1992 and became negative in 1993. Non-oil GDP fell by 1.5 per cent. If by democracy we mean *the popular will*, then democracy and free-market economic reform are uneasy bedfellows in Venezuela. A popular transition had not proved possible.

The deteriorating economic situation provoked a collapse in 1994 of the second largest bank in Venezuela, Banco Latino, followed by further bank crises. Government support for the banking system in 1994 alone amounted to 13 per cent of GDP. This led to capital flight and pressure on the exchange rate, and about $3 billion of foreign reserves were lost in the first half of 1994. In response, the government imposed blanket foreign-exchange and price controls. Inflation, often the barometer of crisis, rose to 71 per cent in 1994, and the fiscal deficit exploded to 14 per cent of GDP. Per capita GDP fell by 5.3 per cent. Venezuela's economic and political system, however, has always been propped up by oil, which is relatively immune to domestic difficulties. In 1994, for example, oil GDP rose by 4.6 per cent, offsetting what would have otherwise been a catastrophic economic performance. The 1990s proved to be as much a 'lost decade' for Venezuela as were the 1980s. Key performance data for the latter part of the decade are summarized in Table 7.2.

Progress towards economic reform had been very slow, and the economy, dependant upon oil, had also been slow to open up to the international economy. The elections of 1998, as was the custom, paralyzed the economy. The new administration under a radical new president was unable, by the end of the 1990s, to reactivate the economy, despite extraordinarily high oil prices. The country has failed to establish a secure environment within which business can flourish. The attempts to create a more open, free-market economy at the start of the decade were reversed by the government in power at the time of writing, which has embraced populist nationalist policies antithetical to the globalization process. Despite the extremely high oil prices of 1999–2000, the country at the end of the 1990s was in severe recession, and incoming multinational investment, recognized as being so vital to the country's future at the start of the decade, returned to its customary very cautious stance. Venezuela has been an economy with the transition programme in reverse.

Table 7.2 Venezuela's economic performance, 1995–9

Year	GDP growth (%)	Inflation (%)	Unemployment (%)
1995	4.0	59.9	10.2
1996	– 0.2	99.9	11.8
1997	5.9	50.0	11.3
1998	0.7	35.8	11.1
1999	– 3.7	29.6	12.5

Source: Data & Forecast Analysis, New York (1999).

We have noted a structural break in Venezuelan economic performance in the late 1970s. The structural break in real per capita GDP growth occurred around 1979. This was not a year marked by a particular crisis, rather to the contrary, in fact, as oil prices doubled. In addition, public investment was running at very high levels of over 40 per cent of GDP in 1979. But pressure had been accumulating for many years through the whole economy. Real per capita GDP increased by an average of 1.7 per cent per annum from 1971 to 1979, but declined at an average rate of 1.9 per cent per annum over the period 1979–90. This trend was paralleled by similar trends elsewhere in the economy. Gross fixed capital formation as a percentage of GDP, for example, grew by 7.7 per cent from 1970–8, but subsequently declined by 9.8 per cent from 1978–90. Real oil income, underpinning the economy as a whole, grew by 10.9 per cent per annum from 1970–80, but declined by 5.8 per cent per annum in the 1980s. The trends in real manufacturing value-added (MVA) and in employment changed markedly in 1979 and 1980, respectively, from growth to volatile stagnation – see the next section for further details.

It is quite clear that Venezuela has been in deep economic crisis for many decades, and its oil wealth has allowed it to continue to postpone the severe reforms that it faces inevitably. Its oil wealth has also propped up a peculiar type of democratic system – a unique symbiosis in which the people depended on the state rather than the other way around. Just as we have observed failing political participation over the decades, so we have also seen failing economic participation. This is also a failure in democracy. Complaints concerning the economic system are numerous in Venezuela, and usually centre on corruption and matters of distributive justice: for example, how the national wealth is shared. Not so well appreciated is that economic democracy is also concerned with access to the capital and productive resources of a nation. These resources have largely been monopolized in the hands of the state and a small group of private interests in Venezuela. The majority of the population have therefore been excluded from productive participation. The wealth of any nation – even Venezuela, with its tremendous natural resources – depends on the creation of new firms, which respond to new, developing technologies, and the dynamic demand conditions and changing market opportunities in a complex global environment. This requires a business environment that allows this process to occur; and this is exactly what Venezuela does not have. The Venezuelan state has been concerned fundamentally with the control and distribution of wealth, rather than its creation. Oil money has been a dangerous luxury, allowing the country to avoid the restructuring of the state and the economy.

SMES IN VENEZUELAN MANUFACTURING

The term *Pequeña y Mediana Industria* (PYMI) refers to small and medium-sized firms[1] within the industrial sector, principally manufacturing. A more general term is *Pequeña y Mediana Empresa* (PYME), which refers to the generality of SMEs within the economy as a whole. The vast majority of the PYME are in the service sector in Venezuela (as in other LDCs) and, of course, many are in the informal sector, where approximately 50 per cent of the labour force are now located. They represent the failure of economic democracy to integrate what is now the majority of the population in the economic system. Venezuela experienced growing unemployment and increased self-employment in the period from 1979 onwards, which fed this growing informal sector rather than helped to create new micro-firms integrated into the economic system. It is estimated that 84 per cent of the 17 million new jobs created in Latin America in the period 1990–5 were in the informal sector.

This informal sector includes a large number of small firms and individuals providing goods and services to the economy, consisting typically of sole proprietors and micro-firms. They are found widely in commerce, and in the electrical repair, auto repair and transport, garment, metal-working, wood and furniture industries. However, most of the informal sector lacks proper skills and education, and is characterized by low incomes, low technology and so on. Its continued existence signifies an economy in a low productivity trap.

From 1979, small firms declined in number, as unemployment and the informal sector grew. Surprisingly, however, there is evidence that the informal sector still continued to grow, even in times of GDP growth (Rivero, 1993). Its growth in the later decades of the twentieth century took place at times of both rising and falling unemployment. Rivero has suggested that 'informalization' has been a strategy by capital in response to the oil crisis. Industry externalized its costs in attempting to deal with the excessive levels of institutionalization of the Venezuelan labour force. This was manifest in the power of the unions, their integration with government parties, and their ability to extract very favourable conditions initially in key state industries, and then more generally throughout the formal economy. The PYMI, of course, also suffered from the imposition of legislation negotiated in the large-firm and government sectors. Labour legislation raised the marginal cost of employing labour in the formal sector. Consequently, with the collapse of oil revenues, the informalization of the labour force became inevitable. Many of the workforce were obliged to be in the informal sector, because firms did not wish to employ labour on the unfavourable terms of formal sector employment. In addition, there were other powerful reasons for entering informal-sector employment: for example, to avoid the high transaction costs associated with taxation, corruption, bribes and bureaucracy linked to formal-sector activity. The growth of the informal sector, the decline of the PYMI, and the attempts by large firms to reduce their costs are therefore all part of the same story of an uncompetitive economy. The marginalization of the majority of the population indicates a profoundly undemocratic system. In developing countries such as Venezuela, we find a distortion of economic democracy expressed in the rise of the informal sector. This can be viewed fruitfully as a form of social exclusion.

A transitional economy with an emphasis on economic democracy normally exhibits a number of features. An important one is the right of individuals to establish small firms. Another is the right to a fair competitive structure, so that these small firms can grow and prosper. These rights have to be established by the political authorities and enforced throughout the economic system. Thus anti-competitive practices have to be discouraged, industrial relations should not militate against the interests of small firms, and so on.

The Venezuelan manufacturing sector is small and inefficient. Statistics are available for 1961 onwards, and Figure 7.2 shows that there was a significant expansion of MVA up to 1979, largely accounted for by the very low base from which the country started. Labour productivity in these years was very slow to increase and, in fact, it declined between 1971 and 1995. From 1979 to 1995, real MVA suffered a volatile stagnation.

This picture is repeated if we look at employment in manufacturing and the number of firms in this sector – see Figure 7.3. Again, we find the structural break around 1979, with significant growth in the period before this date, and decline afterwards.

As an indication of the lack of democratic inclusion (thereby implying a failure of 'transition'), Figure 7.4 shows the participation of SMEs in manufacturing activity since 1961. It shows the percentage share of SMEs in three indicators in the manufacturing sector: employment, number of firms, and value-added. Here, we observe something different.

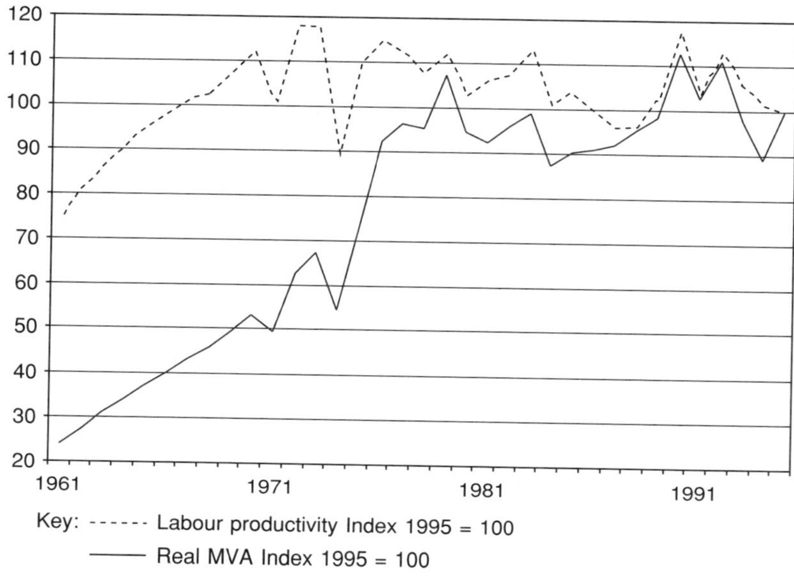

Figure 7.2 Real manufacturing value-added and labour productivity in Venezuela, 1961–95

Note: Both the employment and the numbers of firms indices are calculated with the 1995 values = 100.
Source: Organización Central de Estadística y Información, Venezuela.

Although there is a general and serious decline throughout the whole period, the loss of percentage share was greatest in the periods of expansion and less in contraction.

In Venezuela, the severe decline in the importance of the SMEs in boom periods has arisen for two reasons. First, economic gains are highly politicized. Larger firms take the lion's share of the gains because they have greater economic and political advantage. Second, because the business environment militates against smaller firms, new initiatives from below in the economy tend to be expressed as new start-ups and increased employment in the informal sector. After 1979, stagnation and recession characterize the economy. The SME share still declines from 1979 onwards, but in general at a slower rate. The reason for this is the reverse of the above argument. Smaller firms contract relatively less in recession, since they are operating at a low level and there are so few of them. They are providing essential services for the economy. This is explained further in the following section.

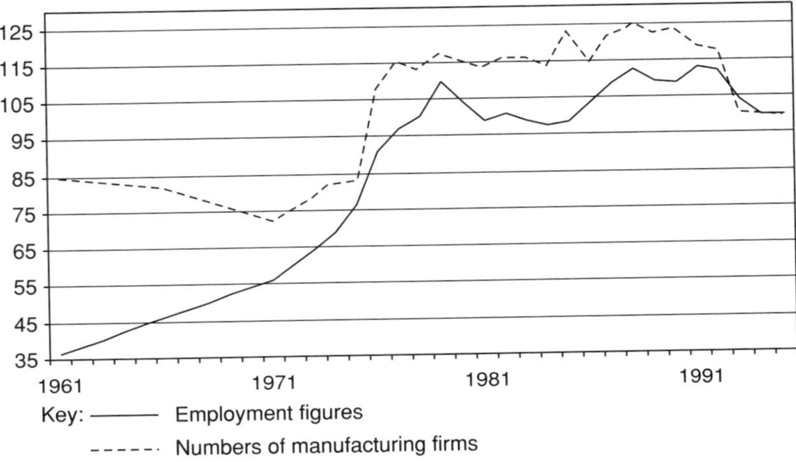

Figure 7.3 Employment and numbers of firms in manufacturing in Venezuela, 1961–95 (1995 = 100)

Note: Both the employment and the numbers of firms indices are calculated with the 1995 values = 100.
Source: Organización Central de Estadística y Información, Venezuela.

MODELLING THE DECLINING SME SHARE OF VENEZUELAN MANUFACTURING

Mulhern and Stewart (1999) used time series data for the period 1961–90 to investigate the declining SME share in Venezuela using the Engle and Granger (1987) error correction methodology. The theoretical model was derived from Acs and Audretsch (1989) who, using US cross-section data, found that industry-wide structural variables (that is, entry barriers such as industry capital intensity, market size, advertising, and concentration ratios) had negative impacts on SME share, while strategic responses by SMEs (innovation and efficiency efforts, especially of the larger SMEs) were found to compensate for these disadvantages and influence SME share positively. These empirical findings for SMEs in the USA have a theoretical base. The structural variables are factors that have a deterrent effect on SME formation and growth. It is well known that economies of scale favour larger firms, since the greater scale of the enterprise may offer significant reductions in average cost. Higher advertising rates in a particular industry are also associated with large-firm domination. Greater

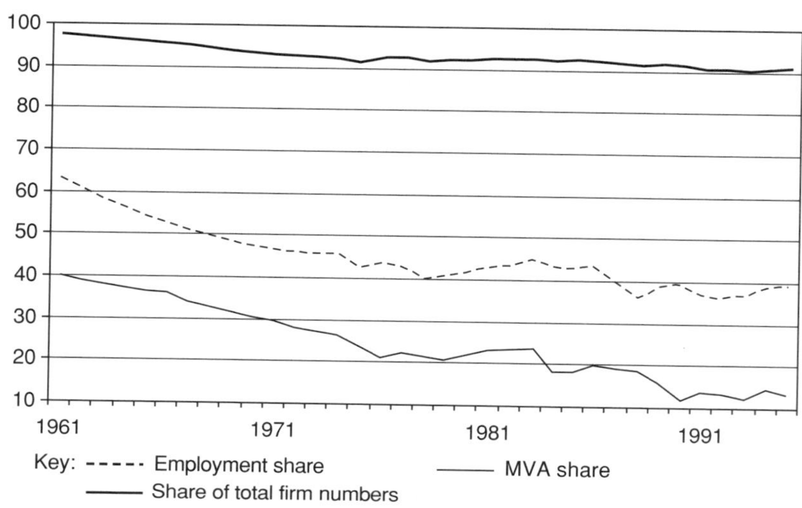

Figure 7.4 The SME shares of employment, total firm numbers, and manufacturing value-added in Venezuela, 1961–95

Note: All three shares are expressed as percentages of the total for the economy as a whole.
Source: Organización Central de Estadística y Información, Venezuela.

capital-intensity in an industry will favour larger firms, who can overcome this obstacle to both enter and grow within an industry.

The dependent variable used in the model measured the change of SME share in manufacturing value-added (*SS*). The independent variables and their expected signs were as follows.[2] First, there were three structural variables. The capital-intensity (*KL*) variable captures the effects of barriers to entry, which discourage the presence of small firms: a negative sign is expected. Market size (*LSZ*) proxies for economies of scale, and has an expected negative sign. Import penetration (*IP*) in the manufacturing sector was also included as a structural variable, but it was not clear a priori whether this should have a positive or a negative impact on SME share.

Clearly, SMEs face structural barriers that affect their share of the manufacturing market negatively, but they can increase their share by demonstrating greater efficiency and productivity *vis-à-vis* larger firms. For example, if SMEs improve their labour productivity relative to larger firms then we would expect, other things being equal, that they would also increase their share of manufacturing output and employment. Three stratum-specific variables were used to capture the effects of changes in labour productivity and enterprise modernization. Labour productivity may be measured by the ratio of output to labour employed (*RES*), and any changes in productivity may be decomposed into adjustments in the relative (capital/labour) factor mix of SMEs (*RKLS*), and improvements in pure efficiency (*VS*). In other words, *VS* measures the efficiency of labour alone after the capital/labour mix has been controlled for; *VS* is not observable, but may be estimated as the residual from an ordinary least squares (OLS) regression of *RES* on *SKLS*; that is,

$$RES_t = \beta_0 + \beta_1 RKLS_t + VS_t,$$

where β_0 and β_1 are the parameters to be estimated.

It is expected that both *RKLS* and *VS* will have positive impacts upon the SME share of manufacturing value-added, as both contribute to competitive advantage. Enterprise modernization is measured by the relative investment intensity (*INVS*) of SMEs compared to industry as a whole – that is, the relative ratio of value-added to capital employed (capital productivity). It is expected that *INVS* will have a positive effect, as the greater relative modernization of the SME stratum, as indicated by a rising *INVS*, should lead to a greater share in manufacturing production.

Total labour costs to the employer (*RWS*) are measured as SME labour costs relative to the manufacturing industry as a whole.[3] The expected sign is negative, since a rising *RWS* for SMEs constitutes competitive disadvantage. GDP was added as an exogenous independent variable. This proxied for the general business environment. It was argued that, in the case of Venezuela during this period, the business environment was hostile to SME progress. The reasoning was as follows. In times of rising GDP, the SME share declines because large firms are able to take greater advantage of favourable conditions such as access to contracts, soft credit facilities,[4] political connections and preferential interest rates, together with easier access to export markets, commercial information and new technologies.[5] Quite simply, access to these advantages is determined by political influence rather than by genuine competition. SMEs are outsiders in the political/economic game.[6] With falling GDP, the SME share increases, not because the SMEs are doing well but because large firms contract production, thus narrowing the gap between them. This was especially noticeable in the recession of the early 1980s. The share of the large firms decreased, reflecting the greater reductions in production in the large-firm strata compared to the SME strata. This greater volatility of the large-firm strata can be observed across a range of important variables such as employment figures, as well as numbers of firms in each stratum. It is not that SMEs are more stable in any positive sense. Rather they are unable, in periods of GDP growth, to take as great an advantage of economic opportunities as large firms, while in recession they have less to lose than the larger firms. In this respect, the Venezuelan SME experience resembles that of certain industrial countries (Spilling, 1998; Trau, 1997). We therefore expect a negative sign for the coefficient of GDP to reflect the fact that rising GDP is accompanied by a declining SME share in Venezuelan manufacturing production.

Mulhern and Stewart (1999) found that the key structural barriers (the capital/labour ratio and the size of market) were correlated negatively with SME share, while the efficiency and modernization measures had the expected positive signs and were significant[7] – see Table 7.3. SME relative labour costs, as anticipated, were related negatively to the SME share, while the relative factor mix, relative efficiency and relative investment effort were correlated positively and significantly to the SME share. Import penetration was found to be insignificant. The study also found a very strong negative correlation between the proxy variable *GDP* and the SME manufacturing share indicating, in the author's opinion, evidence for a business environment hostile to SME interests.

The study distinguished between long-and short-run determinants. The main determinants of long-run SME share were barriers to entry (*KL*), factor mix (*RKLS*), enterprise modernization (*INVS*), and the exogenous *GDP*. *RKLS* and *INVS* had positive influences on the SME share, while *KL* and *GDP* were correlated negatively with it. Changes in SME shares were adjusted by 87.8 per cent of past deviations from this equilibrium. The primary variables that influenced short-run changes in shares were the change in factor mix ($\Delta RKLS$) and the change in enterprise modernization ($\Delta INVS$). Both exerted the expected positive influence. This model explained 86.3 per cent of the variation in the changing SME share.

Overall, the analysis of long-run SME share confirmed the results of Acs and Audretsch's (1989) US investigation, namely that SME share 'is negatively related to the existence of structural barriers, positively related to the extent to which small firms rely on a strategy of innovation, and negatively related to the efficiency differential between small and large enterprises'. Furthermore, the results indicated the importance of investment and technology in the determination of short-run dynamics.

Table 7.3 Estimated regression equation explaining the change of the SME share in Venezuelan manufacturing value-added

Explanatory variable	**Expected sign**	**Estimated coefficient**	***t*-statistic**
Constant		0.119	1.435
KL	negative	– 0.129	2.378
LSZ	negative	– 0.020	1.354
IP	negative	– 0.002	0.411
RKLS	positive	0.296	7.872
VS	positive	0.121	1.290
INVS	positive	0.203	3.973
RWS	negative	– 0.060	1.592
GDP	negative	– 0.0003	4.354
Adjusted R^2		0.995	
DW		2.167	

Notes: The dependent variable is the change in the SME share of manufacturing value-added.
Data for 1961–90 were used to estimate the model. A dummy variable was added for 1978.
Source: Adapted from Mulhern and Stewart (1999), where complete diagnostics and test results for other models can be found.

The above modelling covered the period between 1961 and 1990. This corresponds closely to the first period of attempted transition to a modern economy, between 1958 and 1989. The authors have not yet tested the period from 1989 to the present, because of the unavailability of key data in this period. However, the data that are available up to 1995 – see Figure 7.4 – show the SME share according to the three key measures of share of firm numbers, share of total employment, and share of MVA, and tell a mixed story. By and large, the SME share appears to hold fairly constant in the first half of the 1990s. This probably reflects the economic reforms that were implemented in this period. However, what is certain is that there was no SME revival in this period and, in the second half of the 1990s, the SMEs were under severe stress as interest rates rose and the economy continued to stagnate.

THE POLITICAL ECONOMY OF FAILED TRANSITION

The results from the Mulhern and Stewart (1999) model revealed the relevance of key economic variables in understanding the SME share.

Political economy variables are also likely to be important but, unfortunately, the paucity of reliable data sources in the Latin-American environment makes the testing of such variables or their potential proxies very difficult. Some results of the model point to the political realm, especially the negative correlation between GDP and the SME share. However, besides the declining relative share there is there the very worrying fact of a declining trend in absolute SME MVA levels from around the 1979 structural break. Figure 7.5 tells the story. By 1995, SME production was at the same level as in the 1960s. Now the relative decline of the SME sector might well be explained largely by arguments of relative efficiency and size levels compared to large firms. Venezuela, it could be argued, was in the early stages of industrialization, where larger firms have distinct advantages over smaller ones. However, the absolute decline of the sector over two decades cries out for explanations at many levels.

It should be noted that the absolute as well as the relative decline of SMEs in manufacturing is not something that can be understood by concentrating only on the manufacturing sector, which the above model does in the main. The SME crisis is indicative of the flawed nature of the political and economic system as a whole. From its inception in 1958, this system promised democracy and economic progress, but has failed to deliver either.

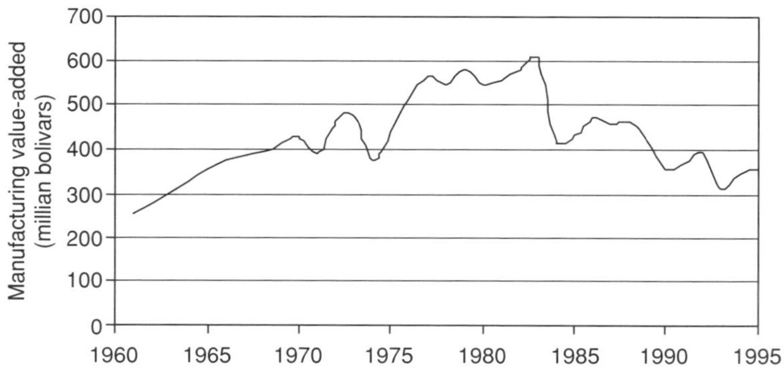

Figure 7.5 Manufacturing value-added in SMEs in Venezuela, 1961–95 (1995 prices).

Note: Manufacturing value-added is expressed in bolivars at 1995 prices.
Source: Organización Central de Estadística y Información, Venezuela.

Venezuela's economic system and the political structure that lies behind it are flawed from two perspectives: first, in orientation; and second, in structure. The first attempt at transition, from 1958 to 1989, was characterized by a development strategy emphasizing state control, import substitution, and large-scale projects. The country relied on its oil revenues to fund its modernization programme. In a very short period of time, Venezuela abandoned large parts of its agricultural system and the population became urbanized. Industry was protected by high tariffs and quota systems, and the government concentrated on large-scale projects such as oil, steel, aluminium, the Guri dam, and, later, petrochemicals. The failure in orientation of ISI strategies has been well documented, and there is no need to repeat this story with respect to yet another country. The illusory success of the early years hid the underlying developing crisis. A protected, highly-subsidized non-market-orientated economic system was destined to become highly unproductive. The state sectors in particular were highly protected, and were suffering annual productivity declines of around 9 per cent in the late 1970s. Even in the restructuring efforts of the 1980s, annual productivity declines of 1.4 per cent were experienced over the period between 1983 and 1988. Labour productivity in manufacturing was no higher in 1995 than it had been thirty years previously.

The Venezuelan economy has not become a modern democratic economic system because, among other reasons, it has failed, and continues to fail, to operate on market principles. If a politically important industry is going bankrupt, then it can be rescued. Populist governments can afford to be magnanimous with oil revenues. After all, such expenditure does not come from taxation, and it is difficult for a population to appreciate the concept of opportunity cost: that is, what could otherwise have been done with the oil revenues in terms of productive investment. The Venezuelan economy is dominated by political decisions (Enright *et al.*, 1996). Extensive red tape and expense characterizes all economic effort. The government has frequently made arrangements with a small group of firms that new entrants to the industry are to be excluded. The government that began the reforms of 1989 acknowledged the faults of these policy orientations openly, and attempted to bring market reforms into the closed economy and open it to the globalization process. The lessons of the Tiger economies such as Singapore and Hong Kong had penetrated parts of the leadership of Venezuelan society (Herring, 1993). Nevertheless it proved to be extremely difficult to change the structure of the Venezuelan economic system.

The Venezuelan economy is dominated by a small number of very powerful groups who operate as 'insiders' to the economic system, and who participate in its benefits. The majority of the country are 'outsiders', at the margins of the economic system. This includes the whole informal sector, and SMEs also fall into this category. The insiders, a small group of powerful vested interests, include the government and the state apparatus, the nationalized industries, the trade unions, a small number of multinationals, and a few powerful families which dominate large areas of industry and the service sector. The industrial structure typically is cartelized and highly concentrated. Barriers to entry are not only economic (for example, economies of scale, capital/output ratios, and so on) but also political, since the government controls entrance to certain industries very actively, and manipulates subsidies and contracts to those whom it favours. Throughout the whole first period (1958–89), the government did not promote competition, or attempt to create a competitive business environment. Quite the contrary, it believed in state control, nationalized industries, and extensive intervention and regulation. Cartels were favoured over more competitive business structures, since they allowed more control. Corruption was rife.

Venezuela's labour policy was designed to protect workers in the formal sector. It was not designed to promote new employment, economic growth or competitiveness. Venezuelan labour laws have given extensive rights to workers and are similar to many that have existed throughout Latin America. They make no distinction between large and small firms. For example, wage increases are often mandated by the government and apply across the board regardless of local market conditions or the size of the company. Dismissal laws and severance payments have been very exacting on the employer. The impact on small firms has been particularly harsh, since they possess none of the advantages of the larger firms, yet they have to abide by the same contracts and laws established in the large-firm and state sectors. For example, small firms contracted to work for the oil industry have to adopt the labour contracts and conditions that exist in the privileged nationalized oil industry. The marginal costs to the employer are thereby substantially driven up. The impact of trade unions and labour laws can also have a negative impact on SMEs. In this, they differ from trade unions in some other parts of the world (for example, Italy) where they have been part of the development of the small-firm stratum.

In Venezuela, there is little opportunity for small firms to gain access to capital markets, since these markets possess no depth. For example, there is no venture capital market. The stock exchange is very weak, with limited dealings that are only for the big players. Sources of funding are extremely limited and depend on very expensive bank loans or access to privileged state credit. Highly discriminatory differential bank lending rates between large and small firms have been common, while interests rates themselves have been prohibitively high (between 30–60 per cent over the 1990s). With the dominance of the state and its major control over credit and monetary policy, deep capital markets that might have helped to fund small firms have failed to develop.

Government regulations and bureaucracy have been extensive and powerful in many Latin-American countries. Traditionally, many governments have not had a pro-business orientation. On the contrary, state enterprises and extensive state intervention were favoured, and protection of privileged interests was rife. Small-business interests have always been marginal to the main thrust of government policy. Governments traditionally have not been concerned with the development of clear market and property rights, or with a well-regulated and functioning market-place. However, this does not imply that Venezuelan SMEs require completely free markets and an absence of intervention. On the contrary, they need extensive government help, but of the right kind: for example, the provision of information, training, enforcement of rights, security, a fair legal environment, access to finance, and protection against uncompetitive practices, monopolies and cartels. They need extensive help in training personnel and access to new technologies. Even more than large firms, they rely on public infrastructure. Large firms can compensate to some extent for the severe infrastructure deficiencies of the country in a way that is impossible for small firms. For example, they can install their own electricity generators to compensate for the frequent cuts in electrical supply; they can have their own planes to transport personnel; and they can invest extensively in information technology and compensate for the deficiencies in communications that plague the rest of the economy. Small firms need, in short, extensive government help to correct the paucity, deficiencies and distortions of their market structures and provision.

Venezuela is not the only economy characterized by the structure briefly outlined above (state dominance, oligarchic private interests, a burgeoning informal sector, declining SMEs in manufacturing, and an over-reliance on a limited range of commodity production). Like the rest of Latin America, Venezuela adopted strategies of import substitution and the dominance of large-scale enterprise. It has had extensive state control accompanied by styles of government that are populist, paternalistic, clientilistic, and socialist-inclined. Its labour markets and labour laws resemble those in many other Latin-American countries. The populist and socialistic policies of Venezuela have been pan-continental. Venezuela is an unusual example of this economic policy genre because its oil wealth permitted the continuances of such policies long past their 'sell-by date'. Venezuela's corruption, market inefficiencies, statist and rentist mentality have been prolonged and believed-in longer than in other Latin-American counties, and have allowed the country to avoid the fundamental reforms it so clearly requires.

The latter half of the 1990s saw a much greater awareness in government circles of the importance of SMEs. International attention is also focused on this question in developing countries. Nevertheless, it is going to be some time before the data emerges so that a proper assessment may be made of the period 1995–2000. However, there is little room for optimism in the case of Venezuela, with a serious decline in GDP in 1999, and with the economic consequences of the natural catastrophes of December 1999, mudslides and floods which claimed the lives of some 50,000 people in a few days, yet to have an impact on the 2000 accounts. The implicit argument of this chapter is that the SME stratum will not be helped until deep structural change occurs in the economy, and that this change needs to be towards the promotion of a competitive business environment in which the state plays the role of helper rather than that of controller. For this to happen, deep vested interests, including those of the state, will have to be challenged, and the mentality of government will have to be changed. The absolute and relative decline of the SME manufacturing stratum is one important symptom of the failure of the economic and political system. Its absence signifies not only a loss of national wealth in terms of employment and production, but also the failure of transition to a modern state.

CONCLUSIONS

This chapter has presented clear evidence of the relative decline of the PYMI between 1962 and 1995, and its absolute decline from the late 1970s. It has also demonstrated the weakness of the manufacturing sector as a whole. Econometric modelling has identified a number of significant 'economic' explanatory variables (both structural, and related to efficiency/innovation) and provided some insight into the reasons behind this decline. However, the roots of this phenomenon lie in deep political and economic structures. It has been argued that Venezuela has a deeply uncompetitive structure, dominated by vested state and private interests that have stymied not only the SMEs but also economic prosperity in general. The chapter also briefly presented the evidence for rising abstention rates, and has put it in the context of economic decline, crisis, and the failure of transition. In particular, it has been argued that the lack of economic participation manifested in the experience of SMEs indicates a profound lack of economic participation without which a genuine transition founders.

Notes

1. SMEs are defined in Venezuela as firms employing between 10 and 100 employees. This is equivalent to the definition of a 'small firm' in the larger industrial economies already mentioned. 'Micro-firms' are those employing up to nine employees.
2. Six of the eight explanatory variables have a history in the literature, especially in Acs and Audretsch (1989), and Thomadakis and Droucopoulos (1996). Two new variables were added: *RWS* and *GDP*.
3. The specific measures used included not only wages, but also bonuses, holiday payments, social security payments, insurance, pensions and so on.
4. For example, it is well known that there is a wide interest rate differential for large and small firms. However, data constraints prevent us from using this as an explanatory variable.
5. Time series data are not available for any of these factors. Hence they could not be used in the model. Their combined effect, producing a hostile business environment, is subsumed within the *GDP* proxy variable.
6. See Roberts and Araujo (1997), ch. 3 for a discussion of the 'blocked society' in Latin America.
7. Previous studies have used advertising as an additional 'structural' explanatory variable. Data constraints prevented this being done for Venezuela. Thomadakis and Droucopoulos (1996) found advertising to be insignificant in the case of Greece, and it is likely that it would also be insignificant in the small manufacturing sector of Venezuela.

References

Acs, Z. and Audretsch, D. (1989) 'Small Firms in U.S. Manufacturing: A First Report', *Economic Letters*, vol. 31 pp. 399–402.
Birch, D. (1981) 'Who Creates Jobs?', *The Public Interest* (Fall), pp. 3–14.
Buxton, J. and Phillips, N. (1999) *Case Studies in Latin American Political Economy*, Manchester University Press.

Engle, R. F. and Granger, C. W. J. (1987) 'Co-integration and Error Correction: Representation, Estimation and Testing', *Econometrica*, vol. 55, pp. 251–76.

Enright, M., Frances, A. and Saavedra, E. S. (1996) *Venezuela: The Challenge of Competitiveness*, London: Macmillan.

Herring, O. (1993) 'El Modelo Taiwanes y sus Lecciones en Beneficio de la PYMI Venezolano', *Corpoindustria Manual de Orientación*, no. 1 (June).

Mulhern, A. and Stewart, C. (1999) 'Long and Short-Run Determinants of Small and Medium-Size Enterprise: The Case of Venezuelan Manufacturing', *Economics of Planning*, vol. 32, pp. 191–209.

Nugent, J. (1996) 'What Explains the Trend Reversal in the Size Distribution of Korean Manufacturing Establishments?', *Journal of Development Economics*, vol. 48, pp. 225–51.

Parades, C. E. (1993) 'Productivity Growth in Venezuela: The Need to Break With the Past', Project Venezuela Competitiva, Key Issue Paper.

Piore, M. and Sabel, C. (1984) *The Second Industrial Divide: Possibilities for Prosperity*, New York: Basic Books.

Rivero, D. M. (1993) 'Informalización de la Fuerza de Trabajo en Venezuela', *Corpoindustria Manual de Orientación*, no. 2.

Roberts, P. and Araujo, K. (1997) *The Capitalist Revolution in Latin America*, Oxford University Press.

Sengenberger, W., Loveman, G. W. and Piore, M. J. (1990) *The Re-emergence of Small Enterprises: Industrial Restructuring in Industrialised Countries*, Geneva: International Labour Organization.

Spilling, O. (1998) 'On the Re-emergence of Small-Scale Production: The Norwegian Case in International Comparison', *Small Business Economics*, vol. 10, pp. 401–17.

Storey, D. J. (1994) *Understanding the Small Business Sector*, London and New York: Routledge.

Thomadakis, S. B. and Droucopoulos, V. (1996) 'Dynamic Effects in Greek Manufacturing: The Changing Shares of SMEs, 1983–1990', *Review of Industrial Organisation*, vol. 11, pp. 69–78.

Trau, F. (1997) 'Recent Trends in the Size Structure of Italian Manufacturing Firms', *Small Business Economics*, vol. 9, pp. 273–85.

8 European Integration and the Survival of Polish Small Enterprises

Subrata Ghatak, George Manolas, Costas Rontos and Ioannis Vavouras

INTRODUCTION

In both developed and transitional economies, small and medium-sized enterprises (SMEs) have a crucial role to play. In the OECD area, for example, the share of SMEs to total employment is between 40 per cent and 80 per cent, while their share of GDP is between 30 per cent and 70 per cent. Poland, an example of a transitional economy, has recently undergone a period of major economic change. This transformation has taken place in the context of its future economic and monetary integration with the European Union (EU). In this context, Polish SMEs[1] have an important role to play. Since they constitute a large part of the Polish economy in terms of output and employment, their survival and development are going to exert a significant impact on Poland's readiness for accession, and on its successful European future. Hence, it is of importance to estimate the ability of SMEs in Poland to survive and develop, and the factors that are likely to determine their survival and growth in the European perspective.

The integration of markets through the European Union, the removal of constraints, and the emergence of new competitive incentives affect SMEs in many ways (OECD, 1997, p. 25):

- through the reduction of administrative procedures for international trade, which allow a better exploitation of economies of scale and scope;
- through improved efficiency in firms resulting from innovations, which are induced by more competitive markets;
- through adjustments between industries, on the basis of a fuller play of comparative advantages;

- through more dynamism and an improved flow of innovations, new processes and new products; and
- through stronger economic growth in the long run, which leads to new market opportunities.

The purpose of this chapter is to investigate the characteristics of the successful Polish SME in the European context, and to construct a model that will enable us to predict the probability of an enterprise surviving and developing in this environment.

The chapter is organized as follows. The second section presents the methodology and the data used, and the third section provides the empirical results of the study. The final section draws conclusions and makes some policy recommendations.

DATA AND METHODOLOGY

The data used in this chapter have been derived from a special statistical survey[2] carried out in Poland in the last quarter of 1999. An extensive questionnaire consisting of fifty-eight questions was employed, and professional enumerators were used to ensure the best-quality data and minimize non-sampling errors.

The sample consisted of 376 small enterprises, each employing between ten and forty-nine persons. The sample constituted 5 per cent of the total SMEs contacted. A proportionate stratification sampling method was used. The stratification factors were the sectors of economic activity selected in the survey. For the purposes of the study, small enterprises were defined as those with fewer than fifty employees. Enterprises with fewer than ten employees were excluded; their data was considered to be unreliable, as they may not have had much knowledge about the European environment. The survey covered two regions of Poland: Gdansk and Lublin, the sample being drawn separately in the two regions. As the two regions have differences in their economic characteristics, many important conclusions could be extracted. Finally, the selected sectors of economic activity were those of particular importance for the transformation of the Polish economy.

A dichotomous logit model was adopted, as we wished to identify the structural characteristics and other factors that explained the choice of individual enterprises over a finite and unordered set of alternatives. More specifically, the dependent variable (Y_i) reflected the views of owners/managers about the influence on the performance of their enterprises of the accession of Poland to the European Union. The dependent variable is thus a dichotomous variable that takes a value of unity when accession is thought to influence performance 'advantageously', and takes a value of zero otherwise. An 'advantageous' influence was assumed when the respondent identified at least one of the following four reasons listed on the questionnaire: better access to EU members' markets; better access to other countries' markets; increase in production effectiveness; 'other' reason.

The independent variables in the model were all categorical variables, related either to the structural characteristics of the enterprises, or to aspects of their economic performance that influenced their ability to survive against the increased competition they would face within the European Union. The variables, and the categories into which they were divided, are shown in Table 8.1, and discussed further in the next section. When categorical variables are used, as here, the predictive ability of the model increases as the values and the direction of the variable coefficients rises. A useful rule is that the larger a positive estimated coefficient of a variable's category, the higher the probability of an enterprise included in this category viewing accession as 'advantageous'; and the smaller, or more negative a coefficient, the lower the probability (Knapp *et al.*, 1982).

Many authors have discussed the standard methods for estimating logit models (Nerlove and Press, 1973; Dhrymes, 1978), and others have suggested improvements (Knapp *et al.*, 1982; Harissis, 1986; Skovgaard, 1990). Here a maximum likelihood approach was used, and a conditional forward stepwise method was adopted. The statistical significance of the coefficients was tested by the Wald statistic, which is equal to the square of the well-known t-statistic, but is preferred in the case of logit analysis. A high level of significance ($\alpha = 25$ per cent) was used to avoid excluding variables that had been hypothesized to be significant in past literature (Harissis, 1986). The overall goodness-of-fit of the various models was assessed on the basis of the likelihood-ratio test statistics. A brief description of the logit model follows:

Let P_i = the probability that the performance of the ith enterprise will be influenced 'advantageously' by Poland's accession to the European Union.

Q_i = the probability that the performance of the ith enterprise will be influenced negatively by Poland's accession to the European Union.

$= 1 - P_i$.

Table 8.1 Explanatory variables in the logit model

Code	Variable	Categories
Structural characteristics		
X59	Region of establishment	Gdansk
		Lublin
X39	Size	Up to 19 employees
		20–39 employees
		40 or more employees
X1a	Branch of economic activity	Manufacturing
		Construction
		Trade
		Hotels/restaurants
		Transport/storage/ communication
		Financial intermediation
		Other services
V03	Sector	Public
		Private
V04	Legal status	State-owned and communal
		Individuals' partnership
		Individuals' business
		Joint stock
		Limited company
		Other
V06	Change of legal status in previous 3 years	No
		Yes
Exposure to international competition		
V20	Origin of competitors	Domestic
		Foreign
		Both
X12	Main destination of production	Local market
		National market
		International market
		Mixed
X16	Efforts made to export/increase exports	No
		Yes
Co-operation with other enterprises		
X9	Ownership of other enterprises	No
		Yes
X10	Ownership of any foreign enterprise	No
		Yes
X17	Is the enterprise based on franchising?	No
		Yes

Table 8.1 (contd.)

Code	Variable	Categories
Research and Development		
V22	Technological level of the enterprise	Medium High Very high
V23	Technological level of the products/ services	Medium High Very high
V24d	IT used in the production process	No Yes, slightly Yes, to a significant extent
V25	Extent of Internet use	No use Yes, to a slight extent Yes, to a significant extent
V26b	Formal co-operation with R&D institutions	No Yes
X28	Existence of R&D department	No Yes
X29	Innovation introduced in 1998–9	No Yes
Staff quality and training		
X40a	Percentage of employees with higher education	Up to 19% 20–49% 50% or more
V42b	Availability of training	No Yes
V43	Existence of written policy on training	No Yes
Knowledge about the European Union		
V48	Knowledge level about EU markets	High Medium Low
V50	Action related to Poland's accession	No Yes
Finance		
V52b	Are bank loans essential for the enterprises's finance?	No Yes
X53	Any difficulty for the enterprise in getting a loan?	No Yes No attempt yet

As P_i must lie between zero and one, it is usual to define P_i as an ordinate of a cumulative distribution function; that is,

$$\begin{aligned} P_i &= F(t) \\ &= \int_{-\infty}^{t} f(z)dz, \end{aligned} \tag{8.1}$$

where $F(t)$ = a cumulative distribution function; and
$f(z)$ = the associated density function.
The upper limit (t) may be expressed as a function of the characteristics of the ith enterprise, thus:

$$t = \mathbf{X}_i\beta, \tag{8.2}$$

where $\mathbf{X}_i$ = a vector of the values of the explanatory variables for the ith enterprise

$$= (\mathbf{X}_{i1}, \mathbf{X}_{i2}, \ldots, \mathbf{X}_{ik});$$

and β = a vector of unknown coefficients (to be estimated).
Hence, Equation (8.3) can be written as:

$$P_i = \int_{-\infty}^{\mathbf{X}_i\beta} f(z)dz = F(\mathbf{X}_i\beta), \tag{8.3}$$

and

$$Q_i = 1 - P_i = 1 - F(\mathbf{X}_i\beta). \tag{8.4}$$

If $F(t)$ is the cumulative function of the standardized logistic distribution, namely:

$$F(t) = \frac{1}{1 + e^{-t}} - \infty < t < \infty, \tag{8.5}$$

then the probability that the performance of the ith enterprise with characteristics given by the vector $\mathbf{X}_i$ will be influenced 'advantageously' by Poland's accession to the European Union is:

$$P_i = \frac{1}{1 + e^{-x\beta}} \tag{8.6}$$

and we can define the logit of P_i as:

$$\log_e \frac{P_i}{1 - P_i} = \mathbf{X}_i\beta. \tag{8.7}$$

Let $Y_i = 1$ if the ith enterprise reports that accession will have an 'advantageous' influence on performance; and
$= 0$ otherwise.

Then we have:

$$\text{Prob}\,\{Y_i = 1\} = F(\mathbf{X}_i\beta)$$
$$\text{Prob}\,\{Y_i = 0\} = 1 - F(\mathbf{X}_i\beta).$$

The model can be estimated by maximizing the likelihood function:

$$L(Y_\mathrm{I}/\mathbf{X}_\mathrm{I}) = \overset{n}{\underset{i=1}{\pi}}[F(\mathbf{X}_i\beta)]^{Yi}[1 - F(\mathbf{X}_i\beta)]^{1-Yi}. \tag{8.8}$$

The log-likelihood is:

$$L = \sum_{i=1}^{n} Y_i \ln F(\mathbf{X}_i\beta) + \sum_{i=1}^{n}(1 - Y_i)\ln[1 - F(\mathbf{X}_i\beta)]. \tag{8.9}$$

Setting the first and second order derivatives of the above equation to zero with respect to β, and specifying the cumulative density function, we can obtain an estimator of β.

The use of a non-linear technique such as logit analysis is appropriate, given that we wish to analyze a situation where all the explanatory factors determine the dependent variable simultaneously. A χ^2 test for independence would not have been satisfactory, as this assumes that the various causal factors work quite independently of each other. Estimation of a linear probability model by multiple regression would have overcome these problems, but would give rise to results that were neither statistically efficient nor unambiguously determined when the dependent variable was a dummy variable.[3]

THE EXPLANATORY VARIABLES IN THE MODEL

The explanatory variables are listed in six groups in Table 8.1. The first group comprises six structural characteristics which are of great importance for a country in transition, such as Poland: the region of establishment, size, the branch of economic activity, public or private sector, legal status, and legal status change. As far as the region (X59) is concerned, Gdansk has more favourable economic characteristics than Lublin. It is postulated that the SMEs in Gdansk will have more to gain from Poland's accession. The size (X39) of the enterprise[4] would seem to be an important factor for the enterprise to be competitive in the wide EU market. It is expected that the larger the enterprise, the higher the probability of a positive impact from accession, as larger enterprises benefit more from scale economies. The branches of economic activity (X1a) that are more likely to have a successful performance in the competitive environment of the EU market are of a great importance. Finally, the ownership status may well be an important factor affecting the survival prospects of enterprises from the previously planned-economy countries. Whether the enterprise is in the public or the private sector (V03), its legal status (V04), and whether that status has changed in the preceding three years (V06) were all included to examine the influence of privatization on the enterprises' survival. Private enterprises are expected to have a higher probability of survival in the EU market.

The second group focuses on the existing exposure to international competition. The origin of competitors (V20) provides evidence as to whether the enterprise has already been affected by international competition. It is expected that those indigenous enterprises who already compete with foreign firms will be better prepared when the trade barriers come down after accession. It is also expected that if an indigenous enterprise is already producing for international markets, it will have an advantage in relation to those who are just producing for the national or local markets (X12). Finally, it is likely that those firms who are already making efforts to export, or to increase their exports (X16), will have a better understanding of the future competitive conditions that will be created after accession, and will have a better chance of survival in the Single European Market.

The third group of variables concentrates on co-operation with other enterprises, Polish or foreign, as an aid to survival. Co-operation can take the form of alliances, participation with other enterprises in order to create a group of enterprises, franchising, venture capital firms and so on. Such co-operation permits enterprises to reach their optimum size, to overcome financial problems, and to approach more readily both national and international markets. These considerations are captured in the model by the variables X9, X10, and X17.

R&D effort is generally recognized as being crucial for endogenous productivity growth and competitiveness at both the microeconomic and macroeconomic levels (Lichtenberg and Siegel, 1991; Basant and Fikkert, 1996). As most of the variables employed in our model (V22, V23, V24d, V25, V26b and X28) represent aspects of the R&D effort that have already been suggested in the literature, or are used in the construction of technology indices (Palaskas *et al.*, 1999), no further explanation is provided. The variable X29 takes the answer 'yes' if at least one of the following was undertaken during 1998–99:

- new or technologically improved goods (services) were produced;
- more modern production methods were introduced;
- significant organizational changes were introduced; and/or
- significant organizational-property changes were introduced.

The fifth group relates to the quality of the staff and of the training provision. It is likely that the higher the percentage of employees with higher education in the total number of employees (X40a), and the higher the specialization of the staff, the higher will be the probability of a successful performance in the European Union. The availability of training for the employees (V42b) reveals the policy of the enterprise in keeping their employees informed about new techniques and methods. Furthermore, the existence of a written policy on training (V43) reveals the degree of interest in staff training needs, and about how a training programme might be implemented. Positive answers to either of these questions suggest that the enterprise might have an advantage following Poland's accession. We could mention the fact that a major contributory factor in the Republic of Ireland's emergence as the seventh most competitive country in the world has been the attention that has been paid to the education and training of the labour force.

Finally, the sixth group of variables concentrated on financial issues. Self-financing is not a sufficient way for enterprises to finance investments nowadays, and the development of a credit system to provide a basic source of financing, and easy access to that system, might be supposed to have a positive impact on the survival of enterprises, especially in a competitive European economic environment. These effects are captured by the extent to which the credit system constrains the financing of the enterprise (X52b), and the difficulty the enterprise has in raising bank loans (X53).

THE EMPIRICAL RESULTS

The empirical results are presented in Table 8.2. In Model (1), all the independent variables were included and the total number of cases was only 182 (out of the total sample of 376 enterprises) as many of the questionnaires had missing values for several variables. This created statistical problems in testing the model's efficiency, as many categories had counts of less than five. Those variables of little significance and/or with large numbers of missing values were thus omitted in Model (2) and the number of cases increased to 270, though efforts were made to include variables from all six groups identified in Table 8.1. Further refinement took place for Models (3) and (4), and 346 cases were included in the latter – that is, only 30 cases were omitted because of missing data.

The stability of successive models is clear, with the same set of explanatory variables being found to be statistically significant in Models (2), (3) and (4). The variables that were considered to be most likely to have an influence on performance after Poland's accession to the European Union were the region of establishment (X59), the branch of economic activity (X1a), the ownership of other Polish enterprises (X9), the extent of internet use (V25), the knowledge level of EU markets (V48), and the difficulty of securing loans (X53). The categorization of the 346 cases used in the estimation of Model (4) according to each of these variables is shown in Table 8.3.

Table 8.4 presents the β values for the categories of each variable included in Model (4), and the statistical significance of each. The expected probability of an enterprise experiencing a positive impact from Poland's accession to the European Union may be calculated using Equation (8.6) on page 142 and the value of the β coefficients in Table 8.4. The probabilities lie between zero and one, with a value of unity indicating certainty of a positive impact, and a value of zero indicating certainty of a negative impact. A positive (negative) coefficient for a particular category shows the higher (lower) probability of a positive impact for enterprises in that category.

As expected, enterprises in the Gdansk region are expected to benefit more from Poland's EU accession than those in the Lublin region ($\beta = 0.31$, $p = 0.027$). In comparison to Lublin, Gdansk has a higher proportion of enterprises with:

Table 8.2 Empirical results from estimation of the logit model

Variable code	**Wald statistics (significance levels in brackets)**			
	Model 1	**Model 2**	**Model 3**	**Model 4**
X59	2.81 (0.09)	2.72 (0.098)	2.82 (0.09)	4.87 (0.03)
X39	ns	ns	ns	
X1a	6.61 (0.36)	9.79 (0.13)	11.97 (0.06)	14.58 (0.02)
V03	ns	ns	ns	
V04	ns	ns	ns	
V06	ns	ns	ns	
V20	ns	ns		
X12	ns	ns		
X16	ns	ns	ns	
X9	0.14 (0.71)	0.23 (0.62)	3.43 (0.06)	3.22 (0.07)
X10	ns			
X17	ns	ns		
V22	ns	ns		
V23	ns	ns		
V24d	ns	ns		
V25	5.32 (0.70)	5.25 (0.07)	6.79 (0.03)	7.96 (0.018)
V26b	2.73 (0.10)	ns		
X28	ns	ns	ns	
X29	ns			
X40a	ns			
V42b	ns	ns	ns	
V43	ns	ns	ns	
V48	ns	2.02 (0.15)	15.73 (0.000)	17.21 (0.000)
V50	ns	ns	ns	
V52b	ns	ns		
X53	5.17 (0.07)	3.63 (0.16)	3.87 (0.14)	3.20 (0.20)
constant	0.29 (0.59)	0.41 (0.52)	2.27 (0.13)	2.34 (0.12)
Cases	182	270	309	346
LRTS	39.28 (0.00)	67.37 (0.00)	77.98 (0.00)	88.70 (0.00)

Notes: ns = the variable was included in the model but was found to be not statistically significant.
LRTS = likelihood-ratio test statistic. The figures in brackets are the associated p values.

Table 8.3 Frequencies of each category in the sample of Polish enterprises

Code	Variable	Category	Number
X59	Region of establishment	Gdansk	223
		Lublin	123
X1a	Branch of economic activity	Manufacturing	70
		Construction	41
		Trade	139
		Hotels/restaurants	12
		Transport/storage/ Communication	26
		Financial intermediation	10
		Other services	48
X9	Ownership of other enterprises	No	322
		Yes	24
V25	Extent of Internet use	No use	137
		Yes, slight	133
		Yes, significant	76
V48	Knowledge level about EU markets	High	62
		Medium	220
		Low	64
X53	Any difficulty for the enterprise in getting a loan?	No	185
		Yes	64
		No attempt yet	97

Note: The sample consists of the 346 enterprises used in the estimation of Model (4).

- greater orientation of production to the international markets;
- advantages over their competitors as far as the price achieved, the quality of the products, the reputation of the enterprise, the effectiveness of marketing and promotion, and the technological level of the products/services; and
- formal co-operation with providers.

In contrast, Lublin has a higher proportion of enterprises than Gdansk with:

- higher effectiveness;
- advantages over competitors as far as the attractiveness and modernity of their products and services are concerned, and the relatively low cost of production;
- formal co-operation with consumers' organizations;

Table 8.4 Detailed empirical results from estimation of the logit model

Code	Variable	Category	β	SE (β)	Wald statistic	Significance
X59	Region of establishment	Gdansk	0.31	0.14	4.87	0.027
X1a	Branch of economic activity				14.58	0.024
		Manufacturing	−1.87	1.48	1.60	0.2
		Construction	−1.26	1.49	0.71	0.39
		Trade	−1.23	1.47	0.70	0.4
		Hotels/restaurants	5.54	8.69	0.41	0.52
		Transport/storage/ Communication	−1.05	1.54	0.47	0.49
		Financial intermediation	−0.30	1.74	0.03	0.86
X9	Ownership of other enterprises	No	−0.73	0.41	3.21	0.07
V25	Extent of Internet use				7.96	0.019
		No use	−0.48	0.2	3.73	0.05
		Yes, slight	−0.36	0.19	3.68	0.05
V48	Knowledge level about EU markets				17.21	0.0002
		High	0.67	0.26	6.55	0.01
		Medium	0.28	0.19	2.32	0.13
X53	Any difficulty for the enterprise in getting a loan?		0.32	0.18	3.20	0.2
		No			3.11	0.08
		Yes	−0.26	0.22	1.35	0.24
	Constant		2.32	1.52	2.35	0.12

Note: The sample consists of the 346 enterprises used in the estimation of Model (4).

- R&D departments in existence; and
- investments in fixed assets made in 1999.

It is expected that the tourism sector (hotels and restaurants) will also be influenced more advantageously by Poland's accession than enterprises in other branches of economic activity. The Polish owners/managers of enterprises operating in the sector consider that the removal of barriers will increase the inflow of tourists from other EU countries. All the entrepreneurs in this branch of economic activity are optimistic about their future in the EU markets, though their views might be influenced by their high rates of profit in 1998 – see Tables 8.5 and 8.6.

In contrast, the prospects in the manufacturing, construction, trade, and other service sectors are more pessimistic, with the results suggesting a higher probability that EU accession will have a negative impact. The owners/managers may believe that they are at a disadvantage in comparison to other enterprises in the developed European countries.

These findings suggest that enterprises in different sectors will be affected in different ways by the accession of Poland to the European Union. However, such conclusions should be treated with some caution, as most of the coefficients are not statistically significant. However, sectoral differences relating to the probability of survival in the European context have been detected in studies of SMEs in both

Table 8.5 Expected impact of accession to the European Union on the sample of Polish SMEs, by branch of economic activity

Branch of economic activity	**Number of enterprises**	**Expected impact of accession**	
		Negative	**Positive**
Manufacturing	70	38	32
Construction	41	18	23
Trade	139	56	83
Hotels/restaurants	12	0	12
Transport/storage/ communication	26	5	21
Financial intermediation	10	1	9
Other services	49	5	44
Total	347	123	224

Note: The sample consists of the 347 enterprises used in the estimation of Model (4). The chi-square test statistic was 39.6 ($p = 0.00$).

Table 8.6 Profitablity of the sample of Polish SMEs, 1998, by branch of economic activity

Branch of economic activity	**Number of enterprises**	**Profitability in 1998**	
		Profit	**Loss**
Manufacturing	71	62	9
Construction	42	39	3
Trade	136	128	8
Hotels/restaurants	9	9	0
Transport/storage/ communication	23	19	4
Financial intermediation	8	7	1
Other services	48	41	7
Total	337	305	32

Note: The chi-square test statistic was 8.8 ($p = 0.72$).

Greece and Poland. Furthermore, the Italian experience demonstrates that participation in the Single European Market has a positive effect on sectors with comparative advantages, while the medium-and high-technology sectors suffered from the increased competition that participation brought (Monaco, 1994).

The enterprises that did not participate with other Polish enterprises have a higher probability of being influenced negatively by Poland's accession to the European Union ($\beta = -0.7$; $p = 0.07$) in comparison to those that did participate. The creation of groups, and of synergy among enterprises, seems to be very important in Poland. The fact that this factor had also been proved to be important in the case of Greece provides a generalized view that enterprises, especially in developing and transition countries, are convinced that this factor is essential for their development in the context of the wider European market.

The extent of Internet use by the enterprise was of high statistical significance ($p = 0.019$) and has a positive influence on the future of the enterprise in the European context. According to the model, those enterprises with no use of the Internet ($\beta = -0.48$), or with only slight use of it ($\beta = -0.36$), have a higher probability of being affected negatively after the elimination of the barriers in comparison with those that use the Internet to a significant extent. The importance of Internet use may well be connected with the possibility of the development of electronic business for Polish enterprises, which is expected to account for a considerable part of future trade. It should be noted that the variable (X25) is the only one in the final model that captures the effects of research and development.

The level of knowledge that the enterprises have about the EU Member States' markets is associated strongly with the impact expected from Poland's accession ($p = 0.0002$). Those enterprises with a high level of knowledge have the highest probability of experiencing a positive impact ($\beta = 0.67$; $p = 0.01$). In addition, those enterprises with a medium level of knowledge have a higher probability of a positive impact ($\beta = 0.28$; $p = 0.13$) than those with a low level of knowledge.

Those enterprises that had not met any problems in securing bank loans have a higher probability of being influenced positively by the accession of Poland to the European Union ($\beta = 0.32$; $p = 0.08$) than those that had either met problems ($\beta = -0.26$; $p = 0.24$), or had not yet tried to get loans. Access to the credit system to finance investments or current obligations seems to be a crucial characteristic for the success of Polish enterprises in the Single European Market. However, 18 per cent of the sample of enterprises had had problems in obtaining a loan, while another 28 per cent had not yet tried to secure a loan and thus were not aware of the difficulties of the whole procedure (see Table 8.3). There are two main problems highlighted by these percentages: the very strict requirements of banks regarding the credibility of the creditor, and the bureaucratic system of loan application. The difficulties associated with obtaining loans seems to affect all branches of economic activity: a chi-square test ($\chi^2 = 121$; $p = 0.43$) revealed no interdependence of the two variables, (X1a) and (X53).

Finally, the positive constant coefficient ($\beta = 2.32$; $p = 0.12$) indicates that the owners/managers of the enterprises in the sample *as a whole* had a positive view of the impact of Poland's accession to the European Union. However, the expected probabilities varied considerably according to the characteristics of individual enterprises. For enterprises that were based in Gdansk; in the tourism sector; participated in other Polish enterprises; made significant use of the Internet; had a good knowledge of the EU market; and had no problems in getting bank loans, the probability was 91 per cent. At the opposite extreme, for an enterprise based in Lublin; in the manufacturing sector; with no experience of participation in other Polish enterprises; no use of the Internet; no knowledge of the EU market; and that had experienced difficulties in obtaining a bank loan, the probability of Poland's accession having a positive influence was only 10 per cent.

CONCLUSIONS

Poland is a country in transition, and its accession to the European Union is in progress. The extent to which this process of accession influences Polish enterprises will be very important to the whole economy. It is of vital importance to determine the characteristics of Polish enterprises that are likely to be associated with EU accession having an advantageous influence on performance, and those characteristics where EU accession might have the opposite effect. This chapter reported the results of a questionnaire survey (carried out towards the end of 1999) of the views of the owners/managers of 376 small Polish enterprises about the perceived impact of EU accession on their enterprises.

The questionnaire data were analyzed by logit analysis, and revealed that the majority of Polish managers were optimistic about the impact that Poland's accession to the European Union was going to have on their enterprises. But there was also considerable variation. For some enterprises, the probability of a positive influence was judged to be as high as 91 per cent, but for others the probability was as low as about 10 per cent. These results highlight the need for a number of important policy initiatives:

- Regional policy to improve the performance of enterprises in the less-favoured regions. The differences found between the Gdansk and Lublin regions must be assessed fully, and an integrated study of regional economic disparities should be undertaken to provide an informed basis for a regional policy.
- Strengthening the enterprises' abilities to participate in other enterprises, to create groups and, in general, to improve their competitiveness through co-operation.
- As Poland seems to have an advantage in tourism, the economic activity of this sector should be encouraged. In general, those sectors in Poland with comparative advantage should be determined in order to gain additional economic incentives for their development in the European context.
- The telecommunications sector should be developed, and further efforts made by the enterprises and more initiatives undertaken by the state to meet these objectives. The use of telemarketing in sales should be exploited further by the small Polish enterprises.
- Information should be collected and disseminated by the state and by official organizations about the needs and other characteristics of the European markets.

- Finally, the access of Polish enterprises to the credit system should be facilitated in order to make easier the access to the banking system. Banks and other financial agencies should reduce the bureaucratic barriers for a loan application. The criteria should be based more on the prospects of an enterprise and less on its assets.

A strategy based on the above initiatives would provide the necessary incentives for Poland's small enterprises not only to survive but to prosper in the environment of increased competition in the Single European Market.

Notes

1. The classification of SMEs in Poland is 0–5 employees for 'micro-enterprises', 6–50 employees for 'small enterprises' and 51–200 employees for 'medium-sized enterprises'.
2. This survey is an offshoot of the research programme undertaken by the authors on 'Small and medium-sized enterprises in Poland: Phase II', financed by the EU Program PHARE-ACE: P–97–8123–R
3. See Goldberger (1964), and Nerlove and Press (1973).
4. The number of employees is used to express the sizes of the enterprises. This variable may not be appropriate if there are substantial variations in capital-intensity between enterprises. Unfortunately, the questions about more appropriate measures, such as the value of sales, had extremely low response rates in the questionnaire survey.

References

Acs, Z. and Audretsch, D. (1989) 'Small Firms in US Manufacturing: A First Report', *Economic Letters*, vol. 31, no. 4, pp. 399–402.

Acs, Z. and Audretsch, D. (1990) *The Economics of Small Firms: A European Challenge*, Amsterdam: Kluwer.

Anagnostaki, V. and Louri, H. (1994) 'Determinants of Entry in the Greek Manufacturing Industry, 1982–88', *Greek Economic Review*, vol. 16, no. 1.

Anagnostaki, V. and Louri, H. (1995) 'Manufacturing Entry in Greece, 1982–99: Did Sectoral Policy Work?', *Journal of Economic Studies*, vol. 22, no. 6.

Balicki, A., Jurkiewicz, T. and Szreder, M. (2000) 'Development of Small Enterprises in Poland: Results of a Sample Survey Conducted in the Province of Gdansk', Paper presented at the ACE Workshop, Kingston, 11–15 March.

Basant, R. and Fikkert, B. (1996) 'The Effect of R&D Foreign Technology, Purchase and Domestic and International Spillovers on Opportunity in Indian Firms', *The Review of Economics and Statistics*, vol. 29, pp. 187–99.

Blawat, F., Ossowski, J. and Zieba, K. (2000) 'Development of Small Enterprises in Poland: Results of a Sample Survey Conducted in the Province of Lublin', Paper presented at the ACE Workshop, Kingston, 11–15 March.

Chassid, I. and Katsos, G. (1992) *European Integration and Greek Industry*, Athens: IOBE (in Greek).

Dhrymes, P. J. (1978) *Introduction to Econometrics*, New York: Springer Verlag.

Draukopoulos, V. and Thomadakis, S. B. (1993) 'The Share of Small and Medium-sized Enterprises in Greek Manufacturing', *Small Business Economics*, pp. 187–96.

Economist Intelligence Unit (1983) *The European Climate for Small Businesses: A 10 Country Study*, London: EIU.

Eurostat (1996) 'Statistics in Focus', *Energy and Industry*, vol. 25.

German Development Institute (1978) *Greece and the European Community: Problems and Prospects of the Greek Small and Medium Industry*, German Development Institute.

Ghatak, S. (2000) 'Small and Medium Size Enterprises in the UK Economy: Lessons for Poland', Paper presented at the ACE Workshop, Kingston, 11–15 March.

Giannitis, T. (1993) 'The Structure of the Technological – Research Activities in the Greek Industry', in T. Giannitis and D. Mavri (eds), *Technological Structures and Technological Transfer in the Greek Industry*, Athens: Gutenberg.

Goldberger, A. (1964) *Econometric Theory*, New York: John Wiley.

Harissis, K. (1986) *Staff Turnover in the Personal Social Services: A Statistical Approach*, Ph.D. dissertation, University of Kent.

Knapp, M., Harissis, K. and Missiakoulis, S. (1982) 'Investigating Labour Turnover and Wastage using the Logit Technique', *Journal of Occupational Psychology*, vol. 55, pp. 129–38.

Liargovas, P. and Tsipouri, H. (1997) *Structural Problems of Greek Industry and the Implementation of the White Paper on Development, Employment and Competitiveness in Greece*, Hellenic Center for European Studies, Research Paper No. 44.

Lichtenberg, F. and Siegel, D. (1991) 'The Impact of R&D Investment on Inquire Productivity: New Evidence using Linked R&D–LRD Data', *Economics*, vol. 29, pp.203–9.

Lymperaki, A. (1991) *Flexible Specialization*. Athens: Gutenberg, (in Greek).

Manolas, G., Rontos, C. and Vavouras, I (1999) 'The Future of SMEs in Poland in the Context of the European Union', Paper presented at the Gdansk Workshop, Poland, October.

Manolas, G., Rontos, C. and Vavouras, I. (2000) 'Research of Small and Medium-sized Enterprises in Poland', Paper presented at the ACE Workshop, Kingston, 11–15 March.

Monaco, T. (1994) 'European Integration and Regional Cohesion: An Evaluation of the Economic Impact of the Single Market on Italian Regional Development', Paper presented at the second meeting of the Economic and Social Cohesion Network, Florence, 3–4 June.

National Statistical Service of Greece, (1997) *Positive and Negative Impacts of SMP on Greek Enterprises*, Athens: NSSG.

Nerlove, M. and Press, J. (1973) *Univariate and Multivariate Loglinear Logistic Models*, R-1306-EDA/NIH, Santa Monica, Calif.: Rand.
OECD (Organization for Economic Co-operation and Development) (1997) *Globalisation and Small and Medium Enterprises, vols 1 and 2*, Paris: OECD.
Palaskas, T., Reppas, P. and Christopoulos, D. (1999) 'An Analysis of the Determinants of R&D Activities in the Greek Industrial Sector', Paper presented at Panteio University of Athens.
Skovgaard, M. (1990) *Analytic Statistical Models: Lecture Notes*, Institute of Mathematical Statistics.

9 The Impact of Adjustment-led Transformation on Small-Scale Manufacturing in Bulgaria

Berhanu Kassayie

INTRODUCTION

The stabilization and adjustment packages of the World Bank group have been subscribed to, and implemented by, governments in most former socialist countries. However, the overwhelming evidence from many studies in adjusting developing countries suggests that the implementation of these policies has been associated with a dismal response in terms of investment and growth in the private-sector economy, including small-scale enterprises (SSEs) (Vitorio and Jaime, 1985; Dornbusch, 1990; Steel and Webster, 1990; Helmsing and Kolstee, 1993).

In November 1989, the reformist flank of the Communist Party in Bulgaria removed President Teodor Zhivkov from power, renamed the party the Bulgarian Socialist Party, and assumed power on winning the first free elections in 1990. The transformation of the Bulgarian system thus started as a top-down reform for democracy and a market-led economic system. During the first two years, the reform measures were primarily in the political sphere, and were characterized by spontaneity and instability. A new constitution came into force in July 1991, which proclaimed Bulgaria as a unicameral, presidential, parliamentary republic, and enshrined the principles of freedom of expression and private property.

In the economic sphere, the reform programme adopted by the Bulgarian government at the end of 1991, in agreement with the IMF and the World Bank, included two main packages of measures: macroeconomic stabilization and adjustment measures to eliminate imbalances in the economy, and structural reforms for the establishment of the institutions of a market economy. The reform measures outlined in the programme included:

- the liberalization of prices, trade and exchange rates;
- the reduction of macroeconomic imbalances through tight monetary and fiscal policy;
- a tight incomes policy and the radical restructuring of the social security system;
- the introduction of a hard budget constraint and the implementation of structural reforms related to the restructuring and privatization of state-owned enterprises (SOEs), and the reform of the banking and financial system; and
- institutional reform and the lifting of all restrictions on private initiative. These measures were similar to the adjustment[1] policies implemented in many developing countries, taking into account the scale and scope of the envisaged transformation. Hence, the Bulgarian reform programme was predominantly 'adjustment-led', in the sense that it was designed to facilitate the transformation to a 'free-market economy' through a process of stabilization and structural adjustment.

This chapter presents the findings of a firm-level survey in Bulgaria,[2] and attempts to assess whether the adjustment-led reform process has had an impact in any way on small manufacturing start-ups and expansion. The chapter starts with a discussion of 'hidden privatization' and the origin of the new manufacturing start-ups, and assesses the effects of reform on the growth and development of the new start-ups during the early 1990s. The following section compares the main features of the Bulgarian survey sample with those of similar surveys of small-scale firms undertaken in selected Central and East European countries.[3] This comparison is undertaken with respect to the regional distribution, the legal form, and the size distribution of the firms. The effects of reform on new manufacturing start-ups, and on the expansion of existing firms, are then investigated. The main finding is a tendency towards larger new manufacturing start-ups in Bulgaria concurrent with the beginnings of institutional transformation and economic reform. Furthermore, this appears to have been effected through favoured access to equipment and external finance for the larger 'small' enterprises. It was also found that reform had a positive impact on the expansion of existing firms, and that this impact was stronger for the larger 'small' firms.

THE ORIGINS OF PRIVATE MANUFACTURING IN BULGARIA

The overwhelming majority of the firms in the sample[4] were reported as new start-ups. In answer to the question 'How did the present owner(s) acquire this firm?', 87 per cent of the respondents reported that they had established the firms themselves. Other forms of acquisition included leases from SOEs, purchase from central or local government auctions, and purchase from private owners and government leases. In fact, except in the case of large enterprises, until 1996 transfers through organized privatization were of little importance at the firm level,[5] and small-scale privatization concentrated predominantly on service units.

Compared to other Central and East European (CEE) countries, the proportion of Bulgarian small private manufacturers that were new start-ups at their inception, is considerably larger – see Table 9.1. In Hungary, where the tradition of some form of private economy survived despite four decades of Communist pressure, new start-ups accounted for 27 per cent of firms. In Bulgaria and Poland, where the implementation of formal privatization was slower, the shares of new

Table 9.1 Origins of private manufacturing firms in selected Central and East European countries

Country	New private start-ups (%)	Privatization (%)	Pre-reform second economy (%)
Bulgaria	87	10	3
Former Czechoslovakia	55	42	3
Hungary	27	60	13
Poland	63	15	12

Notes: The figures provide a percentage breakdown for each country of the origin of the private manufacturing firms in the various sample surveys.
The 'second economy' is a pre-reform sector that existed outside the centrally-planned economy, and consisted of various illegal, semi-legal and legal small-scale activities and co-operative enterprises attached to SOEs and operating with diverse contractual arrangements.
Sources: Bulgaria: survey results.
Former Czechoslovakia: Webster and Swanson (1993).
Poland: Webster (1993a).
Hungary: Webster (1993b).

start-ups in private manufacturing were higher: 87 per cent and 63 per cent, respectively. Interestingly, however, in the former Czechoslovakia, where privatization was relatively comprehensive and swift, the proportion of private manufacturing originating through new start-ups was 13 per cent higher than that originating from privatization. Despite its less comprehensive and less swift character, privatization in Hungary was the origin for 60 per cent of emerging private manufacturing firms, 18 per cent more than in the former Czechoslovakia.

Where there was a relatively more liberalized environment, as in Hungary and Poland, a higher proportion of firms had their origin in the second economy that existed outside the centrally planned economy of state socialism. Overall, the above analysis suggests that differences in the speed and scale of privatization have not been such important determinants of the role of new start-ups in emerging private manufacturing. As economists such as Gelqb (1991) have suggested, comprehensive and speedy privatization has not always led to a significant transfer of production capital to small, private manufacturing. The single most important influence behind the significant role of new inceptions has probably been the dominance of large-scale enterprises in the socialist past, and the 'hidden privatization' that accompanied their restructuring under the market-led transformation.

Although the majority of Bulgarian small manufacturing firms were new start-ups, some local studies (for example, Avramov and Genov, 1995), and my own discussions with local academics, have indicated that, in most cases, these firms were not the result of new investment but rather that their origin may be traced indirectly to former state and co-operative enterprises. The main channels in this process of 'hidden privatization' were the total or partial take-overs of divisions of large state and co-operative enterprises by their former higher or middle management personnel, in most cases with their employees, local customers and overseas markets. A few examples provided some illustrations. A former designer, her husband (the former general manager of a state-owned clothing enterprise), and a former financial manager who, having bought the recently imported equipment, took with them the enterprise's fifty best tailors, and established a women's' fashion clothing firm in a rented property in 1991. A former chief accountant of a soft-drinks-producing subsidiary of a large co-operative who, with her son, secured the entire firm with its workers through an early privatization. Two former departmental managers of a large state-owned machinery plant (restructured in 1991), who managed to secure thirty of its skilled workforce and the necessary equipment to set up an assembly firm in a leased property. Overall, the history of the firms in the sample suggests that the majority of Bulgarian small manufacturers were spin-offs from state decontrol and the restructuring of SOEs.

THE DEVELOPMENT OF PRIVATE MANUFACTURING IN BULGARIA

Economic reform and liberalization in Bulgaria was initiated officially in 1990, and Figure 9.1 shows how the numbers of new manufacturing firms have changed over the period 1989–95. The trend in the rate of emerging private manufacturing depicted by the sample data reflects closely that in the aggregate national data, with the exception of 1993. The variation in 1993 is most probably because of the obligatory re-registration introduced in 1992, which would have inflated the aggregate data for 1993 by including many firms established prior to that date.

The survey data revealed significant differences ($\chi^2 = 197, p < 0.05$) between the year in which firms were established and the year in which they actually became operational – see Figure 9.2. While 43 per cent of the firms in the sample were established during 1990 and 1991, only 28

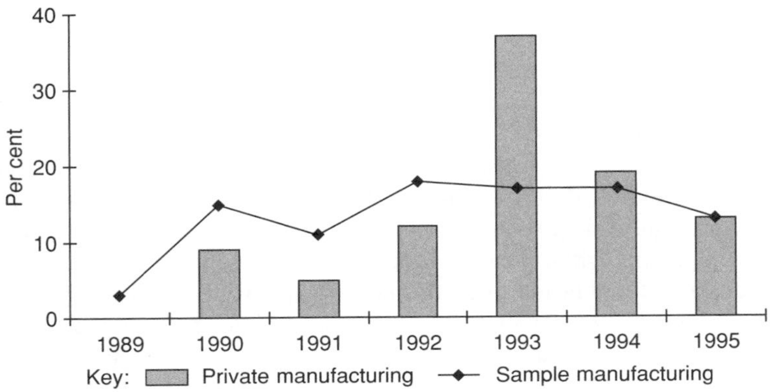

Figure 9.1 New entrants in Bulgarian private manufacturing, 1989–95

Note: The figures refer to the annual numbers of new start-ups as percentages of the total number of sample firms established over the period 1989–95.
Sources: National Statistics Institute (various editions); Survey results.

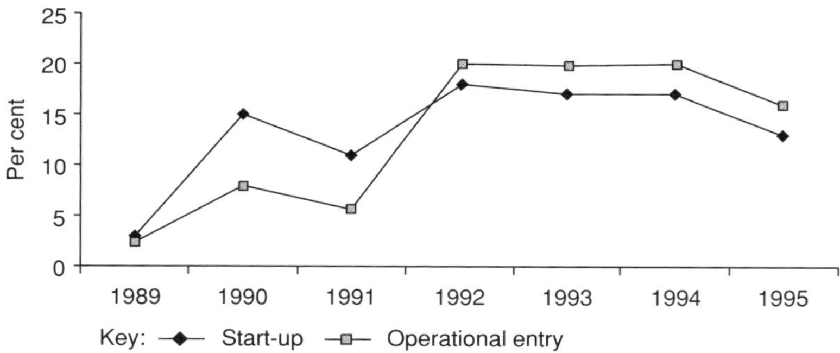

Figure 9.2 The establishment and operational start-up of the sample of Bulgarian firms, 1989–95

Note: The figures refer to the percentage of total entrants over the period 1989–95.
Sources: National Statistics Institute (various editions); Survey results.

per cent started operations during this period. The proportion of enterprises starting operations rose during 1992–5, possibly because of the release of capital goods and skilled labour following the massive 1991 restructuring of SOEs, and the subsequent launch of organized privatization in 1992. Apart from the 1990–1 period, however, a large proportion of small manufacturers became operational, either in the same year or in the year following their inception. Only about 8 per cent of all the surveyed enterprises had not become operational two years after their establishment, and the majority of them were established at the beginning of the Bulgarian transformation. The above findings appear to gainsay the claim, at least for registered small manufacturing, that most emerging Bulgarian private enterprises were non-operating shell companies (Pissarides, 1996).

In general, both the data on firm establishment and on operational start-ups indicate that the official launch of transformation in 1990 had an immediate and marked impact on the rate of emerging private manufacturing. This initial push is revealed by the jumps in the rates of new firm establishments and operational start-ups from 3 per cent and 2 per cent, respectively, in 1989, to 22 per cent and 15 per cent, respectively, in 1990. Given the concurrent economic recession and political instability, the impact of the launch of system reform and of initial liberalization appears to have been very strong. However, the implications for small-firm start-up must be seen alongside the widespread spontaneous and hidden privatization during the early stage of transformation. In the three years following the introduction of a market-led institutional setting and the introduction of economic reform (that is, in 1992, 1993 and 1994), the number of small manufacturing firms starting operations was relatively constant. This suggests that 'reform institutionalization'[6] in 1992 had little more than a stabilizing impact on the emergence of new private manufacturing activity in Bulgaria.

To investigate further the effects of 'reform institutionalization', the survey sample was divided into two groups, according to when the firms became operational. The first group, hereafter referred to as the *pioneer firms*, comprised those firms that became operational during the three years before the end of 1992, and which might be expected to have faced comparatively unfavourable and riskier conditions. The second group, the *advantaged firms*, were those that started operations during the three years after the 'reform institutionalization' in 1992, and which therefore began operations in a rather clearer institutional and market environment. The numbers of pioneer firms and advantaged firms in the sample were similar – see Table 9.2 – suggesting that the 'reform institutionalization' had not had any significant impact[7] on the rate at which small private firms had emerged in Bulgaria's manufacturing industry, despite the more favourable climate. The implication is that the 'push effect' of system reform (in the form of signalling the direction and nature of the future socioeconomic set-up, liberalization of the regulatory framework and political security, and

Table 9.2 Survey sample of Bulgarian firms, analyzed by size and year of entry into operation

Size of firm	**Firms in sample**		**Pioneer firms**	**Advantaged firms**
	Number	**Percentage of total**		
Micro (1–10 employees)	72	51	30 (42)	42 (58)
Medium–small (11–25 employees)	45	32	27 (60)	18 (40)
Small (26–50 employees)	25	17	8 (32)	17 (68)
Total	142	100	65 (46)	77 (54)

Note: Figures in brackets are the percentages of firms within each size category.
Source: Survey results.

the disorder that followed the immediate withdrawal of the state from practising its control rights over the SOEs) was the primary source for the re-emergence of a large proportion of small manufacturers in Bulgaria. At least with regard to small manufacturing, these findings cast doubt on the efficacy of the shock-therapy reform programmes, as prescribed and implemented in many transition economies, as a means of promoting the development of private firms.

The firms in the sample may also be classified by size, according to their levels of employment – see again Table 9.2. Firms with up to ten employees are classified as 'micro' enterprises; those with between 11 and 25 employees as 'medium–small' enterprises; and those with between 26 and 50 employees as 'small' enterprises. Thus, 51 per cent of the sample were micro enterprises, and 32 per cent and 17 per cent were medium–small and small enterprises, respectively. The average employment level of the firms in the sample was fifteen persons, while average sales were US$150 000 – see Table 9.3. The average sales of the micro firms were US$35 000, and those of the medium–small and small enterprises were US$113 000 and US$561 000, respectively. Three-quarters of the firms in the sample had sales of less than US$100 000, but the average figure was raised by three firms with annual sales of over US$1 million. As is the case in other developing and developed countries, sole proprietorship was the most popular legal form for the micro and medium–small enterprises, while the limited liability company was the favoured form for the small firms. Overall, the above analysis demonstrates that the micro enterprise was the dominant size of emerging private manufacturer in Bulgaria, and suggests that firm-level privatization has not made any meaningful contribution to the rebirth of small private manufacturing.

The firms in the sample survey were classified as one of six industrial sectors – see Table 9.4. Twenty per cent were found in each of the 'machinery and metalwork' and 'food and drink' industries, with 'clothing', 'chemicals and plastics' and 'electrical and electronics' accounting for 18 per cent, 16 per cent and 15 per cent, respectively. The 'textiles and knitwear' industry had the lowest representation, with only 11 per cent of the sample. The highest average annual sales were reported by the 'textiles and knitwear' firms, followed by those in 'chemicals and plastics'.

The sectoral distribution of the sample firms was rather different from that of all manufacturing enterprises – see Figure 9.3. The proportions of 'chemicals and plastics' and 'clothing' firms were rather higher than the aggregate figures, while the share of 'textiles and

Table 9.3 Survey sample of Bulgarian firms, analyzed by size and legal form of organization

Size of firm	Number of firms	Average sales (US$000s)	Legal form of organization		
			Sole proprietorship (%)	Limited liability (%)	Other (%)
Micro (1–10 employees)	72	35	74	14	12
Medium–small (11–25 employees)	45	113	53	29	18
Small (26–50 employees)	25	561	24	64	12
Total	142	150	59	27	14

Notes: The 'Other' category includes partnerships, joint stock companies, and co-operatives operating on a lease or a lease-to-buy arrangement.
Source: Survey results.

Table 9.4 Survey sample of Bulgarian firms, analyzed by sector

Sector	Number of firms	Average employment	Average sales (US$000s)
Machinery & metalwork	29	17	112
Electrical & electronics	21	12	102
Chemicals & plastics	23	20	283
Textiles & knitwear	16	14	340
Clothing	25	18	63
Food & drink	28	10	46
Whole sample	142	15	150

Notes: The data on average employment and average sales relate to 1995, when the exchange rate for US$1 was 70.7 lev.
Source: Survey results.

knitwear' firms was rather lower. These differences might have resulted from an unrepresentative sample, or they may reflect differences in the sectoral distributions of small and large firms in the Bulgarian economy. This latter interpretation would be consistent with the view that

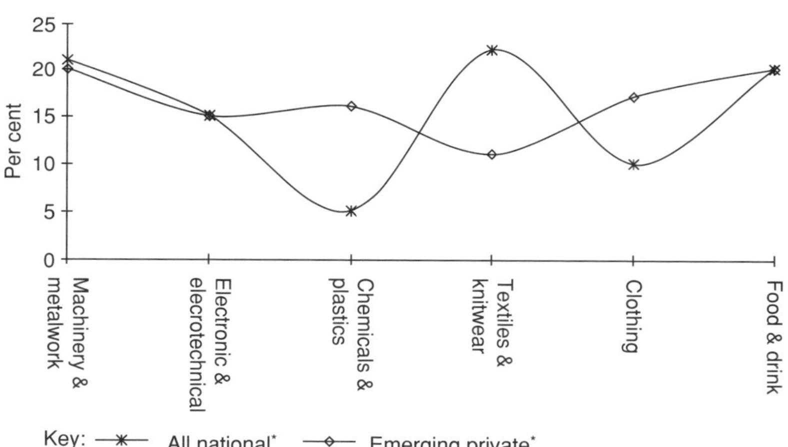

Figure 9.3 A comparison of the sectoral distribution of the Bulgarian sample with the national distribution, 1995

Note: The figures refer to the percentage of total entrants starting operations during 1995.
Sources: National Statistics Institute (various editions); Survey results.

many of the small private manufacturers had emerged not as a result of new investment but rather from within existing company structures. It might be expected that certain sectors (for example, 'food and drink' and 'clothing') would be more attractive to small business in the early stages of transformation. However, a chi-square test ($\chi_2 = 4.87, p < 0.05$) did not support this hypothesis, which suggests that the entry of small businesses had not favoured the above sectors but had also penetrated modern sectors such as 'electrical and electronics'. The inter-industry pattern also did not appear to be influenced by whether the entrants were pioneer firms or advantaged firms. Even during the early years of reform, entrepreneurs were establishing small firms in all sectors of manufacturing. Neither the reforms nor 'reform institutionalization' had had any significant effect on the emerging inter-industry pattern of private manufacturing.

A COMPARISON OF SMALL-SCALE MANUFACTURING IN BULGARIA AND IN OTHER SELECTED CENTRAL AND EAST EUROPEAN COUNTRIES

It is instructive to compare the composition of the sample of firms from the Bulgarian survey with those from similar surveys of small-scale firms in the former Czechoslovakia, Poland and Hungary (Webster, 1993a, 1993b; Webster and Swanson, 1993). This comparison is undertaken with respect to the regional distribution, the legal form, and the size distribution of the firms.

The Regional Distribution of Small Private Manufacturing Firms

The highest concentration of private manufacturers in the Bulgarian sample was found in the regions of Sofia and Plovdiv, with 30 per cent and 27 per cent, respectively. Interestingly, these two regions had a relatively more developed entrepreneurial tradition prior to the 1944 Communist revolution. The next highest concentrations of sample enterprises, with 13 per cent and 12 per cent, respectively, were found in Starazagora and Ruse, while Burgas (one of Bulgaria's largest heavy industry centres) had the lowest proportion of private manufacturing firms. This regional distribution is similar to that demonstrated by the aggregate data for all manufacturing enterprises in the country.[8]

The geographic distribution of Bulgarian private manufacturing firms is similar to those in Poland and Hungary, with the majority

Table 9.5 Regional distribution of private manufacturing firms in selected Central and East European countries

Country	Regional cities (%)	Rural Towns (%)
Bulgaria	65	35
Former Czechoslovakia	38	62
Hungary	60	46
Poland	54	46

Note: The figures provide a percentage breakdown for each country of the location of the private manufacturing firms in the various sample surveys.
Sources: Bulgaria: survey results.
Former Czechoslovakia: Webster and Swanson (1993).
Poland: Webster (1993a).
Hungary: Webster (1993b).

located in the regional cities – see Table 9.5. Sixty-five per cent of the firms in the Bulgarian sample were located in cities, and only 35 per cent in rural areas. The situation in the former Czechoslovakia is rather different, where the concentration of firms is higher in rural towns.

Possible explanations for this regional distribution are many. One factor is the relative cost and marketing advantages emanating from better access to established infrastructure, trade and distribution networks, and markets. A second might be the geographic distribution of the labour force. Under the Communist regime, Bulgaria had urbanized rapidly, and by 1995 over a third of the population lived in urban areas. However, the rural–urban spread of the working population was almost equal; in 1995, 49 per cent of the working population was based in rural areas, and 47 per cent in urban centres (National Statistics Institute, 1995). However, the proximity of the urban centres, because of the small size of the country, and the relatively developed transport network, meant that rural people were easily able to travel to work in urban industrial centres. It thus appears that the regional distribution of labour was not an important factor in determining the geographic spread of emerging small manufacturing. The final, and probably the main, factor influencing the geographic dispersion of small manufacturers, was the inherited distribution of industrial activity. This is consistent with the proposition that the former state and co-operative enterprises were the major source of equipment, labour and entrepreneurs.

The Legal Form of the Small Private Manufacturing Firms

The most favoured legal form among the sample of Bulgarian private manufacturers was sole proprietorship, which accounted for 59 per cent of the surveyed firms – see Table 9.6. Limited liability companies formed the second largest group, with 39 per cent of the sample of firms. There were relatively few partnerships and joint stock companies in the sample, accounting for only 14 per cent of the responding firms. These proportions were quite different from those evidenced in other CEE countries.

Many factors contribute to the explanation of the predominance of sole proprietorship in Bulgaria. In addition to the small amount of required start-up capital, some entrepreneurs were registering their units as sole proprietorships in order to enjoy larger tax concessions than those offered to higher forms of corporate organization. In contrast to the regulations governing the establishment capital of limited liability companies and partnerships, the section of the 1991 Commercial Law on sole proprietorship requires a simple act of registration, with the sole proviso being that bankrupts are ineligible to establish other commercial enterprises. The lack of a recent tradition in entrepreneurship also meant that entrepreneurs were not ready or happy to share and delegate the running of their enterprises. Combined with the pride of owning one's own business for the first time, this factor

Table 9.6 Legal organization of private manufacturing firms in selected Central and East European countries

Country	Sole proprietorship (%)	Limited liability company (%)	Other
Bulgaria	59	27	14
Former Czechoslovakia	–	'nearly all'	–
Hungary	9	91	0
Poland	20	80	0

Notes: The figures provide a percentage breakdown for each country of the legal organisation of the private manufacturing firms in the various sample surveys. The 'other' category includes partnerships, joint stock companies, and co-operatives operating on lease or lease-to-buy arrangements.
Sources: Bulgaria: survey results.
Former Czechoslovakia: Webster and Swanson (1993).
Poland: Webster (1993a).
Hungary: Webster (1993b).

contributed to entrepreneurs' emphasis on controlling decision-making, especially during the start-up and early stages of business operation. Finally, the comparatively unsettled legal and institutional environment in Bulgaria fuelled a lack of trust and insecurity between emerging entrepreneurs. Some entrepreneurs, during the semi-structured interviews, expressed the opinion that sharing managerial control was an unworthy step, and that they preferred their firms to remain and grow as one-person operations.

Seventy-two per cent of the limited liability companies were *advantaged firms*, while 89 per cent of the partnerships were *pioneer firms*. This suggests that the process of 'reform institutionalization' was having an impact on the corporate organization of emerging manufacturers, with limited liability companies increasingly finding favour.

The Size Distribution of the Small Private Manufacturing Firms

As noted above, the average employment of the surveyed firms in the Bulgarian sample was fifteen persons. This is considerably lower than the corresponding figures for the surveyed firms in the former Czechoslovakia, Hungary and Poland – see Table 9.7 – and more in line with that found in other parts of the world, such as Africa.[9] Micro enterprises comprised 51 per cent of the Bulgarian sample, and just under a quarter had 11–20 employees and another charter 21–50 employees.[10] In contrast, about two-thirds of the firms in the other three countries had between 11 and 50 employees. This dominant position of the micro firm in Bulgaria may be explained in part by the entrepreneurs' desire to remain small and 'in the shadow of the economy' (Hillman *et al.*, 1995, p. 50) and thus insulated from the tax authorities.

THE EFFECTS OF REFORM ON NEW MANUFACTURING START-UPS IN BULGARIA

Fifty-four per cent of the firms in the Bulgarian sample were established after 1992: that is, they were 'advantaged' – see Table 9.2. The other 46 per cent were 'pioneer' firms. But there appear to be differences in the size structures of the two groups. Whereas only 12 per cent of the pioneer firms were 'small' at start-up, the corresponding proportion of the advantaged firms was 22 per cent, and accounted for 68 per cent of all 'small' firms in the survey. It appears that reform institutionalization had an impact on the size of manufacturing enter-

Table 9.7 Size distribution of private manufacturing firms in selected Central and East European countries

Country	**Percentage of firms with employment**					**Average employment**
	1–10	**11–20**	**21–50**	**50 +**	**Total**	
Bulgaria	51.4	24.1	24.5	0	100	15
Former Czechoslovakia	16	27	37	20	100	42
Hungary	9	30	36	25	100	44
Poland	20	38	29	13	100	32

Notes: The figures refer to the percentage of private manufacturing firms in each size category in the sample surveys for each country. The size categories are defined in terms of the numbers of employees.

The average employment figure for the firms in the former Czechoslovakia is inflated by the inclusion of a few firms with more than 100 employees.

Sources: Bulgaria: survey results.

Former Czechoslovakia: Webster and Swanson (1993).

Poland: Webster (1993a).

Hungary: Webster (1993b).

prises at start-up, and this is confirmed by the results of a chi-square test ($\chi^2 = 6.06, p < 0.05$).

This size effect may be further explored by examining data on the sale and replacement values of the firms, and the equipment they had acquired – see Table 9.8. The data on the firm values (sale or replacement) show only small differences between the pioneer and the advantaged firms, which were classified as either micro or medium–small. But both the average sale and replacement values of the small advantaged firms were significantly higher than the corresponding values for the small pioneer firms.

The above finding raises the question of whether reform progress had entailed favoured access to capital goods and external finance. It is evident from Table 9.8 that both the average sale and replacement values of equipment acquired by the micro and medium–small advantaged firms were lower than those of the equipment acquired by the micro and medium–small pioneer firms. In contrast, the small advantaged firms acquired equipment with a value, on average, about 2.5 times that of the small pioneer firms. This suggests that the liberalization of prices, trade, and exchange rates, and the restructuring and privatization of the state and co-operative enterprises, that accompanied reform may well have favoured small firms' access to both local and foreign capital goods markets.

Reform institutionalization also seems to have had an impact on the type of acquired technology. The larger firms operate with relatively more new equipment, and reform institutionalization has had a positive effect on this situation – see Table 9.9. Micro and medium–small firms appear to have larger proportions of secondhand equipment.

Another important aspect of the reform process relates to the acquisition of imported equipment. Eighty-three of the firms in the sample had imported equipment, of which 42 per cent were micro, 35 per cent were medium–small, and 23 per cent were small firms. The observed variations in the proportions of pioneer and advantaged firms that had imported equipment were not statistically significant ($\chi^2 = 1.99, p > 0.05$), suggesting that reform progress had not influenced the access of equipment from overseas markets. However, it appears that the proportion of firms within each size category that had imported equipment rises in line with the size of the firm. Thus only 61 per cent of the micro pioneer firms had imported equipment, whereas 87 per cent of the small pioneer firms had done so. The corresponding figures for the advantaged firms were 49 per cent and 86 per cent.

Table 9.8 Survey sample of Bulgarian firms, analyzed by value, and type and size of firm

Type and size of firm	**Firm value (US$)**		**Equipment value (US$)**	
	Sale value	**Replacement value**	**Sale value**	**Replacement value**
Pioneer firms				
Micro	9000	5000	3000	6000
Medium–small	13000	16000	15000	11000
Small	18000	18000	16000	15100
Advantaged firms				
Micro	3000	5000	3000	2000
Medium–small	13000	12000	7000	8000
Small	99000	106000	41000	37000

Note: The data relate to 1995, when the exchange rate for US$1 was 70.7 lev.
The 'sale value' is defined as the estimated market value of the enterprises if the entrepreneurs had sold their firms in 1995.
The 'replacement value' is defined as the estimated value of the capital required in 1995 to re-establish the sample firms from scratch.
Source: Survey results.

Table 9.9 Survey sample of Bulgarian firms, analyzed by source of technology, and type and size of firm

Type and size of firm	Proportion of secondhand equipment			Imported equipment		Formal credit
	≤ 25%	26–50%	> 50%	As % of total firms of each type	As % of total firms of each size	
Pioneer firms						
Micro	52	29	44	42	61	20
Medium–small	35	57	44	39	62	55
Small	13	14	11	18	87	25
Totals	100	100	100	100		100
Advantaged firms						
Micro	23	50	62	42	49	9
Medium–small	30	30	22	31	82	41
Small	47	20	16	27	86	50
Totals	100	100	100	100		100

Notes: 'Secondhand equipment' refers to all used equipment, whether acquired domestically or from overseas. 'Imported equipment' refers to both new and secondhand equipment acquired from overseas.
Except where indicated, the data refer to the proportions of firms of the specified type and size.
Source: Survey results.

Reform progress may also have favoured certain firms with regard to access to external finance. Thirty-four of the sample firms had succeeded in obtaining either formal or semi-formal credit, of which 30 per cent were micro firms, 35 per cent were medium–small firms, and a further 35 per cent were small firms. A chi-square test ($\chi^2 = 6.9, p > 0.05$) confirms that the small firms were disproportionately successful. Of the pioneer firms that had obtained credit, 20 per cent, 55 per cent and 25 per cent were micro, medium–small and small enterprises, respectively. The situation with regard to the advantaged firms was, however, rather different. Only 9 per cent of the successes were micro firms, whereas 50 per cent were small firms. Reform institutionalization thus seems to have favoured small firms' access to external finance, which may explain, at least partially, the increase in their start-up sizes.

It was shown in Table 9.2 that micro firms accounted for over 50 per cent of the sample. However, their percentage share of annual new start-ups declined steadily between 1990 and 1995 – see Table 9.10. In contrast, the share of the medium–small enterprises increased substantially, from 6 per cent in 1990 to 27 per cent in 1995. Eighteen per cent of the new start-ups in 1990 were small enterprises, many of which were likely to have been firms established by insiders capitalizing on the unsettled macro environment in the wake of the initiation of reform. This percentage dipped in subsequent years to a low of 6 per cent in 1993, before increasing thereafter.

Table 9.10 Size distribution of the Bulgarian sample of firms, 1990–5

Size of firm	**1990**	**1991**	**1992**	**1993**	**1994**	**1995**
Micro	76	74	73	73	65	60
Medium–small	6	14	19	21	25	27
Small	18	11	8	6	10	13
Total	100	100	100	100	100	100
Number of firms	17	35	63	87	118	135
χ^2	14.6	26.4	45.8	66.3	57.8	47.6
p	< 0.05	< 0.05	< 0.05	< 0.05	< 0.05	< 0.05

Notes: The number of firms refers to those that have started operations, and that have reported employment figures for each year.
The chi-square statistics (and the p values) relate to tests of whether the size distribution of the firms vary from year to year.
Source: Survey results.

It would be inappropriate to read too much into these figures, as the information is from a small and non-uniform sample. Nevertheless, there does appear to have been a tendency towards larger new manufacturing start-ups in Bulgaria concurrent with the beginnings of institutional transformation and economic reform. Furthermore this appears to have been effected through favoured access to equipment and external finance for the larger 'small' enterprises. An obvious, and related, question is thus whether reform progress has also had an impact on the expansion of firms.

THE EFFECTS OF REFORM ON THE EXPANSION OF MANUFACTURING FIRMS IN BULGARIA

To investigate the effects of reform on the expansion of firms, data were collated on the average annual growth rates of sales, employment, and investment.[11] The figures in Table 9.11 depict these growth rates for the surveyed firms surviving at the end of each year in the period 1991–5. It appears that 1992 – the year in which reform institutionalization was instigated – was a favourable year for small, private manufacturers.

Table 9.11 Average annual growth rates of firms in the Bulgarian sample, 1991–5

	1991	**1992**	**1993**	**1994**	**1995**
Sales					
Percentage growth rate	151.6	433.7	252.8	129.5	689.8
Number of firms	132	132	132	132	132
Employment					
Percentage growth rate	119.4	130.9	128.9	131.9	142.8
Number of firms	130	130	130	130	130
Investment					
Percentage growth rate	(61.0)	458.2	128.4	(28.1)	129.2
Number of firms	124	124	124	124	124

Notes: The growth rates for sales and investment are calculated based on the US dollar equivalent of the lev-denominated figures at each year's average annual exchange rate, and deflated using the consumer price index.
The numbers of firms used to calculate the growth rates for sales, employment and investment varies, because some values were missing for some years.
Source: Survey results.

On average, sales were four times higher than in the previous year. Sales growth slowed in the ensuing two years, before surging again in 1995. This latter period of strong growth coincided with a favourable macro-economic and political environment, as both GDP and manufacturing output grew in that year, by 2 per cent and 5 per cent, respectively (National Statistics Institute, 1996), for the first time since 1989.

Employment figures demonstrate much steadier growth, while the data on investment growth rates reveal substantial annual variations, with negative growth recorded in both 1991 and 1994. The negative figure for 1991 probably reflects the fact that many of the firms had only just been established, and thus may have had little spare capital left after the initial investment. The drop in investment in 1994 can probably be ascribed to the fall in the sales growth rate and the uncertain economic environment of that year, while the improved situation in 1995 gave rise to positive growth once again.

It thus appears that the period of economic reform has been associated with substantial growth in the sales, employment, and investment of small firms in Bulgaria. This proposition was tested formally by the use of repeated-measures multivariate analysis-of-variance, and the results of the statistical analysis are shown in Table 9.12. The results are mixed, in that reform was not found to have had a significant effect on the growth rates of sales, employment or investment for the surveyed firms taken as a whole. However, marked differences were found in the growth rates achieved by firms in the three different size categories, particularly in relation to sales and investment. For the most part, small firms grew at a faster rate than medium–small and micro firms. It thus appears that reform has not only had a positive impact in terms of the numbers of new manufacturing start-ups, but also on the expansion of existing firms, and that this impact has been stronger for the larger 'small' firms.

However, there are two important caveats to the above conclusion. First, reform was not the only factor contributing to the growth and expansion of small manufacturing. Many of the firms in the survey were operating either as suppliers or as customers to the SOEs, and thus there were widespread transfers of value-added from the SOEs to the private sector. Second, the process of reform did not lead to a macro environment that was entirely conducive to the growth and smooth operation of small manufacturing. Not only did the reform strategy introduce many constraints for entrepreneurs; there were also inconsistencies in the implementation of the strategy, and the growth and performance of small manufacturers was heavily cyclical.

Table 9.12 Effects of size on the average annual growth rates of the firms in the Bulgarian sample, 1991–5

Size of firm	1991	1992	1993	1994	1995
Annual Sales					
Micro	173.6	550.1	366.3	331.9	657.9
Medium–small	145.5	562.8	538.9	271.7	428.5
Small	164.1	742.1	508.3	200.9	879.3
Analysis of variance					
Effect of period of operational start-up			$F = 1.00$	$p > 0.05$	
Effect of size			$F = 2.48$	$p = 0.012$	
Within subject effect			$F = 32.52$	$p < 0.01$	
Annual employment					
Micro	177.7	186.6	134.9	138.6	152.1
Medium–small	193.5	154.8	126.9	141.6	166.9
Small	215.7	186.0	190.8	139.5	358.1
Analysis of Variance					
Effect of period of operational start-up			$F = 1.30$	$p > 0.05$	
Effect of size			$F = 1.92$	$p > 0.05$	
Within subject effect			$F = 11.55$	$p < 0.01$	
Annual investment					
Micro	145.5	123.8	197.6	185.5	211.2
Medium–small	129.8	136.5	198.0	163.7	138.6
Small	135.7	157.4	239.3	179.4	321.2
Analysis of variance					
Effect of period of operational start-up			$F = 0.13$	$p > 0.05$	
Effect of size			$F = 0.59$	$p > 0.05$	
Within subject effect			$F = 76.80$	$p < 0.01$	

Notes: The growth rates for sales and investment are calculated based on the US dollar equivalent of the lev-denominated figures at each year's average annual exchange rate, and deflated using the consumer price index.
The figures should be interpreted with care as they have been generated from a sample transformed to minimize the number of missing values and the differences in the numbers of firms reporting on each variable for each year.
Source: Survey results.

CONCLUSIONS

The experience of system reform has had mixed implications for the establishment and expansion of small private manufacturing operations in Bulgaria. The emerging small manufacturing sector was founded primarily on spin-off start-ups from large SOEs during, and in the period immediately following, the initiation of system reform in 1990. It was the initial 'push effect' of the launch of system reform, and the initial liberalization of the legal framework, that had the most marked impact on the numbers of new start-ups, though this must be viewed in the context of the 'hidden privatization' made possible as a result of the disorder following the withdrawal of the state from control of the economy. The rate of new firm entry appeared to slow down in the aftermath of the introduction of the adjustment-led reform programme in 1992, while inconsistencies in reform implementation seem to have eased its negative implications. These findings cast doubt on the argument that the explosion of small firms is testimony to the efficacy of the 'shock therapy' reform programmes prescribed to many transitional economies.

The progress of reform in Bulgaria has been found to be neutral with respect to the spatial and sectoral distributions of the emerging small manufacturing sector, with both being determined largely by the distribution of the SOEs to which the small firms owe their origin. Here again, therefore, the 'shock therapy' adjustment programme appears to have had little impact in initiating 'rational choice' in small manufacturing start-up.

However, reform has had an impact on the size structure of the emerging small manufacturing firms. Notwithstanding the fact that, in contrast to other transitional economies, the micro firm is the dominant size for emerging small manufacturers in Bulgaria, reform has favoured the larger 'small' enterprises through improved access to both domestic and imported capital goods, and to external finance. Furthermore, the average growth rates of sales, employment and investment for existing small manufacturing firms have been enhanced by reform, with the larger 'small' manufacturers exhibiting the best performance. These encouraging findings must, however, be viewed in the context of the constraints on entrepreneurs inherent in the 'shock therapy' programme, the inconsistencies of reform implementation, and the cyclical performance of the economy.

Notes

1. Stabilization and structural adjustment are two distinct but complementary policy packages. Stabilization refers to 'the policy of an orderly reduction in demand to achieve improvements in macroeconomic imbalances', while structural adjustment involves 'reform in macro and microeconomic institutions of an economy to enhance efficient resource allocation' (Khan, 1993). In reality, some measures such as exchange rate liberalization are instrumental to both. Hence, I follow Khan and employ the term 'adjustment' to describe both stabilization and structural adjustment.
2. This chapter arises from a large research project undertaken in Bulgaria in December 1996. The main part of the project was a firm-level questionnaire survey involving a sample of 142 entrepreneurs from a national population of active, private-majority, domestically-owned small manufacturers, employing between three and fifty full-time workers, and located in six regions of Bulgaria. The survey information was complemented by data from separate semi-structured in-depth interviews with entrepreneurs, business association representatives, government officials and local academics, and by data from published sources and other research findings. The information from the field survey was analyzed using the SPSS statistical package.
3. The comparative data on private manufacturers in the other transition economies are from 1992, when the economies were at an earlier stage of reform. However, this should not affect the conclusions to any marked extent.
4. Ninety-nine per cent of the firms in the sample were fully owned by their founders.
5. Similarly, in her study in Sofia, Pissarides (1996) found that 92 per cent of the firms sampled were new start-ups, while only 3 per cent were previously part of a SOE, and 5 per cent were privatized.
6. 'Reform institutionalization' refers to the measures, effective since 1992, which relate to the installation of a market-led legal framework, the elaboration of economic reform policy and strategy, the liberalization of prices, markets and exchange rates, restitution, privatization, and the restructuring of state and co-operative enterprises.
7. An analysis of variance using annual data failed to detect any significant difference between the numbers of operational start-ups before and after 'reform institutionalization' ($t = 0.42, p = 0.713$).
8. See National Statistics Institute (1995).
9. For a series of studies in Africa, see Helmsing and Kolstee (1993).
10. Note that these size categories do not correspond exactly to the 'medium–small' and 'small' categories used elsewhere in this chapter.
11. The initial year of this analysis was 1990. The data from firms started in 1989 and 1990 are grouped together. As most of the 1989 firms were established in the last quarter of the year, this should not affect the interpretation of the data.

References

Avramov, R. and Genov, K. (1995) *Poftorno Radjdane Na Kapitalizma Vef Bulgaria*, No. 2, Sofia: Bankov Pregled (in Bulgarian).

Dornbusch, R. (1990) 'From Stabilisation to Growth', National Bureau of Economic Research Working Paper No. 3302, Cambridge, Mass.: NBER.

Gelb, A. H. (1991) *The Transformation of Economies in Central and Eastern Europe: Issues, Progress, and Prospects*, World Bank, Policy Research Series, New York: World Bank.

Helmsing, A. H. J. and Kolstee, Th. (eds), (1993) *Small Enterprises and Changing Policies: Structural Adjustment, Financial Policy and Assistance Programmes in Africa*, London: Intermediate Technology Publications.

Hillman, A. L., Mitov, L. and Peters, K. R. (1995) 'The Private Sector, State Enterprise, and Informal Economic Activity', in Z. Bogetic and A. L. Hillman (eds), *Financing Government in the Transition – Bulgaria: The Political Economy of Tax Polices, Tax Basis, and Tax Evasion*, New York: World Bank.

Horst, R. V. (1996) 'Entrepreneurship in Western and Eastern Europe,' in M. Dimitrov and K. Todorov (eds), *Industrial Organisation and Entrepreneurship in Transition*, Sofia: Informa Intellect.

Khan, R. A. (1993) *Structural Adjustment and Income Distribution: Issues and Experiences*, Geneva: ILO.

National Statistics Institute (1989–97) *Statisticheski Spravochink* (various issues), Sofia: National Statistics Institute (in Bulgarian).

Pissarides, F. (1996) *Small and Medium Size Enterprises in Transition: Evidence from Bulgaria and Russia*, London: EBRD.

Steel, W. F. and Webster, L. M. (1990) 'Ghana's Small Enterprise Sector: Survey of Adjustment Response and Restrictions', World Bank Working Paper No. 33, New York: World Bank.

Vitorio, C. and Jaime, M. (1985) 'How Firms Adjusted to the Recent Reforms in Argentina, Chile, and Uruguay', World Bank Staff Working Paper No. 764, New York: World Bank.

Webster, L. M. (1993a) 'The Emergence of Private Sector Manufacturing in Poland: a Survey of Firms', World Bank Technical Paper No. 237, New York: World Bank.

Webster, L. M. (1993b) 'The Emergence of Private Sector Manufacturing in Hungary: A Survey of Firms', World Bank Technical Paper No. 229, New York: World Bank.

Webster, L. M. and Charap, J. (1993) 'The Emergence of Private Sector Manufacturing in St. Petersburg: A Survey of Firms', World Bank Technical Paper No. 228, New York: World Bank.

Webster, L. M. and Swanson, D. (1993) 'The Emergence of Private Sector Manufacturing in the Former Czech and Slovak Federal Republic: A Survey of Firms', World Bank Technical Paper No. 230, New York: World Bank.

Part III

Clusters: One Fit for All Situations?

10 A Cure for Loneliness? Networks, Trust and Shared Services in Bangalore

Mark Holmström

INTRODUCTION

> A small firm in an industrial district does not stand alone; a condition of its success is the success of the whole network of firms of which it is a part ... The main problem for small firms is not being small but being lonely.
>
> (Sengenberger and Pyke, 1992; pp. 4 and 11)

Small firms are fashionable, in developed and developing countries alike. If large firms cannot provide enough jobs, or if they are too inflexible to seek and supply new markets, then small and medium-sized enterprises (SMEs) can fill the gap. At least that is the argument for encouraging smaller firms, ranging from the amorphous 'informal sector' to high-technology and sometimes capital-intensive firms supplying world markets.

India, in particular, has long had a policy of encouraging 'small-scale industries' and discriminating against large firms. The intentions were good; the results were sometimes good but often disappointing, and the opportunity cost was high. Many small firms are inefficient, exploitative and a drain on the public purse. The idea, and ideal, of 'small-scale industry' is a distraction from the tasks of achieving high-quality marketable production, employment, and good jobs for workers of both sexes. Policies designed to help small firms have sometimes – but not always – amounted to little more than government aid for the educated unemployed, who can cause more trouble than the uneducated unemployed. Such policies have also given small firms an incentive not to grow beyond a certain level of investment (below which they have certain privileges) or employment (since firms with more than ten workers are subject to social security charges and other costs). Yet some small firms are innovative and market-led, make high-quality products, and teach useful skills.

Which industrial policies, in India or elsewhere, are most likely to achieve quickly the objectives most people probably agree on: *economic growth* (in the short run, this has nothing to do with employment or equity; but in the long run, it could raise living standards for everyone); more *employment*; *good wages* and *security* for those who have jobs; and *better work* (interesting, autonomous work, with chances to learn new skills and to build a career)?

There may be trade-offs: economic growth without new jobs, or more jobs but worse ones, or good work for a privileged elite only. On the other hand, the good things may go together: for example, workers who feel secure and find their work interesting may make better products, leading to faster growth and more jobs.

There is no virtue in smallness, no point in propping up firms simply because they are small. Large firms usually pay better and offer more secure employment and better conditions. If larger firms could provide good work for all who need it, that would be fine; but they cannot. Smaller firms may have reserves of innovative talent; may create employment where large firms cannot or do not; and have the great merit that they exist in large numbers.

Can the disadvantages of smallness be overcome, and its advantages be exploited, through 'flexible specialization', as in north-central Italy (Sabel 1982, Goodman and Bamford 1989)? Flexible specialization happens when clusters or networks of smaller firms, usually but not necessarily in an industrial district, complement each other to achieve economies of scale ('collective efficiency') and co-operate on marketing, improving quality, developing new products, and stages of production for which some firms have specialized machinery or workers. They are interdependent, and independent of large firms when it is to their advantage. This allows them to do things they could not do if they were isolated in a jungle of competing firms. It works only if there is some degree of trust between entrepreneurs, and between them and their workers; and/or collective provision of 'real services' such as training, consultancy and design, which single firms cannot afford to provide for themselves.

Hubert Schmitz (1992: 67) distinguishes between '(a) hierarchical clusters, for example where a large enterprise farms out parts of the production to small enterprises and thus orchestrates the division of labour, and (b) non-hierarchical clusters, in which equals compete or cooperate'. There is nothing wrong with hierarchy – or with large firms – if they can deliver what we want (employment and so on). But where hierarchy stifles innovation, or fails to draw out the smaller firms' potential to create jobs, we should explore ways in which smaller firms can achieve economies of scale ('collective efficiency') without losing independence and flexibility, in the special conditions of India's industrial economy as it is suddenly exposed to fiercer competition with foreign and Indian rivals.

This chapter is based on fieldwork in Bangalore, a city of nearly five million people, containing some of India's most advanced engineering and electronic industries. I know the city well, having done social anthropological fieldwork there over many years (Holmström, 1969, 1971, 1972, 1976, 1984, 1998). I have also drawn on my experience of industrial districts in Emilia-Romagna, the Italian region which is the best known example of flexible specialization (Bagnasco, 1977; Sabel, 1982; Goodman and Bamford, 1989; Trigilia, 1989; Dei Ottati, 1991; Brusco, 1992), where I made a study of the flourishing workers' co-operative movement (Holmström, 1985, 1989). I am now completing a study of industrial districts in the Valencia region of Spain, where the regional government's agency for small and medium-sized enterprises (Impiva) has tried to follow the Italian example.

Bangalore has a dense network of large and small firms using advanced technologies, and abundant skilled labour. The many small engineering and electronic firms depend mainly on large public- and private-sector factories for orders, but some of them market their own products. Increasingly, these small firms are using CNCs (computer-numerically controlled machine tools) and CAD (computer-aided design). If they lack some of the necessary machines and skills, they put the work out to other small firms and consultancies. They use 'real services' – testing, calibration, advice – provided by public-sector bodies. I have written elsewhere (Holmström, 1998) about the ways in which market-led innovation takes place in some of these firms, in spite of all obstacles: how information is transmitted from the market, digested and acted on, to improve the product or to fill a niche in the market. If flexible specialization can succeed anywhere in India, we should expect it do so in the network of large and small firms that make up Bangalore's engineering and electronic industries.

What are the prospects for non-hierarchical clusters, in which equals compete or co-operate? Or clusters where they compete *and* co-operate, as in the 'Third Italy' around Emilia Romagna, where these apparent opposites are combined in 'an industrial community that restricts the forms of competition to those favouring innovation' (Piore and Sabel 1984; p. 17)? Are places like Bangalore moving towards a less hierarchical model, where smaller firms are no longer ancillaries making components and doing subcontracting work to the large firms' designs, but interdependent firms supplying markets that the large firms do not reach? Can smaller firms work together to develop their own products, and compete successfully with large firms on national and foreign markets, creating faster economic growth and more employment than big firms alone could provide?

In principle, everyone can see the benefits of pooling some resources, especially information, if it were only possible to define the limits of competition in the common interest. In practice, this is hard to achieve in a situation where entrepreneurs and workers are afraid – with good reason – of cheats and free riders, those who take but give nothing in return. Competition in India is fierce and getting fiercer, with the liberalization of the economy and the ever more desperate scramble for jobs and higher living standards (Holmström, 1999a, 1999b, 2000).

What are the extent and limits of co-operation and trust between small or medium-sized firms, and the prospects for less hierarchical management within firms and networking between them, for mutual aid and consortia? How can smaller firms make the most of their independence and flexibility, while overcoming the disadvantages of loneliness? And can public provision of 'real services' make up for lack of trust, or *build* trust? This case study of Bangalore is part of a collaborative programme of studies of the prospects for flexible specialization in other Indian cities and industries, and is relevant to other industrializing countries with large labour surpluses.

FORMAL ASSOCIATIONS AND INFORMAL NETWORKS: THE LIMITS TO TRUST

In Bangalore, small or medium firms compete to get subcontract work from larger ones; but they also put out work to each other: manufacture of components, different stages in production, work that requires special equipment like a CNC machine tool, or capacity subcontracting to meet a deadline. They do this whether they mainly do subcontracting or market their own products.

This division of labour between firms cannot depend entirely on short-term considerations of profit in a competitive market. It requires a degree of trust, just as running a successful flexible enterprise depends on some minimum level of trust between employers and workers: not unlimited trust in either case, but some shared understanding about the situations in which conflict or competition are appropriate.

In Bangalore, this trust exists, but within close limits. As the secretary to an association of small firms said, industrialists are far too suspicious of each other, especially where markets are concerned; unlike farmers, who share information because they cannot hide success from their neighbours, and do not compete to sell their produce. Yet it is obvious to all of them that the small or medium-sized firms cannot possibly compete with large ones unless they can rely on other firms for help at short notice. Successful flexible specialization depends on this trust and mutual aid, as in the 'Third Italy', where

> Each firm is jealous of its autonomy, overly proud of its capacities, but fully conscious that its success and very survival are linked to the collective efforts of the community to which it belongs and whose prosperity it must defend.
>
> One kind of dependence on related firms is implicit in the firm's innovative activity – the capacity to tailor a particular part or component to special conditions...The moment the firm begins to expand and move beyond its original specialty it finds itself dependent on the help of neighbors with complementary kinds of specialities; and because the neighbors can never exactly anticipate when they too will need assistance, the help is forthcoming...Mistrust freezes the technological progress of a whole sector; trust fosters it...Where invention creates demand and invention is collective, this is a natural result.
>
> (Sabel, 1982; pp. 225–6)

This shared understanding about the limits to competition must be backed by public opinion within a group. At the last resort, there must be economic sanctions: if you cheat, you lose your reputation and no one will do business with you. The moral community – the group within which trust and reputations are built up and tested – is usually local: for example, the group of small and medium-scale businessmen in an industrial district. In some situations a more effective moral community could be a professional body, or a network of companies in different cities which do business with each other, or a community of birth such as a caste or religion.

This last point could be crucially relevant to countries like India, where the solidarity of small firms, or of craftsmen, is often based on kinship and ethnic ties, which exclude outsiders and limit the scope for growth, especially in employment:

> Trust ... as a foundation of economic relations, is a 'double-edged sword': it can retard economic development where it is a strictly private form of transactional coordination, as in the case of mafias or aristocracies, for these, by definition, restrict the entry of new producers; where trust is highly generalized and public, on the other hand, it serves to sustain transactions and reduce the costs for established producers, while at the same time allowing new entrants into the community.
>
> (Storper, 1991, p. 112)

In the past, many Indian entrepreneurs, especially those with a financial rather than a technical background, have been notoriously suspicious of anyone outside – and sometimes even inside – their own family, caste or religious community, and unwilling to share information. In an industrial district like Bangalore, are relations of trust still confined to closed communities? Or are there ways for new people, from different social origins, to join the networks of mutual aid, and to build up a reputation for competence and honest dealing?

My evidence of the ways in which trust is built up and maintained is anecdotal and one-sided. An entrepreneur (who trusts me) may tell me about particular people he or she relies on or distrusts, and why, and may tell me more about general tendencies – what kinds of information entrepreneurs will share, how they make friends; but there were few occasions when I was able to get the story from both sides (and if I have it, I may be unable to publish it for fear of identifying the actors). In contrast, accounts of how market-led innovation takes place are more specific and easier to check. One can meet customers, service engineers and designers, all on separate occasions; see the old and new designs; watch and talk to workers making the new designs in the factory.

Projects for mutual aid among entrepreneurs have foundered on a pervasive suspicion of each other's motives. Some entrepreneurs are more relaxed, willing to share information and technology with business contacts: as one of them said, we have few secrets – we copy other people's designs ourselves. A state government official said that small or medium-sized firms often help each other to find workers, and pass on technological know-how, which is no secret in any case, since much of it comes from public institutions such as the Small Industries Service Institute or the Central Machine Tools Institute: they are only suspicious where *markets* are concerned, afraid that someone else will undercut their price and steal their market.

Where there is a greater degree of trust, it can spring from a purely business relationship between entrepreneurs, which matures into friendship. Often these friendships go back a long way: colleagues who trained together at an engineering or management college or the Indian Institute of Science in Bangalore, or who worked in the same big factory or an institution such as the Central Machine Tools Institute, before setting up their own business, have a solidarity cemented by fond memories, like French *Polytechniciens*.

Another kind of business friendship is more of a patron–client relationship: small-scale entrepreneurs keep up profitable contacts with the purchasing and other officers of the big firms they once worked for. Some small employers train engineers or skilled workers and then help them to start their own businesses: doing subcontracting work for their ex-employer, developing products, and helping in other ways.

An even stronger basis for trust exists in what Pierre Lachaier (1992) calls the 'Industrial Lineage Firm', where a company is divided and subdivided among the founder's kin; though in India there have been notorious cases of bitter feuds between brothers or between branches of a family, which can break up business empires and close factories. Assuming that relatives remain on speaking terms, this network of kin is usually – but not always – confined to a community of birth, in a society where most people marry within their own caste or religion. However, it does not seem that membership of the same caste, religion or language group is automatically a foundation for trust, or that entrepreneurs will subcontract work to or share information with someone for this reason alone.

There are exceptions – some tightly-knit castes with merchant traditions – but business friendships, unless they began with purely economic relationships, are much more likely to develop in clubs and professional associations, or from chance encounters with neighbours living in the same suburb. Rotary and Lions Clubs, in particular, have local branches with an enthusiastic membership engaged in charitable work and convivial gatherings. Engineers have their professional associations. A Kaizen ('continuous improvement') Study Circle of managers meets monthly. All these clubs and associations invite speakers (like me) and take refreshments. There are seminars and conferences in hotels, with parties and a bar. Entrepreneurs and managers belong, or aspire to belong, to a culture that is consciously modern, meritocratic, cosmopolitan, used to foreign travel, and entertaining each other in the fine restaurants for which Bangalore is justly famous. These are the settings in which ideas are exchanged, and business contacts and personal friendships are formed.

MARKETING AND THE SMALL FIRM

To grow through market-led innovation and continuous improvement, each firm must have access to markets, and a quick feedback of information from those markets about market trends and customers' needs and complaints. It usually gets both these things through the same channel (the firm's own sales staff, or agencies), but there are other ways of getting information: through trade associations, government bodies, the trade press (Indian and foreign), and informal contacts with customers, suppliers and business friends.

Another option for the smaller firm is to go it alone. The owner does all the marketing, and collects the necessary information. A more established firm will employ a specialized marketing manager, and sometimes its own service engineers:

> An engineer employs 40 workers. His steady income comes from job work on his four CNCs, for large and small firms, and 'reverse engineering' for other firms. Engineers constantly discuss problems of production and quality informally with workers on the shop floor, where I spent some days.
>
> His enthusiasm is for the products he designs himself, especially an accessory for CNCs, developed from a standard pattern but with modifications and improvements to meet customers' stated requirements or to fill gaps in the market. He will make, and if necessary design, a single piece, when a large firm would not be interested. Thus one customer asked for a model which tilts; another, for a model which will work when immersed in liquid. He designed these, and advertised them as additions to his standard range.
>
> His products are exhibited at trade fairs all over India, and his marketing manager travels around, asking customers and potential customers what they would like. One manufacturer of CNCs already includes his accessory with its standard products; if others follow, this will build up his reputation. He hopes to start exporting soon. It is hard for him to match the marketing network or design

capability of a large firm, though he can use his access to friends in big firm where he once worked.

Going it alone is costly for a small firm. Thus several entrepreneurs making machine tools or components say the best opportunity to meet customers and pick up ideas is the Hanover trade fair, yet they find it prohibitively expensive to fly to Germany and stay there, knowing they may come back empty-handed. They can market their products through large manufacturing companies which have extensive sales networks throughout India and abroad, but which cannot give priority to the needs of smaller clients. Or they can use agents specializing in a range of products, often a different agent in each major Indian city. An agent may provide useful information about market opportunities, or may simply sell the product.

There appear to be few *local* marketing agents of the kind found in Italian industrial districts, with extensive contacts throughout the country and abroad, each handling similar or complementary products of a few local firms, and providing details and up-to-date information about new demands and trends. However, there are hopeful examples:

> An engineer has long expertise in designing a range of specialized machinery needed for certain industrial processes. His own factory is small (20 workers). Most of his effort goes into solving clients' design problems, turnkey systems, consultancy and training. He is starting an agency to market a range of products from high-tech small Bangalore firms, in India and abroad.

Another obvious – and Italian – solution is to form a marketing consortium:

> A large factory used to make a machine, used by farmers and others, in its own factory. It does not require high precision work. A group of ancillaries on an industrial estate suggested that, instead of making parts, they could form a consortium to make and assemble the whole machine much more cheaply. It is now made in small, poorly equipped workshops. Instead of doing most of the production with cheap labour, as they used to, they now do all of it. Few of the workers are skilled and many are boys and girls, some apparently ten or twelve years old. The parent factory still markets the machine under its own brand name.

Such consortia do collectively what many small firms do separately: subcontracting work for a large firm, to designs and standards set by that firm. There is no innovation at all. Consortia exist, or are being set up, on the national level:

> Indian automobile component manufacturers have come together to set up Inapex Auto Products Export Ltd, with government support. 'While India enjoys significant comparative advantages in the manufacture of these products, there are too many producers making small numbers of disparate items', so that India holds a mere 0.25 per cent of the world market. The chairman pointed out that 'the large global companies are no longer prepared to buy individual components from different vendors. They want matched packages of kits of several components from each source, which Indian suppliers are not currently equipped to supply.' The consortium will place orders with a large number of companies, exercise quality control, and market a common Indian brand. 'If this venture succeeds ... it will provide an example for similar export consortia in other industries, including food processing and electronics.
>
> (*Times of India*, 30 July 1993)

No doubt orders from the new consortium will filter down to the smaller firms; but local consortia, built from the ground up, would be useful to smaller firms, which need both to sell their products and, crucially, to get market information they can use to make profitable innovations. After careful enquiry I found only two such consortia in Bangalore, one of them embryonic:

> Five medium or small machine tool manufacturers – three in Bangalore, two in other cities – have set up a sales and service consortium. The founders of these companies know and trust each other, since they all worked together for the Central Machine Tools Institute in Bangalore.
>
> The consortium has six offices throughout India, and 70 staff. They provide a comprehensive marketing and after-sales service for the five member companies and for a few other firms in Bangalore. The clients are not in competition with each other, since each makes different types of machine tools, for which the consortium has sole domestic selling rights. It does not operate abroad: each firm must make its own export arrangements.

The consortium's sales representatives meet from time to time, to assess market trends; and they regularly pass on information about customers' complaints to member companies, which send their own engineers to solve any problems. Thus the managing partner of one member firm said that if anything goes wrong with one of his machine tools – even because of a mistake by the operator – his customers know the firm's engineer will make as many flights as are necessary and will send a replacement urgently, without question: so he builds up a better reputation than larger firms.

Eight small firms set up a consortium a year ago, to export electronic components; the consortium also acts as agent for ten other local companies, which are not members. They thought it best to begin in neighbouring countries, which have cultural and other links with India (and are cheaper to visit): two journeys to Sri Lanka brought a number of orders and a good chance of others. Then they will try other Asian countries. A partly-retired entrepreneur does most of the work: he has a small office and high hopes.

One success story, another moderately successful so far. Against this, there have been several failed attempts to form marketing consortia:

In the late 1980s a number of small consultancies sprang up, offering CAD to electronic manufacturers. Since there was cut-throat competition between them, an engineer with his own consultancy suggested that eight small firms should form a consortium, sharing out the available work according to their capacities: then they could employ specialized sales staff, and have an impact on the market. But (he says) every small entrepreneur wants to go his own way, and suspects even his partners and employees of plotting to go independent and take away his market. So nothing happened: most of these firms are out of business, and few CAD consultancies survive in Bangalore.

Two young engineers do job work, using two CNC wire-cutters. They cannot think of developing their own product, because of the difficulty of marketing it and knowing what is in demand: for example, they could not afford to visit the Hanover trade fair. I asked one of them: why doesn't a group get together and send one person to Hanover? The reply was that this would never work – no one would trust the others, and each would want to go to Hanover for himself. There are business friendships, he says, especially between people who trained in the same institution, but few entrepreneurs trust each other enough to share information or to form consortia.

If few marketing consortia have succeeded in establishing themselves, there may be a better chance for consortia to purchase components or services. Thus firms in other parts of Karnataka set up formal or informal consortia to calibrate instruments (in Bangalore, the government's Central Machine Tools Institute does it for them). Machine tool manufacturers are setting up a consortium to purchase components:

> For some time, the Indian Machine Tool Manufacturers Association has lobbied the government to reduce duties on imported components in line with the reduction of duty on complete machine tools, in order to make Indian products competitive in India and abroad. While the manufacturers waited for the government to take a decision, they asked a medium-sized Bangalore firm to do the groundwork in setting up an informal consortium of Indian manufacturers, who normally compete with each other, for the joint purchase of foreign or Indian components at the best prices. On behalf of the group, this company has begun to negotiate with Japanese and Indian suppliers of selected components.
>
> One problem is standardization: each manufacturer may have bought components from a different source. If they agree on a single model, this will involve some firms but not others in costly design changes. If the consortium orders a variety of components, it will be difficult to get suppliers to agree on terms for supplying each member with different quantities and specifications; and the smaller the quantities, the harder it will be for the consortium to guarantee orders even for the following year.

NETWORKING FOR INNOVATION AND DESIGN

A flexibly-managed large firm is decentralized internally in many ways, but it has powerful central departments for marketing, and for the design and development of new products. Smaller firms, which cannot do these things by themselves, must look outside, to other firms, public institutions, or consortia. Just as some smaller firms can handle their own marketing while others use selling agents or (rarely) consortia, some are relatively self-sufficient in design, with others needing outside help.

Many of Bangalore's smaller engineering and electronic firms are founded, managed and usually owned by engineers with design experience in large factories or in public institutions, especially the Central Machine Tools Institute. Often their motive for leaving secure employment was not simply economic: it was a passion to develop their ideas creatively. They are prepared to delegate much of the responsibility for marketing, production or labour, in order to spend as much time as possible on design and development.

These designers and designer-entrepreneurs may or may not use CAD, depending on the nature of the job and their own temperaments. Thus a partner in a small firm making machine tools said that most design work consists of thinking, not drawing, so CAD saves very little time: when he needs CAD, he has it done by the Central Machine Tools Institute. Another designer found CAD a distraction. But for some complex shapes, CAD is essential or very useful, the expense is not prohibitive, and skilled assistants are available or can be trained; depending of course on the complexity of the design.

As with CNCs, manufacturing firms with CAD do a certain amount of work for those without it. Thus a small electronic manufacturer does relatively simple 2-D (two-dimensional) CAD for some of the many firms making printed circuit boards (PCBs), and sends them the programmes on a disc.

Even firms with their own CAD facilities cannot handle design problems requiring specialized, and sometimes expensive, programmes run on high-powered computers. One solution is to take their design problems to one of the public institutions with which Bangalore is exceptionally well endowed, especially the Central Machine Tools Institute (CMTI). It is generally agreed that the CMTI does a good job, but is slow and bureaucratic. Others include the National Aeronautical Laboratory and the Indian Institute of Science. The big public-sector factories are sometimes willing to help, particularly since many of the smaller entrepreneurs once worked there and have personal contacts.

The alternative is to use a specialized firm of designers, but these are few. It seems there were more of them in the mid-1990s, but not enough demand for their services. What survive are a number of 'drafting pools' doing simple design work, or digitizing engineering drawings to be retrieved and modified when needed; and firms specializing in simple CAD for makers of printed circuit boards.

For the kind of design that requires original thought and imagination, there are a very few consultancies, which serve both small and large firms, in Bangalore and further afield.

> One such consultant, with eight employees, said that until recently Indian markets were vast and closed. Few firms, large or small, saw any need for design. They just bought foreign designs if they could afford them and copied if they could not, though 'reverse engineering' never produces as good a result as the original. Now there is more competition and more push to innovate. Yet small entrepreneurs are still reluctant to pay for design, and wonder why they should spend good money when all they get for it is a drawing.
>
> His complaint was echoed by another consultant: big firms now do their own designing; small ones do not pay in time, or in full. Many of them think they can manage without CAD: they would rather make a piece in metal and see if it works, which is very wasteful.

In fact, many smaller firms are innovative and see the need for better design, often involving CAD. These are run by engineers with design experience, who are capable of doing much of the work themselves or with a few employees, or they are catered for by public institutions such as the Central Machine Tools Institute. Other small firms do no original design, only subcontract work to other firms' designs. This leaves a number of small firms that try to develop their own products, but they have not yet got the message that good design is worth paying for, at a time when old markets are fast disappearing or fragmenting.

POOLING RESOURCES: CONSORTIA TO DEVELOP NEW PRODUCTS

> The creation of an innovative climate in the industrial sector could be achieved through the further encouragement of research and development in enterprises and the formation of research consortia among companies.
>
> (UNIDO, 1990; p. xxi)

One way to overcome the loneliness of the smaller firm is by networking, interdependence between small firms, between small and large firms, or between small firms and public institutions set up to help them. Going one stage further, they can achieve economies of scale by forming consortia for marketing or purchasing.

The most obvious need is a marketing consortium for firms whose products complement each other, but are not in direct competition, or where the market is big enough for a group of local suppliers to compete with producers elsewhere. Another obvious need is for purchasing consortia, even for firms that compete directly. In practice, there are few such consortia in Bangalore, though there are informal arrangements serving the same purposes.

Taking this a step further, smaller firms can combine their strength and achieve 'collective efficiency' by setting up formal consortia to develop and market new products. As with marketing consortia, there is some talk of this possible solution, but in Bangalore there is now only one successful consortium in which innovative small firms pool their resources to design and develop their own high-quality products.

> When the public-sector Indian Telephone Industries told its ancillaries it was modernizing its products (not before time) and would no longer require their services, they formed a consortium Anco, designed their own telephone, and persuaded ITI to market it. Meanwhile they are developing new products, like small telephone exchanges for particular markets, which the consortium may later market independently.
>
> Some forty firms, employing over 2000 workers, have shares in Anco, which divides the work among member firms and employs 150 people directly, in administration and assembly. These firms' labour is cheaper than in their former parent factory, which not only pays higher wages to a large staff but also subsidizes a large township and a fleet of buses. But low pay is not Anco's only advantage, since it has experienced engineers and the capacity to develop existing designs imaginatively.

Another success story comes from Coimbatore in the neighbouring state of Tamil Nadu:

> Coimbatore has many small or medium firms making domestic pumps. Since each firm had its own design, customers found servicing slow and difficult, and spare parts hard to find. At the suggestion of the State Bank of India, the manufacturers agreed to set up a consortium to standardize products and parts. Each firm still makes and markets its own pumps, but there is a useful division of labour between firms making different parts, and more co-operation and exchange of information between competing firms to maintain and update the system of standardization.

Consortia for research and development, and perhaps production, seem such an obviously good idea that Anco is much talked about, and held up as an example; yet it is the only one of its kind in Bangalore. There have been abortive attempts, before and after Anco, to do something on similar lines.

> In the mid-1980s, an engineer with experience in design and marketing persuaded six other engineer-entrepreneurs to develop and make a machine tool part, similar but not identical to one made by the large factory where most of them had once worked. Their main saving would be on wages. The consortium raised a bank loan, developed the new machines, sold two of them and paid off the loan. But after two years, when the founder wanted to build up their market, he says he encountered petty jealousy from the some of the others, about matters such as paying his air fare to Mumbai. He sees now that he should have been more diplomatic: like him, his colleagues had left the big firm because they wanted independence, and people who strike out on their own are not always suited to working in a team.

Another scheme was more ambitious and innovative:

> Inspired by the example of the Coimbatore pump manufacturers' consortium, and – like that consortium – with State Bank of India support, a number of large and small companies, making computers or computer parts, set up a steering committee to develop an innovative computer that would be competitive on world markets. Financial institutions were sceptical about India's chances of developing a world-class product and unwilling to put up the capital. Each member company was asked to provide part of the capital, but some larger companies were unwilling to make the higher contribution demanded from them; one company wanted the sole right to manufacture the computer; and the project broke down, leaving at least one small firm to develop a new product, benefiting from the work already done.

The success stories, though rare, suggest consortia may have a future, as a way for smaller firms to overcome the weaknesses that are obvious to all of them, and will rapidly become more obvious as the economy becomes more competitive and open to world markets. The most pressing needs are for a marketing network comparable to those of the big firms, providing an efficient feedback of information to innovators and designers, and for well-organized and funded research and development.

Too many hopeful projects have foundered on the rocks of an individualistic and competitive culture. Each entrepreneur treasures independence, which was often the chief motive for leaving employment with a big firm. There are special strains on a consortium that brings together firms of very different sizes, since the small ones fear domination by the large.

TRADE ASSOCIATIONS

Joining a consortium means entering into financial and legal commitments which these individualistic entrepreneurs are reluctant to undertake, unless they see concrete benefits for themselves. Yet they are great joiners of clubs and associations, where the commitment is more limited and the expense modest.

There are trade associations, like KASSIA (Karnataka Small Scale Industries' Association), which provides excellent practical advice and other services to small-scale entrepreneurs, so its resources have to be spread thinly. Groups like Clik (Consortium of Electronic Industries of Karnataka: not really a consortium) publish directories, and in other ways encourage mutual aid among entrepreneurs in one branch of industry. Others are locally-based, like the Peenya Industries' Association in Bangalore, bringing together smaller firms in the Peenya Industrial Area (claimed to be 'the biggest industrial estate in Asia').

In the past, the trade associations' main task was to represent members' interests to national and state governments, in relation to taxes, permits, quotas of raw materials, laws and regulations. Since many of these controls have been swept away in the recent liberalization, this aspect of the associations' work is becoming less important. Now they concentrate on advising new or established entrepreneurs, putting members in touch with markets and suppliers, and publishing newsletters and trade directories, while still lobbying the government where they believe this is necessary. Thus some associations are trying to get a relaxation of labour legislation affecting smaller firms, and to stop inspection of their premises; or to end the daily power cuts that force factories to depend on generators. Some trade associations have more ambitious plans to set up their own technical, quality control or marketing services. They organize meetings for discussion or to hear outside speakers, and social gatherings where business friendships are formed or kept up; though for this purpose they seem less important than social or charitable clubs such as Rotary and the Lions Club. Trade associations are much looser than consortia, yet they are a soil in which consortia might grow. In some cases their office-bearers have actively encouraged members to form consortia: in at least one case, with success.

If consortia or similar forms of networking are to succeed, they need the kind of initial push which the State Bank of India gave to the Coimbatore pump makers' successful consortium, or the abortive computer consortium. Public policies to encourage consortia are probably worthwhile. But consortia for marketing, purchasing, or for the development and manufacture of new products, are unlikely for some time to become as important in India as they are in Italian industrial districts.

'REAL SERVICES': PUBLIC INSTITUTIONS TO HELP SMALL FIRMS

So much for self-help. Are there other ways in which public policy and institutions can help smaller firms to achieve market-led innovation, commercial success, and good jobs? One lesson from the literature on flexible specialization and industrial districts is that successful networks of innovative smaller firms are most likely to emerge where the state, local authority, or public institutions intervene to provide the services that smaller firms cannot provide for themselves, separately or by forming consortia, and cannot easily buy on the market: what Sebastiano Brusco (1992, p. 187) calls 'public provision because of market failure'. Following Italian usage, these are known as 'real services'. They include training workers and entrepreneurs, accountancy, design, management consultancy, advice on marketing and technical standards in export markets, and testing of materials. In the 'Third Italy' these services are often provided by local governments, working closely with associations of local entrepreneurs and with trade unions.

From the 1940s onwards, the big public-sector factories not only produced a supply of skilled, experienced labour, but also continued to provide consultancy and technical services to smaller firms: sometimes officially for a modest fee, but often informally through personal friendships.

Bangalore has also been well supplied with training and research institutions, starting with the Polytechnic and the Tata Institute of Science (now the Indian Institute of Science). Such institutions have operated in Bangalore for many years – long before the rapid growth of electronics in the 1980s; like the Small Industries Service Institute (SISI), they are of a type found in all major industrial cities in India. SISIs provide a range of services under one roof: technical and market advice, training courses for workers, and machining which the small firms lack the equipment or skilled labour to do for themselves. Bangalore's SISI played an important part in building up the dense network of small engineering workshops in industrial estates and back streets, mostly doing subcontract work for larger firms. Like other SISIs, its resources are spread too thinly, because it has to help all 'small-scale industries' indiscriminately, and cannot target its efforts narrowly enough on firms and industries with real prospects for growth.

The Industrial Training Institute, also on a pattern found throughout India, provides subsidized diploma courses for young men and a few women, mostly school-leavers. Their diploma holders try to find work in the bigger firms, where wages are higher and jobs more secure. Here they face stiff competition from young men trained in other public or private institutes equipped with newer machinery; so they enter smaller firms while waiting and hoping for a job in a large firm.

Other public institutions, funded by the central and/or state governments sometimes with foreign financial and technical aid, offer specialized services: among others, the Foreman Training Institute; the Electronics Test and Development Centre; and the Government Toolroom and Training Institute, which makes, sells or leases tools, runs an 'Earn while you learn' training scheme, and offers consultancy. The Bureau of Indian Standards tests samples, inspects factories and awards ISO certificates, which are required for products exported to the European Community and an advantage in other markets.

Tecsok (the Technical Consultancy Services Organization of Karnataka) is a recent initiative of the state government. A small group of engineers advise 'tiny', small and medium entrepreneurs about new technologies. Its fees are subsidized, yet few small firms are willing to pay for detailed feasibility and market studies.

Other government or privately-funded research institutes in Bangalore provide consultancy services, which are used mainly by larger firms and a few of the smaller high-tech companies. The National Aeronautical Laboratory also serves electronic and engineering industries not connected with aircraft production. The prestigious Indian Institute of Science, especially its Centre for Electronic Development and Technology (CEDT), advises companies and trains their engineers.

Two institutions have been of strategic importance in stimulating high-quality innovative production. The Central Machine Tools Institute (CMTI), recently renamed the Central Manufacturing Technology Institute, funded by the national government, was established in Bangalore because India's leading machine tool manufacturers were concentrated around the public-sector giant, Hindustan Machine Tools. The CMTI pioneered research and development of CNC machine tools in India. It is now moving towards an emphasis on whole systems (Computer Integrated Manufacturing) rather than machine tools alone. It trains engineers, designs and now manufactures machine tools, and provides consultancy, machining and design services.

The CMTI exists to serve industry throughout India, but its presence has been of crucial importance for engineering in Bangalore, especially for smaller firms. The CMTI provides technical services, especially calibration and testing. It designs or modifies special-purpose machine tools on request (though many smaller firms are unwilling to pay for new designs, or they design their own tools). The consensus among the CMTI's customers is that its services are of high quality, but delivery is slow, hampered by bureaucratic delays and form-filling: a criticism the Institute is trying to meet. And some of Bangalore's most innovative and successful engineering firms were founded by CMTI designers, who know and trust each other, and exchange ideas and services.

The other institution that provides valuable 'real services' to innovative firms is the Nettur Technical Training Foundation (NTTF), a voluntary institution with seven training centres, all in South India. It began as a joint initiative of the Swiss churches, the Swiss government and the Church of South India. No longer linked to the churches, it now supports itself by running its own factories, and to a lesser extent from consultancy and services to firms.

> The NTTF has two training centres in Bangalore. The older centre provides a rigorously planned four-year diploma course in tool and die making to 120 young men – half of them from village schools – who receive free tuition and subsidized or free hostel accommodation. Tuition is in English, with special help for those whose English is poor. About 30 per cent of those who complete the course find work abroad; the others find work in Indian firms, or become small-scale entrepreneurs. The Foundation also offers a postgraduate

course in tool engineering, besides special programmes and short courses. The new Electronics Centre offers similar programmes for women as well as men, notably in CNC programming and CAD.

The NTTF provides a small but valuable supply of highly skilled and employable young workers; short courses to many more who are already employed, mostly in larger firms; and high-quality consultancy and design services to firms willing to pay for them. Its engineers are involved in other initiatives to raise standards of quality and innovation in Bangalore's engineering industries, such as the Kaizen Study Circle, or workers' conferences organized jointly with trade unions.

Although Bangalore's engineering and electronics industries have access to an unusually wide range of public institutions providing 'real services', none of these institutions is the result of *local* initiative, either by entrepreneurs or by local government, even if they are responsive to local needs. Some are administered by the state government, which has its capital in Bangalore but serves a population of over 40 million. Others come under the national government, like the Central Machine Tools Institute, the only one of its kind in India, which Bangalore is lucky to have. The Nettur Technical Training Foundation is a voluntary organization, not dependent on state aid. Some institutions were founded with financial and technical aid from foreign governments (Czechoslovak, German, Danish, Swiss), though most no longer receive financial aid.

These institutions are important to local industry, not only because of the services they provide directly, but also because of close personal friendships between their staff and the entrepreneurs running innovative smaller firms in the city, many of whom began their careers in institutions such as the CMTI or the big public-sector factories. These people, whether they work in public institutions or in large or small factories, share a professional culture and a network of contacts, which do not guarantee trust, but are sometimes a foundation for it.

THE SOCIAL ANTHROPOLOGY OF EXCHANGE AND TRUST

> Men are able to trust one another, knowing the exact degree of dishonesty they are entitled to expect.
>
> (Stephen Leacock)

Marshall Sahlins (1972), building on social anthropological theories of exchange which go back to Marcel Mauss' *The Gift* (1954, originally 1925), places what we regard as 'economic' relations at various points on a 'spectrum of reciprocities', including social and moral relations not usually regarded as 'economic' at all, and which may or may not involve transfer of material things. This spectrum ranges from 'generalized reciprocity, the solitary extreme' (Malinowski's 'pure gift', Sahlins, 1972, p. 194), through 'balanced reciprocity, the midpoint', to 'negative reciprocity . . . the attempt to get something for nothing with impunity' (Mauss, 1954; pp. 193–5). An example of negative reciprocity is the 'amoral familism' which, according to Edward Banfield, allows one to predict behaviour in a south Italian hill town:

> The Montegranesi act as if they were following this rule: Maximize the material, short-run advantage of the nuclear family; assume that all others will do likewise . . . In a society of amoral familists, no one will further the interest of the group or community except as it is to his private advantage to do so.
>
> (Banfield, 1954; pp. 83–4)

Another example may be contemporary Russia (where 'If you catch someone with his hand in your pocket, he says "You don't understand market forces" ').

Sahlins attempts to classify the spheres of social relations where different rules of reciprocity apply, enforced by economic or legal sanctions, public opinion, or conscience. His examples are from 'primitive' societies, but the idea is also useful in understanding industrial societies. 'Balanced reciprocity' refers to direct exchange. In precise balance, the reciprocation is the customary equivalent of the thing received and is without delay' (Sahlins, 1972; p. 194). In industrial societies, this could be a product, a cheque, or a contract (but for 'customary equivalent' read 'market price'). Our idea of a typical 'economic' relationship is one of balanced reciprocity, sometimes tending towards the negative. In the words of the economist, Robert Kuttner, 'every business relationship is a one-night stand'.

In an ideal-type free market economy, individuals or firms act legally, but otherwise in their own self-interest, so contributing to the common good. Such an economy does not exist: self-interest is always tempered by conventions, trust, moral pressure and mixed motives. Real successful markets lie somewhere between balanced and generalized reciprocity.

Flexible specialization moves the pointer further towards generalized reciprocity: Emilia–Romagna is a long way from Banfield's (one-sided?) picture of southern Italy in the 1950s. An industrial district is a moral community where the limits to trust and self-interest are understood and backed by public opinion, as they apply to different kinds of relationship: contracts, informal co-operation, competition. Here I compete with you vigorously; here I trust you, and you can trust me. Or I work for you and want more pay – I may even strike; at all other times I work hard, loyally and imaginatively to make our business a success.

Self-interest, narrowly defined, only explains so much. To explain or change behaviour in real – not abstract – markets, we need a more complex understanding of motives in a culture: economic self-interest, the social and family reasons why people want money, the respect of others in a moral community, pride in one's work, creativity and independence. Trust and self-interest can go together, provided the boundaries are clearly drawn.

WHAT CAN BE DONE TO BUILD TRUST?

I have described the extent and limits of co-operative networking between smaller firms in Bangalore, the 'real services' that exist, and the use that small firms make of them (for more details, see Holmström, 1998). If networking and 'real services' can sometimes cure the loneliness of the small firm (as they have with spectacular success in the 'Third Italy'), what lessons are there for Bangalore, for India, and for other industrializing countries? Are there critical factors that allow or encourage trust? What is likely to work, and what is not? What is there to build on? Is public provision of real services an *alternative* to trust, *built* on it, or a way to build it and to define its limits?

Experience from Italy and elsewhere suggests that the provision of 'real services' is only likely to be effective when there is strong specific local demand for a particular service: otherwise, well-meaning attempts to guess the demand, and to provide a broad spectrum of possibly useful services, are probably a waste of effort and public money (Nadvi, 1994; pp. 222, 237). But once 'real services' exist and are used, they can be a basis for building up and encouraging trust. They are object lessons in the possibility of common action, and an incentive to organize more of it. This applies even where the state apparatus is sometimes ineffective and sometimes corrupt, provided there are enough people in it who are moved by professional pride and an ethic of public service. Fortunately this is still the case in India. Nor is the national or local state the only supplier of 'real services': if consortia or associations of small firms do not take the initiative, voluntary organizations such as the Nettur Technical Training Foundation can do so.

Bangalore's successes and failures suggest practical steps which those in a position to decide – governments, entrepreneurs, trade or voluntary associations, unions – might take to build successful industrial districts, in India and other developing countries, and to show entrepreneurs and their workers how to break out of dependence on large firms for markets, designs and so on, or how to turn that dependence to their advantage. In particular, to:

- improve and invest in 'real services';
- target public spending and incentives more effectively; and
- foster co-operation between entrepreneurs.

First, improve and invest in 'real services' (training, advice, technical services, consultancy, help with marketing and so on) provided by public institutions. But which public institutions can give the best value for money?

> While state intervention does not actually create industrial districts, such assistance, particularly in the form of 'real services', can be critical in ensuring the overall success of small-firm clusters which lack the capacity to generate internally support infrastructure... Such programmes are likely to be more effective if formulated by levels of government which are politically rooted within the community, in much the same way that the industrial cluster is socially embedded; moreover, they must actively involve the participation of those to whom they are directed through representative sectoral associations.
>
> (Nadvi, 1994; p. 237)

A fine principle, but hard to act on where local government is weak. In places like Emilia-Romagna, local government has provided many of these services, and helped consortia and trade associations to provide others. However, local government in Emilia-Romagna is notably efficient and free from corruption. This is not always the case in India, or in other regions of Italy.

In Bangalore, most 'real services' are provided by agencies of the national or state governments. Some agencies, such as the Small Industries Service Institute, follow an all-India pattern; others, such as the Central Machine Tools Institute, are unique: Bangalore is lucky to have them. There are also specialized research institutes, entirely or partly supported by public funds. The initiative is not local, but the impact is.

One institution could serve as a model for the provision of training and consultancy. The Nettur Technical Training Foundation (NTTF) is a voluntary association, supporting itself from its own factories and receiving no state funds, with two of its seven training centres in Bangalore. Several state governments have approached the Foundation for advice on the possibility of establishing centres on the NTTF model: a training, design and consultancy service, supported by production in its own factories and from fees. It is not clear whether anything will come of these initiatives. But if this were done, is it desirable – or possible – to combine accountability with the independence from state interference, which the NTTF regards as a key element in its success?

Second, target public spending and incentives more effectively. Develop more practical, corruption-proof and influence-proof machinery for intervention by national, state or local governments. Past policies designed to promote 'small-scale industries' have sometimes been indiscriminate, helping the efficient, the inefficient and the fraudulent equally. This is now recognized generally in India. There is, however, the problem of making incentives more selective while avoiding party or communal pressures, and corruption.

Third, foster co-operation between entrepreneurs, especially in marketing and product development: this is easier said than done, when they are often so suspicious of each other. Indian entrepreneurs can see the advantage of consortia for marketing, sometimes for common services such as testing, and for research and development of new products. Yet consortia are difficult to get off the ground, because of suspicion and the personal tensions that arise when fiercely independent entrepreneurs make a sincere effort to work together.

Support consortia and other joint efforts, building on the success of a few (Anco in Bangalore, pump manufacturers in Coimbatore) and holding them up as examples of what can be done. Encourage informal networking and a mutually beneficial division of labour between firms, even those that sometimes compete among themselves. Trade associations, based on particular industries or localities, are sometimes a way to build confidence and trust, a moral community with sanctions against cheats and free riders.

What are the bases for trust? Kinship and birth community (caste or religion) are often effective, but exclusive. Other bases to build on are links between business associates; between colleagues who worked together in big firms, or in public agencies, before starting their own business; or members of social and philanthropic clubs such as the Lions. These people are open to new ideas and anxious to hear about new methods (such as Japanese management). They see themselves as innovators. And this is a propitious moment in India. Because of liberalization, an awareness of new problems and opportunities, there can be no going back to the old days of permits, quotas, and bureaucratic string-pulling. Public agencies could make a concerted effort to spread the message: not just a vague message that trust is a good thing, but a constantly updated appraisal of successes and failures of collective action.

Emphasize the importance of defining the *limits* of trust in different types of relationship, the spheres in which different rules apply legitimately: formal contracts, informal co-operation, competition (in Sahlins' terms, the borders between balanced reciprocity and generalized reciprocity).

This emphasis on trust – rather than power within a hierarchy – applies not only to relations between entrepreneurs, but also between employers or managers and their workers. Distinguish participative management, with the potential to draw on workers' talents and imagination, from the paternalism that some Indian employers still hanker for: the myth that there are no conflicts of interest, that the firm is an organic unit, like an ideal family. As with relations between firms, useful trust needs to be based on clear definition of where interests coincide, and where conflict is recognized, with ground rules for managing conflict. This may mean coming to terms with unions rather than trying to keep them out: collective bargaining can define the limits and rules of conflict (even including strikes).

These are not just abstract reflections on what would be desirable, but rather proposals for what can be done, and who should do it: the various public agencies charged with stimulating industrial growth in general, and small and medium enterprises in particular; research and consultancy institutions, public or private; business associations, local and/or sectoral (sectoral ones are best); social clubs; and trade unions. Smaller firms have no great virtue in themselves, but a cure for their loneliness can take us some way towards curing the real diseases of poverty, unemployment and tedious work.

Acknowledgements

This chapter was first published in the *Economic and Political Weekly* of Bombay (30 August 1997), and then in Italian in M. R. di Tommaso and R. Rabellotti (eds), *Efficienza collettiva e sistemi d'imprese: oltre l'esperienza italiana* (Bologna: Il Mulino, 1999). An earlier version was submitted to a workshop on 'Industrialization, Organization, Innovations and Institutions in the South' organized by the European Association of Development Institutes and the Vienna Institute for Development and Co-operation, held in Vienna in November 1994. Hubert Schmitz made helpful comments on the paper, and the British Council gave me a travel grant to attend the workshop. Some passages then appeared as 'Bangalore as an Industrial District: Flexible Specialization in a Labour Surplus Economy?', in Philippe Cadène and Mark Holmström (eds), *Decentralized Production in India: Industrial Districts, Flexible Specialization, and Employment* (New Delhi: Sage/French Institute of Pondicherry, 1998). Copyright © French Institute of Pondicherry. All rights reserved. Reproduced with the permission of the copyright holders and the publishers, Sage Publications India Private Limited, New Delhi, India. I am grateful for permission to republish here.

My greatest debt is to the people in Bangalore who gave up their time to talk to me, and trusted me with their confidence, when I did the fieldwork on which this chapter is based. The Overseas Development Administration paid my research and subsistence costs; the Department of Human Geography at Amsterdam University paid my fare to India; and the School of Development Studies at the University of East Anglia gave me study leave.

Bibliography

Bagnasco, A. (1977) *Tre Italie: La Problematica Territoriale dello Sviluppo Italiano*, Bologna: Il Mulino.

Banfield, E. C. (1954) *The Moral Basis of a Backward Society*, New York: Free Press.

Brusco, S. (1992) 'Small Firms and the Provision of Real Services', in F. Pyke and W. Sengenberger (eds), *Industrial Districts and Local Economic Regeneration*, Geneva: International Institute for Labour Studies, pp. 177–96.

Dei Ottati, G. (1991) 'The Economic Bases of Diffuse Industrialization', *International Studies of Management and Organization*, vol. 21, no. 1, pp. 53–74.

Goodman, E. and Bamford, J. (eds) (1989) *Small Firms and Industrial Districts in Italy*, London: Routledge.

Holmström, M. (1969) 'Action-sets and Ideology: A Municipal Election in South India', *Contributions to Indian Sociology*, New series, vol. 3, pp. 76–93.

Holmström, M. (1971) 'Religious Change in an Industrial City of South India', *Journal of the Royal Asiatic Society*, vol. 1, pp. 28–40.

Holmström, M. (1972) 'Caste and Status in an Indian City', *Economic and Political Weekly*, 8 April, pp. 769–74.

Holmström, M. (1976/1978) *South Indian Factory Workers: Their Life and their World*, Cambridge University Press (1976) New Delhi: Allied (1978).

Holmström, M. (1984/1986) *Industry and Inequality: The Social Anthropology of Indian Labour*, Cambridge University Press (1984)/Hyderabad: Orient Longman (1986).

Holmström, M. (1985) 'How the Managed Manage the Managers: Workers Co-ops in Italy', *Anthropology Today* (December), pp. 7–13.

Holmström, M. (1989) *Industrial Democracy in Italy: Workers Co-ops and the Self-Management Debate*, Aldershot: Gower/Avebury.

Holmström, M. (1998) 'Bangalore as an Industrial District: Flexible Specialization in a Labour Surplus Economy?', in Philippe Cadène and Mark Holmström (eds), *Decentralized Production in India: Industrial Districts, Flexible Specialization, and Employment*, New Delhi/Thousand Oaks/London: Sage/French Institute of Pondicherry, pp. 169–229.

Holmström, M. (1999a) 'A New Map of Indian Industrial Society: The Cartographer All at Sea', *Oxford Development Studies*, vol. 27, no. 2, pp. 165–86.

Holmström, M. (1999b) 'Employment in Smaller Indian Firms: Choices under Liberalization', *Economic and Political Weekly*, vol. xxxiv, no. 39, (25 September), pp. L2–L9.

Holmström, M. (2000) 'Business Systems in India', in G. Jakobsen and J. E. Torp (eds), *Understanding Business Systems in Developing Countries*, Newbury Park/London/New Delhi: Sage, pp. 42–64.

Lachaier, P. (1992) '"Employeurs–employés" et "Employés–employeurs" dans les Firmes Lignagères Industrielles du Secteur de la Mécanique de Puna', in G. Heuzé (ed.), *Travailler en Inde/The context of work in India*, Collection Purusartha, Paris: Editions de l'Ecole des Hautes Etudes en Sciences Sociales, pp. 31–56.

Mauss, M. (1954) *The Gift: Forms and Functions of Exchange in Archaic Societies*, trans. I. Cunnison, London: Cohen & West.

Nadvi, K. (1994) 'Industrial District Experience in Developing Countries', in United Nations Conference on Trade and Development (UNCTAD), and Deutsches Zentrum für Entwicklungstechnologien (eds), *Technological Dynamism in Industrial Districts: An Alternative Approach to Industrialization in Developing Countries?*, New York and Geneva: United Nations, pp. 191–266.

Piore, M. J. and Sabel, C. F. (1984) *The Second Industrial Divide: Possibilities for Prosperity*, New York: Basic Books.

Sabel, C. F. (1982). *Work and Politics: The Division of Labor in Industry*, Cambridge University Press.

Sahlins, M. (1972) 'On the Sociology of Primitive Exchange', in M. Sahlins, *Stone Age Economics*, London: Tavistock, pp. 185–275.

Schmitz, H. (1992) 'On the Clustering of Small Firms', in J. Rasmussen, H. Schmitz and M. P. van Dijk (eds), *Flexible Specialization: A New View on Small Industry?*, (special issue of IDS Bulletin vol. 23, no. 3), Brighton: Institute of Development Studies, pp. 64–8.

Sengenberger, W. and Pyke, F. (1992) 'Industrial Districts and Local Economic Regeneration: Research and Policy Issues', in F. Pyke and W. Sengenberger (eds), *Industrial Districts and Local Economic Regeneration*, Geneva: International Institute for Labour Studies. Also published in *Labour and Society*, vol. 16, no. 1 (1991), pp. 1–24.

Storper, M. (1991) *Industrialization, Economic Development and the Regional Question in the Third World: From Import Substitution to Flexible Production*, London: Pion.

Times of India (1993) 'Auto Parts Makers Form Consortium', 30 July.

Trigilia, C. (1989) 'Small-firm Development and Political Subcultures in Italy', in E. Goodman and J. Bamford (eds), *Small Firms and Industrial Districts in Italy*, London: Routledge, pp. 174–97.

UNIDO (1990) *India: New Dimensions of Industrial Growth*, Industrial Development Review Series, Oxford: Basil Blackwell for UNIDO.

11 Promoting Small-Scale Industries in Indonesia: A Review of Recent Policies and Programmes

Henry Sandee

INTRODUCTION

During the New Order period under former President Soeharto, Indonesia experienced impressive economic growth and a rapid rise in large-scale manufacturing. To an important extent, this large-scale manufacturing was characterized by its concentration on labour-intensive assembly, and was orientated increasingly towards export markets. However, notwithstanding the impressive growth of the large-scale sector, the relative importance of small-scale industrial enterprises[1] did not decline greatly.

More recently, however, Indonesia suffered a severe economic setback: GDP fell by some 13–15 per cent in 1998, and another 2 per cent in 1999. In 2000, positive growth of about 4 per cent was expected. Hill (1999) reported that the manufacturing sector had contracted significantly since the start of the Asian financial crisis. Many large firms shed labour as they were not able to maintain production and export levels. In comparison, the small-scale industries seemed to be weathering the crisis better than larger companies (Berry *et al.*, forthcoming).

This chapter[2] aims to explain the performance of Indonesia's small-scale industries under different macroeconomic environments. In particular, I shall look at the role that policies and programmes have played in promoting the development of small-scale industries through these years. Subsequently, I discuss the growing attention given to small-enterprise development as an instrument for poverty alleviation and employment generation. I shall also review the recent policy initiatives and programmes that have been formulated to boost the role of small-scale industries.

SMALL-SCALE INDUSTRIES, DURING THE PERIOD 1986–96

The Promotion and Development of Small-scale Industry

It is now acknowledged widely that the policy stance during Soeharto's New Order was not favourable for small-enterprise development. Hill (1995; pp. 21–2) argued that government policies in Indonesia had often discriminated against small-scale industries, in various ways. First, trade policies were biased against small enterprises. For example, large-scale producers of roof tiles, who use cement as the main input, while smaller establishments rely on clay, had benefited from the heavy subsidies on cement prices. Second, some fiscal incentives apply only to firms that plan investments of a certain minimum size. Third, Indonesia has a complex set of overlapping laws, rules, regulations, licences and fees that raise compliance problems, especially for small firms (Van Diermen, 1999). The result is that small firms spend a large proportion of their income on fixed regulatory costs.[3]

The most important technical assistance programmes are the provision of extension services and the creation of (mandatory) partnerships (alliances) between large and small firms. These programmes have not been very successful. Extension services consist of supply-side measures to promote process and product innovations by small-scale producers. A review of these services in the province of Central Java showed that they have had little impact on the growth of small firms. For example, palm sugar producers were taught to use new production methods, although the market for palm sugar in Indonesia is saturated. The effectiveness of these extension services is further circumscribed by their non-recurring nature, and by the limited budgets. A two-day training session and financial assistance of some US$50 is not likely to help small firms switch to more dynamic growth trajectories. Furthermore, the low level of satisfaction of the producers that have received assistance makes it unlikely that there will be much diffusion of the benefits to others (Sandee, 1998).

Programmes aimed at developing linkages between small firms and larger establishments have not had much success. Large enterprises have been encouraged to assist small firms in marketing their products. The government has elevated the partnership programme to a national movement, and it has become the major form of government non-financial assistance. However, there is little evidence that these partnerships have resulted in sustainable alliances. Very few of them have been based on commercial benefit for both partners (Van Diermen, 1999).

A notable feature of small-scale industries in Indonesia has been a tendency to grow in geographic clusters and according to economic subsectors. In rural Indonesia, a large number of villages have specialized in the manufacture of certain specific products only. The government has recognized the importance of such clusters of small enterprises, and it has launched a special programme to promote them. Such cluster development programmes aim to identify local entrepreneurs who can play leading roles in the dissemination of knowledge, skills, and experience of acquiring new production processes. However, several studies have suggested that these programmes have not always succeeded in bringing about technological change. This lack of success may be attributed to the incidental nature of the technical assistance, which fails to have a lasting impact on the behaviour and strategies of the small-scale entrepreneurs (Tambunan, 2000).

Sandee *et al.* (1994) have estimated the participation rates of small firms in the main technical assistance programmes. The study found that participation rates were low; the majority of small firms had not by that time been included in the programmes. Furthermore, the low participation rates imply that, with current budgets, it will be many years before a majority of small firms begin to participate in technical assistance programmes.

Indonesia also has a wide array of credit programmes aimed at various groups in both urban and rural areas. These programmes include, *inter alia*, the requirement that commercial banks should provide 20 per cent of their total credit fund to small enterprises, together with micro credit schemes aimed at the self-employed. Field evidence suggests that credit is highly relevant to accommodate growth. However, participation rates in these financial assistance programmes have been low, and there is little evidence that credit has, in general, played a crucial role in promoting small-firm growth in Indonesia (Agusman, 2000).

The Performance of Small-scale Industry

Given the unfavourable policy stance and the limited impact of the small enterprise programmes, it is interesting that the size structure of the manufacturing sector in Indonesia has changed only marginally in the period 1986–96. Employment growth has been rapid in all size categories. Large differences in labour productivity across the size groups were still apparent, but did not appear to have increased, implying that significant investment and technological upgrading has also occurred among small-scale industrial enterprises. Table 11.1 presents an overview of changes in the size composition of manufacturing establishments on the basis of census data for 1986 and 1996. It shows that total manufacturing employment in Indonesia increased by more than 100 per cent over the period. Meanwhile, the percentage share employed in small establishments[4] declined, from 67.3 per cent in 1986 to 61.9 per cent in 1996 (Berry *et al.*, forthcoming).

In general, the changes in the small industry sector in the period 1986–96 reflect the general overall trends when an economy develops, urbanization proceeds, and per capita income increases (Anderson, 1982). The size structure gradually changes, with smaller units losing their prominent role in the manufacturing sector. However, in absolute terms, employment in the smallest (micro) enterprises has increased by 78 per cent. These enterprises thus remain of utmost importance for employment generation and poverty alleviation. Establishments with 5–19 workers have become somewhat more vital, and their productivity level has increased importantly. Finally, the medium-sized companies do not appear to have performed very well. Van Diermen (1999; p. 12) has suggested that the medium-sized enterprises may be too small to capture government benefits in the way that larger enterprises have, and yet are too large to escape detection by government regulators in the way that small firms have.

An Explanation of the Performance of Small-scale Industry

Liedholm and Mead (1999) found that, in several African and Latin-American countries, small enterprises added to their workforce when the economy as a whole was growing fast, but many micro enterprises, especially one-person establishments, closed down. During good times, small enterprises have been able to profit from new market opportunities. However, for poor households, the need to gain income through (self-) employment is reduced, because there are many more rewarding alternatives as wage workers. In Indonesia too, the period of rapid growth during the New Order contributed to changes in the size structure of manufacturing; with small firms (5–19 workers) gaining in importance *vis-à-vis* micro enterprises (up to 4 workers).

Panel data analysis for Indonesia also shows the dynamics of the small industry sector. An important part of the apparent increase in the share of employment and value-added of large establishments in fact comes, not from the establishments that were large to begin

Table 11.1 Size distribution of Indonesian manufacturing establishments, 1986 and 1996

Year	Size of firm (No. of employees)	Number of establishments	Employment		Labour productivity (output per days worked)
			(000s)	(% of total)	
1986	<5	1,422,593	2,700.1	52.4	n.a
	5–19	98,129	787.7	14.9	2,366
	20+	12,902	1,728.7	32.7	12,627
	20–99	10,008	400.3	7.6	n.a
	100+	2,894	1,328.4	25.1	n.a
	Total	1,533,624	5,286.5	100.0	
1996	<5	2,415,285	4,830.5	44.6	n.a
	5–19	242,067	1,873.2	17.3	2,985
	20+	22,997	4,124.9	38.1	22,143
	20–99	16,317	623.8	5.8	9,913
	100+	6,680	3,501.1	32.3	24,268
	Total	2,680,349	10,828.8	100.0	

Sources: Berry *et al*. (forthcoming); Rice and Abdullah (2000).

with, but from the small ones that grew rapidly to become large enterprises (Van Diermen, 1999).

The rapid growth of the Indonesian economy took place during a period of trade liberalization. There was an export boom for both large-scale and small-scale firms. Small-scale industry exports also benefited from subcontracting networks. Berry *et al.* (forthcoming) found that a significant and rapidly-increasing share of small industry output had been exported through subcontracting arrangements. Large firms from Indonesia and elsewhere buy semi-finished products from smaller units. The buyer firms provide a range of business development services to smaller firms, such as training, advice and so on, finance part of the production process, and are responsible for marketing their output.

The dynamics of the small industry sector also suggests that the expansion of production for the domestic and export markets has been generated to an important extent by enterprise clusters. Clustering allows small enterprises to market output beyond the local community, and to react positively to changes and opportunities in the wider economic environment. There is empirical evidence that small firms in clusters are in a better position to adopt innovation compared with their dispersed counterparts. Clustering facilitates the sharing of the costs and risks of technological change. Virtually all small industry exports from important subsectors such as clothing, footwear, textiles and furniture have come from clustered enterprises (Sandee, 1995; Van Diermen, 1999).

Jepara is a very large cluster, scattered across eighty villages. There are over 40 000 permanent workers in more than 2000 small enterprises and 100 large and medium-sized enterprises (Sandee *et al.*, 1998, p. 3). A craft industry that has changed little over the years, occupies 70 per cent of the cluster's workforce. Domestic demand has risen rapidly since the mid-1980s. About 30 per cent of the value-added is directed towards the domestic market. Producers now often produce for stock without bearing the risk of changing consumer tastes (Sandee *et al.*, 2000). The export industry benefited from the improvement of the provincial harbour in Semarang (which facilitated door-to-door container transport), improved credit facilities, and from the greater participation of foreign traders and producers in the industry. A major breakthrough was participation in a trade fair in Bali in 1989. Professional intermediaries, who place large orders for sale in the West, have gradually replaced Jakarta-based producers who used to buy Jepara's furniture. A few foreign companies have taken up production in the cluster to better control quality. Most foreigners are in partnership with Indonesians, to circumvent the many legal and tax problems frustrating foreign firms. The top ten firms control 50 per cent of exports, so this segment is much more concentrated than the domestic one. Foreigners may account for as much as 25 per cent of exports. The industry is known for its rapid and successful imitation of product lines that are popular in the West. Jepara's exports are aimed at the low-income segment of the markets in the countries to which they go. The value-added per cubic metre of furniture almost doubled during 1986–96, indicating an increase in average quality. Competition from China, Vietnam and Cambodia is on the increase.

Small firms are mainly subcontractees, receiving advance payments to finance production. Large numbers of mobile skilled craftsmen offer services to the highest bidder. In recent years, they have been employed mainly by joint ventures or by foreign firms. Over the period 1986–96, when the number of enterprises went up 3.5 times or so, the average size jumped from 12.4 to 15 workers. Registered foreigners rose from 20 to 154, and others are unregistered.

Regional and local government agencies have created an enabling environment, through various infrastructural projects, harbour improvements and one-stop facilities to curtail bureaucratic delays. The regional government has promoted producers' trade fairs, especially helpful to exports. A specific academy has been created where technical and management training is provided. Basic technical skills and general lessons about the regional furniture industry have been introduced into the primary curriculum. Technical assistance to the industry has come mainly from private channels; government agencies and non-governmental organizations have played only a limited role.

SMALL-SCALE INDUSTRIES AFTER THE ASIAN FINANCIAL CRISIS

The Promotion and Development of Small-scale Industry

The substantial devaluation of the currency was favourable for the development of small enterprises, which were less reliant on imported inputs compared with larger firms. The credit crunch and the substantial increases in the costs of borrowed funds were serious constraints for large firms, but less so for smaller establishments that rely on their own savings. The agreements between the Indonesian government and the International Monetary Fund (IMF) also contributed to the evolution of a business environment that was more conducive to small business growth. The IMF packages aimed to eliminate a large number of distortions in the economy; some distortions (for example, fixed costs) are not related to the size of an enterprise, and their elimination will favour small firms (Tambunan, 2000).

There have been contrasting trends with regard to the provision of direct support to small industries. Technical assistance has suffered budget cuts because of the crumbling financial situation of the government, and the lack of interest among donor agencies to replenish technical support budgets. This does not come as a surprise, given the fact that technical support was not rated very highly, a fact now acknowledged widely by the donor agencies. In contrast, both the Indonesian government and the international donor agencies have attached high priority to the expansion of financial assistance within the framework of social safety-net programmes. Access to micro credit has improved since the crisis, with small amounts being disbursed on a wide scale. Most financial assistance programmes offer credit at subsidized interest rates (Sandee, 2000).

The Performance of Small-scale Industries

It is not yet possible to assess the impact of the crisis on small-scale industry dynamics in Indonesia. There is an absence of aggregate data. It seems, though, that small-scale enterprises have fared very differently according to their individual sector. However, there is a widespread impression that small-scale industries are weathering the crisis better than larger companies. Two distinct interpretations of the resilience of small firms may be highlighted. First, Jellinek and Rustanto (1999) argue that there has been an upsurge of new economic opportunities for many small-scale activities. They report that cottage industries, that were almost completely destroyed over the preceding twenty years, were beginning to find it hard to keep up with new orders. In this view, the policy correction has created growth prospects for 'communal–capitalist systems being created by the people themselves'. A second line of argument suggests that the performance of small-scale enterprises since the Asian financial crisis should be interpreted in the light of their dynamism before the crisis. Being less reliant on formal markets and formal credit funds, the small-scale enterprises were able to respond more quickly and more flexibly to sudden economic shocks than could their larger counterparts. Also, small firms tend to produce 'necessities' rather than 'luxuries', for which demand is unlikely to stagnate significantly, even during a crisis (Hill, 1999).

Liedholm and Mead (1999) found that, during a crisis, micro enterprises gain in importance through the substantial growth of new start-ups. This upsurge may be explained by the loss of income opportunities elsewhere in the economy, and by the need to generate some income, however low. Their findings are reflected in current trends in Indonesia. Berry *et al.* (forthcoming) have analyzed the importance of self-employment *vis-à-vis* other ways of generating income since the crisis.[5] A comparison of the data for 1995 and 1998 shows that businesses with no hired workers moved up some 4 per cent, whilst those enterprises with temporary or family workers dropped by the same percentage. During economic downturns, many enterprises have to lay off employees, who consequently may have to start their own micro enterprises, albeit with very low returns. The expansion of the micro enterprise sector may also result from the social safety-net programmes and the growth of micro credit schemes. The new schemes have also been used by the poor to start up microeconomic activities, especially in ventures with low entry barriers. There has been involuntary growth of the sector, with more enterprises serving an unchanged market.

Scattered evidence on the resilience of firms with 5–19 workers suggests again the importance of clusters. There is evidence that furniture, roof tiles, cloth-weaving and metal-casting industry clusters have been able to adjust to changes in the macroeconomic environment. Small firms' exports have risen importantly since the beginning of the crisis, as they have benefited from the lower exchange rate, the ongoing process of liberalization, and their limited dependence on imported inputs.

The furniture industry in Jepara has done well since the start of the economic crisis. Small firms have benefited from the lower exchange rate, and large buyers have also spotted the increased business opportunities. Small firms that were involved as subcontractors before the crisis are now tied more closely to large firms, but have lost their direct access to markets. In general, however, their profits and turnover are substantially higher. Small firms with no previous experience in the export trade have become 'second-tier subcontractors', taking orders from firms already embedded in export trade networks. In addition, some firms with little export experience have been working with foreign tourists attracted by the low value of the Indonesian currency. However, Jepara's exporters are unhappy about these new 'joint ventures', fearing that the low-quality output may jeopardize the development of the industry in the long run.

A COMPARISON OF THE PERFORMANCE OF SMALL-SCALE INDUSTRY BEFORE AND AFTER THE ASIAN FINANCIAL CRISIS

I have surveyed the evidence that small-scale enterprises in Indonesia performed well before and during the New Order, as well as in the aftermath of the Asian financial crisis. I have discussed several factors that explain the dynamics of small-scale industries in both domestic and export markets. Periods of economic growth offer new market opportunities to small firms, and are conducive for technological upgrading. Such periods also see many micro enterprises closing down. However, during the current economic downturn, there has been evidence of a re-emergence of the micro enterprise sector. The evidence on small-scale enterprises is mixed. Numerous firms employing between five and nineteen workers have been hit by the crisis, though some have been resilient and able to develop new business opportunities.

It is acknowledged widely that, in earlier years, the policy in Indonesia was biased towards larger firms, and not favourable for small business development. The environment has improved since the beginning of the crisis, however, and may improve further when the IMF agreements are implemented fully. However, there are still a number of policy measures that have a negative impact on small-business development.

There is also general agreement that technical and financial assistance programmes for small industries have not been very effective. Although technical assistance is delivered at low cost, there is little evidence that it has contributed to small-firm growth, technological upgrading, or employment generation. Financial assistance has been somewhat more effective. Since the crisis it has contributed to a mushrooming of micro enterprise activities, but many of these do not appear to be viable in the long run. Furthermore, both technical and financial assistance have limited outreach among small firms, and the majority of these firms have not (yet) received any support at all. Consequently, there is extensive debate among Indonesian government agencies and representatives of the donor community about new strategies to promote small-industry development. These will be discussed in the following section.

NEW PROMOTION AND DEVELOPMENT PROGRAMMES FOR SMALL-SCALE INDUSTRIES

In December 1999, the Indonesian government and the international donor community organized a national conference aimed at making an assessment of policies for small-enterprise development (Van Diermen, 2000). The policies were to be complementary to the adjustments due to be made within the framework of the IMF agreements; there is a need for policy reform, the strengthening of programmes, the removal of barriers and biases in policies, the strengthening of support services, and the privatization of programmes. I shall review the various issues below.

First, the need has been identified for a more conducive environment for small-enterprise development, including the simplification of the regulatory framework. At the time of writing, small firms incur high costs when they apply for licences, approvals and permits to start or expand their businesses. This is not only costly and time-consuming, but also creates uncertainty, and hampers investment and technological upgrading. Small producers are reluctant to put in more effort, as they are not sure whether such investment will pay off. Local attempts to develop so-called 'one stop' facilities that allow small producers to process the necessary paperwork in a single visit, have had some success. A pilot project was undertaken in Bali, and led to substantial growth in the number of applications for permits. This positive experience could have a nationwide impact if repeated in other parts of the country.

Second, there is a need to rationalize assistance to small firms. At the time of writing, programmes and projects are 'all over the place' with several ministries executing their own activities with little co-ordination. Programmes of different departments are being executed in the same village without any co-ordination. Similarly, technical assistance is often not tuned to financial assistance, and vice versa. It is proposed to encourage the greater involvement of the private sector, while government support should concentrate on linking producers to markets, rather than offering supply-side services. Visits to buyers (retailers and wholesalers), markets and fairs, would help to establish new trade networks, and outlets for new products. My own experience in Indonesia points to the importance of assisting the mobility of small producers. This would help them to become acquainted with new business opportunities. It is envisaged that technical assistance programmes by the government will concentrate on linking producers to markets, and on paving the way for the development of the private provision of business development services (BDS) to small firms.

Third, it is important to improve the provision of non-financial assistance, or BDS, to small firms. It is envisaged that private agents increasingly will provide BDS. There are two types of private BDS provider. On the one hand, there are business consultants who provide services on a commercial basis, including advice on product design, the renting of equipment and so on. A number of initiatives aim to strengthen the role of such consultants, and make their services more popular, such as through the introduction of voucher schemes. Such schemes may help the dynamic small firms that have the means to pay for services. On the other hand, there are BDS schemes that are relevant even for those small firms that may be reluctant to pay for services. Many firms are already receiving a range of such services through existing trade networks. Traders not only purchase output, but they are generally also involved in the provision of advice on designs and technological processes, while they also supply credit to finance production. Government initiatives, discussed above, aimed at linking producers to markets, could be a good starting-point for strengthening the so-called 'hidden services' provided by traders to the small-business community.[6]

Fourth, discussions have taken place on the development of the small-scale private sector by the private sector generally. This would entail extending collective and collaborative business practices. It is recognized increasingly that a substantial part of the small-industry sector in Indonesia tends to cluster, and that clusters are generally linked to traders who play a key role in marketing output. Clustered small enterprises are characterized by business networking among small firms, and between small firms and traders. These networks frequently are underdeveloped in the case of dormant clusters, while they are strong in dynamic clusters. There is thus a challenge to develop strategies to strengthen the networks in the private sector that may be useful for small-enterprise promotion.

Finally, there is a need for institutional capacity-building at various levels in the government hierarchy. This would help to support the implementation of the proposed policies and programmes. There is considerable expertise among Indonesian government officials, at the national, provincial and local levels, on small-industry issues. Many officials know that present extension services do not have much impact on small firms, as well as what kinds of initiative and support would be relevant to promote those enterprises. Officials are confronted by strict targets set by central government departments concerning the number of small firms that have to be provided with extension services each year. Consequently, the quality of services often becomes a victim of quantitative targets. Furthermore, provincial and local government officials complain about the current incentive systems for the provision of extension services. Their salaries are in no way related to the quality of extension services provided. Institutional capacity-building at the lower levels should aim at making optimal use of the expertise and skills of provincial and local government staff through the development of an environment that enables them to do their job better.

CONCLUSIONS

This chapter has discussed the performance of small-scale industries in Indonesia both before and during the economic difficulties prompted by the Asian financial crisis. In Indonesia, globalization and the government's liberalization policies have had an important impact on small-firm dynamics. Furthermore, we have seen that there is scope for provincial governments to improve the business environment for small firms through policies that have an impact on regional economic development.

We should be cautious in appraising the contribution that the small-enterprise development programmes make to the dynamics of small firms. The programmes were delivered at low cost, but have had a limited impact on employment generation and technological upgrading. These limitations have been recognized increasingly by the Indonesian authorities and the international donor community. Recently, there have been co-ordinated efforts to formulate a new set of programmes that would be more conducive for small-firm development in the post-crisis environment.

The new programmes entail a streamlining of government assistance and regulation, through the establishment of one-stop facilities for support, licences and so on, as well as incentive systems for provincial and local government officials to make more effective use of their expertise. In addition, the new programmes are intended to increase the role of private-sector traders and business consultants. The main challenge will be to find the right balance between government and private provision of services. The involvement of the private sector may well be most effective for small firms that have growth prospects, and where the producers can pay for the services. The government agencies still appear to be important in the many cases where private-sector interest is limited, and where the linking of producers to markets is a prerequisite for business-to-business support.

Notes

1. In this chapter, we follow the definition of the Indonesian Bureau of Statistics: small-scale enterprises are defined as firms with fewer than twenty workers. They are further divided into enterprises with 1–4 workers, and those with 5–19 workers.
2. An earlier version of this chapter was presented at the conference on 'Small-scale Enterprises in Developing and Transitional Economies' at King's College, London in September 2000.
3. Sandee *et al.* (1998) estimated that such transaction costs may be as high as 20 per cent of monthly income in Central Java.
4. Small establishments are defined as those with fewer than twenty workers.
5. The survey was undertaken during the month of January, in the middle of the rainy season, when agricultural activity is most prominent.
6. Anderson (2000) and Sandee and van Hulsen (2000) have recently discussed the importance of strengthening BDS schemes through traders.

Bibliography

Agusman, D. (2000) 'Financing SME Growth in Indonesia: Issues, Constraints, and Prospects', Paper presented at the Workshop on Small and Medium-Sized Enterprise Financing in Asia, Asian Development Bank, Manila, 3–4 July.

Anderson, D. (1982) 'Small Industry in Developing Countries: A Review of Issues', *World Development*, vol. 10, no. 11, pp. 913–48.

Anderson, G. (2000) 'The Hidden Micro and Small Enterprise Service Sector: Research into Commercial BDS Provision to Micro and Small Enterprises in Vietnam and Thailand', Paper presented at the Conference on Business Services for Small Enterprises in Asia, Hanoi.

Berry, A., Rodriquez, E. and Sandee, H. (forthcoming) 'Small Industry Dynamics in Indonesia', *Bulletin of Indonesian Economic Studies*.

Hill, H. (1995) 'Small–Medium Enterprise and Rapid Industrialisation: The ASEAN Experience', *Journal of Asian Business*, vol. 11, no. 2, pp. 1–31.

Hill, H. (1999) *The Indonesian Economy in Crisis: Causes, Consequences, and Lessons*, Singapore: Institute of Southeast Asian Studies.

Jellinek, L. and Rustanto, B. (1999) 'Survival Strategies of the Javanese during the Economic Crisis', Consultancy Report to the World Bank, Jakarta.

Liedholm, C. and Mead, D. C. (1999) *Small Enterprise and Economic Development: The Dynamics of Micro and Small Enterprises*, London and New York: Routledge.

Rice, R. and Abdullah, I. (2000) 'A Comparison of the Development of Small and Medium/Large Indonesian Manufacturing Enterprises from 1986 to 1996 by Sector', Jakarta: USAID, Partnership for Economic Growth Project.

Sandee, H. (1995) *Innovation Adoption in Rural Industry: Technological Change in Roof Tile Clusters in Central Java, Indonesia*, Amsterdam: Free University.

Sandee, H. (1998) 'Promoting Small-scale and Cottage Industry Clusters in Indonesia', *Small Enterprise Development*, vol. 9, no. 1 pp. 52–8.

Sandee, H. (2000) 'SMEs in Southeast Asia: Issues and Constraints in the Pre- and Post-Crisis Environments', Paper presented at the Workshop on Small and Medium-Sized Enterprise Financing in Asia, Asian Development Bank, Manila, 3–4 July.

Sandee, H., Andadari, R. K. and Hunga, I. (1998) 'Pungutan and Sumbangan in a Central Javanese Case Study', Report to the Asia Foundation, Jakarta.

Sandee, H., Andadari, R. K. and Sulandjari, S. (2000) 'Small Firm Development during Good Times and Bad: The Jepara Furniture Industry', in C. Manning and P. van Diermen (eds), *Indonesia in Transition: Social Aspects of Reform and Crisis*, Singapore: Institute of Southeast Asian Studies, pp. 184–98.

Sandee, H. and van Hulsen S. (2000) 'Small and Cottage Industry Clusters and Business Development Services in Indonesia', Paper presented at the Conference on Business Services for Small Enterprises in Asia, Hanoi.

Sandee, H., Rietveld, P., Supratikno, H. and Yuwono, P. (1994) 'Promoting Small-scale and Cottage Industries in Indonesia: An Impact Analysis for Central Java', *Bulletin of Indonesian Economic Studies*, vol. 20, no. 3, pp. 115–42.

Tambunan, T. (2000) *Development of Small-scale Industries during the New Order Government in Indonesia*, Aldershot: Ashgate.

van Diermen, P. (1999) *Competition and SME Programme: Background paper on SME Sector in Indonesia*, Jakarta: Asian Development Bank.

van Diermen, P. (2000) (ed.) *National Conference on SME Development in Indonesia: Proceedings*, Manila: Asian Development Bank.

12 The Determinants of Competitiveness in SME Clusters: Evidence and Policies for Latin America

Manuel Albaladejo

INTRODUCTION

Nearly all Latin-American economies faced a shift towards more liberalized regimes during the 1990s. The opening up to new markets has exposed small- and medium-sized enterprises (SMEs) in Latin America to the benefits and threats of globalization. On the one hand, optimists argue that increased competitive pressures will trigger the upgrading of SMEs through the introduction and absorption of new technologies. Pessimists, on the other hand, point out that trade liberalization has been accompanied by macroeconomic distortions (such as the instability of the real exchange rate) that have posed a special threat to SMEs. All other things being equal, the relative comparative advantage of SMEs deteriorates, as larger firms have more resources to adjust their production systems to changing environments.

As in many other regions in the Third World, industrial clustering in Latin America is significant. SMEs have benefited from geographical agglomeration as proximity breeds external economies and encourages joint action. However, the growth experience of clusters is varied, as new competitive pressures require more than 'collective efficiency' to break into global markets. Indeed, the whole concept of competitiveness has changed from static to dynamic, which requires the ability to supply new market niches constantly with the right product, at the right time, and with the right quality. Under this new scenario, few clusters in developing countries have been able to compete in 'high-street' markets with innovative and high-quality products because of internal and external constraints to growth. But what makes them so different from successful clusters in industrialized countries?

This chapter tries to identify the determinants of competitiveness of SME clusters, with special reference to five clusters in Latin America. It takes the debate forward by adding country-level and firm-level determinants to the cluster-level factors mentioned in the 'collective efficiency' approach. Based on an enlarged analytical framework, policy recommendations to foster clusters' competitiveness are provided at the different levels.

The chapter is structured as follows. The second section presents the conceptual underpinnings. The third section then presents an overview of the importance of SMEs in Latin America, and of the five clusters to be surveyed. The empirical evidence on the determinants of the competitiveness of these five SME clusters is considered in the penultimate section, while the final section lists possible policy recommendations to foster the competitiveness of SME clusters in Latin America.

THEORETICAL UNDERPINNINGS: AN EXTENDED FRAMEWORK

Although there is no generally accepted definition of 'cluster', the concept is used widely in the industrial economics literature. The term could refer to both structured industrial production systems and informal market agglomerations where business arrangements occur. However, it is clear that, in the broadest sense, it denotes 'the geographical and sectoral concentration of firms' and its potential benefits for the smallest companies (Schmitz, 1995a).

The concept of cluster is derived from the idea of an 'industrial district', originally used by Marshall (1920) to stress the economies that arise from the concentration of specialized industries in particular localities. Some decades later, Becattini (1990) reintroduced it in the debate to explain the successful performance of local SMEs in the Italian regions of Tuscany and Emilia-Romagna. Sectoral concentration led to vertical disintegration and flexible specialization where economies of scale could be reaped through inter-firm co-operation. Common goals and sociocultural identities helped to build up trust in the cluster, and self-help institutions were used as vehicles for political lobbying. The 'Italian district model' became a benchmark for policy-makers and researchers to explore how far (or close) were other SME clusters from the *beau idéal*.

However, understanding why some clusters do well, while many others stagnate, requires a more in-depth investigation than a mere comparisan with 'textbook' model. Indeed, the performance of clusters' can be hampered or fostered through a wide array of interconnected factors. Some factors are internal to the clustered firms, while others belong to the economic and social environment in which the firms operate. Some can be fostered directly through government intervention, while others are promoted more effectively through market channels. Research in this topic has so far tended to focus on inter-firm determinants (that is, the factors found to be important in the Italian experience), clearly overlooking the importance of intra-firm and macroeconomic issues. An understanding of the behaviour of clusters requires an integrating framework depicting a wider set of factors that may help to explain differences in economic performance. Drawing on several bodies of literature, Figure 12.1 presents an extended framework of the determinants affecting competitiveness in SME clusters.

Country-level Determinants

General interventions at the macro level reflect overarching concerns with the economic environment in which all firms operate. Under this umbrella fall polices related to macroeconomic stability and the regulatory and policy environment. For instance, there seems to be agreement that clusters (and firms in general) benefit from a stable macroeconomic environment with tight inflation control, low budget

Country-level determinants

General interventions
Macroeconomics
Regulatory and policy framework

SME-specific interventions
Financial services
Non-financial services

Cluster-level determinants

External economies
Joint action
Trust
Connectivity

Firm-level determinants

Skills (management, technology-related)
Technological effort and learning
Working conditions
Physical infrastructure and machinery

Figure 12.1 The determinants of competitiveness in SME clusters

deficits, reasonable interest rates, and a competitive real exchange rate. Indeed, macroeconomic stability provides companies with incentives to save, and mechanisms to channel those savings into investments.

A conducive regulatory environment often requires a market-friendly trade regime, which reduces import controls and tariffs. The reduction in import restrictions, however, needs to be gradual, so that companies have the time to adjust to the new challenges. In order to accelerate the adjustment process, governments need to reduce the transaction costs facing companies, by simplifying and centralizing formal administrative procedures to register businesses (for example, through the provision of 'one-stop' shops), and cutting red tape[1].

Providing macroeconomic stability and a conducive regulatory framework are important preconditions for clusters' competitiveness, but they might not be enough. A second set of determinants relate to the existence (or not) of specific SME interventions. It is necessary to intervene in a direct way as changes in the macroeconomic setting, on their own, will not solve all the problems faced by SMEs. One particular problem is lack of capital. Financing constraints often limit the investment capacity of SMEs, and hence hamper their growth. In general, lending to SMEs is seen as a 'high-risk' business, as most of these companies lack collateral. However, it is worth stressing that the problem does not seem to be the lack of funds, but rather how to make them accessible to SMEs. Research shows that funding often gets diverted to the benefit of larger enterprises, and that only an insignificant number of SMEs have been able to attract bank financing (United Nations,1993).

The difficulties of implementing financing support schemes, and their limited impact on SMEs, has led development agencies to turn their attention to non-financial services as an alternative way to support SMEs. The rationale behind this idea of providing services is that 'small firms need to have a whole range of services and inputs which large firms are normally able to call upon internally but which, for reasons of scale, small firms are unable to provide themselves' (Pyke, 1994, p. 4). Non-financial services broadly cover two areas:

- Services concerned with improving production and innovation capabilities, such as counselling on production layouts, quality standards, and maintenance checks; the provision of information for technology development; launching co-operative joint operations of large-scale and expensive equipment; testing of raw materials; and training of entrepreneurs and workers; and

- Services concerned with developing commercial/marketing activities in firms, such as marketing training, business linkages and co-operative sales initiatives.

These non-financial services can be delivered through public service centres or through the business environment (commercial channels). In the former, such provision involves supplying companies with the services they require in return for a price or a performance-based commission. Although these centres often provide services tailored to the needs of their clients, their affordability by the poorest businesses is debatable. In response to this, services provided by, and channelled through, private enterprises have attracted the attention of donor agencies, though the role of the latter is not defined clearly, as they can generate market distortions. The nature and effectiveness of services provided varies from country to country, and sector to sector. However, a common feature is that they are often designed to offset constraints facing SMEs. Both public and private service providers have adopted a customer-orientated, collective and cumulative approach (Humphrey and Schmitz, 1996) to reduce transaction costs, increase outreach, and stimulate the sustainable growth of SMEs.

Cluster-level Determinants

These are the inter-firm determinants emphasized by the 'textbook' model based on the success of SME clusters in Italy. This approach emphasizes that the problem of many small firms is not their size, but rather their isolation (Sengenberger and Pyke, 1991). Indeed, research has shown that geographical and sectoral concentration breeds external economies and induces joint action.

External economies are the unplanned gains that occur as a consequence of the unintentional influences firms have upon each other when they are in close proximity. The creation of a pool of skilled labour, the diffusion of technological expertise, and the ability to attract foreign buyers are some examples of the spillover effects derived from clustering.[2]

Joint actions represent the planned gains of being clustered. Strong collaborative ties have been shown to be very effective in helping SMEs to overcome structural constraints in their productive, organizational and marketing functions. There are several patterns of co-operation:

- 'Horizontal co-operation' represents a partnership between companies operating at the same (or similar) stage in the production chain. For example, companies may get together to share expensive technology and to purchase raw material at lower cost;
- 'Backward co-operation' comprises any type of contractual or informal arrangement between final producers and their input suppliers and subcontractors. For example, backward co-operation can be strengthened to increase quality standards of the components produced by subcontractors. This may involve technology transfer and training provision from the top; and
- 'Forward co-operation' involves aspects such as the exchange of market information and demand trends between buyers and producers, which gives rise to a *creative milieu*.

The term 'collective efficiency' (Schmitz, 1995a) is an integrating concept that captures both the external economies and the joint action gains that result from geographical agglomeration. It is important to note that the notion of collective efficiency does not deny competition and conflict within the cluster. Rather, it emphasizes the benefits that SMEs would miss if they were not clustered. Indeed, research shows that clustering facilitates the mobilization of financial and human resources, as it breaks down investment into small, 'riskable' steps (Schmitz, 1982). It stimulates a process in which companies create – often unwillingly – a niche for accumulating expertise, skills and capital. But while collective efficiency provides the basic ingredients for clusters to flourish, growth may not follow. The gains resulting from clustering require two other factors; trust and connectivity.

Trust

Political and social life is inherent to clusters. Accepted and respected common values derived from sociocultural identities are shared by people as well as firms. This homogeneity contributes to the achievement of common goals, the strengthening of communication flows, the promotion of co-operative efforts, and trust among producers. Such interconnections help firms to identify themselves with the industry in the area, and to promote the interests of the community as a whole. Social sanctions occur when individuals break rules or act against common goals. Collective efficiency is unlikely to happen without trust and sanctions. Research has shown the importance of the existence of these social rules to strengthen the co-operative ties among firms, therefore accelerating the process of learning in clusters.[3]

Connectivity

A major feature of clusters, especially in developing countries, is being by-passed by international flows of products, technology, information and finance. The insertion (or not) of an SME cluster into global and regional value chains defines its sustainable performance and growth. On the one hand, clusters well-connected to distant markets are more likely to experience evolutionary growth based on the continuous upgrading of products and processes. Global buyers and foreign firms can be a major source of technology transfer, and a learning pool for SMEs.[4] On the other hand, clusters that are limited to domestic markets are likely to experience 'immiserizing' growth, with price being the main basis for competitiveness. There are no incentives to upgrade quality, as domestic markets, especially in developing countries, tend to be less demanding. Firms that follow this strategy are likely to fail in the long run, as they rarely invest in the labour force, and their low wages may generate internal conflicts.

Firm-level Determinants

The overall performance of a cluster reflects the performance of individual firms, or small groups of firms, within the cluster. However, research has tended to focus attention mainly on the socioeconomic context in which clustered firms operate, while little has been said about the firm-level dynamics that occur in clusters. Furthermore, the link between intra-firm factors and a cluster's overall performance has not been explored empirically in the literature.[5]

The point of departure of this approach is that the dynamic competitiveness of clusters depends on a continuous process of technological learning and upgrading within firms. Learning requires the existence of technological capabilities, defined as the knowledge, skills and effort required for firms to bring about an indigenous process of technological development. Technological capabilities can be divided broadly into two groups: those required to increase production efficiency (production capabilities), such as quality control and production scheduling management; and those needed to make major improvements to established technologies, or to create new ones (innovation capabilities).

Such capability acquisition cannot be taken for granted, and often requires purposive and cumulative efforts aimed at assimilating and modifying existing technologies, adapting them to local conditions. This is especially the case in developing countries, since major innovations are still concentrated in technologically advanced countries. The effectiveness of these integral efforts that lead to in-firm technological learning is assumed to depend on the managerial and technical skills of entrepreneurs and the workforce. The importance of technology effort is reflected in how much a firm spends on upgrading and improving existing products and processes, or creating new ones.

Companies with strong technological capabilities are likely to generate 'learning-rich' networks boosting a cluster's technological dynamism. Co-operation ties generate technology-related information flows that may lead to incremental capability building for the parties involved: for example, R&D joint ventures between clustered firms. On the contrary, if technological capabilities are weak, the benefits of joint action are restrained because of obvious limitations in technology-related knowledge. In this context, information flows between clustered companies tend to be 'learning-poor', having little impact on the process of inter-firm technological capability building. Clusters at this level lack technological dynamism and often remain stagnant, production-driven spots of low value-added activities, where cheap and abundant labour prevails as the main competitive factor.

To sum up, the determinants of competitiveness in clusters are many, and located at different levels. Some are external to the cluster, and some are external to the firms but internal to the cluster (inter-firm factors), while others are internal to the clustered firms (intra-firm factors). The 'collective efficiency' framework, which focuses only on the externalities and joint action derived from geographical agglomeration, has so far been the predominant approach in exploring the competitiveness of clusters in the Third World, by comparing them to the ideal 'textbook' model.

SME CLUSTERS IN LATIN AMERICA

In this section, I discuss the relative importance of SMEs in Latin America, and present an overview of the clusters researched. The SME sector accounts for much of the labour force and production in most Latin-American countries, becoming a key player in their economic activities. For example, SMEs in Argentina account for 99 per cent of all firms, employing about 70 per cent of the total labour force. In Brazil, there are around four million SMEs, which account for 40 per cent of GDP. In Paraguay and Uruguay, SMEs account for 60 per cent and 50 per cent of GDP, respectively (*Gazeta Mercantil Latinoamericana* 1996). Breaking down the SME category into smaller units, we find that over 80 per cent of the businesses in Latin America and the Caribbean have ten employees or fewer. These small productive units provide jobs for over 120 million people in the region (Berger and Guillamon, 1996). SMEs in Latin America, as elsewhere in the Third World, are often family-owned and chiefly involved in the production of labour-intensive traditional goods for the domestic market. Many of these local industries are static, as major technological changes in products and processes have rarely occurred.

Clusters in Latin America are diverse, but they tend to consist mainly of micro and small firms involved in low-technology activities (garments, shoes and so on) with low barriers to entry, and low industrial rents which are difficult to sustain because of the increased competitive pressures from catching-up countries.[6] Generally speaking, it seems that SMEs in Latin America have used clustering as a self-defence strategy, rather than as a means of building up dynamic competitiveness through inter-firm learning and technological upgrading (Albaladejo, 1999). The clusters presented in this chapter have been researched in depth. They are listed below.

The Sinos Valley cluster of shoe-makers in Brazil

The Brazilian shoe industry has its main core in the Sinos Valley (Schmitz, 1995a, 1995b, 1999; Schmitz and Bazan, 1997). There are around 1800 firms – most of them SMEs – of which, 500 are shoe producers, supported by 700 service-rendering industries and 200 component firms. Producers in the Sinos Valley have specialized in women's footwear. The spatial concentration of the cluster – a 50 km radius around Novo Hamburgo – has attracted the attention of export agents all over the world. In 1990, the cluster exported 65 per cent of its total shoe production, and employed 150 000 people (Schmitz and Bazan, 1997). Competitive pressures were felt by local producers with the opening of the Chinese economy to international markets. The annual growth rate of shoe imports from China increased to almost 40 per cent, threatening the exports of standardized shoes.

The Mexican footwear clusters of Guadalajara and Leon

Mexico's footwear industry is mainly located in two clusters: Leon, which specializes in men's and children's shoes; and Guadalajara, specializing in women's shoes (Rabellotti, 1997, 1999). Both clusters together account for two-thirds – over 4000 firms – of all Mexican shoe producers. Most firms are small or very small in size, and family-owned. The Mexican shoe-producers were also badly affected by cheap shoe imports from China.

The garment cluster of Gamarra in Peru

Lima's 'Complejo Gamarra' is the most important garment cluster in Peru (Villaran, 1993; Visser, 1997). It has over 3000 businesses including final producers, subcontractors, trading firms and input suppliers, all of them engaged either directly or indirectly in the production and marketing of garments.

The Peruvian cluster of shoe-makers in Trujillo, Peru

The 'El Porvenir' cluster in the city of Trujillo consists of 1000 small and micro firms that account for 35 per cent of the Peruvian domestic shoe market (Tavara, 1993). As in the other Peruvian case, there is no information about how increased competitive pressures have affected the dynamism and growth prospects.

The Brazilian granite industry cluster in Cachoeiro de Itapemirim, Brazil

The cluster of Cachoeiro de Itapemirim in Brazil is a very interesting example of a spatial concentration of SMEs in a resource-based industry (Sabadini, 1998). The cluster contains 500 firms – of which 300 are stage firms – accounting for almost 80 per cent of Brazilian exports of solid ornaments in marble and granite. In his study, Sabadini provides a detailed comparison of the cluster's main features with the Italian model.

These clusters show signs of both success and failure, and have recently felt increased international competitive pressures. Although generalizations cannot be made from these few examples, they provide interesting insights into the kinds of factor that affect competitiveness of similar clusters throughout the region.

THE DETERMINANTS OF COMPETITIVENESS IN THE FIVE CLUSTERS

This section attempts to shed light on the determinants of competitiveness in the five clusters in Latin America. The inter-firm variables emphasized in the 'collective efficiency' approach were used in these cases to determine the level of (dis)similarity of these clusters with regard to the 'textbook' model. We therefore start by exploring the determinants at the cluster level. Complementary research material has been gathered to take into account country-level and firm-level factors as they have been presented in the theoretical framework. This should give the reader a broader view of the factors affecting the competitiveness of these clusters.

Cluster-level Determinants

The decentralization of the production process, firms' specialization on a specific phase of the production chain, and the increase in subcontracting practices are major features of the 'new' competition (Best, 1990). This shift towards post-Fordist ways of industrial organization has also been experienced in the clusters researched.

Decentralization of production and flexible specialization are key features of the SMEs in the Sinos Valley. There is a great range of inputs, components, and intermediate goods to shoe manufacturing, and all provided locally. In the other Brazilian case, Sabadini (1998) points out that 73 per cent of the firms interviewed concentrate on only one phase of the production process. Visser (1997) also acknowledges that Gamarra's economic dynamism results mainly from the fact that wide decentralization of production has taken place, and firms have specialized in particular stages of the value chain.

This pattern is less obvious in Trujillo, where 'individual firms ensure that the initial and final activities of the production process are performed in-house' (Tavara, 1993, p. 102). A shortage of trustworthy subcontractors may be the reason, as in the case of Mexico, where firms 'try to internalise as many phases of the production cycle as possible in order to reduce their dependency on an unstable, low quality supply' (Rabellotti, 1997, p. 44). Although the situation has changed slightly with the opening of the Mexican economy to global markets, the larger and most competitive firms still seem to be highly centralized.

Strong collaborative links among firms is another feature of the 'textbook' model. Schmitz (1995a) coined the term 'collective efficiency' when studying how local shoe producers in the Sinos Valley strengthened their co-operative links to face global competition. Forward ties with export agents played a major role in the breaking of the cluster into international markets. The agents would provide technical assistance to ensure a good-quality product. This quality check would also be reflected in the firms' backward relationships with input suppliers and subcontractors, thus creating a quality-conscious stream from the production process to the marketing phase. In Guadalajara, Rabellotti (1999) states that increased co-operation has contributed positively to the cluster's growth.

Unlike the Sinos Valley and Guadalajara, Cachoeiro de Itapemirim and Trujillo show lower levels of co-operation among firms. Furthermore, the real benefits of joint collaborative efforts seem not to be there. In the Brazilian case, Sabadini (1998) points out that while 46 per cent of firms appear to be involved in co-operative activities with other firms, these arrangements tend to be informal and unstructured, thus having little impact on the firms' capacity to improve production processes.

A shared set of values and common goals are the result of concrete economic, social, cultural and historical conditions. Sociocultural embeddedness implies mutual knowledge and trust among firms, which 'helps to promote the generation and diffusion of innovations within the cluster' (Villaran, 1992, p. 144). The social milieu seems to be strong in the cases of Trujillo and Cachoeiro de Itapemirim. In the Peruvian case, Tavara (1993) reports that there seems to be a high degree of solidarity resulting from communal efforts to improve the living conditions of the cluster's inhabitants. This has facilitated trust relationships among the firms, and led to the formation of local self-help organizations. In Brazil, Sabadini (1998) points out that the common roots of the entrepreneurs in the cluster – 46 per cent of the entrepreneurs interviewed were Italian – has contributed to strong co-operative links to increase productivity.

The Sinos Valley is an interesting case, as it shows how the social milieu can change over time. At the beginning, there used to be strong sociocultural ties because of the German origin of most of its population. The penetration of outsiders – particularly export agents – with a very different set of values diffused the inherent social ties in the cluster. But how can inter-firm co-operation be so high when social and cultural values have become so heterogeneous? Schmitz (1995b) stresses that the increase in co-operation in recent years has not resulted because of sociocultural ties, but rather because of the 'economic costs of not co-operating'.

The active presence of local self-help institutions, such as trade unions and manufacturers, have been integral parts of successful clusters in industrialized countries. They play a key role as they tend to promote initiatives that reflect the needs and concerns of local firms. Strong self-help organizations seem to be present in the selected clusters. In the Sinos Valley cluster, co-operation among local producers led to the formation of FENAC, a professional trade organization that has been used to attract foreign buyers (Schmitz, 1999). The same can be said of the two Peruvian cases, where the National Footwear Makers' Association (APEMEFAC) in Trujillo, and the Peruvian Association of Small-Scale Garment Manufacturers (APIC) in Gamarra, have played significant roles in the development of both clusters.

Firm-level Determinants

Firm-level determinants comprise those intra-firm factors discussed in the 'technological capability' literature. As already noted in the theoretical framework, the dynamic competitiveness of clusters depends on a continuous process of technological learning and upgrading within firms. For such a process to happen, investment in physical and human capital is required.

Unfortunately, the cases studied here do not provide detailed information on the level of technological excellence of the clustered companies. However, Villaran's (1992) analysis of clusters in Peru shows the low competence-level of the SME workforce in Trujillo and Gamarra. Similarly, Sabadini (1998) points out in his study on Brazil that only a few firms care about the training and the skills of the labour force. According to Sabadini's survey, '44 per cent of firms report to do nothing about increasing the skills of the workforce' (Sabadini, 1998, p. 15). Finally, the level of skills in the Brazilian shoe industry is not clear, but one could assume that it is weak, as the industry employs a high number of unqualified teenagers (Schmitz, 1993).

But the shortage of skills is not limited to the shop floor alone. Research published in *La Gazeta Mercantil Latinoamericana* has shown that Latin-American entrepreneurs lack managerial skills and long-term vision (*Gazeta Mercantil Latinoamericana*, 1996). According to this study, managers are apprehensive about change, and stick to traditional and defensive strategies in business practices. Improvements in quality, productivity, and innovation are not seen as ways of increasing firms' competitiveness. Company owners are satisfied with the status quo and only aspire to perform everyday operations, with no thought to the long run. Other research carried out by the Economic Commission for Latin America (ECLA) found that lack of managerial skills and limited technological effort were among the major problems faced by the SME sector in Brazil (*Gazeta Mercantil Latinoamericana*, 1997).

In their comparative study of industrial districts in developing countries, Nadvi and Schmitz (1994) also showed the weak technological standards of Trujillo, Gamarra, Guadalajara and Leon, relative to the Italian ideal model. Sabadini points out the obsolete infrastructure and poor conditions that workers have to put up with in the cluster of Cachoeiro de Itapemirim. He finds the machinery used to be 'old, obsolete and in precarious conditions, being the cause of the high number of working accidents in this particular sector' (Sabadini, 1998, p. 15).

Country-level Determinants

The impact of macroeconomic policies on the performance of clusters was not explored in the case studies selected. Only the Mexican case of Guadalajara suggests that trade reform made firms aware of global competitive pressures. The peso devaluation 'gave some firms the time to respond with greater co-operation with suppliers, buyers, and through the entrepreneurial association' (Rabellotti, 1999, p. 1582).

Among the external constraints faced by SME clusters, the domestic policy environment seems to be dominant. In most Latin-American countries, macroeconomic instability has been present for decades. For example, countries such as Argentina, Brazil, Peru and Venezuela have all encountered periods of unsustainable balance-of-payments deficits and hyperinflation. This resulted in appreciating exchange rates and the imposition of import restrictions, and has created general policy uncertainty. These aspects of the macroeconomic environment were harmful to all private enterprises, but especially to SMEs.

A second major external constraint is the deficient regulatory environment created by many Latin-American governments. Although improvements have been seen in recent years, the complexity of the regulations to register businesses has increased the transaction costs of SMEs *vis-à-vis* large domestic enterprises and foreign firms.[7]

As far as SME-specific interventions are concerned, with only a few exceptions, Latin-American governments have not provided the financial and technical resources to enable SMEs to overcome these structural constraints. Adjusting the productive system of SMEs to compete with more innovative products requires a quick infusion of new capital. In Latin America, the evidence shows that large firms have better access to credit, and that governments protect them more. The ECLA study (*Gazeta Mercantil Latinoamericana*, 1997) found that, from a survey of 400 firms within the MERCOSUR agreement, 87 per cent of SMEs had problems in financing new investments. Other research shows the positive relationship between access to bank finance and increased exports (Miller and Caprio, 1997). Within the MERCOSUR context, the study concludes that larger enterprises have easier access to bank finance than do SMEs.

On the technological side, the ECLA study (*Gazeta Mercantil Latinoamericana*, 1997) exposes the deficient technology and innovation schemes of many supporting institutions in Latin America. In most cases, the main problem is not the existence of such support schemes, but rather the lack of co-ordination and shared objectives among the different institutional actors.

The High Road and the Low Road

According to Sengenberger and Pyke (1992) there are two main industrial strategies that clusters have followed to meet the challenges of international competition: the 'high road' and the 'low road'. Clustered firms that follow the low-road strategy seek competitiveness through low prices. This is achieved by squeezing labour costs and by operating in a deregulated market environment. Working conditions are often poor, as companies rarely invest in physical and human capital. They often supply domestic markets where quality standards are less demanding, and prices are lower. In contrast, companies that follow the high-road strategy base their competitiveness on quality improvements and innovation. This strategy requires the continuous technological learning and upgrading of existing technological capabilities. Export-orientated companies often restructure in this way, as innovation has become an essential factor when competing in the new international context.

Clusters do not always follow these industrial strategies. It is common to find groups of firms that, within the same cluster, follow different restructuring strategies (Brusco, 1992). In the ideal model, however, clustering is a key factor influencing SMEs to take the 'high road'. Indeed, research has shown that the success of industrial districts in Europe has been based on SMEs being able to upgrade and break into export markets (Capecchi, 1990; Benton, 1992; Schmitz,

1992). In contrast, clusters in Latin America have not exploited the enormous benefits of spatial agglomeration to take the 'high road'.

Price competitiveness remains the driving factor in the clusters studied. Take the case of Guadalajara in Mexico. A move towards more quality-conscious products is unlikely, because of 'the low quality of the components and raw materials supplied, and the scarce attention to fashion changes' (Rabellotti, 1997, p. 42). In Cachoeiro de Itapemirim, 95.3 per cent of the companies interviewed reported that low price was the main market strategy. In the Sinos Valley, although firms have become more quality-driven because of international competitive pressures, the cluster presents features (for example, poor wages) common to the 'low road' strategy.

Interestingly, though, is the fact that some changes *alla italiana* have occurred in Latin-American clusters. For example, most of the clusters selected for this study have experienced increased inter-firm co-operation and vertical disintegration of production processes (some more than others). But these positive changes, together with the strong social milieu and the presence of self-help associations, do not seem to be sufficient for the Latin-American clusters to become competitive in more up-market products.

What is missing, then? The 'collective efficiency' approach used in these studies clearly overlooks the national- and firm-level determinants of clusters' competitiveness, as presented in the theoretical framework. Evidence from other sources suggests that the shortage of technological capabilities in these firms might not have triggered technological dynamism in these clusters, and that increased inter-firm co-operation has been used more as a survival strategy rather than as a means of breaking into global markets (Albaladejo, 1999). Following the same line of thought, macroeconomic instabilities, a disabling regulatory environment and a lack of SME-specific policy interventions might have prevented firms from doing better, clearly offsetting the possible benefits of geographical proximity. This would suggest that the challenges resulting from globalization might require more than joint action between clustered companies. Policy interventions to enhance the competitiveness of Latin-American clusters should go beyond the mere promotion of collective efficiency. Such policies should also create a business environment conducive for companies to flourish. Finally, there is also the need for interventions to boost technological capabilities in firms, and promote inter-firm learning. Specific policy recommendations at different levels are spelt out in the final section.

CONCLUSIONS: POLICIES TO FOSTER COMPETITIVENESS IN LATIN-AMERICAN CLUSTERS

One of the main questions faced by policy-makers in the Third World is how to foster the dynamic competitiveness of SME clusters. Policy recommendations have so far been biased by a narrow approach. New empirical evidence for Latin-American countries suggests that policies should not be directed solely towards strengthening inter-firm co-operation within clusters. To be more effective, they should be combined with another set of policies: government interventions at the national level, and specific schemes to build up the technological capabilities of SMEs.

Macro policies are important to enable clusters to break into external markets. Maintaining an open trade regime provides a link to global markets and exposes SMEs to new competitive pressures. Governments can help the export-orientation of SME clusters by promoting gradual cuts in tariff rates, and streamlining import/export regulations. Ensuring macroeconomic stability – for example, controlling inflation and exchange rates – is also an important way of allowing SMEs to emerge, grow and prosper. It is also accepted generally that governments should provide an enabling regulatory and policy framework based upon:

- A stable fiscal and monetary policy environment, with reasonable interest rates, a system of financial markets that provides incentives to save, and mechanisms to channel savings into investments. For example, a lower tax rate on initial profits allows firms to retain some earnings and to increase investment as appropriate;
- Policies that minimize the costs of business licensing and registering, while safeguarding public interests; and
- Policies that facilitate business transactions, such as infrastructure development.

Promoting SME clustering and networking means stimulating inter-firm co-operation and competition among the economic actors, creating specific location advantages for SMEs. This can be achieved through:

- Promoting programmes that favour the vertical disintegration of larger firms and subcontracting arrangements with smaller firms;
- Strengthening self-help institutions, such as employers' organizations and trade unions. If properly co-ordinated, these organizations

can give SMEs a political voice, as well as acting as vehicles for decentralizing initiatives in favour of local producers; and

- Enhancing the role of intermediary institutions easing SMEs' access to finance and technical services. Sector-specific service centres can play a major role, since their services reflect the needs of the clients and they tend to target groups of firms with similar needs rather than individual companies.

At the firm level, initiatives should help SMEs to build up their technological capabilities. Policies should be directed towards tackling the main internal problems faced by SMEs in Latin America. This would boost the technological dynamism and competitiveness of clusters. In broad terms, such initiatives should comprise (among many others):

- The investment in human development to guarantee a pool of skilled labour, and encouragement to firms to train their labour force by, for example, promoting tax reduction schemes;
- The enhancement of the innovation and production capabilities of local firms, making good and rational use of external sources (for example, facilitating the transfer and use of appropriate technology in SMEs);
- The elimination of limitations on innovation by designing support services on the basis of the indigenous capacities of local firms. Service providers should act as intermediary agencies in the spread of technologies through a process of inter-enterprise learning; and
- The design and promotion of R&D-intensive services to encourage SMEs to move towards more innovative, and therefore higher value-added, products.

Clustering on its own does not guarantee industrial success. However, geographical agglomerations create a niche where well-designed and properly implemented institutional interventions could make a difference. In general terms, clusters' competitiveness requires:

- Demand-side stimulants to create a new challenge for Latin American SME clusters, as clusters have been shown to perform better when there is economic dynamism and increased competitiveness; and
- Supply-side responses to cope with the new challenges. It is clear that the opening up of national economies to global markets has

increased SMEs' prospects and opportunities, but it has also increased international pressure to upgrade and become more efficient. Competitive pressures require effective support services at different levels. Latin-American governments need to ensure a stable macroeconomic environment for business development, foster clusters' competitiveness in global markets, and help SMEs to overcome their structural constraints.

Notes

1. For a more detailed study on the constraints facing companies in the regulatory and policy environment, see Späth (1999).
2. Krugman (1991) identifies three types of external economy in SME clusters: labour market pooling, intermediate input effects, and technological spillovers.
3. For research on trust and sanctions in clusters, see Nadvi (1999), Humphrey and Schmitz (1998), and Mead (1984).
4. See Schmitz and Knorringa (1999), and UNCTAD (2000).
5. Bell and Albu (1999) provide an analytical framework for research on this topic.
6. Of course, there are exceptions to the rule. For example, Altenburg and Meyer-Stamer (1999) distinguish between survival clusters, mass production clusters, and clusters of transnational corporations in Latin America. The emergence of an SME cluster centred on Intel in Costa Rica is a good example of more advanced clusters.
7. See De Soto (1989) for the situation in Peru.

References

Albaladejo, M. (1999) 'Clustering in Latin America: Strategy for Survival or Alternative for SME Development', in Y. Koike and K. Horisaka (eds), *New Production Systems in Latin America: An Alternative to Import Substitution Models*, IDE Research Series No. 449, Tokyo: Institute of Developing Economies, pp. 91–133.

Altenburg, T. and Meyer-Stamer, J. (1999) 'How to Promote Clusters: Policy Experiences from Latin America', *World Development*, vol. 27, no. 9, pp. 1693–1714.

Becatini, G. (1990) 'The Marshallian Industrial District as a Socio-economic Notion', in F. Pyke, G. Becattini and W. Sengenberger (eds), *Industrial Districts and Inter-firm Co-operation in Italy*, Geneva: ILO, pp. 37–51.

Becatini, G. and Rullani, E. (1996) 'Sistemas Productivos Locales y Mercado Global', *ICE*, no. 754 (June), pp. 11–24.

Bell, M. and Albu, M. (1999) 'Knowledge Systems and Technological Dynamism in Industrial Clusters in Developing Countries', *World Development*, vol. 27, no. 9, pp. 1715–34.

Benton, L. (1992) 'The Emergence of Industrial Districts in Spain: Industrial Restructuring and Diverging Regional Responses', in F. Pyke and W. Sengenberger (eds), *Industrial Districts and Local Economic Regeneration*, Geneva: ILO, pp. 48–86.

Berger, M. and Guillamon, B. (1996) 'Microenterprise Development in Latin America: A View from the Inter-American Development Bank', *Small Enterprise Development*, vol. 7, no. 3, pp. 4–16.

Berry, A. (1996) 'Small and Medium Enterprises (SME) under Trade and Foreign Exchange Liberalisation: Latin American and Canadian Experiences and Concerns', *Canadian Journal of Development Studies*, vol. 17, no. 1, pp. 53–72.

Berry, A. and Escandon, J. (1994) 'Colombia's Small and Medium-Size Exporters and their Support Systems', World Bank, Policy Research Working Paper No. 1401, Washington DC: World Bank.

Best, M. (1990) *The New Competition: Institutions of Industrial Restructuring*, Cambridge: Polity Press.

Bianchi, P. (1996) 'New Approaches to Industrial Policies at the Local Level', in F. Cossentino F. Pyne and W. Sengenberger (eds), *Local and Regional Response to Global Pressure: The Case of Italy and its Industrial Districts*, Geneva: ILO, pp. 195–206.

Brusco, S. (1990) 'The Idea of the Industrial District: Its Genesis', in F. Pyke, G. Becattini and W. Sengenberger (eds), *Industrial Districts and Inter-firm Cooperation in Italy*, Geneva: ILO, pp. 10–19.

Brusco, S. (1992) 'Small Firms and the Provision of Real Services', in F. Pyke and W. Sengenberger (eds), *Industrial Districts and Local Economic Regeneration*, Geneva: ILO, pp. 177–96.

Capecchi, V. (1990) 'A History of Flexible Specialisation and Industrial Districts in Emilia-Romagna', in F. Pyke, G. Becattini and W. Sengenberger (eds), *Industrial Districts and Inter-firm Cooperation in Italy*, Geneva: ILO, pp. 20–37.

Cuevas, C. (1996) 'Enabling Environment and Microfinance Institutions: Lessons from Latin America', *Journal of International Development*, vol. 8, no. 2, pp. 195–210.

Curran, J. and Blackburn, R. (1992) '*Small Firms and Local Economic Networks: Relations between Small and Large Firms in Two Localities*', Business Paper No. 2, Kingston Business School.

De Soto, H. (1989) *The Other Path*, New York: Harper & Row.

Gazeta Mercantil Latinoamericana (1996) year 1, no. 31.

Gazeta Mercantil Latinoamericana (1997) year 2, no. 57.

Gelbard, E. (1990) 'Changes in Industrial Structure and Performance under Trade Liberalisation: The Case of Argentina', Unpublished Ph.D. dissertation, University of Toronto.

Gray, T. and Gamser, M. (1994) 'Building an Institutional and Policy Framework to Support Small and Medium Enterprises: Learning from other Cultures', USAID Special Studies, no. 8.

Humphrey, J. and Schmitz, H. (1995) 'Principles for Promoting Clusters and Networks of SMEs', UNIDO Discussion Paper No. 1.

Humphrey, J. and Schmitz, H. (1996) 'The Triple C Approach to Local Industry Policy', *World Development*, vol. 24, no. 12, pp. 1859–77.

Humphrey, J. and Schmitz, H. (1998) 'Trust and Inter-Firm Relations in Developing and Transition Economies', *Journal of Development Studies*, vol. 34, no. 4, pp. 32–61.

Julien, P.-A. (1992) 'The Role of Local Institutions in the Development of Industrial Districts: The Canadian Experience', in F. Pyke and W. Sengenberger (eds), *Industrial Districts and Local Economic Regeneration*, Geneva: ILO, pp. 197–214.

Kristensen, P. (1992) 'Industrial Districts in West Jutland, Denmark', in F. Pyke and W. Sengenberger (eds), *Industrial Districts and Local Economic Regeneration*, Geneva, ILO, pp. 122–74.

Krugman, P. (1991) *Geography and Trade*, Cambridge, Mass.: MIT Press.

Loveman, G. and Sengenberger, W. (1990) 'Introduction: Economic and Social Reorganisation in the Small- and Medium-sized Enterprise Sector', in W. Sengenberger, G. Loveman and M. J. Piore (eds), *The Re-emergence of Small Enterprises*, Geneva: IILS, pp. 1–61.

Marshall, A. (1920) *Principles of Economics*, 8th edn, London: Macmillan.

Mead, D. C. (1984) 'Of Contracts and Subcontracts: Small Firms in Vertically Disintegrated Production/Distribution Systems in LDCs', *World Development*, vol. 12, no. 11/12, pp. 1095–106.

Miller, M. and Caprio, G. (1997) *The Role of Credit in Small and Medium-Size Enterprise Exports: The Case of Mercosur*, Latin America and the Caribbean Economic Note 21, Washington DC: World Bank.

Murray, R. (1992) 'Flexible Specialisation in Small Island Economies: The Case of Cyprus', in F. Pyke and W. Sengenberger (eds) *Industrial Districts and Local Economic Regeneration*, Geneva: ILO, pp. 255–76.

Nadvi, K. (1997) 'The Cutting Edge: Collective Efficiency and International Competitiveness in Pakistan', IDS Discussion Paper No. 360, July.

Nadvi, K. (1999) 'Shifting Ties: Social Networks in the Surgical Instrument Cluster of Sialkot, Pakistan', *Development and Change*, vol. 30, no. 1, pp. 143–77.

Nadvi, K. and Schmitz, H. (1994) 'Industrial Districts in Less Developed Countries: Review of Experiences and Research Agenda', IDS Discussion Paper No. 339, January.

Nelson, R. and Winter, S. (1982) *An Evolutionary Theory of the Firm*, London: Macmillan.

OECD (1994a) *Globalisation and Regionalism: The Challenge for Developing Countries*, Paris: Development Centre Studies.

OECD (1994b) *Micro-enterprises and the Institutional Framework*, Paris: Development Centre Studies.

Ohmae, K. (1985) *Triad Power: The Coming Shape of Global Competition*, New York, The Free Press/Collier Macmillan.

Piore, M. and Sabel, C. (1984) *The Second Industrial Divide: Possibilities for Prosperity*, New York: Basic Books.

Pyke, F. (1992) *Industrial Development through Small-firm Cooperation: Theory and Practice*, Geneva: International Labour Office.

Pyke, F. (1994) *Small Firms, Technical Services and Inter-firm Cooperation*, International Institute for Labour Studies, Research Series No. 99.

Rabellotti, R. (1997) 'Footwear Industry Districts in Italy and Mexico', in M. P. Van Dijk and R. Rabellotti (eds), *Enterprise Clusters and Networks in Developing Countries*, EADI Book Series 20, London: Frank Cass, pp. 30–60.

Rabellotti, R. (1999) 'Recovery of a Mexican Cluster: Devaluation Bonanza or Collective Efficiency?', *World Development*, vol. 27, no. 9, pp. 1571–86.

Sabadini, M. de S. (1998) 'Os Distritos Industriais Como Modelo de Crescimento Endogeno: O Caso do Segmento de Rochas Ornamentais (marmole e granito) no Municipio de Cachoeiro de Itapemirim (ES)', Unpublished Ph.D. dissertation, Vitoria, Universidade Federal do Espirits Santo (UFES).

Schmitz, H. (1982) 'Growth Constraints on Small-scale Manufacturing in Developing Countries: A Critical Review', *World Development*, vol. 10, no. 6, pp. 429–50.

Schmitz, H. (1992) 'Industrial Districts: Model and Reality in Banden-Wurttemberg, Germany', in F. Pyke and W. Sengenberger (eds), *Industrial Districts and Local Economic Regeneration*, Geneva: ILO, pp. 87–121.

Schmitz, H. (1995a) 'Collective Efficiency: Growth Path for Small-scale Industry', *Journal of Development Studies*, vol. 31, no. 4, pp. 529–66.

Schmitz, H. (1995b) 'Small Shoemakers and Fordist Giants: Tale of a Supercluster', *World Development*, vol. 23, no. 1, pp. 9–28.

Schmitz, H. (1999) 'Global Competition and Local Cooperation: Success and Failure in the Sinos Valley, Brazil', *World Development*, vol. 27, no. 9, pp. 1627–50.

Schmitz, H. and Bazan, L. (1997) 'Social Capital and Export Growth: An Industrial Community in Southern Brazil', IDS Discussion Paper No. 361.

Schmitz, H. and Knorringa, P. (1999) 'Learning from Global Buyers', IDS Working Paper No. 100.

Sengenberger, W. and Pyke, F. (1991) 'Small Firm Industrial Districts and Local Economy Regeneration: Research and Policy Issues', *Labour and Society*, vol. 16, no. 1, pp. 1–24.

Sengenberger, W. and Pyke, F. (1992) 'Industrial Districts and Local Economic Regeneration: Research and Policy Issues', in F. Pyke and W. Sengenberger (eds), *Industrial Districts and Local Economic Regeneration*, Geneva: ILO, pp. 3–30.

Späth, B. (1999) 'The Institutional Environment and Communities of Small Firms', *IDS Bulletin*, vol. 23, no. 3, pp. 8–14.

Tavara, J. (1993) 'From Survival Activities to Industrial Strategies: Local Systems of Inter-firm Co-operation in Peru', Unpublished Ph.D. dissertation, University of Massachusetts.

UNCTAD (2000) *TNC–SME Linkages for Development: Issues – Experiences – Best Practices*, Proceedings of the Special Round Table on TNCs, SMEs and Development, 15 February, 2000, Bangkok: UNCTAD.

United Nations (1993) 'The Report of the Meeting on Creation of Indigenous Entrepreneurship and Opportunities for Small- and Medium-scale Industrial Investment', 11–13 April Damascus: ESCWA.

Van Dijk, M. P. (1993) 'Small Enterprise and the Process of Globalisation and Regionalisation', *Small Enterprise Development*, vol. 4, no. 3, pp. 4–13.

Villaran, F. (1992) 'Technological Innovation and Industrial Districts: Some Comments and Evidence', in United Nations, *Technological Dynamism in Industrial Districts: An Alternative Approach to Industrialization in Developing Countries?*, New York/Geneva: United Nations, pp. 143–54.

Villaran, F. (1993) 'Small-scale Industry Efficiency Groups in Peru', in B. Späth (ed.) *Small Firms and Development in Latin America: The Role of Institutional Environment, Human Resources and Industrial Relations*, Geneva: ILO.

Visser, E. (1997) 'The Significance of Spatial Clustering: External Economies in the Peruvian Small-scale Clothing Industry', in M. P. Van Dijk and R. Rabellotti (eds), *Enterprise Clusters and Networks in Developing Countries*, EADI Book Series 20, London: Frank Cass. pp. 61–92.

Zeitlin, J. (1992) 'Industrial Districts and Local Economic Regeneration: Overview and Comment', in F. Pyke and W. Sengenberger (eds) *Industrial Districts and Local Economic Regeneration*, pp. 279–94, Geneva: ILO.

Part IV
New Developments: Technology Upgrading

13 Firm Size, Technological Capabilities and Market-oriented Policies in Mauritius

Ganeshan Wignaraja[1]

INTRODUCTION

Mauritius is an outlier in Sub-Saharan Africa for its impressive industrial performance. Since about the 1980s, the Mauritian economy has undergone a remarkable transformation from a mono-crop sugar producer to become one of the leading exporters of manufactures in Sub-Saharan Africa. The share of manufacturing in GDP in Mauritius nearly doubled between 1980 and 1998 (from 15 per cent to 25 per cent).[2] The engine of industrial growth was manufactured exports (primarily garments), which grew at 14.8 per cent per annum during 1980–98. By 1998, the value of the country's manufactured exports per head (US$ 1094) was the highest in Sub-Saharan Africa. This striking performance has led some to regard Mauritius as an economic miracle in paradise (ILO, 1999). Its success in exporting garments is attributed to the adoption of a more market-oriented development strategy since the early 1980s. This emphasized trade liberalization and attracting foreign investment through export-processing zones and attractive investment incentives; reasonable macroeconomic stability in terms of low inflation and a competitive real exchange rate; a business-friendly economic environment, bureaucracy keen to get things done and a low level of corruption; a pool of cheap, literate, bilingual labour (English- and French-speaking); preferential access into the European Union market, as a signatory of the Lomé Convention, and close proximity to the untapped African market; and a high degree of political stability.[3]

In contrast to the attention paid to macro aspects, there are hardly any studies on microeconomic aspects in Mauritius, during the period of market-oriented economic policies. Information on the part played by internal technological factors on the exporting behaviour of Mauritian enterprises is particularly patchy.

Enterprise-level technology issues are attracting increasing interest in the literature on economic development. A distinct body of research has begun to examine the nature of industrial technological development in market-oriented developing economies (Katz, 1987; Lall, 1992; Bell and Pavitt, 1993; Pietrobelli, 1997; Wignaraja, 1998; Romijn, 1999; Metcalfe, forthcoming). This research suggests that industrial technological development should not be viewed as a process that can be promoted easily and quickly by investing in new equipment or buying imported technology. It requires conscious investments by firms in their own technological capability. Technological capability is defined here as the skills, knowledge and experience that enterprises need to operate imported technology efficiently. This research has also found that enterprises in the newly industrializing economies (NIEs) in East Asia have built up relatively good technological capabilities, in a spectrum of industries, compared to international standards, and that this was a major factor in their rapid export growth and technological upgrading (Pack and Westphal, 1986; Hobday, 1995; Aw and Batra, 1998; Ernst *et al.*, 1998).

The few available studies on Mauritius indicate that firms in the garment industry acquired technological capabilities, which enabled them to produce for international markets (World Bank, 1994; Dubois *et al.* 1995; Lamusse, 1995). However, little is known about the nature of technological learning in large firms, and small and medium-sized enterprises (SMEs), and the firm-level influences on this process. There is also a lack of statistical analysis of the relationship between capability building and export performance. Consequently, much of the literature on Mauritius has only been able to provide a limited picture on the dynamics of enterprise performance during the period of market-oriented policies.

This chapter attempts to fill these gaps, and to shed light on the relationship between firm size and the acquisition of technological capabilities in Mauritius. Using cross-section data for the late 1990s, it constructs a technology index for a sample of forty[4] Mauritian enterprises in the garment industry, and analyzes its firm-level determinants (including firm size, ownership, employment of technical manpower, investments in enterprise training, and use of external technical assistance).[5] It goes on to examine the influence of the technology index in an econometric analysis of firm-level export performance.

The structure of the chapter is as follows. The second section surveys the recent literature on technological capabilities in developing countries, focusing on econometric work on firm size and technology development. The third section discusses briefly the experience of market-oriented policies and SME development in Mauritius. The fourth section examines the nature of technological development in SMEs and in the large firms in the Mauritian sample. The penultimate section presents the econometric results, and the final section concludes.

TECHNOLOGICAL CAPABILITIES IN DEVELOPING COUNTRIES: A REVIEW OF RECENT LITERATURE

General Findings

A common perception in the literature is that the successful accumulation of technology in a developing country can be encouraged by a smooth inflow of new information, ensuring conducive macroeconomic conditions and increasing expenditures on education. These factors have a role to play but, on their own, are insufficient to ensure a continuous process of domestic technological development.

A relatively recent development in the literature is the emphasis on manufacturing enterprises as the main actors in the process of accumulating technological capabilities. The capability literature emphasizes the notion that enterprises have to undertake conscious investments to convert imported technologies to productive use.[6] New technologies have a large tacit element (that is, person-embodied information which is difficult to articulate) that can only be acquired through experience and deliberate investments in various inputs (for example, training, information search, engineering activities, and research and development (R&D)). Five features of the process of building firm-level technological capabilities in developing countries are particularly relevant to this study:

- The process of acquiring technological capabilities is unpredictable (Lall, 1992; Metcalfe, forthcoming). Investments in technological capabilities, like financial investments, carry considerable risk, and the outcome is uncertain. Firms face technical difficulties and financial uncertainties, especially in research activities. Moreover, rarely can firms insure against failure in capability building. The implications of fundamental uncertainty are clear: the reality cannot be fully modelled, and the direction of change never achieves equilibrium.

- Capability building is an incremental and cumulative process (Bell and Pavitt, 1993; Hobday, 1995; Aw and Batra, 1998). Enterprises rarely develop diverse capabilities simultaneously. Nor do they make jumps into completely new areas of technology. Instead, they procesed in an incremental manner by building on past investments in technological capabilities, and typically move from simpler to more technologically complex activities.
- Capability building involves close co-operation between organizations (Lall *et al.*, 1994; Mytelka and Farinelli, 2000). Firms rarely acquire capabilities in isolation. When attempting to absorb imported technologies, they interact and exchange technical inputs with other firms (for example, competitors, suppliers, and buyers of output) and support institutions (for example, technology institutions, training bodies, and SME service providers) in a national innovation system. Hence, interaction and interdependence between organizations (that is, collective learning) in a national innovation system is a fundamental characteristic of capability building.
- Success in acquiring firm-level technological capabilities can spill over into industrial success (Pack and Westphal, 1986; Katrak, 1996; Ernst *et al.*, 1998). Differences in the efficiency with which firm-level capabilities are created are themselves a major source of differences in comparative advantage between countries.
- Capability building is affected by a host of national policy and institutional factors (Katz, 1987; Lall, 1992; Westphal, 2001; Metcalfe, forthcoming). Firm-level learning can be stimulated by the trade, industrial and macroeconomic regime as well as be supported by institutions of different kinds (including those providing industrial finance, training, and information and technological support). Prominent among the factors that have a positive influence on capability building are: macroeconomic stability, outward-oriented trade and investment policies, ample supplies of general and technical manpower, ready access to industrial finance, and comprehensive support from technology institutions.

The bulk of the empirical work on technological capabilities in developing countries has been based on case studies of enterprises in particular industries.[7] These detailed studies of individual firms and groups of firms have offered valuable insights into the nature of technological activities in developing countries, the utility of different learning mechanisms, and factors affecting firm-level capability building. A significant contribution from case study research has been to suggest ways of classifying the technical functions performed by manufacturing enterprises to assimilate imported technology. One of the most elaborate taxonomies of technological capabilities is the one proposed by Lall (1992), which breaks them down into investment, production and linkages as follows:

- *Investment* is represented by project execution activities including feasibility studies, equipment search, assessment of equipment, employee training during start-up, and involvement of the firm in detailed engineering;
- *Production* is subdivided into process technology and product technology. Process technology includes quality control, maintenance, plant layout, inventory control, and various improvements in equipment and processes. Product technology covers copying imports (or buyers), improving existing products, introducing new products, and licensing product technology; and
- *Linkages* are considered under supplier firm linkages, subcontracting linkages, and linkages with institutions that provide troubleshooting, testing, training, and product design assistance.

The advantage of this framework over other approaches is that it provides a clear continuum of technical functions from the time that new technology enters a given firm, to when it exits to other firms and institutions. Furthermore, as this framework has been used successfully in past empirical work on technological capabilities in developing countries, it will be also used here to examine firm-level technological development in Mauritius.[8]

The Determinants of Technological Capabilities

One of the major challenges facing researchers working on technological capabilities is to summarize inter-firm differences in capabilities. It is convenient to develop a simple summary measure to permit statistical analysis of the influences on capability acquisition. Recently, some studies have begun to rank the technological capabilities of individual firms and attempt statistical analysis of their determinants.[9] The ranking integrates objective and subjective information into measures of the enterprises' capacity to set up, operate, and transfer technology. To create an enterprise score, the information from these indicators is converted into a summary measure of capabilities. The typical approach adopted by this literature is to highlight the various technical functions performed by enterprises to manage imported technology, and award a given firm a score for each technical activity, indicating its level of technical competence in that activity. An overall capability score is obtained for a given firm by taking an average of the scores for the different technical functions.

Two qualifications on the interpretation of the firm-level scores should be noted. First, the estimates contain an element of subjectivity, which can lead to bias in the absolute values of the technological capability scores. However, this may not matter much for the purpose of inter-firm comparisons. As Westphal *et al.* (1990) explain in the context of their study of Thailand:

> the capability scores are biased estimates with respect to the measurement of capabilities cum capacities *per se*. The degree of bias depends on the respective weights placed on capability and sophistication in the researcher' scoring. Unfortunately, it is not possible to state these weights. However, the bias that is present in the absolute values of the scores does not necessarily affect the relative values obtained when the scores are considered in comparison to one another. Intra-firm comparisons (across capabilities for one firm) and inter-firm comparisons (across firms for one capability) are biased with respect to indicating differences in capabilities cum capacities only to the extent that sophistication levels differ intra and inter-firm respectively. Since most of the analysis is concerned with relative values, it is possible that the bias has minimal consequences for the analysis.
>
> (Westphal *et al.* 1990, pp. 87 and 91)

Second, the weights attached are subjective, with all activities being given equal weights by averaging.

Cross-section econometric work on the determinants of technological capabilities (henceforth termed a 'technology index' for short) reports some interesting findings, particularly with regard to the relationship between firm size and the technology index in five developing economies that had adopted market-oriented policies (Thailand, Pakistan, Sri Lanka, Tanzania and Kenya).[10] Ordinary Least Squares (OLS) regressions were run, relating technology indices to particular characteristics of enterprises. These studies have attempted to test the hypothesis that there is a positive relationship between the technology index and firm size. The expectation of a positive relationship is based on the argument that the returns from capability acquisition are higher where a firm has a larger volume of sales to spread the fixed costs of capability acquisition, and large firms can have more specialized technical manpower. Moreover, it is argued that capital market imperfections confer an advantage on large firms in securing finance for risky technological activities, and size is correlated with the availability and stability of funds.

The earliest study by Westphal *et al.* (1990) included firm size as one of four variables determining the technology index: the other variables were ownership, market orientation and incentives given by the Board of Investment. The sample covered 100 Thai enterprises in the electronics, biotechnology and materials technology industries. Firm size was found to have a positive effect on the production technology index, and was significant at the 10 per cent level.

Using a sample of forty-six engineering firms in Tanzania, Deraniyagala and Semboja (1999) attempted to estimate the influence of several firm-level characteristics (firm size, foreign equity, firm age, entrepreneur's education level, and a skill index) on a production-based technology index. Interestingly, they found that firm size and foreign equity were not significant. Of the other explanatory variables, the entrepreneur's education level and the skill index both had positive and significant (5 per cent level) effects, while firm age was also significant (5 per cent level), but negative in sign.

Wignaraja (1998) tested an overall technology index and one for production alone, against several firm-level characteristics (including firm size, foreign equity, technical manpower and technology imports) in a sample of twenty-seven garment and engineering enterprises in Sri Lanka. In both regressions, firm size turned out to be significant (5 per cent level) and positive, while technical manpower and technology imports were also significant (1 per cent level) and positive.[11]

Using a sample of forty-one Kenyan garment and engineering enterprises, Wignaraja and Ikiara (1999) regressed an overall technology index against firm size, foreign equity, the entrepreneur's education level, technical manpower, and employee training. They report that firm size, foreign equity, and the entrepreneur's education were all significant (5 per cent level) and positive.

Finally, in a departure from the studies mentioned above, Romijn (1999) conducted econometric work using technology indices based on the manufacturing complexity of products. The sample covered 100 engineering firms in Pakistan. In her best two regressions, firm size was found to be significant (1 per cent level) and positive. Among the other explanatory variables, external technical assistance and improvements made to products were both significant (1 per cent level) and positive, while the search for information had a positive sign and was significant at the 5 per cent level. Surprisingly, entrepreneurs' education level and firm age were not significant.

This handful of econometric studies thus seem to provide some empirical support for the hypothesis that firm size is associated positively with the acquisition of technological capabilities. The entrepreneur's education level, technical manpower, external technical assistance, and foreign equity also show up as important determinants of capability building in some studies. This chapter builds further on this econometric work, and explores the relationship between firm size and technological capabilities in the garment sector in Mauritius.

MARKET-ORIENTATED POLICIES AND ENTERPRISE PERFORMANCE IN MAURITIUS

The Trade and Industrial Regime

In terms of its trade, industrial and macroeconomic regime, Mauritius is an outlier from other African developing economies. The country did not subscribe to the prevailing orthodoxy of the 1960s and 1970s that emphasized stringent import substitution coupled with heavy state intervention in the economy, unlike many African developing economies. Instead, in the 1970s, Mauritius followed a mixed trade policy of import substitution coupled with incentives for exports through the Export Processing Zone (EPZ).[12] These two trade regimes coexisted, influencing the enterprises that produced for the small home market as well as those producing for export. In the early 1980s, Mauritius introduced a stronger market-oriented stance to its economic policy. As a part of a structural adjustment loan agreement with the World Bank, Mauritius embarked on a process of trade liberalization and industrial adjustment in 1983.

Three distinct phases of trade liberalization and industrial reforms can be identified since the mid-1980s, each with a different rate of reform and coverage.

- The first phase, between 1983 and 1985, consisted of the rapid elimination of most quantitative restrictions on imports, and their replacement by tariffs. Existing incentives for exporting – granted via the EPZ since 1970 – were maintained, and macroeconomic stability (low inflation and competitive exchange rates) became an explicit policy objective. Despite these early reforms, however, the domestic manufacturing sector remained relatively highly protected, and restricted by a plethora of bureaucratic regulations.

- The second phase, between 1986 and 1993, was marked by the gradual reduction in the dispersion of effective protection rates between industries, and by the more vigorous promotion of exports through the provision to exporters of overseas marketing support, preferential interest rates, and tax concessions. Export and investment promotion was strengthened greatly by the creation of the Mauritius Export Development and Investment Authority (MEDIA) in 1985. Emphasis was also placed on maintaining macroeconomic and price stability. There were also cuts in bureaucratic procedures affecting imports, exports and foreign exchange. The net result of these reforms was that the economy became more outward-oriented and private-sector focused than in the past.
- The third phase, from 1994 to date, cut protection further by reducing import tariffs and attempted to develop new areas of comparative advantage. In 1995, the number of tariff bands was reduced, and the maximum import tariff rates were cut. New institutions were also established to promote new skill-intensive exports (for example, the Mauritius Productivity and Competitiveness Council was created in 2000).

By the mid-1990s, Mauritius had become considerably more open and market-friendly than in the past, and was one of the most liberal economic regimes in Africa. Substantial progress had been made in reducing tariffs and non-tariff barriers to imports. The main changes included: quantitative restrictions being eliminated in the main, and the few that remain are largely on health, sanitary and security grounds; there are few import prohibitions (with the exception of commodities such as secondhand motor vehicle spares and explosives); the level of nominal tariffs fell, as well as its dispersion (the number of rate bands were cut from sixty to eight, and the maximum rates were reduced); there are no local content programmes to assist local suppliers; and public procurement policies are minimal. One indication of the greater openness in Mauritius was that the average tariff rate on manufacturing imports fell from 86.2 per cent in 1980 to 30.1 per cent in 1994.[13]

Progress in achieving an open, market-friendly policy regime, however, was not matched by similar reforms in the human resource base and the technology support system for industry.[14] Mauritius has a good record in educational investment that is reflected in a relatively good base of primary- and secondary-educated manpower by regional standards. In 1993, its primary enrolment ratio was 106 per cent,[15] while its secondary enrolment ratio was 59 per cent. This primary- and secondary-level education base provided a pool of literate (bilingual), trainable workers for the industrial sector in Mauritius. However, the country suffers from a severe shortage of tertiary-level manpower, particularly in technical subjects (for example, mathematics and computer science, engineering, and natural science), which will be needed for the technologically sophisticated industries of the future. University enrolments in these technical subjects were tiny in relation to its population (only 0.04 per cent in 1991, compared with 0.56 per cent for Singapore, and 1.5 per cent for Taiwan). Moreover, teacher quality, materials, and equipment were often poor, with a mismatch between the skills produced by tertiary-level institutions and those needed by industry.

Mauritius has a reasonable technology support system for industry. Several institutions are involved in providing metrology, standards and quality services; productivity improvement; SME extension services; training; and the diffusion of technologies.[16] This support has been improved in recent years, particularly with the Mauritius Standards Bureau and the Technology Diffusion Scheme (part of a World Bank competitiveness project). The Export Processing Zone Development Agency and the SME agency were also doing useful work in relation to productivity and SME extension services though their efforts were not adequate in terms of what was needed to transform SMEs into efficient subcontractors for export. The institutions in general were inadequate, in terms of size, financial resources and technical manpower, to respond to the technical challenges facing the industrial sector. Moreover, there were some function needs that no institution was meeting – the most prominent among these were research, development and design, productivity improvement.

The Performance of Large Firms and SMEs

The transformation of the Mauritian economy since the 1970s from a low-productivity, subsistence base to a producer of labour-intensive manufactures for export is a remarkable developmental achievement.

It has built up a significant base of export-related skills, information and institutions, far ahead of neighbouring countries in Africa, and is regarded by some as a candidate for newly industrializing economy (NIE) status. Its manufactured exports grew at 14.8 per cent during 1980–98, compared with 8.1 per cent for South Africa, 9.0 per cent for Zimbabwe, 4.8 per cent for Kenya, 10.2 per cent for the Ivory Coast, 6.6 per cent for Nigeria, and 1.7 per cent for Uganda.[17] By 1998, its manufactured exports per head (US$ 1094) were the highest in Africa, and among the highest in the developing world.

However, the bulk of the growth in manufacturing in Mauritius during this period can be attributed to a single export item – garments. Garments accounted for over 82 per cent of total manufactured exports in 1998, and Mauritius's dependence on this item is greater than that of other garment-dependent economies in South Asia (for example, Sri Lanka and Bangladesh). To date, there is little evidence of diversification into other labour-intensive exports (for example, toys or footwear), or of industrial upgrading into more technologically sophisticated exports (for example, electronics and engineering industries) that was witnessed in the East Asian economies in the 1960s and 1970s. The high degree of dependence on garments makes the country vulnerable to competitive pressures from cheaper producers of garments (for example, China and Vietnam) particularly after the expiry of the Multi-Fibre Agreement in 2005.

There is a dearth of information on the relative economic contribution or performance of large firms and SMEs in Mauritius. However, a recent study provides some insights[18]:

- There were 411 large firms and 5320 SMEs in the manufacturing sector in Mauritius in 1997;
- SMEs accounted for 21.7 per cent of manufacturing employment in 1997, and large firms for the rest;
- SMEs accounted for manufactured exports worth only US$ 23.5 million, and large firms for US$1.1 billion in 1997 (2.2 per cent and 97.8 per cent of total manufactured exports, respectively);
- SMEs produced only 1.1 per cent of clothing exports (the dominant industry), while large firms accounted for 98.9 per cent; and
- The labour productivity of the SMEs was below that of the large firms in most industries.

The available evidence thus indicates that there is a distinct pattern of manufactured export performance by firm size. Large enterprises seem to account for most of the country's manufactured export dynamism. SMEs have hardly participated in exports. Further insights into national export performance may be derived from micro-level analysis.

THE TECHNOLOGICAL CAPABILITIES OF THE MAURITIAN SAMPLE

This section examines the nature of industrial technological development in large firms and SMEs during the market-oriented period in Mauritius. The analysis is based on the concept of a firm-level technology index (TI), which has been used successfully in other technology studies in developing countries (see above).

The sample of forty garment firms used in the analysis was fairly evenly distributed between firms of different size classes: there were nineteen SMEs (<100 employees) and twenty-one large firms (>100 employees). The average number of employees for the large firms was 536, compared with 38 employees for the SMEs. Four micro-enterprises with fewer than 10 employees each were included in the SME category. Only thirteen enterprises had some proportion of foreign equity, hence the sample consisted mainly of local firms.

There was a high propensity to export among the sample enterprises. Twenty seven enterprises were exporting some proportion of their sales, and ten enterprises exported 100 per cent of their output. The large firms were more export-oriented than the SMEs. The two groups had average export-sales ratios of 75.8 per cent and 12.3 per cent, respectively.

Computing the Technology Index

The technology index (TI) used for this study of Mauritian garment enterprises is a variant of those used by Wignaraja (1998) for Sri Lanka, and by Wignaraja and Ikiara (1999) for Kenya. The TI draws on the threefold classification of firm-level technological capabilities into investment, production and linkage activities, developed by Lall (1992). Information on the technical functions performed within a given industrial enterprise is used to compute a TI for each of the forty garment firms in the Mauritian sample. The TI scoring system for the Mauritian firms – see Table A1 in the Appendix – consists of two sets of technical functions: production and linkages.[19] The larger category (production) is represented by ten separate technical activities, which range from common process engineering tasks (such as measurement of internal reject rates and ISO 9000 quality management status) to product engineering tasks (such as copying existing products, improving existing products, and introducing new products). Productivity improvement, a key industrial engineering activity, is also included under this heading. The other category (linkages) is represented by two technical activities. It highlights technology transfer via two kinds of inter-firm relationship: those with subcontractors and those with overseas buyers of output. Each of the twelve activities is graded at different levels (0, 1 and 2) to represent different levels of competence within that function. Thus a given firm is ranked out of a total capability score of 24, and the result is normalized to give a value between 0 and 1. The TI scores will be used first as the dependent variable, and then as an independent variable in the econometric analysis of the next section.

The Composition of the Sample in Terms of the Technology Index

Table 13.1 shows the frequency distribution of the overall TI scores for the forty garment firms in the Mauritian sample. The data suggest that there is a wide variation in TI scores between garment firms. One firm has a score in excess of 0.81, a further six have scores in excess of 0.61, and the remainder have scores well below those of the best firms.

This technological capability gap is linked to firm size. Table 13.2 shows the overall TI scores for the twenty-one large firms (>100 employees), and for the nineteen SMEs (<100 employees) in the sample. It also shows the scores, by firm size, for the main sub-categories of the TI,

Table 13.1 Technology index of the sample of Mauritian firms

Technology Index	Number of firms	Percentage of total sample
0.00–0.20	14	35.0
0.21–0.40	10	25.0
0.41–0.60	9	22.5
0.61–0.80	6	15.0
0.81–1.00	1	2.5
Total	40	100.0

Note: The technology index (TI) takes a value between 0 and 1; high values indicate high levels of technical competence.
Source: Survey results.

namely process engineering, product engineering, and linkages.[20] The overall TI scores suggest a striking difference in the level of technological development between the large firms and the SMEs. The large firms record an average TI score (0.51), which is three times higher than that for SMEs (0.17).

Much of the technology gap between the size classes is due to differences in process engineering capabilities. The large firms have an average process engineering score (0.53) that is more than double that for the SMEs (0.20). In part, this reflects the fact that large firms have much better quality management capabilities. The evidence from our sample shows that large firms (2.6 per cent) typically record lower average internal reject rates for their main product than do SMEs (3.9 per cent).[21] Furthermore, the large firms have also moved into comprehensive quality management by adopting ISO 9000 quality management standards to enhance their export competitiveness. Four large firms were certified to ISO 9000 standards, and another four were in the process of being certified; none of the SMEs had received certification, and only two were being certified. Most SMEs rely on the final inspection of goods at the end of a line rather than employing a comprehensive quality management system. In some cases, the entrepreneur does *ad hoc* checks on finished goods, and reject rates are not recorded. The majority of SMEs did not know about the ISO 9000 system and its many advantages (including the improvement of quality, more rapid productivity growth, and increasing the attractiveness to overseas buyers of output).

Table 13.2 Average technology index for large firms and SMEs in the Mauritian sample

Average score	Large firms	SMEs
Overall technology index	0.51	0.17
Process engineering	0.53	0.20
Product engineering	0.37	0.23
Linkages	0.40	0.04
Number of firms	21	19

Notes: SMEs have fewer than 100 employees; large firms have more than 100 employees.
The indices take values between 0 and 1; high values indicate high levels of technical competence.
Source: Survey results.

The large firms also seemed to have better maintenance capabilities than the SMEs. Nearly all the large firms had a regular routine for the maintenance and servicing of equipment, and a maintenance shop with specialized manpower (including some brought in from overseas). Some SMEs did conduct routine maintenance of their equipment, but tended to undertake repairs only when the equipment broke down. SMEs also lacked in-house maintenance shops and specialized maintenance manpower,[22] and tended to rely on contract maintenance staff hired from the local market.

The large firms were also more active in ensuring that equipment was calibrated properly, that equipment was upgraded regularly through purchases of new machines and technologies,[23] and that local raw materials were substituted for imports where possible.

In the case of the product engineering scores, a somewhat smaller gap between the large firms (0.37) and SMEs (0.23) is indicated by the data. This may be slightly deceptive, as our firm-level interviews indicated that there was considerable variation in the emphasis on product technology in the sample firms. At one end are the large firms that, typically, receive new products and designs from foreign buyers of output, and make periodic visits to international trade fairs. On the whole, the large firms are making garments in line with trends in international market demand. A core of large enterprises have even tried to create independent design capabilities by hiring trained designers, investing in computer-aided design (CAD) systems, and formulating strategies for interaction with a range of foreign buyers. The survey revealed that thirteen large garment enterprises had full-time designers; some of them had even qualified overseas. In comparison, only six SMEs had designers, and many of these lacked formal design qualifications.[24]

Some SMEs tend to copy imports or rely on local sources of information for product information and design. A high proportion of their products cater for consumer tastes in the local/regional markets, and are not in line with international trends. Relatively few SMEs had long-term marketing relationships with foreign buyers, or had made efforts to develop independent design capabilities.

Finally, the large firms (0.40) had better linkages scores than the SMEs (0.04). There are a limited number of contract-based intra-firm technological transfers in Mauritius, either through subcontracting, or buyer–seller relationships with foreign buyers. To the extent that these occur, large firms (and, to a lesser extent, medium-sized firms) are involved in exchanges of information, skills and technology. The lack of linkages involving small firms seems to be related to weaknesses in their price, quality and delivery performance.[25]

THE ECONOMETRIC RESULTS

This section uses cross-section data from the late 1990s to provide an econometric analysis of (a) the determinants of the technology index (TI); and (b) the determinants of firm-level export performance. Student's *t*-tests were also conducted to explore the differences in the means of various characteristics of large firms and SMEs, and so shed further light on the technological and exporting behaviour of the two enterprise groups.

The Determinants of the Technology Index

The full regression model used to investigate the determinants of the technology index (TI) is as follows:

$$\mathrm{TI} = \beta_1 + \beta_2 SIZE + \beta_3 FE + \beta_4 AGE + \beta_5 ET + \beta_6 TB + \beta_7 EXTA + \varepsilon_1,$$

where

SIZE	=	total employment;
FE	=	the share of foreign equity;
AGE	=	years of production experience;
ET	=	the share of engineers and technicians in employment;
TB	=	expenditure on employee training as a percentage of sales;
EXTA	=	the number of times the firm has used an external technical consultant or local technology institution over the previous three years; and
ε_1	=	random disturbance term.

Total employment (*SIZE*) was expected to have a positive influence on TI. Larger firms have more specialized manpower, and can spread the fixed costs of capability acquisition over a larger volume of sales. Moreover, capital market imperfections confer an advantage on large firms in securing finance. The share of foreign equity (*FE*) is also expected to have an influence on TI. There are two possible reasons for this. On the one hand, foreign affiliates are better placed to acquire technological capabilities because of their ready access to the 'ownership advantages' (for example, technologies, skills and marketing expertise) of their parent corporations. On the other hand, foreign affiliates may have relatively greater learning expertise and accumulated technological capabilities. The years of production experience (*AGE*) might also be expected to have a positive impact, because such experience may capture 'learning by doing', among other effects.

The share of engineers and technicians in total employment (*ET*) can be expected this to have a positive effect on TI. Engineers and technicians can influence the process of building technological capabilities (even in simple industries, such as garments) through new quality management methods, equipment maintenance and upgrading, productivity improvement, training, minor adaptations to process technologies, and energy-saving measures. The expenditure on employee training as a percentage of sales (*TB*) is expected to have a positive sign. Explicit employee training is crucial during enterprise start-up, to create the requisite capabilities to use new production technologies. As technologies evolve, a continuous process of training and retraining is needed to supply the technical and managerial skills needed by new process and product innovations. Finally, the number of times a firm has used an external technical consultant or local technology institution during a three-year period (*EXTA*) should also have a positive influence.[26] Long-term relationships with individuals and institutions that provide training, technical information and technical services can be a valuable input into the acquisition of technological capabilities. Such linkages enable exchange of information, skills and technologies, and can contribute directly to improvements in productive efficiency as well as the diffusion of technologies throughout the industry.

The econometric investigation proceeded as follows. I started with a simple model incorporating just three explanatory variables: *SIZE*, *FE* and *AGE*. Then we added the remaining explanatory variables (*ET*, *TB* and *EXTA*) one by one. Finally, I estimated a model with only the significant explanatory variables from the previous models. The results are shown in Table 13.3. I consider the results of Equations (4) and (5) in the table.[27] Both have been checked for multicollinearity and heteroskedasticity. The former contains all the explanatory variables, whilst the latter includes only those variables that are statistically significant.

The adjusted R^2 (0.53) in Equation (4) is reasonable for a cross-section study based on a small sample. Of the six explanatory variables, four are significant (one at the 1 per cent level, two at the 5 per cent level, and one at the 10 per cent level) and have the expected sign. Firm size, engineering and technical manpower, employee training and

Table 13.3 Estimated regression equations explaining the technological capabilities of garment firms in Mauritius

Variable	Equation				
	1	2	3	4	5
Constant	0.278 (4.40)***	0.204 (3.15)***	0.178 (2.99)***	0.153 (2.57)**	0.193 (5.48)***
SIZE	0.210 E-3 (3.64)***	0.193 E-3 (3.59)***	0.172 E-3 (3.50)***	0.158 E-3 (3.25)***	0.175 E-3 (4.05)***
FE	0.511 E-3 (0.60)	0.658 E-3 (0.82)	0.509 E-3 (0.70)	0.349 E-3 (0.56)	
AGE	– 0.157 E-4 (– 0.003)	0.001 (0.28)	0.001 (0.32)	0.003 (0.75)	
ET		0.066 (2.64)**	0.058 (2.57)**	0.052 (2.29)**	0.050 (2.25)**
TB			0.236 (2.91)***	0.232 (2.08)**	0.184 (2.21)**
EXTA				0.008 (1.77)*	0.007 (1.74)*
Adjusted R^2	0.29	0.39	0.49	0.53	0.55
F-statistic	6.35***	7.29***	8.78***	8.30***	12.68***
Number of firms	40	40	40	40	40

Notes: The dependent variable in each regression is the technology index (TI). See the text for definitions of the explanatory variables.
The *t*-statistics are shown in brackets. The coefficients marked by * are significant at the 10% level; those identified by ** significant at the 5% level; and those identified by *** significant at the 1% level.
Source: Survey results.

external technical assistance have a positive and significant relationship with TI. The lack of significance of the foreign ownership variable might reflect the fact that there are too few foreign majority-owned firms in the Mauritian sample for this effect to show up. The years in production (*AGE*) have no significance.

Equation (5) produces somewhat better results than Equation (4). There is a small improvement in both the adjusted R^2 (from 0.53 to 0.55) and the F-statistic (from 8.30 to 12.68). There is also some improvement in the significance of two of the explanatory variables.

The role of firm size, as an important determinant of TI, is now further examined. Table 13.4 shows the results of *t*- tests comparing the means of some characteristics of the large firms and the SMEs. The following conclusions may be drawn:

- Large firms have significantly higher levels of technological capabilities than SMEs (the means for the technology indices are 0.51 and 0.17, respectively);
- The export–sales ratio is significantly higher for the large firms (the means are 75.7 per cent and 12.3 per cent, respectively);
- Large firms have significantly higher foreign equity than SMEs (the means are 43.1 per cent and 5.1 per cent respectively);
- There is a significant difference between the training expenditures of the two groups (the means are 0.27 per cent of sales for large firms and 0.08 per cent for SMEs);
- There is a significant difference in the use of external technical assistance between the two groups (the mean usages over the three-year period are 6.7 and 1.3 for the large firms and the SMEs, respectively); and
- The years in production, and engineering and technical manpower, do not show up as being significantly different between the two groups.

The Determinants of Firm-Level Export Performance

Although there is a growing literature on firm-level export performance in developing countries,[28] no previous work has been undertaken

Table 13.4 Mean values of the variables for large firms and SMEs in the Mauritian sample

		Large Firms	**SMEs**	**t-statistic**
Technology index	TI	0.51	0.17	6.9**
Export-sales ratio (%)	EXSH	75.7	12.3	6.7**
Share of foreign equity (%)	FE	43.1	5.1	3.4**
Years of production	AGE	10.3	10.4	– 0.06
Engineers and technicians (%)	ET	1.20	0.62	1.6
Training expenditure	TB	0.27	0.08	1.9*
External technical assistance	EXTA	6.7	1.3	2.7*
Number of firms		21	19	

Notes: SMEs have fewer than 100 employees; large firms have more than 100 employees.
*indicates significance at the 10% level; ** indicates significance at the 5% level.
The figures for external technical assistance (EXTA) indicate the number of times used in the previous three years.
Source: Survey results.

for Mauritius. This literature suggests that firm-level export performance is influenced by factors such as skills, ownership, technology, and firm size. The regression model used to investigate the determinants of export performance (EXSH), as measured by the export–sales ratio, is as follows:

$$\text{EXSH} = \gamma_1 + \gamma_2 FE + \gamma_3 SIZE + \gamma_4 AGE + \gamma_5 TI + \gamma_6 ET + \varepsilon_2,$$

where

FE	=	the share of foreign equity;
SIZE	=	total employment;
AGE	=	years of production experience;
TI	=	technology index;
ET	=	the share of engineers and technicians in employment; and
ε_2	=	random disturbance term.

The share of foreign equity (*FE*) is expected to have a positive influence on export performance. Access to the marketing connections and expertise of their parent companies, as well as the accumulated learning experience of production and exporting, make foreign affiliates better placed than local firms to tap international markets. Total employment (*SIZE*) is also expected to have a positive sign, because exporting allows large firms, particularly in small economies, to exploit economies of scale in production by relieving the disadvantage of the small home market. The years of production experience (*AGE*) may also be expected to have a positive effect as accumulated experience of different kinds (including performing repetitive technological tasks) is a means of improving firm-level production efficiency, and hence export performance.

The technology index (*TI*) is expected be have a positive impact on export performance, because the process of acquiring technological capabilities in enterprises is the outcome of conscious investment in creating skills and information. Finally, the share of engineers and technicians in employment (*ET*) is expected to have a positive effect on export performance, as higher levels of technical manpower are likely to give firms a competitive advantage in exporting.

Four econometric models were estimated, and the results are shown in Table 13.5. I consider the results for Equation (2) for the full model, and for Equation (4) that contains only the significant variables.[29] The adjusted R^2(0.47) for Equation (2) is reasonable for a cross-section model. Two of the five explanatory variables (that is, *FE* and *TI*) have the expected signs, and are significant at the 1 per cent

Table 13.5 Estimated regression equations explaining the export performance of garment firms in Mauritius

Variable	Equation			
	1	2	3	4
Constant	21.840	1.472	– 0.372	0.389
	(1.69)*	(0.11)	(0.41)	(0.97)
FE	0.463	0.397	0.394	0.383
	(2.90)***	(2.80)***	(2.99)***	(2.97)***
SIZE	0.170	– 0.002		
	(1.59)	(– 0.20)		
AGE	– 0.111	– 0.240		
	(– 0.12)	(– 0.30)		
ET	8.856	2.256	2.590	
	(1.77)*	(0.47)	(0.56)	
TI		99.841	95.511	100.929
		(3.36)***	(3.90)***	(4.53)***
Adjusted R^2	0.31	0.47	0.49	0.51
F statistic	5.41***	7.85***	13.74***	20.84***
Number of firms	40	40	40	40

Notes: The dependent variable in each regression is export performance (EXSH). See the text for definitions of the explanatory variables.
The *t*-statistics are shown in brackets. The coefficients marked by * are significant at the 10% level; those identified by ** significant at the 5% level, and those identified by *** significant at the 1% level.
Source: Survey results.

level. Equation (4) produces better results than does Equation (2). The R^2 and the F-statistic increase to 0.51 and 20.84, respectively, and there is an increase in the significance of both explanatory variables.

CONCLUSIONS

Drawing on the recent literature on technological development in developing countries, this chapter has attempted to provide some evidence on the relationship between firm size and the acquisition of technological capabilities in Mauritius. Following a decade of import substitution and export promotion via EPZs, the country began to emphasize market-oriented policies strongly in the early 1980s. By the mid-1990s, Mauritius had become considerably more open and market-friendly than in the past, and at the time of writing is one of most liberal regimes in Africa. Since the 1980s, Mauritius has witnessed double-digit manufactured export growth (particularly in garments), which has resulted in a per capita manufactured export value that is far ahead of other African countries. While this is a considerable industrial achievement, the available evidence suggests that the bulk of this export growth has come from large firms, and that SMEs have not played much of an active part in this process.

Micro-level evidence from a sample of forty garment enterprises suggests that the differential export performance is related to the acquisition of technological capabilities. The large firms seem to have acquired the requisite competitive capabilities to produce to the high standards of price, quality and delivery demanded by major foreign buyers of output, but the SMEs lag behind the achievements of the large garment firms. Quality control and quality management systems are inadequate. Few SMEs have planned systems for equipment maintenance. Their capacity to copy, adapt and design new products is weak. They make little use of contractual technology imports, and have few relations with foreign technical consultants.

Using the information from the sample enterprises, I constructed a technology index in an attempt to quantify inter-firm differences in technological capabilities, and conduct econometric analysis. The econometric analysis of the determinants of the technology index and of export performance in Mauritius produced some interesting results. The econometric analysis of the determinants of the technology index showed that firm size, technical manpower, employee training and external technical assistance had significant and positive effects, whereas firm age and foreign equity were not significant. Simple *t*-tests were used to highlight further the differences between the large firms and the SMEs. This analysis indicated that, when compared with the large firms, the SMEs had lower levels of technological capabilities, were less export-oriented, had less foreign equity, conducted less employee training, and made less use of external technical assistance.

The econometric analysis of the determinants of firm-level export performance indicated that foreign equity and the technology index were significant and positively associated with export shares. Meanwhile, firm size, firm age and technical manpower were not significant.

These results confirm the usefulness of recent attempts in the literature to quantify enterprise-level technological capabilities in developing countries. By providing new conceptual tools and analytical methods, this new strand of econometric research into technological capabilities complements nicely previous work based on detailed technology case studies of individual enterprises. Further work will lead to the refinement of the technology index presented here, the collection of larger enterprise datasets, and the use of more sophisticated econometric methods, such as simultaneous equation models.

This research on Mauritian garment enterprises reaffirms the case for policy support to improve the competitiveness of SMEs in market-oriented developing economies. Providing support in existing marketing relationships between large local firms and foreign buyers is recognized increasingly as a powerful mechanism for accessing overseas markets, and new production technologies and capabilities. In this vein, it is necessary for the SMEs in the Mauritian garment industry to be incorporated into effective clusters around the large enterprises, in order to facilitate upgrading. This may in part occur spontaneously over time, but policy can also encourage the process of clustering. The experience of both developed and developing countries suggests that supplier linkage programmes and focused business development services (training, productivity improvement, quality management and technical information) are useful ways of connecting SMEs into clusters, and of improving their technological capabilities (Altenburg and Meyer-Stamer, 1999; Mytelka and Farinelli, 2000).

Appendix

Table 13A.1 The technological capability scoring scale

	Score
Production capabilities	
Process Engineering	
Internal defect rates	
No measurement	0
High (>2%)	1
Low (<2%)	2
ISO 9000 status	
No accreditation	0
ISO 9000 in progress	1
ISO 9000 obtained	2
Maintenance awareness	
None	0
Only repair when breakdown	1
Preventative system	2

Table 13A.1 (*contd.*)

	Score
Calibration of equipment	
None	0
Little	1
Frequent	2
Substitution of local raw materials	
None	0
A little	1
A lot	2
Buy new equipment	
None	0
A Little	1
A lot	2
Product Engineering	
Copying	
None	0
Ad hoc	1
Systematic	2
Improving existing products	
None	0
Some	1
Considerable	2
Introducing new products in-house	
None	0
Some	1
Considerable	2
Industrial Engineering	
Productivity Improvement	
None	0
Some	1
Systematic	2
Linkage capabilities	
Subcontracting linkages	
None	0
Ad hoc technology transfer	1
Systematic technology transfer	2
Systematic receipt of technology from buyers	
None	0
Ad hoc technology transfer	1
Systematic technology transfer	2

Table 13A.2 Correlation matrix

	TI	*SIZE*	*FE*	*AGE*	*EXSH*	*ET*	*TB*	*EXTA*
TI	1							
SIZE	0.58	1.00						
FE	0.31	0.40	1.00					
AGE	0.08	0.15	−0.06	1.00				
EXSH	0.65	0.43	0.52	−0.02	1.00			
ET	0.37	0.08	−0.02	−0.08	0.25	1.00		
TB	0.48	0.20	0.14	0.01	0.37	0.12	1.00	
EXTA	0.51	0.25	0.23	−0.20	0.31	0.24	0.43	1

Notes

1. An earlier version of this chapter was presented at a conference on 'SMEs in Developing and Transitional Economies' at Kings College, London in September 2000, and at seminars at Queen Elizabeth House, Oxford in November 2000, and UNU INTECH, Maastricht in February 2001. I benefited greatly from comments received from participants at these events and am particularly grateful to Homi Katrak, Sanjaya Lall, Lynn Mytelka, Rose Kiggundu and Roger Strange. The views expressed in this chapter are entirely mine, and should not be attributed to the Commonwealth Secretariat.
2. Calculated from World Bank (2000).
3. See Woldekidan (1996), WTO (1996), Milner and McKay (1996), ILO (1999) and UNCTAD (2000).
4. An SME is defined here as a firm with 100 or fewer employees, while those with over 100 employees are taken to be large firms. According to this definition, there were nineteen SMEs and twenty-one large firms in the sample of forty Mauritian enterprises. Thirteen firms had some proportion of foreign equity, and twenty-seven were exporting some proportion of their sales.
5. The enterprise data for this chapter were collected during fieldwork in Mauritius in 1996 and 1998 in the course of studies on national competitiveness strategy and SME exports (see Lall and Wignaraja, 1998; Wignaraja and O'Neil, 1999).
6. See Pack and Westphal (1986), Katz (1987), Lall (1992), Bell and Pavitt (1993), Ernst *et al.* (1998) and Metcalfe (forthcoming).
7. See Katz (1987) for a survey of early studies in Latin America, and Bell and Pavitt (1993) for studies on other developing countries. Recent examples include: Lall *et al.* (1994) on food processing, wood working, textiles and garments, and metal working in Ghana; Hobday (1995) on the electronics industry in East Asia; Pietrobelli (1997) on food processing and other industries in Chile; Wangwe (1995) on food processing, wood working,

and metal working in several African economies including Mauritius, Kenya and Tanzania.

8. See, for example, Lall *et al.* (1994) on Ghana; Biggs *et al.* (1995) on Kenya, Zimbabwe and Ghana; Pietrobelli (1997) on Chile; and Wignaraja (1998) on Sri Lanka.
9. The pioneering work on this subject is Westphal *et al.* (1990) on Thailand. Subsequent work includes SRI International (1992) on Indonesia; Gosen (1995) on Mexico; Deraniyagala (1995) and Wignaraja (1998) on Sri Lanka; Romijn (1999) on Pakistan; Deraniyagla and Semboja (1999) on Tanzania; Wignaraja and Ikiara (1999) on Kenya; and Latsch and Robinson (1999) on Zimbabwe.
10. Lall *et al.* (1994) on Ghana, and Latsch and Robinson (1999) on Zimbabwe, also attempt to relate inter-firm differences in capabilities to firm characteristics (including firm size) using *t*-tests and rank correlation measures.
11. In neither the Sri Lanka study nor the Kenya study was the industry dummy variable significant.
12. Woldekidan (1994), Milner and McKay (1996), Lall and Wignaraja (1998) and UNCTAD (2000).
13. WTO (1996).
14. See Bheenick and Hanoomanjee (1988) , and Lall and Wignaraja (1998).
15. Primary school enrolment data are estimates of the ratio of children of all ages enrolled in primary schools to the country's population of school-age children. Although many countries consider primary school age to be 6–11 years, others use different age groups. Gross enrolment ratios may exceed 100 per cent because some pupils are younger or older than the country's standard primary school age.
16. This assessment of the technology support system in Mauritius is drawn from Lall and Wignaraja (1998).
17. Calculated from World Bank (2000). The same data source shows that the 1980–98 manufactured export growth rates achieved by Mauritius were closer to East Asian levels. For example, Singapore experienced manufactured export growth rates of 15.4 per cent, Taiwan of 11.6 per cent, and Hong Kong of 15.7 per cent.
18. See Wignaraja and O'Neil (1999) which defined SMEs as less than 50 emplayees. Additional insights are provided by survey data. The De Chazal Du Mee (1998) survey of forty Mauritian SMEs found that only seven were engaged in export sales (mainly towards the regional African market), and they concluded that SMEs were weak exporters relative to large firms.
19. A lack of data on investment functions performed by the Mauritian sample enterprises meant that investment capabilities could not be incorporated into the technology index. As achievements in investment capabilities are likely to be correlated closely with those on production and linkage capabilities, this is not expected to affect a given firm's technology ranking.
20. There are six categories of technical function under process engineering – see Table A13.1 – and a score for this is obtained by ranking firms out of 12. Similarly, a score for product engineering can be computed by ranking firms out of 6, and one for linkages by ranking out of 4. Size class scores are obtained by averaging the requisite enterprise scores. As industrial

engineering only had one technical function listed, it was decided not to compute a separate score for this activity.

21. The World Bank (1994) argues that quality management in Mauritius 'needs dramatic improvement'. It found that average reject rates in Mauritius were around three times higher than in developed countries, despite the use of considerable numbers of quality control personnel on the line. It also found that few firms had good systems that would prevent defects from arising. The World Bank concluded that the spread of ISO 9000 accredited quality management systems should be encouraged in Mauritius.
22. Dubois *et al.* (1995) report that local firms (particularly SMEs) lack the ability to undertake major maintenance, citing the following reasons for this: unavailability of qualified manpower and servicing equipment for undertaking major maintenance work; maintenance crews being more oriented towards routine maintenance; few people being involved in the maintenance department, poor maintenance planning; and inadequate status being allocated to the role of maintenance in the organization.
23. The World Bank (1994) noted that a number of medium-sized and large Mauritian firms have adopted computer-aided design and manufacturing. Computer-aided cutting is rare, since it is much more expensive; however, some large firms have made the necessary investment. Wider application of this technology is, however, needed if quality is to be raised in general. The study also commented that some large firms have also adopted computerized sewing in order to reduce labour costs, cut defects and realize more complex designs. Meanwhile, the bulk of Mauritian firms (particularly SMEs) rely on outdated basic sewing machines.
24. The acquisition of design capabilities in some large local firms is impressive. One large local garment firm had set up a fully-equipped design centre with the latest CAD facilities from Japan, and employed two overseas-trained designers and ten assistants. The firm said that it was able to offer several styles of a particular garment from which foreign buyers could choose. This was by no means an isolated case. Another large local garment firm had a CAD system and a nine-strong in-house design team. Such design capabilities seem to put Mauritius garment firms ahead of rival garment exporters in competitor countries such as Sri Lanka, Bangladesh and Vietnam.
25. The interviews shed some light on these issues. Two large garment MNC affiliates said that they had subcontracted orders to SMEs previously, but finding that the quality of output was below international standards (and the SMEs were unable to meet tight deadlines) had stopped subcontracting to SMEs altogether. Similarly, one large local garment firm reported that the quality of subcontractors' output was very irregular; it rejects 20 per cent of its subcontractors' output on an average order.
26. Expenditure on external technical assistance as a percentage of sales is a better measure of external technical assistance than the one used here, but the data were not available from the Mauritian firms.
27. Correlation analysis suggests the absence of multicollinearity amongst the explanatory variables in Equations (4) and (5). Using the White test, I reject the hypothesis of heteroskedasticity in Equations (4) and (5).

28. Recent examples include Wilmore (1992) on Brazil; Kumar and Siddharthan (1993) on India; and Wignaraja (1998) on Sri Lanka.
29. Correlation analysis suggests the absence of multicollinearity in Equations (2) and (4). Using the White test, we reject the hypothesis of heteroskedasticity in Equations (2) and (4).

Bibliography

Altenburg, T. and Meyer-Stamer, J. (1999) 'How to Promote Clusters: Policy Experiences from Latin America', *World Development*, vol. 27, no. 9, pp. 1693–714.

Aw, B.-Y. and Batra, G. (1998) 'Technological Capabilities and Firm Efficiency in Taiwan (China)', *World Bank Economic Review*, vol. 12, pp. 59–79.

Bheenick, R. and Hanoomanjee, E. (1988) *Mauritius: Towards an Industrial Training Strategy*, Port Louis: Ministry of Planning and Economic Development.

Bell, M. and Pavitt, K. (1993) 'Technological Accumulation and Industrial Growth: Contrasts Between Developed and Developing Countries', *Industrial and Corporate Change*, vol. 2, no. 2 pp. 157–210.

Biggs, T., Shah, M. and Srivastava, P. (1995) 'Technological Capabilities and Learning in African Enterprises', World Bank Technical Paper No. 288.

De Chazal Du Mee (1998) *Research Study on Small and Medium Enterprises in Mauritius: First Interim Report*, Port Louis: De Chazal Du Mee.

Deraniyagala, S. (1995) *Technical Change and Efficiency in Sri Lanka's Manufacturing Sector*. Unpublished PhD thesis, University of Oxford.

Deraniyagala, S. and Semboja, H. (1999) 'Trade Liberalisation, Firm Performance and Technology Upgrading in Tanzania', in S. Lall (ed.), *The Technological Response to Import Liberalisation in SubSaharan Africa*, London: Macmillan, pp. 112–47.

Dubois, P. R., Beedasy, J., Hurreeram, D. K., Ramgutty-Wong, A. and Seebaluck, D. (1995) *Technological Competence in Mauritian Small and Medium Enterprises*, Port Louis: University of Mauritius.

Ernst, D., Ganiatsos, T. and Mytelka, L. (eds) (1998) *Technological Capabilities and Export Success in Asia*, London: Routledge.

Gosen, R. (1995) 'Technological Capability in Developing Countries: A Case Study of Biotechnology in Mexico', Unpublished Ph.D. thesis, University of Oxford.

Hobday, M. (1995) *Innovation in East Asia: The Challenge to Japan*, Cheltenham: Edward Elgar.

International Labour Organization (1999) *Studies in the Social Dimension of Globalisation: Mauritius*, Geneva: ILO.

Katrak, H. (1996) 'Trade Policies, Enterprise Characteristics and Technological Effort in Developing Countries', *Journal of International Development*, vol. 8, no. 1, pp. 39–51.

Katz, J. M. (1987) 'Domestic Technology Generation in LDCs: A Review of Research Findings', in J. M. Katz (ed.), *Technology Generation in Latin American Manufacturing Industries*, Basingstoke: Macmillan, pp. 1–30.

Kumar, N. and Siddharthan, N. S. (1993) 'Technology, Firm Size and Export Behaviour in Developing Countries: The Case of Indian Enterprises', UNU INTECH Working Paper No. 9, Maastricht.

Lall, S. (1992) 'Technological Capabilities and Industrialisation', *World Development*, vol. 20, no. 2, pp. 165–86.

Lall, S. and Wignaraja, G. (1998) *Mauritius: Dynamising Export Competitiveness*, Commonwealth Economic Paper No. 33, London: Commonwealth Secretariat.

Lall, S., Barba-Navaretti, G., Teitel, S. and Wignaraja, G. (1994) *Technology and Enterprise Development: Ghana Under Structural Adjustment*, London: Macmillan.

Latsch, W. and Robinson, P. (1999) 'Technology and the Responses of Firms to Adjustment in Zimbabwe', in S. Lall (ed.), *The Technological Response to Import Liberalisation in SubSaharan Africa*, London: Macmillan, pp. 148–206.

Lamusse, R. (1995) 'Mauritius', in S. Wangwe (ed.), *Exporting Africa: Technology, Trade and Industrialisation in Sub-Saharan Africa*, London: Routledge, pp. 350–75.

Milner, C. and McKay, A. (1996) 'Real Exchange Rate Measures of Trade Liberalisation: Some Evidence for Mauritius', *Journal of African Economies*, vol. 5, no. 1, pp. 69–91.

Metcalfe, S. (forthcoming) 'Science, Technology and Innovation Policies in Developing Countries', in G. Wignaraja (ed.), *Competitiveness Strategy and Industrial Performance in Developing Countries: A Manual for Policy Analysis*, London: Routledge.

Mytelka, L. and Farinelli, F. (2000) 'Local Clusters, Innovation Systems and Sustained Competitiveness', Mimeo, Maastricht, UNU INTECH.

Pack, H. and Westphal, L. E. (1986) 'Industrial Strategy and Technological Change: Theory versus Reality', *Journal of Development Economics*, vol. 22, no. 2, pp. 87–128.

Pietrobelli, C. (1997) *Industry, Competitiveness and Technological Capabilities in Chile: A New Tiger from Latin America*, London: Macmillan.

Romijn, H. (1999) *Acquisition of Technological Capability in Small Firms in Developing Countries*, London: Macmillan.

SRI (1992) *Industrial Restructuring in the Electronics Sector*, Singapore: SRI International.

UNCTAD (2000) *Investment Policy Review: Mauritius*, Geneva: UNCTAD.

Wangwe, S. (ed.) (1995) *Exporting Africa: Technology, Trade and Industrialisation in Sub-Saharan Africa*, London: Routledge.

Westphal, L. E. (2001) 'Technology Strategies for Economic Development in a Fast Changing Global Economy', Mimeo, Swarthmore College, Penn.

Westphal, L. E., Kritayakirana, K., Petchsuwan, K., Sutabutr, H. and Yuthavong, Y. (1990) 'The Development of Technological Capability in Manufacturing: A Macroscopic Approach to Policy Research', in R. E. Evenson and G. Ranis (eds), *Science and Technology: Lessons for Development Policy*, London: Intermediate Technology Publications. pp. 81–134.

Wignaraja, G. (1998) *Trade Liberalisation in Sri Lanka: Exports, Technology and Industrial Policy*, London: Macmillan.

Wignaraja, G. and Ikiara, G. (1999) 'Adjustment, Technological Capabilities and Enterprise Dynamics in Kenya', in S. Lall (ed.), *The Technological Response to Import Liberalisation in SubSaharan Africa*, London: Macmillan, pp. 57–111.

Wignaraja, G. and O'Neil, S. (1999) 'SME Exports and Public Policies in Mauritius', Commonwealth Trade and Enterprise Paper No. 1, London: Commonwealth Secretariat.

Wilmore, L. (1992) 'Transnationals and Foreign Trade: Evidence from Brazil', *Journal of Development Studies*, vol. 28, no. 2, pp. 314–35.

Woldekidan, B. (1994) 'Export-led Growth in Mauritius', Australian National University, National Centre for Development Studies, Indian Ocean Policy Paper 3.

World Bank (1994) *Mauritius: Technology Strategy for Competitiveness*, Report No. 12518–MAS, Washington DC: World Bank.

World Bank (2000) *World Development Indicators 2000*, Washington DC: World Bank.

World Trade Organization (1996) *Trade Policy Review: Mauritius 1995*, Geneva: World Trade Organization.

14 Information, ICTs and Small Enterprise: Findings from Botswana

Richard Duncombe and Richard Heeks

RESEARCHING INFORMATION, ICTs AND SMALL ENTERPRISE

Much is being made of the potential for information and communication technologies (ICTs) to assist small enterprise development (Mansell and Wehn, 1998; World Bank, 1998). This potential has spawned a good deal of comment, much of it based on speculation rather than research. A few research studies are now being undertaken and reported (for example, Kole, 1998; Barton and Bear, 1999; Ferrand and Havers, 1999). However, many – if not most – such studies have taken a technocentric approach. That is to say, they have made technology the starting point and the main focus. Such studies typically take a predetermined view that new technology is the solution to development problems; that it should be applied as liberally as possible; and that initiative failures result from technical issues or the inability of the humans involved to appreciate and champion the wonders of ICTs.

The research project reported here[1] sought to understand the potential for application of information and communication technologies to small enterprise development. However, it took a broader, more critical and more systemic approach that had three main components (summarized in Figure 14.1):

- Information is the key to understanding ICTs. Information and communication technologies may be defined as 'electronic means of capturing, processing, storing, and disseminating information'. All these technologies do is to provide new mechanisms for handling an existing resource: information. We can therefore understand nothing about ICTs unless we first understand information practices and needs. This research therefore began not with the technology as its starting point, but with the existing information and communication practices of small enterprises, with the role of those practices within the enterprise's main business systems, and with enterprise requirements for improvements in those practices.

- ICTs are not the only 'technology' that handles information. ICTs are based on digital information held as 1s and 0s, and comprise computer hardware, software and networks. Other information-handling technologies include (Heeks, 1999):

  - 'intermediate' technology, still based largely on analogue information held as electro-magnetic waves such as radio, television and telephone;
  - 'literate' technology, based on information held as the written word, such as books and newspapers; and
  - 'organic' technology, based solely on the human body, such as the brain and sound waves.

Any study of information and small enterprise must therefore encompass these other technologies, since there may be situations in which they are more appropriate than ICTs.

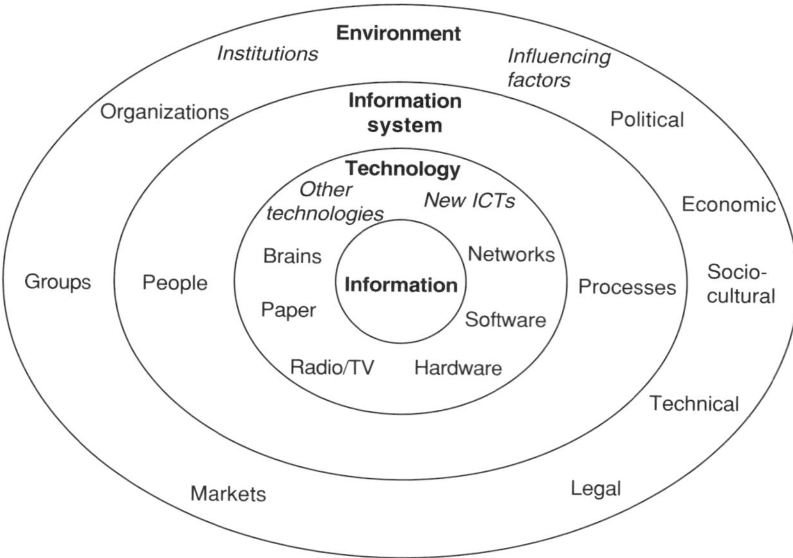

Figure 14.1 A systemic view of information and communication technologies

- Information systems are more than just technology and information. In building up a systemic model of ICTs, two separate elements have already been identified: the technology itself, and the information on which it operates. In order to make this useful, we add two further components: processes of purposeful activity, and people to undertake those processes. These together now make up an 'information system', such as a support system that helps staff in an enterprise share information with suppliers via electronic mail. But this information system cannot sit in a vacuum. It exists within an environment of institutions (organizations, groups, markets) and of influencing factors (political, economic, sociocultural, technical and legal). Recommendations, in particular, need to understand this environment and the constraints it might impose.

THE BOTSWANA RESEARCH PROJECT

Botswana was chosen as the site for fieldwork for three main reasons. First, there are a large number of small enterprises of many different types in many different sectors that are relatively easily accessible.[2] This provided a broad spectrum from which to sample. Second, Botswana's ICT infrastructure is relatively well-developed, and usage levels are higher than in many developing countries.[3] It was therefore possible to cover a very broad range of use, from enterprises without access to even a telephone up to those making intensive use of Internet-enabled applications. The findings could also move beyond the 'intermittent electricity; bad phone lines; lack of spares' issues that appear repetitively in many reports on ICTs and development.

Third, there is a favourable policy environment. There has been a high level of interest in small, medium and micro-enterprise (SMME) development in Botswana since the approval of a new SMME policy in December 1998 (Ministry of Commerce and Industry, 1999). The policy's prime aim is to encourage further expansion of the SMME sector. In addition, Botswana's 'Vision 2016' document (Presidential Task Group, 1997) makes a strong commitment to the development of competitive enterprises through the use of modern technology, including the implementation of ICTs across all manufacturing and service sectors.

The initial research reported here was targeted at formal sector enterprises, drawn from those recorded in the Botswana Registry of Establishments (CSO, 1997). Two data collection techniques were focused on enterprise information practices and needs:

Table 14.1 Respondent profile from the questionnaire survey in Botswana

Entrepreneur gender	Male *(77%)*	Female *(23%)*		
Entrepreneur age	<31 years *(8%)*	31–40 years *(30%)*	>41 years *(62%)*	
Entrepreneur education	Primary schooling *(12%)*	Secondary schooling/above *(88%)*		
Enterprise size	<5 employees *(26%)*	5–29 employees *(50%)*	30–99 employees *(24%)*	
Enterprise ownership	Botswana citizen-owned *(57%)*	Foreign citizen-owned *(30%)*	Joint ownership *(10%)*	Foreign subsidiary *(3%)*

- semi-structured interviews, carried out with an initial sample of twenty enterprises; and
- a questionnaire sent to 480 small, medium, and micro-enterprises covering non-exporting manufacturers, exporting manufacturers, and service-based enterprises.[4]

Sixty-one usable questionnaires had been returned at the time of writing (a 13 per cent response rate). The response profile is summarized in Table 14.1.

The profile components of sex, age and ownership are in line with previous formal sector profiles (BOCCIM, 1994; Briscoe, 1995). However, as was to be expected from a postal questionnaire, there was some bias. In particular, there was a higher proportion of educated entrepreneurs and of larger enterprises than in the main population. There is also likely to have been a bias towards ICT users. The figures given below on technology use may therefore be somewhat greater than those for the whole population of formal sector enterprises.

ENTERPRISE INFORMATION SYSTEMS

Figure 14.2 presents the model of enterprise information systems used as the basis for investigation. Before exploring the findings about these information system components in more detail, though, the balance between informal and formal information practices must be highlighted. The evidence of both questionnaires and interviews shows that current information practices within the survey group are

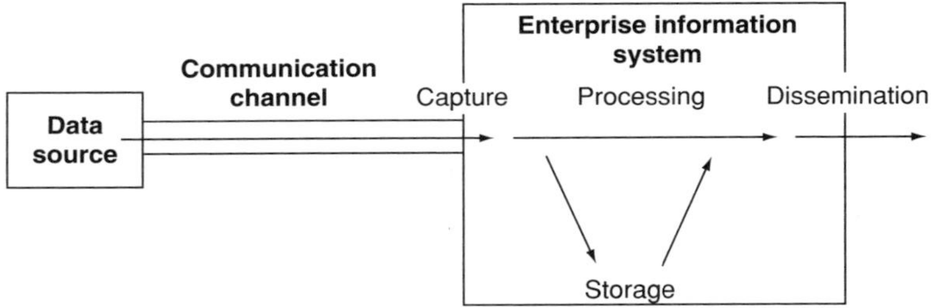

Figure 14.2 The enterprise information systems model

overwhelmingly informal in nature. This was true not only in 'traditional' sectors such as the manufacture of clothing, leather, wood products, and construction materials, but also in 'non-traditional' sectors such as tourism, engineering, and IT services. The sources and channels of informal information were characterized by:

- a high degree of reliance on information obtained through the knowledge and experience of the business owner;
- information received through informal local networking within the business community;
- information received through contacts with family and friends; and
- information accumulated through enterprise-specific learning.

The evidence from the interviews shows that the exchange of informal information is common across all areas of business activity. For example, information about loans often comes from family and friends (as do the loans themselves); on-the-job training allows information to pass directly from more experienced to less experienced employees; business associates will provide information in the form of informal advice or technical assistance; and market information leading to a new contract may frequently be received through the business grapevine or from a family member.

Determining the comparative quality of formally- and informally-provided information is not easy. On the one hand, informal information can be constrained and insular if the entrepreneur's social network is small, closed and knowledge-poor (Barton, 1997). Informal information systems may be particularly deficient for marginalized or displaced entrepreneurs who lack a coherent social network. For them, formal (potentially ICT-based) systems may hold more promise. However, information received through informal sources and channels was rated more highly by most business owners than information from formal institutional sources. This tends to be because entrepreneurs value the time, cost and convenience benefits of informal information systems. For example, information relating to the implications of a new law or regulation is more likely to be accessed from a business associate than a government institution, because the former is quicker and easier. Entrepreneurs also trust informal information sources and find them easy to process.

The exception was enterprises exhibiting a high degree of dependency on government contracting: these firms tended to be locked into more formalized information practices. Many of these enterprises seemed to lack access to the informal business networks that are valued by the wider business community, and their entrepreneurs placed a far greater emphasis on information received from external governmental and non-governmental support organizations.

Data Sources

The results suggest that entrepreneurs depend predominantly on their own 'internally generated knowledge and experience', which has been built up within their present business or as a result of previous employment/business ownership. As just noted, 'externally generated information' is sourced primarily through informal business networks of customers and suppliers, or family and friends. In contrast, formal institutional data sources, such as banks, consultants and business support agencies are not seen as being particularly important. The exception, also noted above, are non-exporting manufacturers, many of whom are relatively dependent on such institutions. Half of these felt that business support institutions were their single most important source of external business information. Other entrepreneur groups found information from formal institutions was not targeted at them, and they were generally less dependent on – and less inclined to deal with – such institutions.

Communication Channels

The vast majority of the respondents in all categories regarded direct contact with customers through face-to-face meetings as the single most effective method of business communication. About 70 per cent of respondents also used fixed-line telephone and fax frequently for their business dealings. Around a quarter of the enterprises were using mobile telephones and e-mail, though far more of these were service than manufacturing enterprises; and far more exporters than non-exporters.

Telephone services (including fax) represent the most popular initial investment for businesses. The rapid growth of mobile communications in the late 1990s/early 2000s is also proof of the value that entrepreneurs place on real-time voice communication. The evidence shows that even very small businesses find telephone services advantageous. For example, one rural artisan producing leather goods used telephone-based communications to contact market traders in distant towns, and materials suppliers in an adjoining country. The extension of telecommunication services, providing for direct voice (and fax) communication, has been of particular value to SMMEs operating in Botswana, given its large land mass and dispersed population.

As yet, the appeal of e-mail and Internet-mediated communication remains confined largely to certain specific sectors. The vast majority of formal-sector SMMEs serve local markets and rely primarily on locally-generated information. Internet use remains in its infancy and, until the amount of local content is expanded in terms of both volume and quality, it is unlikely that the benefits of information access through networked services will justify the cost for most formal-sector SMMEs.

Investments for Internet access are significant in terms of initial financial outlay, running costs, and investment of time and skill. Because of this, such investments would need to be accompanied by significant benefits in terms of regularity of use and quality of information provided. The evidence shows that it is only in specific sectors, such as technical services, the IT sector, and travel and tourism, that information-access benefits can be achieved as yet. These are all sectors that require regular access to information and/or software across borders, both regionally and world-wide. In contrast, the benefits of access to telephone services seem likely far to outweigh the comparatively low investment and training costs for a much wider spectrum of enterprises.

Information Storage and Processing

The majority of entrepreneurs still stored information on paper/cards or in their heads, and processed it manually. Use of computers for information storage and processing was highly uneven. Taken overall, the initial fieldwork results suggested significantly higher levels of computer use among service-based enterprises than either manufacturing exporters or non-exporting manufacturers. Among service-based businesses and manufacturing exporters, information relating to company accounts, for example, was held on computer by nearly 70 per cent of the enterprises surveyed, but only 9 per cent of the non-exporting manufacturers had computer-based accounts.

Dissemination of Information

The primary formal objective of all enterprises was to sustain/increase their sales by means of retaining existing customers and/or locating new customers. There is evidence from the survey that, when promoting their products and services, entrepreneurs have a strong preference for personal contact with customers. Ninety per cent of all business owners regarded face-to-face contact as being very effective for promotion.

Other forms of communication were not considered to be so effective. This was particularly the case among service-based enterprises. At the time of writing, formal methods of media-based marketing are generally not used in Botswana by the small enterprise sector. The postal and telecommunications infrastructure is thought to be insufficiently developed and not reliable enough for effective direct telephone sales or the use of direct-mail marketing techniques. Marketing and advertising services in Botswana are at an early stage of development, and cater predominantly for the corporate sector. And, quite apart from these environmental constraints, such services would generally not be affordable by SMMEs.

Approximately 50 per cent of those who responded to the survey had Internet access, 43 per cent used the Internet 'very often', and 30 per cent rated it 'very important' as a source of business information. However, there was far less use of the Internet as a means of disseminating information about enterprise products and services. Only 13 per cent of Internet users regarded it as a very effective product/service promotion tool, and a further 47 per cent had not yet used the Internet for business promotion.

In serving domestic markets, Internet-based marketing is not likely to offer any substantial benefits in comparison with other forms of media, which are themselves under-utilized at the time of writing. There are, however, likely to be considerable benefits for enterprises whose customers are located outside Botswana. For manufacturing exporters and the tourist industry, a strong Internet presence may become a powerful marketing tool, both for raising the profile of the business and for the rapid dissemination of information to existing and potential customers.

ENTERPRISE INFORMATION NEEDS

Critical Problem Areas

Information is not the be-all and end-all of enterprise development, and the study of information and ICTs must set these factors alongside the others that enterprises require. The research therefore investigated enterprise problems generally in order to understand the relative importance of information-related problems. Three general problem areas were identified as being equally 'critical' by around 40 per cent of enterprises:

Access to skills

This was the main issue, being cited as 'very important' by an additional 52 per cent of enterprises. The respondents most often identified poor existing management skills, lack of access to improved management skills, inability to acquire and retain skilled workers, and lack of access to skills training as their most significant constraints.

Access to markets

The main issues here were the need to increase sales to existing customers, and to expand/diversify the customer base.

Access to finance

This was identified as a key problem by non-exporting manufacturers. Manufacturing exporters and service enterprises were much less concerned about finance, and much more concerned about skills and sales.

Enterprise Information Gaps

Overall, within formal-sector SMMEs, the evidence suggests there is a large 'information needs gap' across a wide range of business activities. This gap was measured as the difference between the stated demand for information from entrepreneurs, and their success in obtaining a supply of such information.

Each of the problem areas identified above has an associated information component. It was therefore no surprise that information gaps accorded largely with prioritization of these problems areas. For example, the largest gaps for particular enterprise categories were as follows:

- *For non-manufacturing exporters*, the greatest need was for information that would lead to advice and/or assistance in accessing external financing and in solving internal financial problems;
- *For manufacturing exporters*, the greatest need was for information concerning access to trained personnel and assistance with workforce training; and
- *For service enterprises*, the greatest need was for information concerning management training opportunities and sources of new, skilled employees.

In addition, 72 per cent of all enterprises had an urgent need to access information that would lead to increased sales by obtaining new local customers and/or by expanding into export markets.

However, a distinction emerged between two root causes of the information gap. Information relating to management skills training, skilled employees, availability of land/premises, export markets and technical expertise was difficult to obtain, primarily because those commodities/services were themselves in short supply locally. In contrast, the difficulty in obtaining information relating to finance and new local customers (and, to a lesser extent, rules/regulations) related more to a lack of access for SMMEs, rather than a more general lack of availability. In relation to finance, for example, the difficulties of accessing information were both the result of information barriers erected by lending institutions, and of the lack of ability among business owners to search out and access such information effectively.

Of course, these are general observations, and it should be emphasized that enterprises are characterized by their diversity: depending on the markets within which they operate; the goods and services they provide; and the capacities of business owners and employees. Each enterprise has its own individual problems and priorities, and hence 'enterprise-specific' information needs. Nevertheless, the findings suggests at least one priority for all enterprises: the provision of better market/demand information. There have been a number of successful initiatives introduced to improve the provision of demand information for entrepreneurs in developing countries (Van Crowder, 1997; World Bank, 1998). These have used both ICT-based and non-electronic methods to disseminate quantitative information such as market prices, and qualitative information such as details of distribution channels. Initiative sustainability is an issue, but sales growth has been an outcome in some cases.

CONCLUSIONS FROM THE SURVEY

The findings reported here are drawn from an initial fieldwork survey, based solely on formal sector SMMEs in Botswana, with partial response bias towards larger enterprises and ICT-using enterprises. The conclusions presented must therefore be regarded as somewhat tentative.

In relation to the investigation approach, we reassert the point made at the beginning of the chapter: in order to understand ICTs, one must first understand information. Taking information as the starting point requires the modelling and investigation of current enterprise information systems and information needs. This forms an essential basis for understanding the role that ICTs can, and cannot, play in the enterprise. Without such a 'bedrock', decisions about ICTs become merely reactive to the whims of current technology fads and fashions. As with the technology, we must also take a systemic view of the enterprises themselves, as shown in Figure 14.3.

Such systemic views are a reminder, as were the questionnaire results, that information must be kept in perspective. Information gaps are certainly an issue for small entrepreneurs, but resources such as skills, markets and money are a more important part of the total small-enterprise development picture. Addressing information alone may be a necessary step in small-enterprise development, but it is very far from being a sufficient one. And what is true for information, must necessarily be true for the ICTs that provide more efficient or more effective means of handling that information.

Entrepreneurs and support agencies must therefore take a multidimensional approach to enterprise development that encompasses a package of related resources. This is particularly true of information, since the information component of all other resources is bound up so intimately with the resource itself. Information-related interventions, by entrepreneurs or institutions, must also recognize the critical and

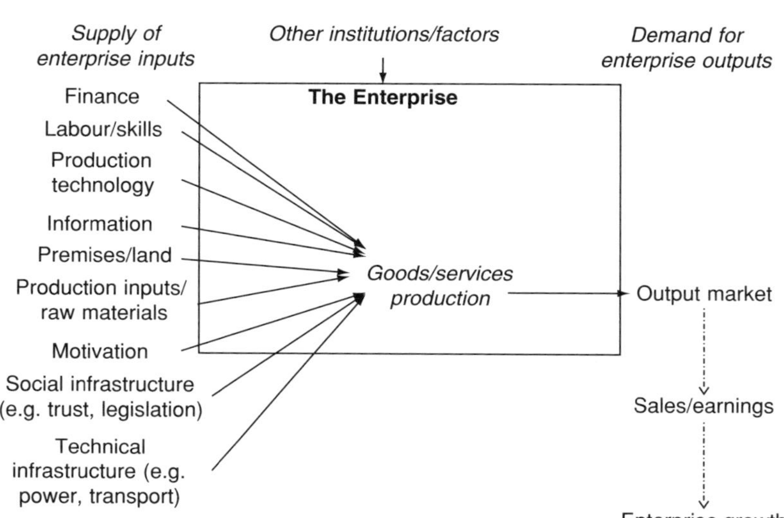

Figure 14.3 A systemic view of enterprise

continuing role to be played by informal information systems, and by 'non-electronic technologies' such as telephone, newsletters, and the human brain. The seductive nature of ICTs can easily pull interventions down a single, narrow track that deals just with ICT access and skills. Instead, a more holistic approach is required that provides information skills, communication skills, and assistance with improving organic-, literate- and intermediate-technology-based systems as well as the more obvious ICT-focused areas.

Therefore, computing/Internet skills training should not be split, but should form one component of task-focused training. The training programme should be, for example, 'better marketing', not 'using the Internet'. Similarly, organizational change interventions should concentrate on improving particular organizational systems by whatever means are appropriate, rather than focusing just on the introduction of a new technology. The intervention aim should be, for example, 'to improve the enterprise's accounting systems', not 'to introduce computers'.

Such a task/systems approach and not a technology-driven one is all the more vital given the environmental constraints that hold back ICT use. In Botswana, these include a lack of knowledge about ICTs, a lack of ICT implementation and user skills, a lack of finance, and a lack of connectivity. Such constraints suggest that informal/non-electronic information system improvements may often be more feasible than those aimed at ICT-based systems.

A DIFFERENTIATED APPROACH TO ICT DEVELOPMENT

The very diverse nature of the enterprises surveyed suggests the need for a differentiated development approach. One obvious differentiation would be between the needs of service, manufacturing export, and non-exporting manufacturing enterprises. Certainly, those exporting and those not have a very different information systems profile, and very different information needs.

Here, though, we shall look at a slightly different categorization, based on the sophistication of information systems in use in the organization. Despite the caveats about technocentrism, we shall use technology-based categories because they are easy to identify and understand, and because they can be related relatively easily to different information practices and interventions. This categorization therefore provides a way of targeting particular enterprises for particular information-related interventions. Five different enterprise categories emerged from the survey:

Non-ICT users

Enterprises that make no use of computers and have no immediate access to telecommunication services.

Non-IT users

Enterprises that make no use of computers but have access to, and make regular use of, telecommunication services; primarily telephone and fax, but with increasing use of mobile communications.

Non-networked ICT users

Enterprises with one or more computers on their premises, but with no network connections; they will have access to telecommunication services.

Networked ICT users

Enterprises with stand-alone computer(s) that lack internal networking, but which have an external e-mail/Internet connection.

Intensive ICT users

Enterprises using two or more internally-networked computers that also have e-mail/Internet connectivity.

The following observations may be made regarding the enterprise size, ownership, and sectoral distribution of the enterprises thus categorized:

- more than 70 per cent of the non-ICT/non-IT users had fewer than five employees, while a similar percentage of medium-sized enterprises (30–99 employees) fell into the networked/intensive ICT user categories;
- all but one of the non-ICT/non-IT user enterprises was owned by Botswana citizens, while two-thirds of the networked/intensive ICT user enterprises were owned by foreigners; and
- more than half of the non-exporting manufacturers were non-ICT/non-IT users, while 80 per cent of manufacturing exporters and service enterprises were networked/intensive ICT users.

Non-ICT Users

Very few non-ICT users emerged from the initial round of fieldwork, but previous studies indicate that the majority of such enterprises are located in the non-formal sector (Daniels and Fisseha, 1992; Lisenda, 1997). Given the predominant role of the non-formal sector, this type of enterprise therefore constitutes the majority of enterprises within the SMME sector as a whole, and creates livelihoods for the largest number of people.

The potential for information- and ICT-related interventions is unclear, but we can surmise from other work (Heeks, 1999) that the information needs of such enterprises will be met more by informal, organic information systems than by formal, ICT-based information systems. Within the non-formal sector, there is strong evidence that business owners place greater value on information received through personal contact, and are able to build up greater trust in personalized information channels and sources. Conversely, information received in a digitised form is generally non-personalized and distant, and lacks the trust components necessary when making decisions that may involve an element of risk. Environmental analysis suggests there are also likely to be substantial long-term financial, sociocultural, and knowledge barriers that would need to be overcome before most business owners in this category could effectively utilize both ICTs and the information they handle.

There are two corollaries for ICT use. First, that where ICTs are used, they should provide a supplement, not substitute, for existing information systems. Second, that in most cases, 'intelligent intermediaries' will be needed to bridge the financial, sociocultural, and knowledge gaps between what non-formal entrepreneurs have and what they would need in order to access and use ICT-borne information.[5]

The priorities for the application of such intermediated access to ICTs probably lie in communication more than in the processing of information. The formal information-processing requirements of such enterprises are relatively limited, and typically can be met cost-effectively by improved paper-based methods. In communication of information, though, ICTs can substantially reduce costs and greatly increase access.

ICTs can provide infusions of external information that break the insularity and quality deficits of some informal social networks. They can be a means for communicating market/demand information (though this can equally, and perhaps more appropriately, be delivered by non-ICT means). They can also disseminate information most eye-catchingly through Internet-mediated marketing of enterprise products and services. However, it must be recognized that the Internet is no panacea, and that many complementary inputs and actions are required if enterprises are to make use of the technology, even via intermediaries.

Non-IT Users

The lack of finance and lack of management/workforce skills were perceived as key problems for this enterprise group, with over 90 per cent of business owners in this category regarding them as critical or very important. These enterprises have an obvious potential for expanding their use of IT systems. However, the lack of finance and skills will be a major constraint. Most could not afford to buy a personal computer and, if one was bought, most would find it difficult to obtain commensurate benefits in the short/medium term.

Current non-IT users are more likely to benefit from improvements in their existing information practices using the information systems and technology to which they already have access. There are various ways in which business owners and employees can be helped to improve their capacity for information access, processing and dissemination. These would include access to training for improving interpersonal communication skills, enhanced financial management skills to improve business efficiency, and training in sales and marketing techniques.

Within such enterprises, it is only when basic skills and/or financial stability have been significantly improved that any true benefit is likely to be gained from applying ICTs. Of course, as with the non-ICT users, they would find value in intermediated access to ICTs. Again, communication is likely to be a priority: both receipt (for example, of market prices) and dissemination (for example, of product/service details).

Non-Networked ICT Users

Non-networked ICT users can be described as 'first-footers' in small-business computing, and they are widespread throughout the manufacturing and service sectors covered in the survey. Although they have access to computers on the premises, levels of computer use typically are low. Thirty-nine per cent of 'users' in fact made no use of their computers for everyday business activities. Among the remainder, by far the main use (71 per cent of actual users) was word processing. In contrast, only 20 per cent of actual users had computerized basic business functions such as customer invoicing and internal accounting.

Non-networked ICT users frequently lack managerial capacities, and they share many of the characteristics of non-IT users. The same preconditions for enhancing basic management and information skills would apply before investments in enhanced ICTs should be considered. Similarly, these enterprises will also benefit from improving their informal/non-electronic information systems. Nevertheless, there are greater ICT-related pressures within this group than those felt in the previous two categories:

- such enterprises may have specific needs for ICTs, as in the printing and publishing sector, where competitive pressures driven by rapid technological change mean enterprises must 'adapt or die' in relation to ICTs;
- such enterprises may feel pressurized to expand their use of ICTs in order to achieve compatibility with customers or suppliers; and

- such enterprises may feel pressurized to adopt ICTs to keep up with competitors and to create an aura of modernity.

Such pressures were reflected in the 50 per cent of respondents in this category who regarded the upgrading of their computer systems as being critical to future business success.

However, the evidence from the interviews suggests significant problems among this category of 'first-footer' computer users. As reflected in the figure of 39 per cent given above, it was not uncommon to find computers not in use or consigned to a back room, after initial failed attempts to adapt unfamiliar software to the needs of the business. This failure, in turn, arises from the gap that exists between the design conceptions of much business software and the organizational realities of many small enterprises (Heeks and Bhatnagar, 1999). Closing the design–reality gap will be a key priority, which will draw in issues of IT production strategy and software production skills within the country.

Networked/Intensive ICT Users[6]

These enterprises – found mainly in the technical services, IT services and tourism sectors – make considerable, networked use of ICTs. Three-quarters of them had computerized accounting and customer invoicing systems. Most other business functions, such as inventories, customer and supplier records, were computerised in about 60 per cent of enterprises. E-mail and the Internet were used very or quite often by 85 per cent of these enterprises, and computers were used for more complex business activities such as project planning by 50 per cent of respondents.

All respondents regarded further upgrading and continued expansion of ICT-based systems as critical or very important to the future success of their businesses. However, the interview evidence showed that such enterprises had applied and adapted such systems on a largely *ad hoc* basis. In many cases, they lacked the employee skills to manage effectively the systems that had been developed. In other cases, the development process was deficient.

Overall, such enterprises will benefit from a more strategic approach to managing information, in order that the costs and benefits associated with improving both ICT-based and non-electronic systems can be evaluated. They also require complementary inputs to support their current systems, such as a better understanding of marketing and promotion as a precursor to making more effective use of the Internet. Lastly, better or best practice needs to be disseminated about the development and management of computerized information systems.

Notes

1. The work reported here was supported by a research grant from the UK Department for International Development.
2. In total, there are estimated to be around 50 000 micro-enterprises (informal sector, one or two paid employees, family-run); 6000 small enterprises (registered, employing fewer than 25 employees); and 300 medium-sized enterprises (registered, 25–100 employees) in Botswana (SMME Task Force, 1998). Some 70 per cent of micro-enterprises are rural-based; some 80 per cent of small and medium-sized enterprises are urban-based. Sixty per cent of registered enterprises are in the retail sector, mainly small food retail outlets and general stores. However, there are also significant numbers in manufacturing, construction, tourism, transportation, finance and business services.
3. Countrywide, Botswana has a telecommunications density of 4.83 main lines per 100 inhabitants, compared to a low-income country average of 2.48. It has 33.42 Internet users per 10 000 inhabitants, compared to a low-income country average of 0.89 (ITU, 1998).
4. The sample was drawn equally from manufacturing and services. The four manufacturing sub-sectors covered were: textiles, clothing and leather products; wood products, furniture and crafts; building and construction materials; and printing and publishing. The four services sub-sectors covered were: tourism; IT and computing; transport; and engineering and technical services.
5. For an assessment of different intermediary models, see Barton and Bear (1999).
6. For the purposes of discussion, the networked ICT user and intensive ICT user categories are combined below.

References

Barton, C. (1997) *Microenterprise Business Development Services*, Bethesda, Md.: Microenterprise Best Practices.

Barton, C. and Bear, M. (1999) *Information and Communications Technologies: Are They the Key to Viable Business Development Services for Micro and Small Enterprises*, Bethesda, Md.: Microenterprise Best Practices.

Botswana Confederation of Commerce, Industry and Manpower (BOCCIM) (1994) *Industry Survey*, Gaborone: BOCCIM.

Briscoe, A. J. (1995) 'Assisting Small Businesses: Findings from a Study of Botswana's New Generation of Entrepreneurs', University of Botswana, Business School of Botswana, Working Paper No. 2.

Central Statistical Office (CSO) (1997) *Botswana Registry of Establishments*, Gaborone: Government of Botswana, Central Statistical Office.

Daniels, L. and Fisseha, Y. (1992) *Micro and Small-Scale Enterprises in Botswana: Results of a Nationwide Survey*, Gaborone: Ministry of Finance and Development Planning.

Ferrand, D. and Havers, M. (1999) 'Information Systems for Microfinancial Services', *Small Enterprise Development*, vol. 10, no. 1, pp. 4–16.

Heeks, R. B. (1999) 'Information and Communication Technologies, Poverty and Development', University of Manchester, Institute for Development Policy and Management, Development Informatics Paper No. 5 (http://www.man.ac.uk/idpm/idpm_dp.htm)

Heeks, R. B. and Bhatnagar, S. C. (1999) 'Understanding Success and Failure in Information Age Reform', In R. B. Heeks (ed.) *Reinventing Government in the Information Age*, London: Routledge.

International Telecommunications Union (ITU) (1998) *World Telecommunications Indicators*, Geneva: ITU.

Kole, E. (1998) 'Supporting Small Enterprise with New Technology', *Appropriate Technology*, vol. 24, no. 4, pp. 21–3.

Lisenda, L. (1997) 'Small and Medium Enterprises in Botswana: Their Characteristics, Sources of Finance, and Problems', Botswana Institute for Development Policy Analysis, Working Paper No. 14.

Mansell, R. and Wehn, U. (eds) (1998) *Knowledge Societies*, Oxford: Oxford University Press for UNCSTD.

Ministry of Commerce and Industry (1999) *Policy on Small, Medium and Micro Enterprises in Botswana*, Government Paper No. 1/1999, Gaborone: Government of Botswana, Ministry of Commerce and Industry.

Presidential Task Group (1997) *Vision 2016: Long-Term Vision for Botswana*, Gaborone: Government of Botswana.

SMME Task Force (1998) *Small, Medium and Micro-Enterprise Task Force Report*, Gaborone: Ministry of Commerce and Industry.

Van Crowder, L. (1997) 'Marketing Information Systems for Small-Scale Farmers', *Information Development*, vol. 13, no. 4, pp. 179–83.

World Bank (1998) *World Development Report*, Washington DC: World Bank.

Index

Note: f = figure; n = endnote; t = table.

acknowledgements, 97(n1), 211, 279(n1), 302(n1)
acquisitions, 87, 90, 95
Acs, Z., 115, 125, 128, 135(n2), 135
adjustment, 157–8, 179, 180(n1)
advantaged firms (Bulgaria), **163**, 163t, 167, 170, 172, 173t, 174t, 175
advertising, 125, 135(n7), 292
Africa, 100, 170, 180(n9), 217, 262, 265, 276, 280(n7, n18)
agencies, 2, 31, 69, 112, 192, 208, 210, 223, 226–7, 232, 246
Agra, 71(n18)
agriculture, 11, 38–9, 95, 131, 189, 193, 227(n5)
Ahmad, J., 99, 112(n1), 113
Albaladejo, Manuel, x, 7
Albu, M., 247(n4), 248
Altenburg, T., 247(n6), 247
Amsterdam University: Department of Human Geography, 211
Anco (consortium), 199–200, 209
Anderson, G., 227(n6), 227
Anhui, 39
APEMEFAC (National Footwear Makers' Association, Peru), 241
APIC (Peruvian Association of Small-Scale Garment Manufacturers), 241
Araujo, K., 135(n6), 136
Argentina, 236–7, 242
Asian financial crisis, 7, 80, 214, **220–3**, 226
Audretsch, D., 115, 125, 128, 135(n2), 135
Avramov, R., 160, 181

Bala Subrahmanya, M.H., 100, 113
Bali, 219, 224
Banco Latino (Venezuela), 119
Banfield, Edward, 206, 207, 211
Bangalore, 6, **185–213**
Bangladesh, 55, 70(n11–12), 265, 281(n24)
banks, 141t, 145, 152, 154, 200, 232, 243
banks/banking, 119–20, 133, 158, 216, 290
bankruptcy, 81, 87, 131, 169
Barba-Navaretti, G., 283
barriers, 55, 87, 88, 97(n3), 125, 126, 128, 132, 190, 222, 237
Barton, C., 302(n5), 302
Basant, R., 114
Bear, M., 302(n5), 302
Becattini, G., 230, 247, 248
Beedasy, J., 282
Beedis, 103
Bell, M., 247(n4), 248, 279(n7), 282
Berry, A., 30, 219, 222, 227
Bhagwati, Jagdish, 31, 32, 34, 46
Bhalla, A. S., 100, 113
Biggs, T., 280(n8), 282
Birch, D., 115, 135
Botswana, 8, **285–303**, 288t, 302(n3), 302(n4)
Brazil, 12, 13t, 15, 16, 17t, 26t, 27f, 29, 36t, 47(n2), **237**, **238**, 241, 242, 282(n28)
Brusco, Sebastiano, 202, 211
budget deficits, 118, 119, 120, 231–2
Bulgaria, 6, 157–8, **157–81**, 159t, **161–7**, 167–8, 168t, 169–70, 171t, 175t, 180(n2)
bureaucracy, 118, 119, 123, 131, 133, 210, 220, 232, 255, 263
Burgas (Bulgaria), 167
business,
  development services (BDS), 219, 225–6, 227(n6)

business (*contd*)
environment, 120, 121–2, 124, 127, 128, 132, 133, 134, 135(n5), 220, 221, 224, 226, 233, 255
friends, 192, 193, 195–6, 202, 205, 210
owners (Botswana), 294, 299, 300
registration, 245
services (Botswana), 302(n2)
buyers, 242, 258, 259
foreign, 40–1, 235, 241, 269, 276, 281(n24)

Cachoeiro de Itapemirim (Brazil), **238**, 240, 242, 244
CAD, *see* computer-aided design
Cadène, Philippe, 211
Calcutta, 58, **60–2**, **62–3**
Cambodia, 220
Canada, 88, 97(n3)
capital, 3, 19, 22–3, 23f, 28, 51, 55, 56, 57, 59, 69, 70(n1), 88, 91, 96t, 121, 122, 127, 144, 160, 169, 200, 232, 234, 243
capital goods, 103, 108, 162, 172, 179
capital intensity, 19, 90, 93, 95, 112(n1), 125, 126, 154(n4), 185
Caribbean, 237
cartels, 132, 133
caste (India), 189, 190, 191, 210
Central and Eastern Europe (CEE), 77, 158, 159, 159t, **167–70**, 168t, 171t, 180(n3)
central effluent treatment plants (CETPs), 54, 55, 70(n10)
CFCs (chloro-fluoro-carbons), 52
Chile, 279(n7), 280(n8)
China, *see* People's Republic of China
China Cocoon and Silk Exchange (Jiaxing, Zhejiang province, 1993–), 42, 48(n11)
China National Silk Import and Export Corporation (CNSIEC, 1987–), 38, 39, 40, 41, 42, 47(n4)
China Silk Corporation (1982–6), 38, 47(n3)
Chinese silk industry (cautionary tale), **31–49**
'churning', 82, 83, 95, 96
Clarke, R., 112(n3), 113
Clik (Consortium of Electronic Industries of Karnataka), 201
clothing, 22, 164, 166t, 166f, 167, 219, 265, 289, 302(n4)
clusters, 4, 6–7, **183–251**, 277
CNC (computer-numerically-controlled) machine tools, 187, 188, 192, 195, 197, 204, 205
CNSIEC, *see* China National Silk Import and Export Corporation
co-operation, 153, 208, 230, 244, 258
co-operative enterprises, 160, 168, 172
co-operative movement (Italy), 187
cocoons, 40, 41, 42, 43
Coimbatore (Tamil Nadu), 199, 200, 202, 209
collectively-owned enterprises (COEs), 5, 81, 83, 84f, 87, 89, 92t, 93, 94t, 95, 96
Colombia, 12, 13t, 16, 17t, 19–22, 20t–21t, 25, 26t, 27f, 29, 55, 70(n11)
Commonwealth of Independent States (CIS), 36t
Commonwealth Secretariat, 279(n1)
communication channels, 289f, 290–1
Communist Party of Bulgaria, 157
Communist Party of China, 78–9, 80
comparative advantage, 137, 151, 258, 263
competition, 2, 3–4, 29(n1), 41, 47, 77, 78, 81, **82–6**, 90, 100, 104, 111, 119, 127, 137, 144, 154, 187, 188, 195, 198, 200, 201, 203, 210, 220, 234, 237, 240, 242, 243, 244, 245, 247, 301
competitiveness, 7, 58, 85, 132, 145, 153, 196, 236, 241, 243, 264, 268, 276, 277, 287
competitiveness in SME clusters: **229–51**, 231f
components, 58, 188, 189, 193, 194, 195, 196
spare parts, 70(n1), 199, 263

computer-aided design (CAD) 187, 195, 197, 198, 205, 269, 281(n23–24)
computers, 200, 202, 292, 296, 297, 298, 299, 300, 301, 302
Confederation of Indian Industries, 100, 113
consortia, 193–6, **198–201**, 202, 208, 209
consultancy, 186, 187, 193, 197–8, 202, 203, 204, 205, 208, 209, 210, 225, 226, 270, 271, 281(n26)
consumers, 34, 47, 47(n1), 57, 106, 148, 219, 269
contracts, 127, 132, 210, 269
cooperation, 188, 209, 210, 233–4, 240, 245
cooperative enterprises: Bulgaria, 180(n6)
corporate governance mechanisms, 5, 96
corruption, 121, 123, 132, 134, 207, 208, 209, 255
  bribes, 123
Cortes, M., 11, 15, 30
costs, 1, 23, 28, 68, 88, 90, 122, 123, 125, 190, 219, 221, 224, 245, 261, 270, 291, 299
Cournot model, 112(n5)
Cox, D., 93, 97
crafts/handicrafts, 111, 220, 221, 302(n4)
credit, 1, 56, 57, 66, 70(n12), 118, 127, 133, 141t, 145, 152, 154, 174t, 175, 216, 219, 220, 221, 222, 225, 243
Czech Republic, 63, 64
Czechoslovakia/Former Czechoslovakia, 159t, 159–60, **167–70**, 171t, 205

Dalian, 83
Das, K., 114
Dasgupta, Nandini, x, 4, 50, 51, 52, 54, 70(n2), 71–2
DCSSI, *see* India: Development Commissioner – Small-Scale Industries
De Chazal Du Mee, 280(n18), 282
De Soto, H., 247(n7), 248
Delhi Pollution Control Committee, 54, 70(n8)
demand, 34, 100, 102, 118, 121, 180(n1), 246, 295
democracy, 5, 77, 119, 121, 130, 157
Denmark, 205
Deraniyagala, S., 261, 280(n9), 282
deregulation, 78, 119, 243
design, 186, 193, **196–8**, 199, 200, 202, 204, 205, 208, 209, 225, 259, 264, 269, 276, 281(n24)
  capability, 192–3
designers, 190
developed countries, 12, 14t, 59, 89, 112(n4), 115, 137, 164, 185, 241, 277, 281(n21)
developing countries, 1, 2, 4, 6, 7, 11–30, 47, 51, 53, **55–7**, 58, 59, 151, 157, 158, 164, 185, 208, 229, 235, 236, 237, 242, 245, **257–62**, 265, 266, 277
division of labour, 100, 188, 199, 209
Doeleman, J. A., 52–3, 72
Droucopoulos, V., 135(n2, 7), 136
Dubois, P. R., 281(n22), 282
Duncombe, Richard, x, 8

East Asia, 256, 265, 279(n7), 280(n17)
EC (European Community), 48(n18), 203
Economic Commission for Latin America (ECLA), 242, 243
economic democracy, 115, 122, 123, 131
economic growth, 55, 57, 58, 87, 99, 119, 132, 138, 157, **186**, 214, 223
economic liberalization and growth of SSEs (India 1991–), **99–114**
  data, 102f, 105f, 107–8, 109t, 110t
Economic and Political Weekly (Bombay), 211
economies of scale, 15, 81, 90, 125, 126, 132, 137, 198, 230, 274
  'collective efficiency' (Schmitz), 6, 186, 187, 199, 229, 230, 234, 236, 239–40, 244
economies of scope, 137

education, 59, 60, 122, 141t, 145, 257, 261, 262, 264, 280(n15)
efficiency, 2, 3, 5, **24**, **24f**, 90, 125, 126, 127, 128, 130, 137, 258, 271
electrical and electronics sector:
  Bangalore, 6
  Bulgaria, 164, 166t, 166f, 167
electrical engineering, 77–8, **82–6**, 90, 91–5, 96
electricity (Venezuela), 133
electronic components, 195
  goods, 58
  industries, 203–4
  mail, 287, 291, 298, 301
  manufacturers, 195
  electronics, 187, 194, 197, 205, 261, 265, 279(n7)
employees, 1, 12, 87, 100, 140t, 141t, 138, 154(n1, n4), 160, 163t, 164, **170**, 171t, 180(n2), 193, 195, 198, 222, 227(n1), 266, 273t, 279(n4), 289, 294, 300, 301, 302(n2)
employment, 1, 2–3, 4, 16, 22–3, 24–5, 24f, 26t, 31, 37, 55, 56, 57, 58, 77, 78, 87, 90, 93, 99, 100, 115, 121, 123, 124, 125f, 126f, 126–7, 128, 129, 132, 134, 137, 187, 190, 197, 217, 270, 271, 274, 275t
  Bulgaria, 166t, 176, 176t, 177, 178t, 179, 180(n11)
energy saving measures, 271
engineering, 187, 197, 203–4, 205, 257, 261, 265, 267, 271, 289, 302(n4)
engineers, 67, 191, 192, 193, 195, 197, 198, 199, 200, 204, 205, 270, 271, 273t, 274, 275t
Engle, R. F., 125, 136
enterprise information needs: **293–5**
enterprise information systems, **288–93**
enterprises, **22–8**, 81, **90**, 95, 96, 112(n1), 127, 128, 144, 295, 296f
entrepreneurs, 60, 168, 169–70, 177, 179, 186, 188, 195, 197, 190–1, 201, 202, 204, 205, 208, 209, 210, 236, 240, 290, 292
entry, exit and the role of the small firm (PRC), **77–98**
environment
  impact of growth of SSEs, 4
  environment-employment dilemma, 58, 70(n14)
  agencies, 53, 64
  problems, **57–9**
  protection and small industries in India, 50–74, 50–2, 50, 51, 52, 52–9, 53, 53–5, 54–5, 55–7, 57–9, 59–65, 60–2, 62–3, 63–5, **65–6, 65–8, 66, 66–8, 67, 69**
EPZ, *see* export-processing zones
equipment, 6, 47, 65, 103, 158, 160, 168, 172, 173t, 173n, 174t, 176, 203, 232, 256, 259, 269, 276, 278t, 281(n22–23)
equity, 186, 261, 262, 266, 270–1, 272, 273, 273t, 274, 275t, 276, 279(n4)
Ericson, R., 88, 97
European Association of Development Institutes, 211
European Community (EC), 48(n18), 203
European integration and the survival of Polish small enterprises, **137–56**, 140–1t, 147–8t, 149t, 150t, 151t
European Union (EU), 5–6, 40, 42–3, 44, **137–56**, 255
Evans, D. S., 105, 113
exchange
  direct, 206
  social anthropology, **205–7**
exchange control, 40
exchange rates, 40, 41, 42, 118, 119, 120, 158, 180(n1), 180(n6), 222, 229, 232, 242, 245, 255, 263
exit behaviour:
  empirical analysis, **86–91**
  hazard rate model, **91–5**, 96
experience, 100, 256, 257, 270, 271, 289
export incentives (Mauritius), 262, 263
export licences, 40
export performance, 7, 255, 256, **273–5**, 279(n4)

export-processing zones (EPZ), 255, 262–3, 275
export promotion (Mauritius), 263
export strategies: silk (PRC), 37
export tax rebate, 43
  export taxes, 40, 42
exports, 44, 100, 119, 138, 140t, 192, 195, 214, 220, 222, **237**, 238, 243, 263, 264, 265–6, 280(n18)

factories, 54, 55, 187, 190, 193, 197, 199, 200, 201, 202, 204, 205, 209
family, 2, 56, 57, 70(n12), 132, 190, 191, 207, 289, 290
FAO (UN Food and Agriculture Organization), 39
FDI, *see* foreign direct investment
FENAC, 241
finance, 6, 8, 99, 133, 158, 172, 175, 176, 179, 235, 246, 258, 261, **293**, 294, 295, 297, 299, 302(n2)
financial, 80, 89, **91**, 141t, 145, 151t, 158, 200, 221, 223, 224, 242, 245
firm
  age, **89**, 93, 262, 276
  ownership (Botswana), 298
  size, 7, 22, 23f, 24, 25, 83, **96**, 158, 170, 256, 261–2, 271, 276, 298
  size, technological capabilities and market-orientated policies in Mauritius, **255–84**
  value, 172, 173t, 173n
firms, 4, 22, 23f, 24f, 26t, 58, 64, 68, 81, 82, 88, 89, **91–5**, 96, 121, 123, 124, 125, 125f, 126, 126f, 127–8, 129, 130, 131, 132, 133, 134, 135(n4), 137, 140t, 144, 158, 162, 164, 167–8, 169–70, 186, 187, 203, 204, 206, 220, 235, 242, 256, **273–5**, 279(n5), 298
flexible specialization, **186**, 187, 189, 202, 207, 230
food and drink sector (Bulgaria), 164, 166t, 166f, 167
food industry, 22, 194, 279(n7)
footwear, 219, **238**, 265
foreign aid (to India), 205
foreign direct investment, 27, 80, 83, 84f, 87, 120
  'foreign investment', 44, 255
foreign exchange, 31, 37, 44, 80, 118, 263
Fournier, Olivier, 43
France, 12, 14t, 37
free markets, 5, 118, 119, 120, 133, 206
Fujian, 39
furniture, 122, 219–20, 222, 302(n4)

Gamarra (Peru), 238, 239, 241, 242
garment
  firms, 261, 266, 267t, 277
  industry, 7, 122, 255, 256
garments, 37, 43, 44, 45–6, 237, 255, 265, 269, 271, 276, 279(n7), 281(n25)
GATT Multi-Fibre Agreement, 43, 265
Gdansk region, 138, 140t, 144, 146, 148t, 148, 149t, 152, 153
GDP, 116t, 118, 119, 120, 120t, 121, 122, 127, 128, 130, 134, 135(n5), 137, 177, 214, 237, 255
Gelb, A. H., 160, 181
Genov, K., 160, 181
Germany, 37, 97(n3), 193, 205
Ghana, 279(n7), 280(n8, n10)
Ghatak, Subrata, x, 5–6
glass industry (Ferozabad), **63–5**, 71(n17)
globalization, 120, 131, 226, 229, 244
Goldberger, A., 154(n3), 155
Gosen, R., 280(n9), 282
government, 31, 42, 46, 50–1, 79, 80, 81, 90, 91, 99, 100, 112, 113(n6), 117, 118–19, 120, 131, 132, 157, 196, 201, 202, 203, 204, 205, 208, 215, 220–1, 223, 224–5, 225–6, 242–3, 247, 290
government
  bodies, 192
  intervention, 7, 231
  recommended (Latin America), 245
  procurement (India), 100
  revenue (Venezuela), 117
  support, 4, 194

Granger, C. W. J., 125, 136
Greece, 135(n7), 151
Guadalajara (Mexico), **238**, 240, 242, 244
Guangdong trade fair, 38
Guri Dam (Venezuela), 131

Hamza, A., 50, 72
Hardoy, J., 50, 73
Harlankar, S., 72, 54–5
Hart, P. E., 86, 97
hazard rate model of exit behaviour, **91–5**, 96
Heeks, Richard, x–xi, 8
Hemlin, M., 73
Hill, H., 214, 215, 227
Hobday, M., 279(n7), 282
Holmström, Mark, xi, 6, 187, 190, 207, 211, 212
Hong Kong, 12, 13t, 15, 16, 17t, 25, 26t, 27f, 28, 29, 40, 41, 51, 66, 83, 89, 116, 116t, 131, 280(n17)
Hopenhayn, H., 88, 97
human resources, 56, 58, 234, 246, 264, 294
Hungary, 159t, 159–60, **167–70**, 171t
Hurreeram, D. K., 282

ICT, *see* information and communication technology
Ikiara, G., 261, 266, 280(n9), 284
ILO (International Labour Office), 55, 70(n14), 72
IMF, *see* International Monetary Fund
immiserizing growth, 3, 4, **31–49**, **44–6**, 235
Impiva (Spain), 187
import, 101, 103, 126, 128, 196, 232, 242
import-substitution industrialization (ISI), 117, 131, 133, 262, 275
imports, 3, 47(n6), 99, 100, 101, 103, 111, 112(n4), 113(n8), 259, 262, 263, 269, 276
Inapex Auto Products Export Ltd, 194
incentives, 41, 44, **65–6**, 69, 137, 153–4, 208, 209, 235, 245
  fiscal (Indonesia), 215
  need to be more selective, 209
income, 106, 222
  effects, 57, 59
  levels, 57
  per capita (Indonesia), 217
incomes, 58, 122
  incomes policy (Bulgaria), 158
India, 5, 6, 36t, 50–74, **53–5**, **59–65**, 70(n9), 70(n11), **99–114**, 101, 185, 282(n28)
  Census of Industrial Production, 108
  Census of Registered Small-Scale Industrial Units, 107–8
  Central Pollution Control Board, 54
  Department of the Environment, 62
  Department of Industrial Policy and Promotion, 108
  Development Commissioner – Small-Scale Industries (DCSSI), 63–4, 108
  Directorate General of Technical Development (DGTD), 108
  National Aeronautical Laboratory, 197, 203–4
  National Productivity Council (NPC), 67, 68
  Small Industries Development Organization (SIDO), 108
  State Pollution Control Boards, 54, 61–2
  Waste Management Circles Programme, 67
  Water Act (1974), 54
  Indian Institute of Science, 197, 203, 204
    Centre for Electronic Development and Technology (CEDT), 204
  Indian Machine Tools Manufacturers' Association, 196
  Indian Standard Industrial Classification, 108
  Indian Telephone Industries (ITI), 199

individualism, 200, 201, 206, 209
Indonesia, 7, 51, 55, 66, 70(n11), **214–28**, 280(n9)
  capacity, 111, 112, 113(n6)
  districts, 6, 185, 202, 207, 208, 230, 242
  engineering, 278t, 280–1(n20)
  estates, 203
  growth, 210
  licensing, 101, 103
  lineage firm (Lachaier), 191
  production (India, 1989–97), 100
  reform (Mauritius), 262
  relations, 123
  research institutes, 113(n12)
  sectors, 25, 26t, 27f, 32–3, 198, 264
  societies, 206
inefficiency, 61, 67, 89, 185
informal sector, 118, 122, 124, 132, 133, 185
information, 56, 59, 63–4, 127, 133, 153, 188, 189, 190, 192, 195, 196, 199, 201, 232, 235, 236, 257, 258, 262, 269, 271, 274, 277, 285–6, 288–90, **292–3**, 295, 296, 300
information and communication technology (ICT), 8, **285–303**
information, ICTs, and small enterprise: findings from Botswana, **285–303**
information
  storage and processing (Botswana), **291–2**
  systems, 286f, 286–7, 296
information technology (IT), 58, 70(n1), 133, 141t, 289, 301, 302(n4)
infrastructure, 133, 168, 208, 220, 242, 245, 292
innovation, 5, 89, 125, 128, 137, 138, 141t, 186, 187, 190, 192, 194, **196–8**, 199, 201, 202, 215, 232, 240, 241, 243, 246
input
  effects, 247(n2)
  prices, 22
  suppliers, 240
input-output analysis, 67
inputs, 1, 22–3, 23f, 100, 220, 222
institutional capacity-building (Indonesia), 225–6
inter-firm
  factors, 236
  relationship, 267
interest rates, 91, 119, 127, 135(n4), 232, 263
International Labour Office (ILO), 55, 70(n14), 72
International Monetary Fund (IMF), 157, 221, 223, 224
International Silk Association, 43
International Trade Centre (Geneva), 37
Internet, 141t, 146, 148t, 149t, 151–2, 287, 291, 292–3, 296, 298, 299, 301–2, 302(n3)
intra-firm factors, 231, 235, 236, 241
investment, 15, 57, 58, 62, 64, 65, 90, 119, 127, 128, 131, 145, 150, 152, 157, 160, 167, 176, 176t, 177, 178t, 179, 180(n11), 185, 217, 224, 232, 234, 243, 245, 246, 256, 257, 258, **259**, 280(n19), 281(n23), 291
Ireland, 145
Ishaq, A., 30
ISO 9000 status, 203, 267, 268, 277t, 281(n21)
IT, *see* information technology
Italy, 37, 115, 132, 151, 186, 187–8, 189, 193, 202, 206, 207, 208, 230, 231, 233, 238, 242, 243, 244
Ivory Coast: manufactured exports (1980–98), 265

Japan, 12, 14, 14t, 36t, 37, 40, 44, 281(n24)
Japanese suppliers, 196
Java (Central), 215, 227(n3)
Jellinek, L., 221, 227
Jepara (Indonesia), 219–20, 222–3
Jiangsu, 39
joint ventures, 41, 87, 220, 222–3, 236
Jovanovic, B., 88, 97

Karshenas, M., 57, 58, 72
Kashy, A., 114

Kashyap, S. P., 100, 114
Kassayie, Berhanu, xi, 6
Kassia (Karnataka Small-Scale Industries' Association), 201
Katrak, Homi, xi, 5, 100, 103, 113(n12), 114, 279(n1)
Katz, J. M., 279(n7), 283
Kenya, 51, 260, 261, 265, 266, 280(n7–8, n11)
Khan, R. A., 180(n1), 181
Khemani, R. S., 88, 98
Kiggundu, Rose, 279(n1)
kinship, 190, 191, 210
knitwear (Bulgaria), 164, 166, 166t, 166f
knowledge, 51, 56, 58, 59, 61, 62–3, 64, 69, 240, 256, 289, 299
Korea, Republic of, 12, 13t, 15, 16, 17t, 19–22, 20t–21t, 26t, 27f, 28, 29, 115
Kritayakirana, K., 283
Krugman, P., 247(n2)
Kumar, N., 282(n28), 283
Kuttner, Robert, 206

labour, 2–3, 16, 19, 22–3, 23f, 39, 51, 55, 56, 57, 58, 59, 69, 82, 95, 100, 123, 162, 187, 193, 197, 199, 202, 203, 214, 233, 236, 246, 247(n2), 264
  costs, 127, 128, 243, 281(n23)
  employed, 127
  intensity, 11, 15–16, 17t, 19–22
  laws (Venezuela), 132
  legislation, 201
  markets (Venezuela), 134
  policy (Venezuela), 132
  productivity, 126–7
Lachaier, Pierre, 191, 212
Lall, Sanjaya, 259, 266, 279(n1, n7), 280(n8, 10), 283
Lardy, N. R., 47(n6), 49
large enterprises (LEs) / large firms, 1, 2, 4, 7, 25, 27–8, 59, 84f, 86f, 90, 96t, 99–114, 102f, 159, 166, 185, 187, 188, 189, 191, 192, 193, 194, 196, 201, 203, 208, 214, 215, 219, 220, 223, 229, 232, 242–3, 256, 261, 265–6, 267–8, 269, 270, 272–3, 273t, 276, 277, 279(n4), 280(n18), 281(n22), 281(n23), 281(n25)
larger firms, 3, 5, 7, 172, 205, 221, 245
Latin America, 7, 116, 116t, 117, 122, 130, 132, 133, 134, 135(n6), 217, **229–51**, 279(n7)
Latsch, W., 280(n9–10), 283
law, 59, 132, 201, 215, 220, 290
Leacock, Stephen, 205
learning, 235, 236, 237, 244, 246, 256, 258, 259, 271, 289
leather (Botswana), 289, 291, 302(n4)
legal framework, 133, 179, 180(n6)
Lei, P. C. K., 66, 73
Léon (Mexico), **238**, 242
LEs, *see* large enterprises
Letteri, C., 29, 30
Liaoning province, 78, **82–6**, 94t
liberalization, 4, 5, 6, **38–44**, 46, 80, 158, 161, 162, 172, 179, 180(n6), 188, 201, 210, 222, 226, 229
Liedholm, C., 217, 222, 227
limited liability companies, 164, 165t, 169, 169t, 170
linkages, **259**, 266, 267, 268, 269–70, 277, 278t, 280(n19–20)
Little, I. M. D., 15, 30, 55, 73, 100, 114
living
  conditions, 240
  standards, 78, 186, 188
loans, 133, 141t, 146, 148t, 149t, 289
Lomé Convention, 255
London: King's College, 227(n2), 279(n1)
Loveman, G. W., 136
Lublin region, 138, 140t, 144, 146, 148t, 148, 150, 152, 153

Maastricht: UNU INTECH, 279(n1)
Macau, 83, 89
machine tools, 194, 195, 197, 200, 204
machinery, 204, 242
  and metalwork sector (Bulgaria), 164, 166t
  plant, 160–1

macroeconomic, 157, 158, 175, 177, 180(n1), 214, 222, 229, 231, 231–2, 242, 244, 245, 247, 255, 257, 258, 262, 263
Makarim, Nabiel, 66
Malinowski, B., 206
management, 51, 87, 69, 160, 196, 210, 242, 268, 271, 276, 277, 281(n21), 294
  consultancy, 202
  input, 64
managerial ability, 56
managers, 138, 150, 152, 153, 191, 195, 210, 241
Mannan, M. A., 70(n12), 73
Manolas, George, xi, 5–6
manpower, 258, 261, 269, 270, 271, 273, 276, 281(n22)
manufacturers, 241, 290, 292, 293, 297
manufacturing, 4, 5, 6, 15, 22, 55, 78, 82–3, 95, 97(n3), 108, 115, 118, **122–5**, 133, 134, 150, 150t, 151t, **157–81**, **167–70**, 177, 214, 216, 217, 218t, 263, 265, 281(n23), 287, 302(n2, 4)
  enterprises, 257, 291
  establishment, size, 12, 13t–14t
  exporters (Botswana), 292–3, 294, 297
  sector (Botswana), 300
  value-added (MVA), 16, 17t, 19, 25, 121, 123, 124f, 126f, 126, 129, 130, 130f, 220, 246
market, 3, 4–6, 15, 16, 27, 38, **75–181**, **91**, 77, 80, 82, 88, 101, 121, 125, 126, 128, 132, 134, 138, 194, 203, 206, 217, 223, 231, 299
  market-based instruments, 52, 53, 59
  market-led economic system, 157
  market-orientation, 3, **90**, 275
marketing, 1, 67, 89, 90, 99, 113(n6), 148, 168, 186, **192–6**, 193–6, 196, 197, 200, 201, 202, 208, 209, 215, 219, 225, 233, 263, 270–1, 274, 277, 292–3, 296, 299, 300, 301
markets, 3, 7, 8, 38, 39, 40, 44, 46, 58, 67, 70(n1), 127, 137, 139, 140t, 141t, 144, 148, 148t, 149t, 150, 152, 153, 160, 168, 180(n6), 185, 188, **191**, 192, 194, 195, 200, 201, 202, 203, 207, 208, 214, 221, 222, 224, 227, 235, 239, 243, 244, 245, 246–7, 255, 256, 262, 269, 274, 277, 280(n18), 291, **293**, 294, 295
Markov process, 88
Marshall, A., 12, 29(n1), 230
Marx, Karl, 12, 29(n1)
Mauritius, 7, 255, 255–6, **255–84**, 262–4, **262–6**, 264–6, 265, 266, 266–7, **266–70**, 267t, 267–70, 268t, **270–5**, 272t, 273–5, 273t, **275–7**, 276, 280(n7), 280(n17)
  Export Processing Zone Development Agency, 264
  SME agency, 264
  Technology Diffusion Scheme, 264
  Export Development and Investment Authority (MEDIA, 1985–), 263
  Productivity and Competitiveness Council (2000–), 263
  Standards Bureau, 264
Mauss, Marcel, 206, 212
Mazumdar, D., 30, 73, 114
Mead, D. C., 217, 222, 227
medium-sized firms/enterprises, 1, 2, 3, 4, 8n, 25, 27–8, 59, 84f, 86f, 96t, 154(n1), 196, 217, 219, 298, 302(n2)
  smaller than 'small', 8n, 172, 173t, 174t, 175, 175t, 177, 178t
  Bulgaria, 163t, 164, 165t
MERCOSUR, 243
mergers, 81, 87
metal-working, 122, 222, 279–80(n7)
Mexico, **238**, 239, 280(n9)
Meyer-Stamer, J., 247(n6), 247
micro firms/enterprises, 8n, 67, 68, 70(n3), 122, 135(n1), 154(n1), 163t, 164, 165t, 170, 172, 173t, 174t, 175, 175t, 177, 178t, 179, 217, 222, 223, 237, 266, 302(n2)
minimum efficient scale, 88
monetary policy, 133, 158
monopoly, 91, 133

Morris, S., 100, 114
Mulhern, Alan, xii, 5, 125, 128, 129–30, 136
Multi-Fibre Agreement (GATT), 43, 265
Mumbai, 200
MVA, *see* manufacturing value-added
Mytelka, Lynn, 279(n1)

Nadvi, K., 208, 212, 242, 249
Nairobi, 58
Nerlove, M., 154(n3), 156
networking, 207, 209, 289
networks, **188–92**, **196–8**, 225, 299
New Order (Indonesia), 215, 217, 223
Newton, Jim, xii, 4, 48(n13), 49
Nickell, S., 89, 98
Nigeria: manufactured exports (1980–98), 265
non-tariff barriers, 3, 99, 263
Norway, 115
Novo Hamburgo (Brazil), 237

O'Neil, S., 280(n18), 284
OECD area, 137
oil, 63, 71(n19), 116, 117, 120, 122, 131, 132
  prices, 117–18, 120, 121
  wealth (Venezuela), 118, 120, 121–2, 123, 131, 134
one stop shops, 224, 226, 232
output, 3, 22–3, 23f, 77, 78, 81, 84f, 85f, 90, 91, 100, 103, 104, 106, 110, 111, 112(n5), 126, 127, 137
  growth, 101
overseas buyers, 267, 268
owners, 67, 68, 138, 150, 152, 180(n4), 192
  ownership, 78, **89**, 96, 274
Oxford: Queen Elizabeth House, 279(n1)

Page, J. M. Jr., 30, 73, 114
Pakes, A., 88, 97
Pakistan, 12, 13t, 19–22, 26t, 27f, 29, 260, 261–2, 280(n9)
Paraguay (SMEs), 237
Parker, R. L., 100, 114
partnerships, 169, 215, 220
Patel, S. V., 56, 73
Pavitt, K., 279(n7), 282
penalties, **65–6**, 69
People's Republic of China (PRC), 5, **31–49**, 32, 36t, 37, 37t, 38, 39, 40, 41, 44, 45, 47(n5), 47(n6), 48(n9–10), 48(n18), **77–98**, 77, **78–80**, 78, 80, 81, 84f, 85f, 91, 220;, **237–8**, 265
  China National Textiles Import and Export Corporation, 38
  Ministry of Commerce, 38
  Ministry of Foreign Economic Relations and Trade (MOFERT), 39, 47(n4)
  Ministry of Textile Industry, 38
  National Federation of Supply and Marketing Co-operatives, 38
  National Silk Textile Trading Market, 42
  State Council, 42, 47(n3)
Peru, **238**, 241, 242, 247(n7)
Petchsuwan, K., 283
Pietrobelli, C., 279(n7), 280(n8), 283
pioneer firms (Bulgaria), **163**, 163t, 167, 170, 172, 173t, 174t, 175
Piore, M. J., 136
Pissarides, F., 180(n5), 181
Plovdiv, 167
Poland, **137–56**, 159t, 159–60, 167–8, **167–70**, 168t, 169–70, 171t
political, 127, 162, 163, 255
pollution, 3, 4, 54, 57, 58, 61, 62, 63, 68, 71(n19)
pollution-control equipment, 66
  see also environmental protection
poverty, 4, 51, **52–9**, 70(n13), 210, 217
Pradhan, B. K., 108, 114
Prais, S. J., 86, 97
Press, J., 154(n3), 156
price
  competition, 43–4
  controls (Venezuela), 118, 120
  inelasticity, 34
prices, 32, 34, 39, 41, 45, 46, 47, 89, 102, 112(n4), 118, 158, 180(n6), 191, 243, 244, 295, 300

private
ownership, 80
property, 157
sector, 62, 65, 118, 140t, 144, 157, 177, 187, 225, 226, 227, 233, 263
privatization, 7, 77, 78, 81, 119, 144, 158, 159t, 159–60, 162, 164, 172, 179, 180(n5–6)
process
engineering, 268, 277t, 280(n20)
technology, **259**, 271
processes, 138, 193, 235, 236
product
development, 209
engineering, 268, 269, 278t, 280(n20)
production, 1, 19, 51, 52, **65–8**, 69, 79, 101, 102, 113(n8), 127, 128, 130, 139, 140t, 148, 185, 186, 192, 197, 214, 225, 232, 236, **259**, 261, 266–7, 270, 271, 272, 273, 273t, 280(n19)
capabilities, 246
costs, 148
experience, 274, 275t
possibility frontier (PPF), 32–3, 33f, 48(n19)
processes, 240, 244
techniques, 18f, 29(n2)
technology, 261
units, 4, 11, **11–30**
productivity, 58, 78, 81, 85–6, 86f, 88, 89, 90, 93, 95, 96, 100, 118, 126, 131, 145, 217, 241, 264, 267, 268, 271, 277, 278t
product quality, 100, 103–4, 106, 108, 112(n4), 113(n8), 148, 186, 192, 194, 240, 241, 243, 244, 264, 281(n25)
profits, 15, 18f, 18–19, 40, 88, 96, 101, 103, 112(n5), 188, 222, 245
short-term maximization, 55–6, 58, 59
public, 119, 121, 123, 131, 140t, 144, 187, 189, 196, 197, 199, 202, 203, 204, 205, 207, 208, 209, 233, 263
Pyke, F., 185, 213, 243, 250

quality control, 7, 201, 234, 235, 268, 270, 276, 281(n21)
quotas, 42–3, 46, 48(n13), 131, 201, 210

Rabellotti, R., 211, 240, 250
Ramachandran, K., 114
Ramaswamy, K. V., 100, 114
Ramgutty-Wong, A., 282
reform, 4, 6, 177, 179
'reform institutionalization', 163, 167, 170[-]172, 175, 176, 180(n6–7)
reform models: absent, 78, 79
regulation, 1, 14, 53, 59, 62, 100, 132, 133, 201, 215, 224, 226, 232, 242, 244, 245, 247(n1), 290
regulators (Indonesia), 217
regulatory policies, 2, 3
Rekhi, S., 103, 114
research and development (R&D), 64, 68, 89, 90, 141t, 145, 150, 152, 198, 200, 201, 209, 236, 246, 257, 264
research institutions, 203, 209, 210
restructuring, 87, 131, 158, 161, 172, 180(n6), 243
retail sector, 41, 45, 224, 302(n2)
Ricardo, David, 12
Rietveld, P., 228
risk, 58, 219, 257, 261, 299
Rivero, D. M., 122, 136
Roberts, P., 135(n6), 136
Robinson, P., 280(n9–10), 283
Rodriguez, E., 227
Rodriguez, E. R., 99, 114
Romijn, H., 261–2, 280(n9), 283
Ronnas, P., 55, 73
Rontos, Costas, xii, 5–6
rural areas, 70(n13), 216, 291, 302(n2)
Ruse (Bulgaria), 167
Russia, 206
Rustanto, B., 221, 227

Sabadini, M. de S., 238, 239, 240, 241, 242, 250

Sahlins, Marshall, 206, 210, 213
sales, 1, 3, 164, 165t, 166t, 176t, 176–7, 178t, 179, 180(n11), 261, 270, 271, 281(n26), 292, 294, 295, 300
Saluja, M. R., 108, 114
sanctions, 50, 51, 55, 65, 66, 69, 189, 206, 209, 247(n3)
Sandee, Henry, xii, 7, 216, 227, 227(n6), 228
Sandesara, J. C., 55, 70(n12), 73, 100, 114
Satterthwaite, D., 50, 73
Schmitz, Hubert, 186, 211, 213, 239–40, 242, 249, 250
Schumpeter, J. A., 82
Seebaluck, D., 282
self-employment, 122, 216, 217, 222, 227(n5)
Semboja, H., 261, 280(n9), 282
Sen, A. K., 70(n13), 73
Sengenberger, W., 115, 136, 185, 213, 243, 248, 250
service sector, 115, 122, 124, 132, 148, 150, 150t, 151t, 187, 188, 196, **202–5**, 207–8, 271, 287, 291, 292, 293, 294, 297, 300, 302(n4)
Seth, A., 100, 114
Sethuraman, S. V., 56, 57–8, 74
Shah, M., 282
Shanghai, 81
Shapiro, D., 88, 98
Shenzhen, 81
shock therapy: doubtful efficacy, 164, 179
shocks, 89
shoes, **237**, 238, 239, 240, 241, 244
Siddharthan, N. S., 282(n28), 283
silk (raw), 31, 32, 35, 36, 36t, 37t, 38, 42, 44, 45, 46
  industry, 4, 31, **31–49**, 47(n8), 48(n20)
Singapore, 116, 116t, 131, 264, 280(n17)
Single European Market, 144, 151, 154
Sinos Valley cluster of shoe-makers (Brazil), **237**, 239, 240, 241, 244
Sjoberg, O., 73
skills, 8, 56, 57, 58, 69, 122, 186, 234, 241, 256, 265, 269, 271, 274, **293**, 295, 296, 297, 299, 300, 301
small is beautiful? a reappraisal, 4, **9–74**, 11–30, 31–49, 50–74
small firms/enterprises, 6, 8n, **31–49**, (conclusion, 46–7), 133, 154(n1), 163t, 164, 165t, 170, 172, 173t, 174t, 175, 175t, 176, 177, 178t, 179, 185, 187, 188, **192–6**, 192, 194, 196–7, 198, 199, 203, **285–303**, 295, 302(n2)
small, medium and micro-enterprise (SMME) development, 287, 291, 292, 293, 294, 295, 298
small and medium-sized enterprises (SMEs), 5–6, 5, 7, 8n, 55, 115, **122–5**, **125–9**, 130, 132, 133, 134, 135, 135(n1), **137–56**, 154(n1), 185, 188, 189, 190, 199, 210, **229–51**, 256, 264, 265–6, 267–8 269–70, 272–3, 273t, 276, 277, 279(n4), 279(n5), 280(n18), 281(n22), 281(n23), 281(n25)
small-scale enterprises (SSEs), 1–2, **1–8**, 2–3, 1, 2, 4–6, 4, 5, 6, ch2, 7, 8n, **11–30**, 15–17, 18–22, 27, 28, **50–74**, 70(n3), **75–181**, **99–114**, 99–114, 157, **214–28**, 227(n1, 4)
  in india, **50–74**
  and market competition, **75–181**
small-scale manufacturing in Bulgaria, **157–81**
smaller firms, 201, 202, 204
social, 80, 89, 123, 135(n3), 158, 186, 187, **205–7**
socialist market economy (PRC), 5, 78–9, **80–2**, 87, 95
Soeharto, President, 214, 215
SOEs, *see* state-owned enterprises
Sofia, 167, 180(n5)
sole proprietorship, 122, 164, 165t, 169, 169t
South Africa, 12, 14t, 25, 26t, 27f, 28, 29, 265
Soviet Union, 77
Spain, 116, 116t
Späth, B., 247(n1), 250
Spence, L. J., 53, 74

SRI International, 280(n9)
Sri Lanka, 195, 260, 261, 265, 266, 280(n8–9, n11), 281(n24)
Srinivasulu, K., 103, 114
Srivastava, P., 282
SSEs, *see* small-scale enterprises
stabilization, 157, 180(n1)
stagnation (Venezuela), 121, 123, 124, 129
standardization, 196, 199
standards, 7
Starazagora (Bulgaria), 167
start ups, 124, 158, 159, 159t, 160, 161f, 162, **170–6**, 179, 180(n5), 222, 259, 271,
state
  control, 117, 131, 132, 133, 134, 179
  intervention, 133, 208, 262
state-owned enterprises (SOEs)/ nationalized industries, 5, 6, 78, 79, 80, 81, 83, 84f, 87, 89, 92t, 93, 94t, 95, 96, 118, 132, 158, 159, 159n, 161, 162, 164, 168, 172, 177, 179, 180(n5–6)
Stewart, C., 125, 128, 129–30, 136
Stockholm Conference on Human Environment (1972), 53
Storey, D. J., 115, 136
Strange, Roger, xii, 4, 48(n13), 49, 279(n1)
structural
  adjustment, 180(n1), 262
  barriers, 128
  reform (Venezuela, 1989–), 118–19
sub-contracting, 5, 111, 188, 191, 198, 203, 219, 239, 259, 269, 278t, 281(n25)
sub-contractors, 220, 222, 234, 238, 239, 240, 264, 267
subsidies, 1, 28, 55, 87, 90, 99, 119, 132, 215
suppliers, 89, 177, 192, 199, 201, 234, 242, 258, 300
supply-side responses, 246–7
Supratikno, H., 228
survival, 3, 57, 68, 85f
Sutabutr, H., 283
Switzerland, 37, 205
Taiwan, 83, 89, 264, 280(n17)
Taj Trapezium, 63, 71(n18)
Tanzania, 260, 261, 280(n7, n9)
tariffs, 3, 34, 41, 99, 119, 131, 232, 245, 263
Tavara, J., 240, 250
tax/taxation, 1, 40, 90, 99, 123, 131, 169, 201, 220, 245, 246, 263
  authorities, 170
technical, 7, **18–22**, 59, 202, 204, 208, 215, 216, 220, 221, 223, 224–5, 242, 246, 262, 272, 273, 273t, 276, 281(n26), 294, 301, 302(n4)
technicians, 270, 271, 273t, 274, 275t
technological
  capability, 7, 235–6, 241, 244, 246, 256, **257–9**, **257–62**, **259–62**, 259, 267–8, 267t, 267, 271, 276, 277
  change, 59, 219
  development: market-orientated developing economies, 256
  dynamism, 15
  expertise, 233, 247(n2)
  innovation, 31, **32–5**, 44
  support, 258
technology, 1, 39, 41, 51, 54, 55, 57, 58, 64, 69, 89, 101, 103, 104, 111, 112, 112(n4), 113(n6), 113(n12), 121, 122, 127, 128, 133, 141t, 145, 148, 151, 172, 187, 190, 203, 234, 235, 242, 243, 256, 257, 258, 260, 269, 271, 274, 278t, 281(n23)
technology index (TI), 7, 256, 259–61, 261, **266–70**, 266, 270–3, **270–5**, 270, 273t, 274, 275t, 275–7, 276, 277 277–8t, 279t, 280(n19)
technology transfer, 27, 234, 235, 246, 259–60, 267, 269
technology upgrading, 1, 4, 7–8, 64, 68, 69, 99, 100, 112, 113(n6), 145, 217, 223, 226, 229, 235–6, 237, 243, **255–303**
Teitel, S., 283
telecommunications, 81, 153, 297
telemarketing, 153
telephones (Botswana), 287, 290, 291, 292, 296, 297, 302(n3)
Temple, Paul, xiii, 4–5

terms of trade, 33f, 34, 46
Tescon, G., 99, 114
textiles, 33, 33f, 34, 35f, 40, 43, 164, 166, 166t, 166f, 219, 279(n7), 302(n4)
Thailand, 51, 260, 261, 280(n9)
Thomadakis, S. B., 135(n2, 7), 136
Tommaso, M. R. di, 211
tourism, 150, 150t, 151t, 152, 153, 222, 289, 291, 292–3, 301, 302(n2, 4)
trade, 44, 47, 137, 150, 150t, 151t, 152, 158
 barriers, 111, 112, 113(n8), 144, 150
 fairs, 192, 193, 195, 219, 220, 224, 269
 liberalization, 219, 229, 242, 255, 262
 unions, 3, 16, 70(n9), 118, 122, 132, 202, 205, 208, 210, 241, 245
training, 6, 7, 63, 133, 141t, 145, 186, 191, 193, 202, 203, 204, 208, 209, 215, 219, 220, 232, 234, 241, 257, 258, 259, 270, 271, 273, 273t, 276, 277, 289, 291, 294, 296, 300
transaction costs, 215, 232, 242
transitional economies, 47, 77, 87, 89, 90, 120, 123, **129–34** 137, 151, 164, 179, 180(n3),
transport, 122, 133, 151t, 168, 302(n2, 4)
Trujillo (Peru), **238**, 239, 240, 241, 242
trust, 6, 186, **188–92**, **205–7**, **207–10**, **234–5**, 240, 247(n3), 290, 298, 299

Uganda, 265
uncertainty, 224, 242, 257–8
UNDP (United Nations Development Programme), 55, 72, 99, 114
unemployment/layoffs, 58, 81, 100, 120t, 122, 185, 210
United Kingdom, 37, 53, 63, 97(n3), 115
 Department for International Development (DFID), 71(n17), 72, 302(n1)
United Nations Industrial Development Organisation (UNIDO), 28, 74, 198, 213
United States of America, 12, 14, 14t, 37, 40, 42, 43, 44, 46, 97(n3), 125, 128, 135
urban areas, 1, 3, 216, 302(n2)
 urbanization, 131, 168, 217
Uruguay, 237

Valencia (Spain), 187
value chains, 235
van Diermen, P., 217, 228
van Hulsen, S., 227(n6), 228
Vavouras, Iohanies, xiii, 5–6
Venezuela, 5, **115–36**, 116t, 117f, 120t, 124f, 125f, 126f, 129t, 130f, 242
Vienna Institute for Development and Cooperation, 211
Vietnam, 51, 220, 265, 281(n24)
villages (Indonesia), 216, 224
Villaran, F., 241, 251
Visser, E., 239, 251

wages, 4, 11, 15–16, 17t, 18f, 18–19, 27–8, 56, 132, 135(n3), **186**, 199, 200, 203, 235, 244
Wang, Y., 97(n2), 98
Wangwe, S., 279(n7), 283
waste, 58, 66, 67
Watkins, P., 40, 49
Wazirpur, 70(n10)
'wealth' effect, 33
wealth distribution, 121–2
Weeks, John, xiii, 4, 29, 30
Westphal, L. E., 260, 261, 280(n9), 283
Wignaraja, Ganeshan, xiii, 7, 261, 266, 280(n8–9, n18), 282(n28), 283, 284
Wilmore, L., 282(n28), 284
women, 43, 203
wood, 122, 279(n7), 289, 302(n4)
work practices, 64, 67, 68, 69
workers, 15, 56, 59, 67, 81, 122, 168, 188, 189, 191, 202, 203, 205, 208, 210, 217, 219, 235, 236, 237, 241, 255

World Bank, 47(n6), 49, 67, 157, 262, 264, 281(n21, 23), 284
World Development (Elsevier), 69

Yang, D. S. C., 66, 73
Yang, Qing Gong, xiii, 4–5
Yao, Y., 97(n2), 98
Yuthavong, Y., 283
Yuwono, P., 228

Zhejiang, 39
Zhivkov, President Teodor, 157
Zimbabwe, 265, 280(n8–10)